This book considers the consequences of the natural sciences (physics, biology, neurosciences) for our view of the world. Drees argues that higher, more complex levels of reality, such as religion and morality, are to be viewed as natural phenomena and have their own concepts and explanations, even though all elements of reality are constituted by the same kinds of matter (ontological naturalism). Religion and morality are to be understood as rooted in our evolutionary past and our neurophysiological constitution. This book takes a more radical naturalist position than most on religion and science. However, religion is not dismissed: religious traditions remain important as bodies of wisdom and vision, and the naturalist view of the world does not exclude a sense of wonder and awe, since at the limits of science questions about the existence of natural reality persist. As well as defending a particular position, Drees also includes a survey and classification of discussions on science and religion and a substantial introduction to contemporary studies on the history of science in its relation to religion.

RELIGION, SCIENCE AND NATURALISM

RELIGION, SCIENCE AND NATURALISM

WILLEM B. DREES

*Nicolette Bruining Professor of Philosophy of Science and of Technology from a
Liberal Protestant Perspective, University of Twente, Enschede, the Netherlands*

 **CAMBRIDGE**
UNIVERSITY PRESS

Published by the Press Syndicate of the University of Cambridge
The Pitt Building, Trumpington Street, Cambridge CB2 1RP
40 West 20th Street, New York, NY 10011-4211, USA
10 Stamford Road, Oakleigh, Melbourne 3166, Australia

First published 1996
Reprinted 1997

Transferred to digital printing 1997

Printed in the United Kingdom by Biddles Short Run Books

A catalogue record for this book is available from the British Library

Library of Congress cataloguing in publication data

Drees, Willem B., 1954
Religion, science and naturalism / Willem B. Drees.
p.   cm.
Includes bibliographical references and index.
ISBN 0 521 49708 6 (hardback)
1. Religion and science   2. Naturalism.   1. Title.
BL240.2D74 1996
215 DC:20   96-8813   CIP

ISBN 0 521 49708 6 hardback

To Zwanet Drees-Roeters

Contents

Preface

Who shall count the host of weaker men whose sense of truth has
been destroyed in the effort to harmonise impossibilities – whose life
has been wasted in the attempt to force the generous new wine of
science into the old bottles of Judaism? (Thomas Huxley 1894, 52)

We need to be honest to science. Through the natural and social
sciences we know in considerable detail the reality in which we live,
move and have our being (to adapt a phrase from Acts of the Apostles
17: 28). We should not sacrifice our sense of truth 'in the effort to
harmonise impossibilities', nor should we waste our time on attempts to
adapt new insights to old views of the world. Rather, we need to adapt
our view of the world to the best available insights we have.

Emphasis on the sciences does not imply that other types of human
discourse are irrelevant. Even if morality, politics, art, the love for
another person, and the love of music can be understood within a
naturalist framework informed by the natural and social sciences, they
are still real and rich human practices. This applies to religion as well:
I do not see religiously relevant gaps in the natural and human world,
where the divine could somehow interfere with natural reality. The
origins and functions of religions may be intelligible. However,
religion can be seen as an important, real, and rich human phenomenon. Furthermore, the whole of reality is not itself understandable
within a naturalist framework; in response, a sense of gratitude and
wonder with respect to the reality to which we belong may be
appropriate.

I do not consider an intellectual study like this one the most
important thing in the world. When we stand before the divine
throne on the day of judgement, if I may for the moment use this
image, God will not ask 'How did I do it?' Rather, the question might
be: 'What did you do with it?' With Calvin DeWitt, from whom, this
set of questions has been taken, I agree that issues which are within

our responsibility, in our time especially environmental issues, are extremely urgent. However, here I will be concerned with 'the voice that speaks' rather than with 'what the voice speaks'. If there is no throne in the clouds, how then should we think about God (if at all), about the world, and about ourselves in this world?

Many believers do not take the natural and social sciences seriously enough. Some do not pay any attention to the sciences at all. Among those who do, various strategies for coping with the sciences may be found in both naive and sophisticated forms. Some concentrate on gaps in our current knowledge. This strategy reinforces others in the impression that the advancement of science has to imply the retreat of religion. Others do not concentrate on specific gaps, but play down the status of scientific knowledge – a 'scientific agnosticism' which has to make room for religion. Then there are others who adopt a 'scientific method' in theology, with an elaborate formal apparatus, while avoiding engagement with scientific knowledge. Quite a few traditional and New Age believers embrace science uncritically; they run away with a mystification of quantum physics or chaos theories. And, for the moment last but not least, science may be taken seriously, but used only as a source of analogies and models, rather than as a source of knowledge about the world of which humans are a part.

I consider such responses half-hearted. They diminish the relevance of science. This becomes especially clear when we note that the sciences offer not only insights into the world, but also insights about ourselves. Not only did the world evolve – an evolution which might be seen as God's mode of creation – but we humans, with our religious beliefs and moral codes, are the product of evolution as well. The sciences are not only about the world out there, but also about ourselves; they inform us about our constitution in relation to our environment (brains, genes, culture, etc.) and about the way this constitution and this environment became what they are through evolution. The challenge is to accommodate religious positions not merely to contemporary physics, but also to insights gained through evolutionary biology and the neurosciences, and beyond that to knowledge acquired in, for instance, cultural anthropology and comparative studies in the histories of religions. In this study the emphasis is on the natural sciences, but the impact of such social sciences needs to be taken into account. The social sciences may be less precise due to the complexity of their subject matter, but they complement the natural sciences in an important way, especially when human practices and beliefs are considered.

Many non-believers take science seriously, and consider this to be the end of all religion. The loss of interest in religion is, in my opinion, an impoverishment of our lives. Science is not the only, and perhaps not even the most important, factor in the declining importance of religion in the Netherlands and other Western countries. The rise of historical consciousness, respect for the plurality of cultures and traditions, and indignation with the way religious traditions have fuelled intolerance and cruelty have certainly contributed to sceptical attitudes towards religious truth claims. The decline of the importance of church membership for social careers has also contributed to indifference with respect to religion. However, even if its traditional truth claims are questioned and its social power is gone, religion may still be important as one of the factors that shape our way of life, our experiences, and our view of the world. It is to such an appreciation of the possible importance of religion that I hope to contribute.

In the first chapter of this book the central notions 'science', 'naturalism', and 'religion' will be explored, and various strategies and views of the relationship between science and theology will be considered. Chapter 2 considers some historical episodes in interactions between science and religion and evaluates views of these episodes. Then, we will turn towards theological responses to contemporary scientific knowledge of *the world* (chapter 3) and of *human nature* (chapter 4). The final chapter (5) returns to the understanding and defence of science and of religion. In the text, numbers placed in square brackets will be used to refer to sections of the book.

Proper sensitivity to disadvantages and prejudices related to gender as it has arisen over the last decades has resulted in uneasiness with respect to the use of personal pronouns when referring to humans. Rather than alternating gender by occasion or chapter, I have decided to use the female and the male pronouns for two slightly different purposes: when referring to a human as the subject who studies reality as a scientist, scholar, or theologian, I will use female pronouns, whereas I will use male pronouns when referring to humans as objects of study. Thus, when an anthropologist studies the beliefs of a tribe, I will refer to 'his beliefs' and 'her studies'. This, of course, in no way implies that scholars are always female or that male persons are the proper representatives of humans.

I was trained in theoretical physics at the University of Utrecht, the Netherlands. Out of interest I studied theology and philosophy of religion at the Universities of Amsterdam and of Groningen. My dissertation on theological and philosophical issues related to astrophysical cosmology was published as *Beyond the Big Bang: Quantum Cosmologies and God* (Drees 1990). Cosmology, and certainly quantum cosmology, is a peculiar and a-typical branch of science, more prone to philosophical and religious speculations than most other areas of the natural sciences. I felt challenged to reflect upon the implications of more regular branches of the sciences, and especially those that impinge upon our understanding of ourselves, such as evolutionary biology and the neurosciences.

When engaged in critical discussion of other positions I sometimes feel ungrateful, as I am mostly taking things apart without being able to put all the pieces back together. I am grateful that there have been persons who dare to elaborate creative proposals and to explore their possibilities; I could not have embarked upon this project without such constructive contributions. I am thinking with gratitude especially of Robert J. Russell, my host at the Center of Theology and the Natural Sciences, affiliated with the Graduate Theological Union in Berkeley, in the Fall of 1987, and of Philip Hefner, who hosted me at the Chicago Center for Religion and Science, linked with the Lutheran School of Theology at Chicago during the Winter and Spring of 1988. Among the many others who through their constructive writings made my work possible, I mention Ian Barbour, Ralph Burhoe, Michael Heller, Nancey Murphy, Arthur Peacocke, John Polkinghorne, and Luco van den Brom, with all of whom I had discussions on various occasions, and Gordon Kaufman and Gerd Theissen, whose constructive writings I appreciate more than may be apparent from the discussion in this book.

The first draft was written during the first half of 1993 in the Center of Theological Inquiry in Princeton, a hospitable and stimulating environment sustained by the leadership of Dan Hardy. I express my gratitude to the Department of Philosophy of Princeton University, which granted me a visiting fellowship during those seven months, and especially to Bas van Fraassen, my friendly host. I also thank the

Netherlands American Committee for Educational Exchange for giving me a grant as a Senior Fulbright Scholar.

I have had the opportunity to present earlier versions of some parts of this book in various contexts. I think with gratitude of the research conferences organised by the Vatican Observatory and the Center for Theology and the Natural Sciences (Castel Gandolfo, Italy, September 1991, and Berkeley, USA, August 1993); the conference on 'Physics and Our View of the World' organised by the Praemium Erasmianum Foundation (Oosterbeek, NL, 1992); the Fourth and Fifth European Conferences on Science and Theology, organised by the European Society for the Study of Science And Theology (Rocca di Papa, Italy, March 1992, and Freising, Germany, March 1994); lectures at the Princeton Theological Seminary and at the Chicago Advanced Seminar on Religion and Science (April 1993); two consultations organised by the Center of Theological Inquiry in Princeton (June 1993 and 1994); and meetings of the research group on knowledge and normativity of the Department of Philosophy of the Vrije Universiteit and of the working group on science and theology initiated by the Bezinningscentrum of the Vrije Universiteit, chaired by Professor Maarten Maurice, a generous supporter of work on the relationship between theology and the natural sciences. I also acknowledge the importance of meetings on (socio)biology and theology organised by the Evangelische Akademie in Loccum (Germany) and the Chicago Center for Religion and Science (May, Striegnitz, and Hefner 1989, 1990), even though I did not present any material there myself. The Prins Bernhard Fonds Prize, awarded in 1992 by the Dutch Academy of Sciences in Haarlem, and the 1994 prize from the Legatum Stolpianum of the University of Leiden, both for my book on cosmology and theology, and prizes in 1994 and 1995 from the John Templeton Foundation in its programme on 'humility theology' were valuable encouragements to academic work which cuts across contemporary disciplinary boundaries.

Peter Kirschenmann, philosopher of science at the Vrije Universiteit in Amsterdam, has contributed enormously to the maturation of this book through critical questions and comments. I also thank the Department of Philosophy for accepting this thesis as a serious contribution to an important debate, even though most faculty members heartily disagreed with the position defended here. Ernan McMullin, John Cardinal O'Hara Professor of Philosophy, emeritus, of the University of Notre Dame is to be thanked not only for his willingness to act as referent, but also for the way he challenged and encouraged me to articulate central elements more clearly. Bas and Tina Jongeling corrected the English of an earlier version as well as some of my arguments. I am also grateful for the many other individuals who responded to drafts of various chapters, or who through discussions contributed to the development of some of the ideas presented here. With the certainty that I am omitting some persons, I recall responses by, ideas from, and conversations with John H. Brooke, Calvin B. DeWitt, S. J. Doorman, Corby Finney, Owen Gingerich, Gary Green, Niels Henrik Gregersen, Casper Hakfoort, Dan Hardy, Philip Hefner, Rob Hensen, Piet Hut, Chris Isham, Wim de Jong, Evert Jonker, Bernd-Olaf Küppers, Theo Kuipers, Huib Looren de Jong, Maarten Maurice, Cees de Pater, Arthur Peacocke, Herman Philipse, John Puddefoot, Hans Radder, Helmut Reich, Robert J. Russell, Robert Scharlemann, Bas van Fraassen, Wentzel van Huyssteen, Wim van der Steen, René van Woudenberg, Bas Verschuren, Christoph Wassermann, and an anonymous referee for Cambridge University Press.

My employer, the Bezinningscentrum of the Vrije Universiteit, graciously allowed me a leave of absence for the seven months in Princeton during which the first draft of this book was conceived, and my colleagues created the atmosphere in which I could complete the book. My closest colleagues, Bert (A. W.) Musschenga and Anton van Harskamp, have responded to drafts of sections and exerted even more influence through many incidental conversations. However, it is likely that neither they nor the board of the Bezinningscentrum, nor any of the persons mentioned, fully agrees with my position as developed here. While they all deserve positive credit, they all must be excused from any blame.

Last but not least, Zwanet graciously allowed me many leaves of absence, both physical and mental, taking care of our children Johannes, Annelot, and Esther, while encouraging me to complete my work. In line with the main thrust of my argument, I believe that her love and support is not less real for being embodied. This book is dedicated to her.

I

Religion and science: strategies, definitions, and issues

1. INTRODUCTION: A VARIETY OF STRATEGIES

Mountain peaks do not flow unsupported; they do not even just rest upon the earth. They *are* the earth in one of its manifest operations. (John Dewey 1934, 3)

Humans too 'are the earth in one of its manifestations'. We are part and parcel of nature. Our mental life, consciousness, and culture, our sciences and our religious convictions 'do not flow unsupported', nor do they merely 'rest upon' our physical constitution. We are natural, limited, biological beings. This has consequences for our self-understanding, our views of human religion and science included.

We are atoms and molecules, but we are not just piles of them. We are much more structured and shaped. Reality allows for a rough division into levels of complexity, from quarks to atoms, and from molecules to organisms and cultures, and our knowledge ranges accordingly from physics and biology to the social sciences and humanities. Religion and morality belong to the 'highest' level, that of human persons, cultures, and traditions. However, that level does not 'flow unsupported', but is rooted in, or rather a manifestation of, the rich possibilities of the natural world. In this study I seek to articulate such a view of reality and attempt to think through perspectives for religion in a world best understood in scientific terms. In chapter 1 I will articulate my understanding of the main partners, that is, of science and the naturalist view of reality which, in my opinion, is the most adequate interpretation of the sciences [2], and of religion [3]. After these reflections on the partners and on definitions of central terms, we come to discussions about the relationship between science and religion [4, 5]. But first, we will consider some strategies for dealing with religion in relation to the natural sciences.

1

My strategy with respect to the sciences is in contrast with various other interpretations of the natural sciences.

(1) Some *play down science* in order to make room for existing beliefs. In their opinion, science offers knowledge which may be instrumentally useful, but this knowledge is not significant when it comes to matters of meaning, where we have to turn to subjective experience and inter-personal relations. Either the status of scientific insights or the extent of the domain of science is supposed to make the sciences irrelevant for reflections on religious life. With such thinkers I agree that religion and science are quite different enterprises. However, humans are part of the natural world; the sciences may well have something to say about interpersonal relations and subjective experiences too. At various places in this study I will attempt to make it clear that such modest, *agnostic views of science*, with respect to its domain and the nature of its claims, underestimate the scope and strength, and thus the relevance of the natural sciences.

(2) Others do not so much play down science, but rather embrace it while arguing that the sciences result in a 'holist' or 'organic' view of reality, which incorporates notions such as values and feelings. In some such approaches the standard disciplinary order of the sciences is rejected, and mental or personal phe-nomena are taken to be more basic than physical ones, or at least equally fundamental (e.g., process metaphysics, as inspired by Whitehead). Reality is seen as more meaningful than the dominant, physicalist view of the sciences seems to suggest. I will argue that such *romantic or metaphysical interpretations of science* are, if not at odds with the best available knowledge, unwarranted when they postulate more fundamental entities or relations than one needs to account for all our experiences.

(3) In this study I opt for an interpretation of the sciences which takes them very seriously (though cautiously so, since current scientific theories are not final) and as relevant to our understanding of the natural world, humans included (against 1). I accept the current disciplinary structure of the sciences, which gives physics a prominent place when it comes to the most basic laws and constituents of reality, while life and consciousness are taken to be phenomena which depend on complex organisations and are studied by 'higher-level' sciences such as biology and psychology. The sciences say what they seem to say; the interpretation need not always be obvious or unique, but a radical reinterpretation and reshuffling of the sciences allows more

liberty from accepted scientific practice than I consider warranted (against 2).

Among those who take the sciences as relevant and as saying what they seem to say, various positions with respect to religion can be found.

(a) Some authors give the sciences full reign in the domain of knowledge, and conclude that science has made all religion futile. I agree with them on the primacy of science in the realm of knowledge; claiming science and religion as separate cognitive enterprises of equal status is too easy. I also agree on a sober rather than a romantic naturalist framework as the best interpretation of modern science, and conclude that science challenges religious views. However, contrary to *polemical anti-religionists*, I hold that religion continues to be an important phenomenon in our reality. Even when religion is explained, if ever, it will not thereby be eliminated even though it will have to change. Furthermore, I will argue that a naturalist understanding of phenomena in reality leaves some questions about the framework as a whole open; questions which such authors dismiss too easily.

(b) This brings me closer to those who do science-and-theology in a way which takes the natural sciences seriously. However, within this approach I will distance myself from those who do *science-and-theology* as if science offers evidence for divine design, as if there is room for particular divine actions within the natural world, or as if we have two enterprises of equal cognitive status which need to be integrated. In my opinion, such a position runs the risk of demanding 'less than it could of theologians and more than it should of scientists' (Eaves 1991, 496). It demands more than it should of the scientists since such an approach threatens the coherence of the sciences; this coherence I articulate in the notion of 'naturalism' [see below, 2]. Equally important, if one relates scientific understanding *of the world* to theological convictions [chapter 3], without taking into account scientific insights *about human nature* [chapter 4], one demands less than one *should* of theologians. I have two reasons for this position.

(i) We should not combine a sophisticated understanding of physics with a pre-scientific understanding of human nature, for example, by talking about mind, subjective experience, affections, or decisions without taking into account the way such aspects of personal life are rooted in our constitution. In our anthropology, which is essential to any theological position which is existentially relevant, we should take the appropriate sciences into account. A jump from quantum physics to the self, or from non-linear thermodynamics and chaos theory to human nature is inadequate since it bypasses many relevant 'intermediate' disciplines such as neurophysiology, behavioural genetics, and sociobiology [22–6, 28].

(ii) Theologians not only have to develop a view of creation and providence which does not conflict with the evolution of species and our knowledge of physical processes. They also have to take into account that religious beliefs and interpretations arose in various historical and pre-historical circumstances. That such beliefs arose in certain circumstances does not imply that they must be wrong, but their historical contingency in relation to human history and human nature raises the question of why we would consider particular beliefs of an earlier epoch as serious candidates for truth or as existentially relevant insights, worth reformulating in our time. Translating theological convictions into new terms by finding new models and metaphors is, in my opinion, inadequate if questions concerning the evolved, historical character of human religious traditions are passed by.

Whether theologians can respond adequately to these insights, is something that depends on the criteria by which one evaluates the results of projects like the one undertaken here. I will articulate a minimum number of elements which I consider essential [3], and seek to argue in this book that these can find a place in a naturalist view of reality.

My approach is minimalist with respect to religion (Stone 1992), but this is, in my opinion, a consequence of taking science seriously. The challenges from the sciences to religion are such that significant *changes* in our understanding of religion are called for. Religion is too important to leave to conservatives who attempt to save faith by keeping science at bay with the help of formal arguments, by rejecting science, or by replacing it with a reconstruction of their own. The rise of conservative positions, both inside and outside the Christian churches, is 'a sign not so much of a recovery of faith as of a loss of nerve before the onslaught of new perceptions of the world' (Peacocke 1993, viii). Theologians and other thinkers about religion should not be satisfied with less than honestly facing the challenges. The hope, and for Gerd Theissen (1985, xi) the 'surprising experience', is 'that precisely when we refuse to stop short at the innermost "sanctuaries" of the tradition with our modern scientific questioning, the tradition shows up in quite a new light'. I am less confident about this 'new light' than Theissen. However, whatever the outcome, intellectual honesty compels us, in my opinion, to take science with utmost seriousness, since it is the joint, cumulative and successful enterprise of many individuals.

By arguing for a naturalist view of religion, for the importance of religion, and for the persistence of limit questions despite the success of the scientific understanding of reality, I will probably offend persons in opposite camps: both those with a more traditional view of religion and those who totally dismiss religion. Many adherents of these two opposite positions share a static cognitive understanding of religion, which is challenged here. Just as politics is too important to leave to extremists on the left and the right to define the issues, so too are religion and science too important to leave their fates to conservatives and eliminators.

This book serves two purposes. One objective is to provide a survey of various positions on, and of issues in, the relationship of religion and science – many of which merit further attention. This survey has to be selective and limited in view of the second goal: the articulation of my own position, and its defence against various challenges, some of which arise from the other positions considered. Though the book presents a personal perspective, I hope that those who do not share my position will none the less find the reflections on various challenges to religion in relation to the natural sciences relevant. The following is an argument, but it is also a map, providing an overview which may be useful whatever the direction in which one may intend to go.

If one were to study all individual trees at length one would not notice the forest. The analysis of the positions of individual authors may leave much to be desired; a complete presentation of each view would have to be much more nuanced. Besides, there are important books which have not been considered, and British and American authors have received much more attention than authors from the European continent. I apologise for any biased representations. However, the aim of this book – an argument about the field as a whole – is at odds with a detailed analysis of individual authors or single issues and with the attempt to be complete.

The focus is on Christianity as it is prominent in Western Europe and in the United States of America. This is not in any way based upon an informed judgement about the value of other traditions. Some limitation is necessary to acquire some depth with respect to the area chosen. The particular limitation and approach adopted here are contingent upon my own background and context, that of a late twentieth-century Dutch academic, who was raised in a religiously liberal and politically social-democratic atmosphere, who was trained in one of the natural sciences, and whose primary professional responsibility is intellectual rather than pastoral. Whether a similar analysis could be made in other contexts, would have to be considered by persons more versed in other traditions.

There may not be a neutral, objective stance; even the mixture of empirical and analytical attitudes assumed here is the product of tradition, namely of the intellectual traditions of modern science and of the European Enlightenment. This tradition has moral and intellectual merits in its ideal of an impartial view and in its intended attitude to put any assertion as much as possible to the test, and therefore its willingness to abandon any belief if it were to fail seriously. This tradition is not neutral, maybe not even self-referentially consistent, as problems of tolerance with respect to intolerant ideologies and persons show. However, as a moral and intellectual tradition it is mine, and that of many others both within and outside the churches in Western Europe and North America. It is in that spirit of inquiry that I offer the following reflections on religion in relation to the natural sciences.

2. SCIENCE AND NATURALISM

The 'Legend' was, and in some circles still is, that science discovers *the* true story of the world by using *the* scientific method (Kitcher 1993, 3). This view has come under attack during the last three or four decades. Studies of actual science showed that some successes had been achieved by violating officially acknowledged methods. Subsequent scientific accounts and paradigms were shown to exhibit substantial discontinuities, even though each story was in its time held to be almost, approximately, or partially true. The relevance of social relations among scientists and between scientists and the wider community to the development of science has been brought to light. Such studies have led to criticisms of the traditional view of science.

One possible response to the criticism of the legendary view of science is to question and dismiss science. Another possible response is to conclude that we should develop a better understanding of science in the conviction that 'Legend offered an unreal image of a worthy enterprise' (Kitcher 1993, 5). I take the latter course. The epistemic status of science can be defended even while the importance of the social dimensions of scientific practices and the reality of discontinuities in the history of various disciplines is accepted. This position can be argued for in a general way on the basis of our successes in manipulating the world and in unifying our understanding. More specific arguments come from detailed studies, for instance of the social dimensions in consensus formation and of continuities and discontinuities during various historical transitions. P. Kitcher's *The Advancement of Science* offers, in my opinion, a promising example of such a revised view of science. He concludes:

Flawed people, working in complex social environments, moved by all kinds of interests, have collectively achieved a vision of parts of nature that is broadly progressive and that rests on arguments meeting standards that have been refined and improved over centuries. Legend does not require burial but metamorphosis. (Kitcher 1993, 390)

A few characteristics of the understanding of science that lies behind my approach:

a. Science is taken in a *realist* way in the sense that it is supposed to study a reality which is to a large extent independent of humans, and even more independent of human attempts to find out about reality. However, science is not restricted to phenomena which are independent of humans. Even though large parts of the biosphere have been modified by humans, a biologist can still study an ecosystem as a reality which precedes her current study. A recently discovered class of materials which exhibit superconductivity at relatively high temperatures exists, as far as currently known, only in so far as these materials have been made by humans in laboratories. However, a physicist who studies these materials after producing them still investigates a reality 'out there', even though that reality has been constructed. Even the study of human consciousness by physiologists and psychologists, to take another example, is in many cases the study of other persons, and if it is self-reflection there still is the assumption that the reflection concerns one's own inner feelings and thoughts – a reality on which one reflects.

b. However, such a realism does not carry us very far in debates on *scientific realism*, which are, in my view, not debates about the existence of 'reality out there' but debates about the quality of our knowledge. Do our terms refer to entities out there? Can we say that these entities exist? Do our theories express relations between entities out there? Or, less generally, which theories, or which elements in our theories, can we take seriously as 'depicting' the way reality is, and to what extent? What criteria should we apply when we attempt to answer such questions? Are there mature sciences in which there is convergence to a true account of the world? Unqualified realism, in the sense that we take all our current theories to be the truth, or at least part of the truth or increasingly better approximations to the final truth, seems too strong, and thus too vulnerable to criticisms. Scientific explanations and concepts are provisional human constructs organising the natural world; they are not wholly independent of human intellectual capacities, social interactions, and contingencies of history.

Debates about realism sometimes become heated due to conflation of this debate about the quality of our knowledge with the debate about the existence of reality out there referred to above (a), especially when the dispute concerns not only the knowledge and existence of ordinary reality but also knowledge about, and the existence of, God. To some extent this conflation of the two debates on realism is to the point when it comes to religious issues, since the consequence of a certain view of our knowledge (the second debate, b) may be that one has a low regard for the belief that religious terms refer to a particular existent with the characteristics ascribed to God without, however, challenging the existence of reality as such; perhaps the religious terms are understood psychologically or sociologically [see below, 20, 22, 24]. To meet the challenge of a non-realist understanding of religious terms, a general defence of realism in the first sense (in contrast with idealism, [17]) is insufficient, since the challenge concerns not so much the existence of a reality, but rather the nature of that reality.

c. One major characteristic of the sciences is their wide *scope*; their domain seems to be without obvious boundaries. In the course of history, terrestrial physics turned out to be applicable to heavenly phenomena as well, and chemistry can be applied to all processes in living beings. The domain of the sciences extends from the smallest objects to the universe at large, from extremely brief phenomena to the stability of rocks, and from heavy objects to massless light. The same physics and chemistry seem to apply everywhere and at all times.

d. Correlated with the extension of science is the inner *coherence* of our scientific knowledge. While I do not claim that theories in one science, for instance biology or chemistry, can be exhaustively reformulated in terms of another science, such as biochemistry or physics, the coherence between different sciences has proved to be a heuristically fruitful guide in the development of the sciences, and, if temporarily strongly violated, has at least re-established itself as a result of later scientific developments.[1] Coherence has become a criterion which makes us reject, or at least consider with the utmost suspicion, purported knowledge which stands in splendid isolation, even if it does not conflict with the rest of our knowledge. This coherence is such an effective heuristic guide that I take it to be informative about the reality with which our knowledge deals, but I will articulate that when we come to 'naturalism'.

e. Science *enlarges and changes* our view of the known world.[2] In science there is more risk involved than in formal demonstrations (as in mathematics) since the scientific theories are not in a strict sense implied by the data. The development of scientific theories is also more risky than induction or extrapolation, since theories may postulate entities and concepts of a kind not found in the data; theories are more than generalisations of facts. The debate about scientific realism (see above, b) can also be interpreted as a debate about the way we should consider the theories of science given the 'risk' involved in the process by which we come to these theories: is the process to be understood as a form of inference on which we can rely (and to what extent and for what purposes)? Whatever we think of the realist status of scientific theories, they offer us *scientific images* of the world which *differ* from our

---

[1] The coherence need not have been heuristically fruitful at all moments in the history of science, as J. H. Brooke pointed out to me with the help of some examples. For instance, in the late nineteenth century there was no coherence between the best physical estimates of the time available for terrestrial evolution (e.g., Kelvin calculated on the basis of known sources of energy a solar lifetime of approximately 20 million years) and the time assumed in evolutionary biology and geology. Too stringent opinions on coherence would have hampered the development of biology. However, in this case coherence was established later, with the discovery of nuclear fission and fusion. Coherence can also be artificial and unfruitful, for example by making too facile claims about similarities and relations between quantum and mental phenomena; this would be a claim to coherence which leaves out many relevant 'intermediate' disciplines, such as the neurosciences and thus is not the kind of coherence referred to in the text.

[2] The expression that science enlarges our view of the known world has been taken from the title of an essay by McMullin (1994); see also (McMullin 1992, 92), where he argues that the scientific 'process *as a whole* is the inference by which we transcend the limits of the observed, even the instrumentally observed'.

manifest images (Sellars 1963). This is especially relevant when we consider religion, since religion is in general intimately related to manifest images. This has to do with the importance of tradition for religion, and hence that of symbols and myths from earlier times. It has also a 'public relations' side, since most religions reach out to a wide audience which understands and relates to manifest images more easily. The difference between manifest and scientific images is also conceptually important. For instance, our concept of a person (with an inner life, emotions, responsibilities, etc.), as it is central to most religious views, is rooted in our manifest images of the world.

f. Contemporary natural science is *stable and provisional.* It is stable in the sense that many branches of science seem to be cumulative, building upon knowledge acquired in the last few centuries. Whereas there was a time when the existence of atoms was seriously disputed, it seems extremely unlikely that physicists and chemists ever will abandon belief in atoms and, for instance, in the periodic table arranging the various elements. It seems equally unlikely that biologists will abandon evolution, both as a view of the natural history of organisms and as a theory explaining this natural history in terms of transmission of properties (in genes) and of differences in survival and reproduction between various variants. However, science is also provisional, and this provisionality is not merely that we may extend our knowledge into new domains (for instance by creating and studying super-heavy elements), but also that we may reach a further understanding of domains already known, and thereby modify our views. For instance, our understanding of the particles that make up atoms (protons, neutrons) has changed; they now are taken to consist of quarks and gluons. And if one probes further, one comes into a domain where the physics is very speculative, and certainly not as stable as our belief in atoms.

Naturalism
Among those who intend to take science seriously, various views of the world may be found, but one of these seems to me to be the most adequate view of the world given contemporary natural science. It is this view which I label 'naturalism'.

There are at least two ways of using the label 'naturalism'. Strawson (1985, 38ff.) distinguishes between 'soft' or 'non-reductive' and 'hard' or 'reductive' naturalism. Upon the 'soft' understanding, naturalism refers to what we ordinarily do and believe as humans, say about colours, feelings, and moral judgements. When a painting is considered 'naturalist', it is so in this 'soft' sense. The 'hard' version, according to Strawson, attempts to view human behaviour in an 'objective', 'detached' light as events in nature. This distinction corresponds to some extent with the distinction made above between 'manifest' and 'scientific' images. Strawson argues that these two ways of viewing the world are compatible when each is considered relative to a certain standpoint; however, if he has to choose, he opts for 'soft naturalism' (Strawson 1985, 95). In contrast, I am of the opinion that in the light of the successes of science we have to give 'hard naturalism' priority over 'soft naturalism' if there appears to be a conflict; science not only supplements, but, in many instances on good grounds, *corrects* our (soft) 'natural' understanding of reality.

One could interpret this study as an attempt to understand what happens to our self-understanding, our 'soft naturalism', when we think through the results of the 'hard' approach. If 'hard' naturalism is to be considered successful, it has to be able to make intelligible why we perceive the world and ourselves the way we do, *i.e.* our 'soft naturalist' view of the world. Physics not only offers a different description of a table, say as empty space dotted by a few nuclei surrounded by fast electrons, but also an explanation of the appearance of substantial solidity. Some elements of our manifest images may be shown to be illusions, but many elements of human self-understanding and manifest images of the world can perhaps be recovered with minor reinterpretations, for instance as valid relative to a certain point of view and a certain level of description. In this study I use the label 'naturalism' for 'hard naturalism'; 'materialism', 'physicalism', and 'physical monism' may be construed as near synonyms.

My naturalism is a metaphysical position. It goes beyond the details of insights offered by the various sciences as an attempt to present a general view of the reality in which we live and of which we are a part. However, it is a rather 'low-level' metaphysics in that it stays close to the insights offered and concepts developed in the sciences, rather than that it imposes certain metaphysical categories on the sciences or requires a modification of science so that it may fit a metaphysical position taken a priori. Thus, the view may seem to share in the provisional character of scientific theories (see above, f). As a general view my position is not dependent upon the fate of speculative theories, say on superstrings. However, it is dependent upon the fate of major scientific insights, and especially on the standard view of matter as constituted of atoms (physics) and on the standard view of organisms as having arisen through an evolutionary process. At various places in this study we will consider the question of how to deal with disagreements in science (especially in [16]), and how the presence of such disagreements affects our view of the current consensus. The fact that there are disagreements, especially disagreements with respect to traditional metaphysical issues such as ultimate origins and the temporality of the universe, does support the conviction that one should be modest in building metaphysical claims upon contemporary science. On the other hand, we cannot do better than accept the best available knowledge, and thus build upon the most stable insights about the constitution of worldly entities and the processes by which they came to be what they are.

The following is an attempt to define some central terms of my naturalism. It is not thereby decided by definition that these definitions of naturalism apply to our world. Rather, it is claimed that these definitions are useful in dealing with our knowledge of the world; this claim to adequacy is to be supported by actual cases. Later chapters thus not only consider the implications of such an understanding of the world, but also explore the viability of a naturalist way of looking at the world.

My own naturalism, informed by the natural sciences, can be articulated in six claims. The first is a consequence of our experience with the wide *scope* of the natural sciences. Non-material aspects of reality, such as music, science, and social meanings, are not studied as such by any of the natural sciences, but they seem to be always embodied, and therefore causally efficacious, in forms which are in the domain of the natural sciences, whether as ink on paper, sound waves in the air, or neural patterns in a brain. Let us call the domain of the natural sciences – a domain which includes stars and planets, living beings and non-living objects, stable entities and ephemeral events, physical objects and embodied mental and cultural entities – the natural world. The first claim is then the following:

1. The natural world is the whole of reality that we know of and interact with; no supernatural or spiritual realm distinct from the natural world shows up *within* our natural world, not even in the mental life of humans. This claim I will call *ontological naturalism* (ON).

The 'within' natural reality has been italicised to signal an important qualification, to which I will return, namely that answers to questions *about* the natural world as a whole may perhaps require reference to something beyond the natural world (see below, LQ).

Above we already noted the *coherence* of our knowledge. This coherence might be seen as an artifact: we might have restricted ourselves to phenomena which could be dealt with in a coherent way. However, such an understanding of the coherence of the sciences seems to do insufficient justice to the historical development and to the contemporary situation of the sciences.

In the course of the development of the sciences, the understanding of various phenomena which once were dealt with separately, has become integrated, or at least linked. Apparent boundaries have dissolved and phenomena which once seemed scientifically inaccessible are now dealt with successfully. A recent example of increasing coherence is the rise of theories which describe complex and chaotically behaving systems with the help of differential equations on the basis of the same physical principles as earlier Newtonian mechanics.

The enormous variety of specialisations in contemporary science may seem to count against this understanding of coherence. A working scientist has no need to reflect on the coherence of all the sciences; a biochemist need not read any astrophysical cosmology. However, scientists do pay attention to disciplines which deal with similar phenomena in a different context, disciplines which study processes or systems which are believed to be involved in the object of their own study, and disciplines which assume certain conclusions about their research. Thus, an astrophysicist studying nuclear processes during stellar evolution may fruitfully relate to specialists in nuclear physics and in plasma physics (who in different ways study the underlying processes and the same processes in other contexts) and to cosmologists, who consider the distribution throughout the universe of the various elements produced in stars. The disciplinary organisation, as expressed in academic careers and professional journals, is to some extent arbitrary and pragmatically justified. However, there is a coherence across the variety of sciences which is not an artefact due to the way we organise science, but which tells us something about the natural world.

If we accept this interpretation of the coherence of the sciences, the question becomes *what* the coherence of the sciences tells us about the natural world. Some seek to interpret it as an indication of some kind of holist or organic unity of the world. However, given the actual shape the coherence of the sciences has taken – which resembles a hierarchy with more fundamental sciences describing the behaviour of the constituents of the more complex systems described by 'higher' sciences, with physics as the most fundamental science at the basis – I take it that the unity of the sciences arises due to the fact that different entities are constituted from the same basic stuff, say atoms and forces. Interactions and spatial relations between constituents are, of course, included in this view of reality; contemporary physics treats forces, particles, and space-time together. Thus, I accept the following two claims:

2. Our natural world is a unity in the sense that all entities are made up of the same constituents. This I label *constitutive reductionism* (CR).

3. Physics offers us the best available description of these constituents, and thus of our natural world at its finest level of analysis. This could be called the *physics postulate* (PP).

Constitutive reduction does not imply elimination, as if the entities or processes are not real; rather the reverse; pain does not become less real or painful when its physiological basis is unravelled [see below, 22]. However, elimination might happen with regard to concepts used in our descriptions: an exhaustive description in terms of constituents might make concepts which were originally employed to analyse the phenomena at the higher level superfluous, as mere convenient devices for something which could be reformulated without recourse to such terms. A major philosophical question is whether all our concepts can be reduced, translated, and thus eliminated, in this epistemological sense – a move which would make physics the only vocabulary which we would, in principle, need. Elimination is especially an important threat to any attempt to salvage religion in a naturalist perspective.[3] There is no such risk when one holds that God intervenes occasionally in the natural world (at odds with my first claim, ON), since religious language is thereby provided with a unique domain of events. However, if one accepts the naturalism described so far, one cannot

---

3   For instance, Viggo Mortensen points out that Burhoe's attempt to revitalise religion by integrating God into the sciences by, apparently, identifying God and natural selection, as both refer to the power to which we owe our being and to which we have to bow our heads and adapt, (see below, [26]) may 'lead to the abolishing of religion', since 'then religion becomes nothing but words – words that we could just as well do without' (Mortensen 1987, 197).

relate religious language to a domain of its own, except for philosophical limit questions about reality as a whole (see below). For further meaningfulness of religious language some form of irreducibility is essential. Such an irreducibility can be defended in relation to the natural sciences.

One way to approach the issue is to consider the division of labour in contemporary science. This is possible due to the considerable stability and independence of 'higher sciences' relative to fundamental physics and cosmology. Various sciences have developed their own ways of describing and analysing the phenomena with which they are concerned. If one accepts constitutive reductionism (CR), every biological, mental, or social change is at the same time a change in the physical state of the system (token–token identity). However, regularities described in processes at higher levels need not correspond to regularities at the physical level. Constitutive reductionism does not necessarily imply conceptual reductionism, or type–type identity, even though some programmes which seek to reformulate theories at higher levels in terms of lower levels may be successful and fruitful. Naturalism need not exclude the meaningfulness and non-superfluous character of concepts which are involved in explanations in sciences other than physics.

This is not merely a philosophical claim, added independently from physics just to mitigate its significance. It can be argued in relation to ideas that have arisen in modern physics: 'The ideas of symmetry breaking, the renormalization group and decoupling suggest a picture of the physical world that is hierarchically structured in quasiautonomous domains, with the ontology and dynamics of each layer essentially quasistable and virtually immune to whatever happens in other layers.' Physicists studying scaling, renormalization, and critical phenomena have come to the conclusion that 'much of the macroscopic behaviour was quite independent of the microscopic forces' (Schweber 1993, 36f.; similarly Anderson 1972). This view could be labelled ontological non-reductionist, in the sense that successful causal explanations at a certain 'level' use terms which relate to real causal dependencies and natural kinds at that level. Protons attract electrons. The fact that at a different level of description protons are understood as being constituted of quarks and gluons is no reason to deny the ontological status of protons. Nor does the role of 'protons' in certain causal explanations imply that they are fundamental rather than constituted of other particles.

I do not expect that many readers will disagree with this point when it is made with respect to protons, but it also applies to notions at higher levels. Carnivores, green plants, and humans are carnivores, green plants, and humans even though at the atomic level they all are carbon, phosphorus, hydrogen, and other well-known atoms. Desires and emotions may perhaps be fundamental concepts in a psychological analysis, even when affective and mental phenomena are rooted in physiological processes, which are, 'further down', identical with physical processes. The whole is not immediately understood in terms of its parts as they function separately, as if someone could predict the occurrence of emotions on the basis of knowledge of the behaviour of individual molecules. Rather, our understanding of the behaviour of a whole organism contributes to our understanding of the parts (nerve cells, transmitters, etc.), and that understanding of the parts as they function in that whole contributes to our understanding of the whole, even though it need not always be possible to understand the whole in the terms used to describe the parts.

The acceptance of the reality of 'higher level' entities may mislead some to forget the physical realities underlying such entities; a risk which is especially relevant in the context of a study of the implications of a naturalist view for religion. The conclusion of the relative independence of various sciences is conceptual and explanatory rather than ontological in the constitutive sense. Therefore, I prefer to abstain from speaking of 'ontological non-reductionism', and label the next claim *conceptual and explanatory non-reductionism* (CEN):

4. The description and explanation of phenomena may require concepts which do not belong to the vocabulary of fundamental physics, especially if such phenomena involve complex arrangements of constituent particles or extensive interactions with a specific environment.

In the natural sciences, research may be oriented in two 'opposite' directions. Some speculative thinkers, also outside the professional communities, are attracted to the quest for an understanding of the most fundamental laws and constituents of reality (e.g., quantum physics, relativity theories, grand unified theories, etc.). But most scientists work on the understanding of phenomena and on the discovery and construction of new phenomena, assuming that the constituents and laws relevant to their purposes are sufficiently well known. This second approach is not only characteristic of disciplines such as chemistry, material sciences, or astrophysics, but also of large parts of physics.

This division of work among scientists is successful. Chemists can go on with their work, even though particle physicists may lack consensus on the most fundamental theory (quarks, superstrings, quantum gravity, etc). Physics is not fundamental to the building of scientific knowledge, since most modifications in fundamental physics do not affect 'higher sciences'. While fundamental physics is fundamental as inquiry about the fundamental ontology of the world, it is the most speculative of the sciences, the pinnacle rather than the foundation of the building of scientific knowledge. Fundamental physics shares this status with cosmology, the study of our particular universe in relation to the possibilities relative to the fundamental laws and constituents.

While one may consider humans as 'inventions' of the evolutionary process, the question arises of 'whose invention' that process itself is. The intentional language is a metaphor conveying an insight: reductionistic explanations within a naturalist framework do not explain the framework itself, as a thumbnail sketch of the sciences may illustrate. Concerning the properties of genes a biologist may refer to the biochemist in the next office. When asked 'when and where did the 92 elements arise?' the chemist can refer to the astrophysicist. The astrophysicist might answer that question in terms of nuclear processes in stars and in the early universe, referring for further explanations to the nuclear physicist and the cosmologist. This chain of referring to 'the person in the next office' ends, if successful at all, with the cosmologist and the elementary particle physicist, the one concentrating on the ultimate historical questions and the other on the most basic structural aspects of reality.[4] Physicists and cosmologists cannot refer to a 'person in the next office'. Due to this particular situation they sometimes engage in philosophical and theological speculation with much less embarrassment than scientists from other disciplines, though not necessarily with greater competence.

5. Fundamental physics and cosmology form a boundary of the natural sciences, where speculative questions with respect to a naturalist view of our world come most explicitly to the forefront. The

---

[4]   The image of referring questions has been taken from Misner (1977, 97); see also Weinberg (1992, 242). It may be the case that historical (cosmological) and structural (fundamental physical) questions converge on one desk, that of the quantum cosmologist (Isham 1993, 52f.).

questions which arise at the speculative boundary I will call *limit-questions* (LQ).

The questions which are left at the metaphorical 'last desk' are questions about the world as a whole, its existence and structure. Such limit-questions are persistent, even though the development of science may change the shape of the actual ultimate questions considered at any time. Naturalism does not imply the dismissal of such limit-questions as meaningless, nor does it imply one particular answer to such limit-questions. Religious views of reality which do not assume that a transcendent realm shows up *within* the natural world, but which understand the *natural world as a whole* as a creation which is dependent upon a transcendent creator – a view which might perhaps be articulated with the help of a distinction between primary and secondary causality, or between temporal processes in the world and timeless dependence of the world (including its temporal extension) on God – are consistent with the naturalism articulated here [13.3, 31].

So far the account of the natural sciences and naturalism has been very general. When we come to humans and their cultural creations, such as moral systems and religions, we may consider various levels of analysis. Physics is fundamental, but not very informative in this case. However, with respect to living organisms we have a powerful pattern of explanation which is not primarily in terms of constituents and laws (physics), but in terms of interactions between organisms and their environments, namely evolutionary biology. An informed contemporary naturalism has to accept this part of science, since it is very successful in dealing with a wide variety of phenomena. Its explanatory schemes are primarily functional: within the constraints due to natural history, traits which contribute to the functioning of an organism (or, more precisely, to the propagation of that trait in a given environment) are likely to become more abundant than other traits which are functionally neutral or disadvantageous.

The emphasis on biology may seem arbitrary: why would biology deserve a more prominent place in this discussion than, for instance, chemistry? However, in physics and in chemistry phenomena are primarily classified in terms of what they do and in terms of their micro-structure, whereas in biology phenomena are primarily classified in terms of their purpose or function (as explicated by Mackor (1994, 542), who develops arguments from Millikan (1984, 1989)). Hence, there is a fundamental difference between physics and chemistry on the one hand and biology (and, beyond biology, psychology and the social sciences) on the other. In biology there is a greater variety of types of explanations (Mackor 1994, 551f.), since one may explain in functional terms what happens, in causal terms how it happens, and in evolutionary terms why the organism is structured so that this behaviour can happen (an 'ultimate' functional explanation in terms of reproductive success).

That traits arose via biological evolution does not imply that every trait must have been optimal in its original context; contingencies of natural history may have determined to a large extent which traits developed. Traits are likely to function well in circumstances similar to those in which they arose, and likely to function less adequately when the circumstances and the interests of the organism differ significantly from those which occurred in the relevant segment of its evolutionary past. Capacities may also be employed for new purposes; this is called 'plasticity'. Consider, for example, humans: our fingers did not evolve to play the piano. Consciously or unconsciously, traits which had evolved because they conferred certain advantages on their possessors have been deployed for novel tasks; perhaps the ability to read animal tracks endowed us with brain structures which we now deploy for reading texts.

An evolutionary view does not imply a particular position in debates on the role of the environment versus the role of the constitution of an organism, such as the debate on whether intelligence is due to nature (genes) or to nurture (education); it is probably due to a complex interplay of both.

Whether evolutionary biology is sufficient for the understanding of humans, their individual and social life and their cultural creations, such as morality and religions, is to be considered in a later chapter. I will argue that culture is not independent from biology, but that an evolutionary treatment of morality, religion, and other cultural phenomena which does not take into account the contribution of culture to human life (and human evolution) is insufficient [24, 25]. Here I want to underline the importance of evolutionary biology:

6. Evolutionary biology offers the best available explanations for the emergence of various traits in organisms and ecosystems; such explanations focus on the contribution these traits have made to the

inclusive fitness of organisms in which they were present. Thus, the
major pattern of evolutionary explanation is functional. This claim
could be labelled the *evolutionary explanations postulate* (EEP).

The evolutionary perspective has consequences for epistemology. We
are able to acquire knowledge since we are endowed with sense organs,
certain mental capacities, and a body of implicit knowledge, much of
which is developed and acquired in early childhood with the acquisi-
tion of language. This background knowledge forms the core of our
manifest image of reality, as distinct from scientific images (see above,
e). This background to our capacity to acquire further knowledge of
natural reality is, upon an evolutionary view, itself a product of natural
reality, and thus a capacity which can be studied in the light of
evolutionary biology. Our epistemic capacities arose because they were
advantageous to our hominid ancestors (and further back in time to
earlier organisms); it is unlikely that traits would have evolved which
would have been costly but ineffective in the actual circumstances our
ancestors encountered. Thus, evolution has endowed us with capacities
and limitations. Our knowledge arises in particular contexts and is tied
to particular interests, though it may subsequently be sustained and
modified if and when the horizons of the 'world' in which we live
expand and our interests change.

Our knowledge of the world is always conditional upon our
capacities, contexts, and interests, and therefore never final or absolute.
Hence, naturalism is not to be identified with scientific realism without
further qualifications. Naturalism informed by the natural sciences
does take mental processes to be secondary relative to physical
processes (PP), and thus is a form of realism if realism is contrasted with
idealism (see at the beginning of this chapter, a). However, as argued
for example by Giere (1988, 8), with respect to a more epistemological
variant of naturalism, naturalism does not imply a scientific realism
which claims that our scientific theories are accurate representations of
reality (see above, b); we may have adopted our theories because of
certain non-representational virtues they have, such as enhancing
human functioning in certain environments (EEP). However, I believe
that non-representational virtues of certain theories and insights, if
these virtues are maintained and extended while new experiences are
incorporated, support a moderate realist attitude towards our insights;
it is hard to have wrong beliefs which none the less support right
behaviour, and even harder to persistently modify wrong beliefs on the

basis of new experiences with the world into other wrong beliefs, which are again successful (as I argue against the philosopher Plantinga; see below and [18]).

This concludes the presentation of the overall view of science and reality. In the remainder of this section I will consider two further issues, namely differences between ontological naturalism as described above and methodological and epistemological naturalism, and the impossibility of a justification of naturalism which would satisfy all non-naturalists.

Ontological, methodological, and epistemological naturalism
Some define naturalism primarily in terms of scientific method; Danto (1967, 448) defines it as 'a species of philosophical monism according to which whatever exists or happens is *natural* in the sense of being susceptible to explanation through methods which, although paradigmatically exemplified in the natural sciences, are continuous from domain to domain of objects and events. Hence, naturalism is polemically defined as repudiating the view that there exists or could exist any entities or events which lie, in principle, beyond the scope of scientific explanation.' Such a naturalism is 'ontologically neutral in that it does not prescribe what specific kinds of entities there must be in the universe or how many distinct kinds of events we must suppose to take place ... it is a methodological rather than an ontological monism ... a monism leaving them [philosophers] free to be dualists, idealists, materialists, atheists, or nonatheists, as the case may be' (Danto 1967, 448).

With respect to ontology, my definition of naturalism is more restrictive than Danto's. In another sense my naturalism is less restrictive than his naturalism, because of conceptual and explanatory non-reductionism (CEN); upon my definitions, there may well be phenomena which are intractable in terms of the natural sciences, even though we can still locate (and thus to some extent understand) such phenomena within our naturalist framework. On my version of naturalism, one may take Danto's reference to scientific method as heuristically useful advice: one seeks to explain phenomena preferably in terms which refer to the most basic sciences which might be relevant. The more successful such a strategy is, the more the ontological unity of reality (CR) becomes explicit.

My definition of naturalism is also less restrictive, compared to

Danto's, with respect to questions which cannot be answered with the help of scientific methods, such as the question of why there is something rather than nothing. On a definition which emphasises methods, questions which cannot be answered by these methods may, in consequence, be dismissed as meaningless. If one defines naturalism in ontological terms, such questions may need to be formulated in accordance with our knowledge of reality (and some such questions may then turn out to be inappropriately formulated), but there is no ground to dismiss such questions a priori.

The philosopher Alvin Plantinga has recently argued against attempts to understand the world exclusively in terms of natural causes, an approach which he calls 'methodological naturalism' (Plantinga 1991). He has also articulated in epistemology a view of warrant, which he considers a version of 'epistemological naturalism' (Plantinga 1993, 46). This is taken to be in contrast with epistemological deontologism, the view that acquiring knowledge is to be understood as fulfilling epistemic duties. His epistemological naturalism relates acquiring knowledge to the proper function(ing) of our epistemic apparatus (sense organs, brain, etc.), and proper function relates to the way something was intended or designed. Since he thinks about our capacities in terms of 'intention' or 'design', he is in a position to argue that 'naturalism in epistemology flourishes best in the context of supernaturalism in metaphysics', and that 'metaphysical naturalism when combined with contemporary evolutionary accounts of the origin and provenance of human life is an irrational stance' (1993, 46 and ix). I will return to these challenges to my approach [18]. I accept most of Plantinga's reflections on epistemology, but I will argue that his argument against an ontological naturalist understanding of our cognitive capacities rests upon a problematic use of possible states of affairs and is wrong with respect to evolutionary biology.

A naturalist view of naturalism

A naturalist approach treats humans as part of the natural world. But humans are also subjects in the world, who describe the world, make judgements about it, and act upon it. 'Naturalism' is one particular human description of the world. A naturalist description of the world (including ourselves) aspires to objectivity, to a *view from nowhere* (Nagel 1986), while naturalism denies us access to such a view; we cannot escape being somewhere, and thus being shaped by a particular historical and cultural context. Therefore, an irksome philosophical question is whether naturalism as a general view of the world is able to deal with itself as a view that arose in a particular context.

One of the difficulties one might see in applying naturalism to itself is that of giving an independent, non-circular definition of 'naturalism'. I do not consider this to be a fatal problem. Any definition of naturalism introduces other terms in need of definition, and thereby leads on to still further terms – including notions such as atom, evolution, fossil, and clock. Thus, the meaning of 'naturalism' is part of an extremely large web of meanings (cf Quine and Ullian 1978). This semantic web is not closed within itself; some terms are tied to phenomena and experiences. Thus, there is no reason to suspect that definitions of naturalism are viciously circular.

Another difficulty might be the possibility of a naturalist explanation of adherence to naturalism. Is naturalism able to explain the fact that some people hold a naturalist view? If a certain conception leads to inconsistencies when applied to itself, it would be ruled out, just like the male barber who shaves all men who do not shave themselves, or the man from Crete who says that all men from Crete always lie. However, a naturalist account of the emergence of persons who hold such a view of the world (and, at the same time, an explanation of the fact that there are persons with other views) does not seem to be inconsistent, since the self-reference considered here is of a much more limited character than the self-reference in the statements about the man from Crete and the barber. Here we consider a certain pattern of explanation, a naturalist one, which is called to explain certain phenomena, namely that some persons hold a naturalist view and that other persons have other views.

A more serious philosophical problem arising as a consequence of self-reference is the justification of naturalism. Can one offer – independently from a naturalist view – a justification for holding a naturalist view? Some justification can be found if one is able to develop a naturalist view which is comprehensive, coherent, and fruitful (or satisfying other such criteria which themselves might perhaps be justified by their past successes), and without an equally satisfactory alternative. However, such arguments assume criteria such as coherence or success. If all such criteria are rejected, or applied in a fundamentally different way, any attempt to justify naturalism comes to a halt. A completely independent justification of naturalism is impossible, since naturalism attempts to deal with everything.

The aim of this study is to develop a naturalist view of reality,

including the phenomenon of religion, and to argue that it is superior
to other ways of considering religion in relation to the natural sciences.
To the extent that this programme is successful, it offers some support
for naturalism (see also [27, 28, 30]).

3. RELIGION

If one defines religion as 'belief in God', one may be asked what is
meant by 'God' and what is meant by 'belief in'. The question 'What
do you believe?' (as a question about the content or object of belief)
may be distinguished from the question 'What is it to believe?' It is the
latter question which will be considered here. Is it primarily a belief
that something is true (e.g., that God exists)? Or is it belief in a person,
as a conviction about a person's trustworthiness and good intentions?
What other kinds of 'belief' are there, apart from 'belief' in the non-
religious sense of thinking that something is the case, even though one
is not completely sure?

In order to avoid premature exclusion of relevant aspects, I opt for a
broad understanding of religions in their variety by presenting various
concepts of religious faith. The term 'religion' covers a wide variety of
beliefs, attitudes and the like, but has also some discriminatory power
in that it allows one to say of certain individuals that they are non-
believers, even though differences among believers are very significant
and interesting [3.2]. We will also come to consider how views of the
nature of faith correlate with views of the agenda for a dialogue
between religion and the sciences [5]. In this section, I will also
formulate some of the main elements of religious views which I
consider important [3.3]. A major aim of the later parts of this book
will be to show that these elements can be accounted for in a
satisfactory way in a naturalist view informed by the sciences.

Before coming to the understanding of religion, I will discuss a
general issue which is important to the present study, namely the
distinction between the point of view of a believer and the point of view
of a modern scholar (including historians, anthropologists, psychologists, etc.; here we reach clearly beyond the natural sciences), who may
or may not be a believer. A study like this one has a hybrid character in
that it seeks to accept a 'detached' scholarly approach but nonetheless
also seeks to argue for a particular stance towards religious beliefs [3.1].

Another general issue is the relation between individual believers
and communities, but I will not consider this point here separately. For

the present purposes I assume that focusing on individuals is a way of focusing on communities in their effects and their constituents. The term 'faith' primarily refers to individuals; the term 'religion', and even more its plural 'religions', refers more often to communities and their traditions as they have been passed on from generation to generation. The terms are also used with a slightly different contrast, when 'religion' is used as the most encompassing term, covering religious behaviour, attitudes, sentiments, institutions, myths, and more systematically articulated sets of convictions, whereas 'faith' more explicitly indicates personal commitments like trust and assent. 'Theology' is used specifically for systematically articulated sets of religious convictions and the structure of such convictions.

3.1. The believer and the scholar

The way a believer *qua* believer approaches his religion is in a fundamental way different from the way a scholar as scholar studies religion; this distinction is similar to the one which arises in the context of sciences such as psychology and anthropology between the scientist and the people studied. Daniel Dennett (1991, 66–98) speaks of 'heterophenomenology' as the attempt to describe neutrally in the other's own terms the way the other understands the world. In normal relationships one expects a conversation partner to respond to one's beliefs by expressing recognition, or disbelief, in some way which reveals his/her own attitude, but in the heterophenomenological phase of research, a scientist should seek to record as neutrally and faithfully as possible, nodding at all utterances without affirming or challenging. 'That deviation from normal interpersonal relations is the price that must be paid for the neutrality a science of consciousness demands' (Dennett 1991, 83). Approaches can be distinguished in many ways; these may differ in details, but such differences do not undermine the usefulness of emphasising that there are two families of approaches. One way in which the difference arises with respect to the natural sciences is the distinction between 'the manifest image' of reality, as it appears to us, and 'the scientific image', as it is constructed or inferred (see above [2, e]).

A scholar studying religion seeks a neutral way of describing the beliefs, suspending her judgement on their truth or accuracy (even when convinced of the sincerity of the speaker). For example, the anthropologist Clifford Geertz (1973, 90) defines a religion as

'(1) a system of symbols which acts to (2) establish powerful, pervasive, and long-lasting moods and motivations in men by (3) formulating conceptions of a general order of existence and (4) clothing these conceptions with such an aura of factuality that (5) the moods and motivations seem uniquely realistic'. And the anthropologist J. van Baal defines 'religion or the religious as: *all explicit and implicit notions and ideas, accepted as true, which relate to a reality which cannot be verified empirically'* (Van Baal and Van Beek, 1985, 3). Even though Van Baal speaks of truth and of a relation with a reality which transcends the empirically verifiable, the issue for these anthropologists in their professional work is not the truth of the ideas, but rather the fact that these ideas are *accepted* by certain individuals in certain circumstances as true (Van Baal) or factual (Geertz).

This distinction between two approaches does not necessarily imply a conflict between the conclusions of a scientist and the convictions of a believer; the one separates judgement and description as far as possible, whereas the other, the believer, makes a positive judgement. Whether there is a conflict depends on the convictions of the believer and of the scientist. The ontological naturalism presented above seems to imply a conflict of this kind. However, even then the conclusion that there is such a conflict, and the precise understanding of the character of the challenge, still depends on the understanding of religion (see below).

There is a related but slightly different conflict between two approaches in the study of religion. A methodological naturalist approach assumes 'that religion could be understood without benefit of clergy – that is, without the magisterial guidance of religious authorities – and, more radically, without "conversion" or confessional and/or metaphysical commitments about its causes *different* from the assumptions one might use to understand and explain other realms of culture' (Preus 1987, x). A religionist approach, such as advocated for instance by Mircea Eliade, assumes that the study of religion is *sui generis*, involving, for instance, a 'transconscious' element, archetypes, or a relation with 'the sacred' which may be illustrated by examples but cannot be defined, analysed, or explained without losing its character as sacred.[5]

In the dialogue about religion and the natural sciences, some have argued for a religionist approach towards religion. In such a way one might understand the approach of T. F. Torrance who, under the inspiration of the theologian Karl Barth, has argued that theology has

---

[5]   A recent discussion of 'religionist' approaches can be found in Platvoet (1994).

to adopt a method appropriate to its object, *i.e.* God. A quite different example of religionism in the dialogue about religion and the natural sciences can be found in approaches which, with the help of science, seek to point out certain phenomena which are *sui generis*. For instance, in *The Encyclopedia of Religion* edited by Mircea Eliade, one finds an entry under neuroepistemology defending a separate kind of experience of the Absolute (D'Aquili 1987; see [20.4]).

In line with my earlier remarks about the coherence of the sciences, I opt for a non-religionist approach in the study of religions. In so far as possible, they should be approached in the same way as other human phenomena. Thus, one should attempt to understand their origins in the context of the rise of human cultures, and their actual functioning in the context of psychological and social mechanisms. If this approach is successful in accounting for the phenomena (including the subjective experiences of individuals and their religious interpretations of the phenomena), it is thereby intellectually justified. If the approach were to fail because one would be unable to account for all details of religious beliefs, practices, and myths of a community, or because one would be unable to specify the actual historical path along which the beliefs of that community were shaped, this might well be acceptable within a naturalist approach. An incomplete understanding is also accepted for other phenomena, both in evolutionary biology and in the understanding of cultures; specifying possible explanatory histories which are compatible with the best available evidence may be the best that can be achieved. However, if one were to fail to find any possible history of the phenomena consistent with the rest of our knowledge, then one would have reason to doubt the naturalist approach as such.

Let us return from the competition between two approaches in the study of religion to the relations between the perspective of a believer and that of a (non-religionist) scholar. The individual believer may be influenced by the scientific study of these phenomena, which may, for example, modify the way the beliefs are held (e.g., not literally but in some other way) or which may modify the content of his beliefs and the vocabulary used to express them. It is such a modification of beliefs that I seek when I suggest that some elements can be maintained in a naturalist approach, though not all. The dependence the other way round is obvious: the scientific study has to do justice to the phenomena, and the phenomena include beliefs and experiences people have. The scientist need not agree with the beliefs, but she needs to explain both the objective and the subjective aspects of the experiences; the advocate of a Copernican view had not only to explain the celestial movements, but also why everybody experiences the earth as stable and sees the sun rise.

Believers may seem more naively credulous than scientists, in that they take their beliefs to be true in some way or another. However, this is not necessarily the easier side. Believers who take their beliefs seriously have to resolve (or live with) problems such as contradictions, whereas, for instance, an anthropologist studying the beliefs of a certain tribe may just record inconsistent beliefs, since she does not take the beliefs as claims about the world but as the beliefs of the tribe she studies. Furthermore, the evaluation itself is not so much an evaluation of beliefs with respect to their truth, but rather an analysis which asks about their antecedents and their psychological and social functions and consequences.

In this light, my study – and many other studies on the relationship between science and religion, except most historical studies – has a hybrid character. On the one hand, I seek to adopt a scientific stance towards all aspects of reality, including a critical analysis of religious beliefs in all their varieties. On the other hand, I go beyond the neutrality of the historian or social scientist studying certain interesting phenomena, or that of the analytical philosopher analysing the concepts used. Most authors on religion in relation to science, including myself, do so from the stance of a believer, in that they seek to answer the question of which intentional stance to take towards religious beliefs. The suspension of judgement, and especially of affirmative judgements, is not maintained, even when in many places a third-person view of religious beliefs is taken.

3.2. Concepts of faith

Not only may different believers have different beliefs, but they may differ in their notion of what 'having a belief' is. W. L. Sessions (1994) distinguishes six models of religious faith; many individual believers and religious traditions combine elements from different models.

(1) Belief may be understood as *faith in a person*. Faith in this sense requires a personal relation with characteristics such as love and trust, as well as, perhaps, 'negative' characteristics such as fear and awe.[6] Propositional belief is, upon this view of faith, secondary, but cannot be

---

[6]   Sessions does not discuss 'negative' characteristics such as fear and awe, which mark distance rather than closeness within personal relationships, but I do not see why they should be excluded, even if positive characteristics such as trust are necessary to the model.

absent, since any kind of faith of a subject S in a person A implies propositions about A and about A's relationship to S, such as claims that A exists and has a personal character, that A is related to S in faith, and that S's trust in A is not misplaced (Sessions 1994, 36f.).

(2) Belief may also be understood as a firm *belief that such-and-such (p) is the case*, especially when 'S has inadequate evidence for p, and S's belief that p is nonevidentially based' (Sessions 1994, 50). Understood thus, faith is an attitude towards propositions. Sessions explicitly distinguishes this model from a more epistemic notion of 'belief that', as advocated by the philosopher of religion Richard Swinburne, according to which religious and non-religious forms of 'belief that' are all in some sense beliefs which should be held in proportion to the available evidence (see [19]). In my view, even if one accepts that 'belief that p' is not based upon overwhelming evidence (or inference to the best explanation, etc.), and thus is not to be argued *for* on the basis of evidence, it still can be confronted with evidence which suggests that p is not the case.

Neo-orthodox Protestant theologians such as Barth, Brunner, and Ebeling have severely criticised the understanding of faith as 'belief that' on theological grounds (Sessions 1994, 151); this kind of criticism is also present in accounts of the history of science and theology by Dillenberger and Buckley (see [11]).

(3) Faith may also refer to a person's *attitude towards the world*; an attitude which constitutes the person who has the belief and at the same time the world as seen by that person. Saying that the world is created is, upon this concept of faith, an expression of a certain way of looking at the world and having a certain attitude towards the world, even though it also implies some claims (such as that the world is not identical with God). Seen thus, beliefs are self-involving (Evans 1963; Kelsey 1985). Such an attitude is total, fundamental, and significance engendering, and therefore a kind of faith (Sessions 1994, 69).

(4) Sessions considers also a non-relation 'confidence model' of faith as *an attitude which qualifies a person* without essential reference to anything else. It may be a kind of self-confidence accompanied by serenity, tranquillity, calm, and peace. It may also be faith as realising one's deeper self, or realising pure awareness, without an object of which one is aware. Such an understanding of faith may be more appropriate to Asian traditions than to Western theistic traditions, even though elements such as self-realisation are not absent from other models of faith.

(5) *Devotion*, with features such as volition and commitment, can be devotion *to a way of life*. On this model of faith 'a devotee treats the way of life to which she is committed not as a mere means to something better, but as an end in itself, something worth pursuing for its own sake even if it does not lead to something else. A way of life requires no goal or end or result beyond itself' (Sessions 1994, 104). Devotion to a person can be understood as devotion to a person exemplifying a way of life.

(6) Rather than faith as feeling or volition, the central feature of faith may also be the *hope for some important future good* G, which the believer 'greatly desires and confidently awaits, anticipates, and expects, despite G's improbability' (Sessions 1994, 114). The latter clause, about the improbability of the realisation of G for S, distinguishes such faith from a warranted expectation that G will come about, a conviction which one would not consider as a variety of religious faith.

Among the differences between these six models are differences in the kind of object of faith, which may be a person, a proposition, an attitude towards the world, a way of life, and a future good; the confidence model has no object at all (Sessions 1994, 131). The six models differ in the role of propositional beliefs and in the kind of beliefs that may be entertained. Debates about propositional beliefs about the world seem to be the main area of engagement of theology with the natural sciences. However, most models also relate to our understanding of human nature, for instance of relations, attitudes, volitions. This too is an issue where there can be engagement with the sciences. This is not immediately obvious if one thinks of physics or cosmology as the typical sciences to be considered, but it becomes a major area once one widens the range of sciences to include a biological view of human origins (including the origins of human desires, attitudes, and ways of life) and a genetic and neuroscientific perspective on human constitutions (including, for instance, human dispositions towards certain attitudes, desires, and ways of life). The claim that this is a major area of discussion is reflected in this study by the fact that chapter 3, on the implications of scientific knowledge of the world, is followed by chapter 4 on the implications of knowledge of human nature.

Given the insight that the debate is not restricted to one about the understanding of the world, I find the way the theologian George

Lindbeck has structured views of doctrine (in three rather than six types) helpful in explicating various areas of discussion on relations between science and religions (see also below, [5]). One view is labelled by Lindbeck a *propositional-cognitivist* view. Upon this view, religion, and especially its systematic articulation in theology, is an attempt to grasp the true, ultimate nature of reality. Another view, called *experiential-expressivist*, 'interprets doctrines as noninformative and nondiscursive symbols of inner feelings, attitudes, or existential orientations' (Lindbeck 1984, 16). This emphasises elements of attitude, especially as related to the impact of the world on humans and the human response to the world as something given. The third view considered by Lindbeck, the *cultural-linguistic* one, understands religions as traditions by which people live, which shape their lives, both individually and communally. This relates to the active side of various models of Sessions, especially to the way a human subject structures the world (the third, attitude, model) and the way of life to which humans devote their lives (the fifth model).

The propositional-cognitivist view of religion correlates with an understanding of the dialogue with the natural sciences as a dialogue about scientific knowledge of the world (and thus often correlates with a major interest in fundamental sciences such as physics and cosmology). The experiential-expressivist view of religion does not have much interest in the details of scientific knowledge, nor in questions of origin and history; upon such a view of religion the main issues of discussion in the interaction with the natural sciences can be in the study of the human constitution (and hence the neurosciences) and in the way this constitution allows humans to experience the world, themselves, and, perhaps, God. The cultural-linguistic view of religion pays much more attention to historical dimensions, since religions as traditions which shape the way people live have a historical dimension. Thus, for such an understanding of religion an evolutionary view of human nature and culture can be much more relevant.

Whereas a propositional-cognitivist understanding of religion directs the discussion towards ontological issues (about time, the openness of natural processes, etc.), the other kinds of understanding religion also bring in axiological issues: how do affective aspects of experience relate to the subject of the experiences and the object experienced? And, thinking of religions as ways of life in relation to an evolutionary understanding of human reality, what are the goods which people have come to desire? Can these desires be understood evolutionarily? How much freedom do humans have with respect to their historically conditioned desires? Understanding the origins of certain human values may explain why they are valued, even if it leaves open the question of why they should (or should not) be valued.

Is everybody religious?

Some aspects of these models of faith are almost universal: everybody has some propositional beliefs and attitudes towards the world, desires some future good, and lives in some way. However, the various models have been qualified by Sessions in important ways. For instance, desiring some future good is not sufficient for that model of religious faith; Sessions has added the condition that the believer confidently awaits and expects that future good despite its improbability if one does not hold the belief. There is a certain attitude which goes with the desire. Essential to these models of faith is the combination of different elements. In that sense, the six models of Sessions (or the three approaches of Lindbeck) cover a significant variety of positions, but not every relationship, attitude, or belief counts as religious.

I add a different argument to the effect that not everybody is religious. This argument relates back to the conceptual and explanatory non-reductionism articulated above (CEN, [2]). With respect to religious language as an articulation of important aspects of human existence, some would argue that it can be eliminated and replaced by a non-religious vocabulary, which does without notions such as mystery and without some articulation of the distance between what is and what is believed should be (see below, [3.3], 1a and 1b). Someone who believes that all religious language can be exhaustively replaced by non-religious language, would not be religious even with respect to the broad concept of religion presented here.

Even if the concept of religion presented here is not all-encompassing it has to be admitted that it is very broad. Hence, many interesting differences will be seen to arise between authors who can be considered religious in different ways (just as a distinction between science and non-science leaves open that many interesting disagreements take place within the broad ambiance of science).

3.3. Essential elements (in my opinion)

Consensus formation, which works quite well in the natural sciences, seems almost totally absent with respect to religious views. Thus, any proposal as to which are the most important characteristic elements of religions is disputable and relative to the person who makes the proposal (and, often, to a larger community with which he or she identifies). Whereas the preceding subsection sought to sketch a variety of religious positions without defending one particular position on the map, this section will indicate what I consider to be the most relevant elements of a religious view. I will not add qualifications such as 'in my view' to all the sentences, but do so here for this whole subsection at once. As I said before, a major aim of the later parts of this book will be to explore whether and to what extent these elements can be articulated in a satisfactory way within a naturalist view informed by the sciences.

1. Two kinds of human experiences
A concept of God as a transcendent and/or immanent reality may be the central symbol of religion, but I do not see how it can be the point of departure of a non-religionist approach to religion. For such an approach, we have to start from human experiences, desires, needs, or reflections. I propose to understand religion as a human response to two kinds of experiences, namely experiences with aspects of reality (a) which we will not accept or (b) which we do not understand or control, but to which we feel positively related.

(a) If religion is seen as a response to *aspects of reality which we will not accept*, it might be called a *prophetic* religion, since it relates to the experience of a discontinuity between values and facts, axiology and cosmology. To articulate this dimension of religion, there should be a dualist element in religious language, articulating a contrast between what is and what should be. Such a dualism can be expressed in religious terms as the difference between earth and heaven, between the city of man and the city of God, between the present and the paradise, between the present and the Kingdom of God, between nature and grace, and in many other ways. Thus, Gerd Theissen (1985, 4) wrote:

Every faith contradicts reality in some way. That is inevitable, if faith is to be an unconditional 'Yes' to life. Think of all the horrors that could contradict this 'Yes'! Think of all the oppressive experiences against which it has to be affirmed: all the probabilities and certainties, including the certainty of one's own death!

Seen in this light, religion is not a reflection of positive experiences, of a sense of divine presence, but rather a critical response, a protest against experiences of injustice or human disorder.

(b) Religion is also a response to encounters with *aspects of reality which we may not understand or control, but to which we feel positively related or for which we feel grateful.* This dimension of religion I call *mystical*, since it has to do with a sense of being related to, or belonging to, something which surpasses us and our understanding. This is a dimension of religion which many authors on the relationship between science and religion seem to identify with when they emphasise elements which correspond to an, affectively speaking, positive view of reality, such as order, creativity, purposiveness, coherence, beauty, or mystery. In my approach, the persistence of limit questions (LQ) will be explored as a possible ground for a 'mystical' sense of belonging and an attitude of wonder and grate-fulness [31], whereas the 'prophetic' duality will be approached through the evolutionary understanding of particular religions with their regulative ideals [26, 32].[7]

2. *A view of reality and a way of life*

If a response is to be considered religious, it has to be related to a view of life and a way of life.

A religious view relates existentially significant human problems (such as sin, death, injustice, and an uncertain future for our descendants and for other living beings; see 1a) and existentially rich human experiences (of love, joy, personal understanding, recovery and transformation; 1b) to a view of reality as a whole, of 'ultimate reality', 'a general order of existence' (as in the definition by Geertz,

---

[7] Barbour (1990, 47f.) offers another angle on mystical and prophetical elements in religion when he, following Ninian Smart, distinguishes between mystical union and numinous encounter (where the sense of distance and contrast is prominent). For a study of biblical theology which focuses especially on divine presence and absence, see Terrien (1978). The issue could perhaps also be argued in the context of the history of religions. John Hick (1989), following Karl Jaspers, distinguishes between the tribal religions which preceded the axial (transition) period around the middle of the last millennium BCE and the post-axial religions. The earlier religions located the individual within the social and cosmic order (and thus are typical examples of religions which stress continuity between cosmological and axiological aspects), whereas the later one's emphasised transformation, salvation, or redemption (and thus, in one way or another, a distinction between the actual social and cosmic order and the destiny of the individual). Platvoet (1993) offers a more elaborate analysis of the history of religions; according to him, the most recently emerged religions (e.g., New Age) have some of the characteristics of earlier types of religions.

above). The experiences do not stand alone, in isolation from convictions about reality as a whole.

The religious responses amount to a stance towards reality, which shapes and guides the interactions of the believer with his environment in the light of the believer's view of his relation to reality as a whole. As a way of life it covers his responsibility for the relevant environment and his way of coping with events in that environment – the second and third view discerned by Lindbeck. (By the way, in the contemporary situation, in my opinion, the relevant environment cannot but include humans of all ethnic and religious backgrounds as well as all other living beings on earth in their ecological relations.)

3. Resources

A religious view is not merely an intellectual position, comparable to a scientific theory which aims at a univocal description and explanation of certain phenomena. Rather, it is an existential response which has elements of all three views described by Lindbeck: propositional beliefs (e.g., about the 'general order of existence', see above), attitudes which structure the world and qualify the subject's relation to himself and others, and a way of life, including regulative ideals distinct from the actual situation in which one finds oneself.

This complex response is nourished by and expressed in various symbols, narratives, and practices, such as singing, breaking bread, burning a candle, meditating and praying, reading poetry, and so on. Thus, religious believers draw on the resources (narratives, commandments, rituals, etc.) of particular communities and traditions. Critical consideration of those resources is intellectually and morally necessary, since symbols, images, and rituals may be powerful and evocative, but they need not be wise in our situation; they developed in other circumstances (see [2], EEP).

4. Coherence

There is another intellectually desirable but problematic characteristic of religion, and that is coherence. The two kinds of experiences considered above (1a, 1b) are quite different; one might say that they point in opposite directions. A mystical view correlates with some sense of continuity between the understanding of the world and the understanding of the central religious symbol God, whereas the prophetic view emphasises discontinuity. I find the combination of continuity and discontinuity between the understanding of the world and the understanding of God, or, in other terms, between what is and what should be, or between facts and values, to be a major characteristic of interesting religious views. Views that lean towards the side of continuity seem insufficient with respect to the existential response to evil, whereas those that lean towards the side of discontinuity are in danger of being too much tied to dualist views of the world, as expressed, for example, as a dualism of heaven and earth, or a distinction between God as creator and as the loving father of Jesus Christ. An important issue is whether an adequate religious view (also adequate with respect to our scientific knowledge) is able to combine mystical and prophetical elements in a consistent and fruitful way.

4. CONTEMPORARY CONTEXTS FOR RELIGION'S RELATION TO SCIENCE

So far we have considered science, naturalism, and religion more or less separately. In this section and the next one, we will begin with an exploration of discussions on their relationship. We will begin with one specific voice among those who give priority to *ethical* issues, that of the Brazilian theologian Rubem Alves, as he spoke at a conference of the World Council of Churches (WCC) on 'Faith, Science, and the Future' in 1979.

When we become concerned about making room for God in the physical universe or when biology becomes the model for our speech about God, have we not departed from the voice of the oppressed? Have we abandoned our tradition? (Alves 1980, 375f.)

Participants from Africa, Asia, Latin America, the Middle East, and the Pacific Islands supported Alves's position when they urged 'scientists to leave their ivory tower and wealthy temples and join this humble Man in his service to the suffering people of our world' (in Abrecht 1980, 171f.). These people from the Third World emphasised the need for action in response to the social and ethical impact of science, especially the role of science in the global imbalance of power.

Ethical issues were central for Western delegates as well, but in a different way. Seven of the ten sections dealt with social responsibility in relation to genetics, pollution, energy, industrial and urban environments, economy, technology and political power, and the social role of Christian churches. This conference stood in the tradition of social ecumenical engagement as it has developed from the conference on

'Life and Work' at Stockholm in 1925 into the work of the section 'Church and Society' of the World Council of Churches. The other major tradition within the WCC, 'Faith and Order', dealing with the understanding of faith, liturgy, and church order, played no major role in the conference. Despite the shared interest in ethical aspects, Alves dismissed the Western discussions as politically inadequate: 'as we have been speaking about the future of mankind we have indeed been speaking about the future of the rich, since the whole was not questioned' (Alves 1980, 374).

Emphasis on the Western ethical agenda is also explicit in a book with the title *The New Faith–Science Debate* (Mangum 1989). In the Foreword, Paul Abrecht – a long-time ecumenical leader who had also been involved in the conference referred to above – writes on a shift in the interaction of science and theology around the middle of the twentieth century, with the discovery of nuclear energy and its use in nuclear weapons.

In the earlier confrontation the fundamental issue was the clash between Christian belief and scientific knowledge, especially between the scientific understanding of the world and Christian views on creation. In that debate the churches were generally on the defensive ...
   The contemporary encounter between faith and science is quite different from the earlier one ... Today, as a result [of the rapid progress of modern science], science and science-based technology are on the defensive, and religious faith, speaking in the name of troubled and anxious humanity, has begun to ask questions about the consequences of the scientific world view. (Abrecht 1989, viii)

The claim that the earlier discussion on 'the clash between belief and knowledge', and thus the challenge to the credibility of belief, has been *replaced* by a new one on the consequences of technology, seems to me incorrect. It would be wonderful if religious traditions could offer some guidance in dealing with the choices we have to make. However, to present oneself as an advocate of a 'troubled humanity' facing the consequences of science and technology does not resolve the doubts one may have about one's intellectual credentials, even if the churches' moral credentials were unproblematic. Those who seek guidance from faith may intend well, but they still have to account for their claim to authority. What is the nature and credibility of religious traditions in connection with our 'scientific world view'? It is not clear that Christianity would become more credible intellectually by exploiting concern and anxiety about moral issues. One might even question the morality of trying to resolve one's own problem, that of the credibility of religious beliefs, by exploiting concerns about the problematic consequences of science.

Even though 'the new science–faith debate' does not replace other intellectual debates, in fact not even in the book with that title, it is important to see that there are such differences in topics to be discussed. I focus in this study on intellectual issues, but I do not intend to play down the urgency of reflection on, and of appropriate responses to, ethical and social issues.

Within the Western part of the world the specific context is relevant to the concerns addressed in intellectual reflections on the relationship of religion and science. Many American contributions are clearly related to the strong presence of creationism. When the astronomer Howard Van Till from Calvin College argues in his *The Fourth Day* that science and religion deal with different questions, and hence that their answers are not of the same kind, so that there cannot be a genuine conflict, his readers are primarily Christians whom he wants to steer away from a creationistic view of science and the Bible. This is not a minor issue in the general population. According to a Gallup Poll of November 1991, 47% of the Americans interviewed opted for the view that 'God created man pretty much in his present form at one time within the last 10,000 years', whereas 40% opted for a view which accommodated religion to science, 'Man has developed over millions of years from less advanced forms of life, but God guided this process, including man's creation', and only 9% opted for the naturalist alternative 'Man has developed over millions of years from less advanced forms of life. God had no part in this process.' Among those with at least college education the figures were 25% for the creationistic view; 54% for the religious accommodation, and 16.5% for the naturalist position.[8]

[8] *US News and World Report* (23 December 1991), 59; among those with incomes above $50 000 the distribution is 29%–50%–17%), similar to the distribution among those with at least college education. In a poll in 1982 on the same three alternatives, the figures for the general population were about the same: 44% recent creation, 38% evolution guided by God, and 9% evolution in which God played no part (*New York Times* 29 August 1982, 22; also quoted in Numbers (1986), 391 and 415 note 1). And, even before the revival of creationism, in 1963, almost 30% of white church-members polled in northern California were against evolution (Bainbridge and Stark 1980, 20). A recent Dutch survey had no question on evolution (which is itself an indication of the minor relevance of the issue compared to issues which were included, such as church participation, and the role of churches in society). The following two items may give an indication of the situation concerning issues relating to creationism in the Netherlands. Eleven per cent supported a literalist interpretation of the Bible; 47% considered the Bible inspired but not to be taken literally, and 43% regarded the Bible as an

Even when they do not deal directly with creationism, American books and journals on theology and science can be read as *apologetics of science* in a culture in which the status and acceptance of the natural sciences is less prominent than in Western Europe. American books (e.g., Barbour 1990, Rolston 1987), tend to be critical of scientism, naturalism, reductionism, and secular humanism as views which might inhibit the acceptance of science. British authors such as Arthur Peacocke and John Polkinghorne, or Dutch authors do not primarily view scientism, naturalism, and reductionism as challenges to the acceptance of science, but as challenges to religion. As concerns the Dutch scene, this applies not only to my own work, but also to that of others who hold a more orthodox religious position, such as Van den Beukel (emphasising religious experience) and Van den Brom (proposing models for conceptualising divine omnipresence and divine action). Regional differences are not to be overemphasised, as Americans and Europeans discuss the same issues with each other, but Europeans seem to be less involved in an apologetics of science, and more in an *apologetics of religion*, against those who are tempted to dismiss all religion.[9]

5. CLASSIFICATION OF AREAS OF DISCUSSION IN SCIENCE-AND-RELIGION

Three challenges to religion

A single synthesis of religious convictions and pre-scientific insights is often assumed to have characterised the late Middle Ages. It is dubious whether such a medieval synthesis actually existed; conflicts between faith and philosophy occurred, no system was complete and comprehensive, and people disagreed: 'The learned Latin culture of the 13th century was no more unitary than ours' (Mark D. Jordan).[10] However, as a construction of later times the mythical medieval synthesis offers a

ancient book with human legends, fables, histories, and moral codes. However, to a question about the historical existence of Adam and Eve, 37% answered in the affirmative (Becker and Vink 1994, 142f.).

9   Daecke (1987, 33) points to another difference between German authors and English and American authors on the relationship between science and religion: the latter aim more often at some kind of integration, whereas German authors more often take the position that the two enterprises are distinct and mutually irrelevant.

10   Mark D. Jordan develops his case for tension and diversity by considering Roger Bacon, Thomas Aquinas, and Bonaventure in *'By whom all things were made': Christology and Cosmology in the Thirteenth Century*, presented at the conference 'Our Knowledge of God, Christ, and Nature' at the University of Notre Dame, April 1993.

nice contrast to our situation. A major example of a systematic synthesis is the work of Thomas Aquinas (thirteenth century). A literary expression of an integration of theology, ethics, politics, and geocentric astronomy is Dante's *Commedia* about hell, purgatory, and paradise (early fourteenth century). In discerning the order of things, the higher creatures trace God's footsteps, as Beatrice tells the poet in the first canto of Paradise. In such medieval syntheses, ideas from Greek philosophers (Plato, Aristotle), from Scripture, and from earlier theologians came together. Medieval views had a static character and a hierarchical structure, and they were geocentric. The order, understood in terms of Aristotle's doctrine of 'natural place', was also normative, as is still reflected in some uses of the words 'natural' and 'counter-natural'. None of the medieval syntheses is tenable any longer.

(a) *New knowledge* separates us from the medieval synthesis. The geocentrism of medieval astronomy has been abandoned. Static views have been replaced by an evolutionary one with time scales far exceeding any scholarly chronology based on the Bible or on knowledge about the ruling dynasties in Egypt and Mesopotamia, such as the date given by Archbishop James Ussher (1581–1656) for the moment of creation, namely the beginning of the night preceding 23 October 4004 BC, a date which became incorporated in the margins of the authoritative King James version of the Bible.[11] Not only have we become aware of a long pre-human history of the earth, but evolutionary biology and the neurosciences have given humanity a new position among other living beings. Some people have attempted to adapt theology to contemporary changes in our view of the world, for instance by seeing God's creative activity in the evolutionary process. Ascribing the problems for theology to 'an outmoded world picture' (Wildiers 1982, 235) is, however, incomplete and inadequate. It is not only the knowledge of nature that has changed.

(b) Ideas about the *nature of knowledge* and about methods for acquiring knowledge have changed, as is exemplified by the role of experiments and of mathematical idealisation. With the rise of modern science the conception of science changed. The changes at this level during the seventeenth century 'were those that most clearly, in retrospect, mark this century as the age of the scientific revolution' (McMullin 1990, 28). The ideal of purely deductive or inductive

---

[11] Ussher's date is too often only mentioned to ridicule religion. However, it deserves to be understood against a much wider discussion of knowledge in that period, as is done, for instance, by Rudwick (1986, 296) and North (1977).

knowledge was gradually replaced by the ideal of hypothetico-deductive (or retroductive) reasoning. The eighteenth-century philosopher Immanuel Kant made the creative role of the subject more explicit. According to him, the world as it is in itself is inaccessible; the accessible, knowable world is the world as we describe it in terms of our categories. Subsequent developments have shown that Kant's categories and forms of perception, such as Euclidean space, were not necessary. But the insight still stands that knowledge is shaped by our categories, and not only by the reality it purports to be about. The shift to the subject of knowledge was followed by an increased emphasis on the role of language and context, by a decline in the belief in secure foundations of knowledge, and by disputes over the demarcation between science and other human activities. Theology has responded to the increased emphasis on the role of the human subject, for instance by focusing on the personal (e.g., Martin Buber's distinction between 'I–thou' and 'I–it' relations).

(c) A third change regards *our appreciation of the world*. The medieval synthesis took the world to be God's good creation. Today some consider the world existentially meaningless, neutral or ambivalent, whereas other thinkers, both secular and religious ones, still find our reality meaningful. The emergence of mixed feelings about the world can be illustrated by the poem John Donne wrote in 1611 during a time of turmoil in Europe, with the oft quoted line, 'And new philosophy calls all in doubt'. It is dubious whether the poem's original intention was a lamentation over the loss of the medieval world view, but this passage has often been used to refer to this loss.[12] Over a century later, the changing appreciation of the world is exemplified by the cultural impact of the earthquake that destroyed Lisbon in 1755. The French philosopher Voltaire gave his *Poème sur le désastre de Lisbonne* (1756) the subtitle 'Or an examination of the axiom "All is well"'. This theme returns in Voltaire's novel *Candide ou l'optimisme* (1759). There the philosopher Pangloss defends the view that this is the best of all possible worlds. The more Pangloss, who stands for Leibniz, argues his case, the less convincing it becomes. Another illustration of changes in the appreciation of the world, again

[12] Stephen Toulmin (1990, 65ff.) is one of the advocates of the view that the poem is about the decline of the cosmopolis, the sense of cosmic and social order. Toulmin's reading can, however, be disputed. Manley (1963, 44) claims that 'the passage is usually taken out of context to illustrate the impact of scientific rationalism on the Medieval world picture'. Donne's poem can be seen as a methodical religious meditation, similar to the Jesuit exercises (Martz 1947).

a century later, can be taken from Dostoyevsky's *The Brothers Karamazov*. One of the brothers, Ivan, wants to return to God his ticket of entry into the world. The suffering in this world is not justified by heavenly meaning. 'And if the sufferings of children go to swell the sum of sufferings which was necessary to pay for truth, then I protest that the truth is not worth such a price.'[13]

Changes in the appreciation of the world have affected theology as well. This is most explicit in those theologians who have moved from an understanding of God in metaphysical terms, say God as the Ground of Being, to an understanding of God as being on the side of the victims or of the poor (e.g., Alves, see [4]). The 'Death of God' discussion of the 1960s reflects the stronger emphasis on human autonomy in creating knowledge (b), but it also fits in with a strong sense of the reality of horror and injustice in the world (c).

Three views of religion

Not only are there different challenges to religion due to the rise of the natural sciences and other developments (such as changes in the understanding of history and in appreciation of other cultures). Our understanding of religion has also diversified. Each particular way that religion is understood gives a certain shape to its interaction with the natural sciences. George Lindbeck has attempted to clarify the nature of ecumenical (dis)agreements by distinguishing between three views of religious doctrine (see above, [3.2]). I will adapt his categories here for my purposes as describing core elements which are combined in various ways in actual religions and theologies.

1. *Cognitive* claims are central to some views of religion. Religion, and especially its systematic articulation in theology, is an attempt to grasp the true, ultimate nature of reality. Lindbeck (1984, 16) has it that such a propositional-cognitivist view 'was the approach of traditional ortho-doxies (as well as many heterodoxies), but it also has certain affinities to the outlook on religion adopted by much modern Anglo-American analytical philosophy with its preoccupation with the cognitive or informative meaningfulness of religious utterances'.

2. Religious *experiences*, or religious interpretations of experience, are at the heart of religion according to other views, especially in liberal positions influenced by Schleiermacher. Lindbeck calls this an 'experiential-expressivist' view of religion; 'it interprets doctrines as

---

[13]   Quoted from the Constance Garnett translation, revised by R. E. Matlaw (New York: W. W. Norton, 1976), pp. 225f.

noninformative and nondiscursive symbols of inner feelings, attitudes, or existential orientations' (1984, 16).

3. Religions can also be seen as *traditions* by which people live, which shape their lives, both individually and communally. This aligns well with anthropological and sociological approaches. Lindbeck speaks of a 'cultural-linguistic' view of religion. Religions resemble languages and forms of life; they are 'idioms for the construction of reality and the living of life' (1984, 18).

A 3 × 3 classification[14]

Given these two ways of structuring the arena of debate, in terms of three challenges to religion and in terms of three views of religion, a total of nine areas of debate may be distinguished. Ideally, each theological or philosophical proposal would cover all these areas; the

[14] On differences with other current classifications. Ian Barbour (1988, 1990: 3–30) uses four major categories: 1. Conflict (scientific materialism; biblical literalism); 2. Independence (contrasting methods; differing languages); 3. Dialogue (boundary questions; methodological parallels); 4. Integration (doctrinal reformulation; systematic synthesis). The categories 'conflict', 'independence', 'dialogue', and 'integration' express strategies for handling tensions: choosing either one position or the other (conflict), separating the contending claims as different and independent, adapting one's views to some extent (dialogue) or accommodating both claims in an interwoven whole (integration). The four categories do not pay attention to the question as to which kind of religion is supposed to be in conflict with, independent from, or to be integrated with, which kind of science. However, the conclusion that there is a 'conflict' between science and religion (or that they are independent, or that they can be integrated), can be drawn for quite different reasons. For instance, Barbour is in a position to dismiss 'scientific materialism' by lumping it together with 'biblical literalism' under the heading *conflict*. The suggestion is that both are mistaken in relying on an all-too-straightforward realism with respect to texts and theories. This is an attractive rhetorical move, but not adequate since it neglects the fact that the challenges are different. 'Biblical literalism' ('creationism') collides with new knowledge and with modern ideas about the nature of knowledge, whereas 'materialism' tries to accommodate maximally to these new insights. 'Scientific materialism' is much more of an intellectual challenge than biblical literalism. Biblical literalism moves from experiences, in this case the words of a text, directly to convictions. The path from experience to theories is much more elaborate in science. This distance between convictions and experience carries over from science to 'scientific materialism', which is therefore – at least in this respect – much more sophisticated than 'biblical literalism'. Clustering by strategical stance also lumps together various views of *independence*. This too is unsatisfactory, as underlying views of religion may be very different. For instance, some pleas for independence are based upon the distinction between primary and secondary causation, maintaining a metaphysical understanding of religion as dealing with the Primary Cause of everything. But independence might also be the strategy adopted when religion is understood as dealing with moral and emotional issues in human existence. It is not illuminating to treat such different ways of separating science and religion together. The scheme not only lumps together arguments and positions which are different in fundamental respects, but also separates views which are similar in important respects. A materialist view of religion, here listed under 'conflict', may be close to a metaphysical 'integration', since both expand the realms of religion and science to encompass the whole of reality.

scheme can be seen as a way to delineate the target area.[15] However, in practice, most authors focus on one area, a single column, or a single row, or at least have a characteristic emphasis there. For instance, the theologian Philip Hefner writes in intense dialogue with an anthropological understanding of religion, and thus most of his writings primarily deal with the areas of discussion in the third column. However, this does not keep him from making cognitive claims. Rather,' myth provides a picture of *the way things really are*' (Hefner 1993, 202). Such a shift of column signals an important (and problematic) element in his approach, as we will have to consider when we come to theologies which take the evolved character of human religions into account [26].

Strategies discerned by Barbour (1988, 1990; see note 14) can be recovered in some of these areas, especially in the one which focuses on

Viggo Mortensen (1987, 1988) uses two major categories to describe the field, restriction and expansion. One might defend the coexistence of science and religion by arguing that they deal with different, restricted aspects of reality. Or one might consider their relation by arguing that each deals, in principle, with the whole of reality. The attractive feature of this distinction between restriction and expansion is that it focuses immediately on the underlying views of science and of religion. However, the two categories do not pay attention to the way the challenges to religion deriving from science are perceived.

Another scheme, which conceives of eight (4 × 2) possible relationships between science and theology, has been developed by Arthur Peacocke (1981, xiiiff.; see also 1993, 20) and Robert J. Russell (1985, 49f.). Russell distinguishes four 'dimensions' in Peacocke's proposal, namely approaches, languages, attitudes, and objects. Along each of these four dimensions, science and theology may be considered as similar (and thus fairly close to each other, positively related) or dissimilar. I appreciate the four dimensions, which I understand as referring to epistemological, semantical, axiological, and ontological issues. My list of three challenges is somewhat similar, except that I explicitly add the issue of the content of scientific knowledge. I also refer to epistemological and axiological issues; I treat issues of semantics and ontology when they come up in the reflection on knowledge and views of knowledge, rather than listing them separately in advance. Whether reflections in these four areas of discussion lead to a 'positive and reconciling' or a 'negative and non-interacting' relationship (Peacocke 1993, 20) is to be seen; I would not make the result an element in the classification itself, and I doubt that a single scale from negative to positive is adequate here. A disadvantage of this scheme is that it emphasises the cognitive aspects of religion. In my opinion this leaves important areas of discussion out of sight. The natural sciences have consequences for theology, understood as cognitive affirmations, but also for experience and tradition, which are central notions in other views of theology. Therefore, I propose a more elaborate scheme of nine areas of discussion.

[15] I owe this metaphor to A. Peacocke. At the Fifth European Conference on Science and Theology (March 1994) he, R. J. Russell, N. H. Gregersen, H. Reich, C. Wassermann, and various others gave helpful responses to an earlier version of this scheme. Russell suggested calling it a typology rather than a classification, since the latter might suggest that the various categories are mutually exclusive. However, I prefer to speak of a classification, since 'typology' carries other undesirable connotations (symbolic representation), whereas classification may be, as intended here, 'a useful schema for stating some of the problems and disputes' (R. Abelson in *The Encyclopedia of Philosophy*, vol. 2, ed. P. Edwards (New York: Macmillan, 1967), 314).

cognitive elements in religion (1a). I prefer to distinguish these strategies as follows: i. conflicts over specific issues; ii. separation of domains and claims; iii. partial adaptation, for instance by developing models which borrow from the sciences to explicate religious notions; and iv. the development of an integrated view, and the debates over various integrated systems, or world views.

Other classifications (see note 14) give most prominence to the way cognitive claims in religion (theology) and in science are related. This is only the first column, and often only one area (1a), in the scheme proposed here. And especially with respect to this area I intend to make it clear that debates do not stand in isolation, but require consideration of other views of religion (other columns) and other views of the challenges (other horizontal rows).

Table 1. *A classification for areas of discussion concerning the relationship of religion and science*

	Character of religion		
Challenge	1. Cognitive	2. Experience	3. Tradition
a. New knowledge	1a. Content: i. Conflicts ii. Separation iii. Partial adaptation iv. Integration	2a. Opportunities for experiential religion? Religious experience and the brain.	3a. Religious traditions as products of evolution.
b. New views of knowledge	1b. Philosophy of science and opportunities for theology.	2b. Philosophical defences of religious experiences as data.	3b. Criticism and development of religions as 'language games'.
c. Appreciation of the world	1c. A new covenant between humans and the Universe?	2c. Ambivalence of the world and implications for the concept of God.	3c. A basis for hope? Or religions as local traditions without universal claim?

I will now give examples of discussions on relations between science and religion in the various areas, with reference to parts of this book where such positions are considered at greater length.

1a. Cognitive claims in religion and new knowledge about the world
i. Various conflicts have arisen over the truth of the Bible: the world either came into being a few millennia ago or it has existed for billions of years; there has either been a world-wide flood or there has not; species are either fixed or they are not; the Sun either stood still at Gibeon (Joshua 10: 12) or it did not, etcetera. We will come across creationist controversies on various occasions during this study, but we will also consider other alleged examples of a straightforward conflict, especially the condemnation of Galileo [7] and the conflicts surrounding Darwin's theory [8]. It will be argued that in these cases, as well as in the 'creationist' controversies of the last decades, the conflicts were also conflicts among believers about the understanding of religion and conflicts among scientists about the interpretation of science [9]. Hence, whereas the popular picture might be that science and religion have collided over facts, further analysis shows that other issues are involved, such as the flexibility of religious expressions (and hence the possibility of partial adaptation (see below, iii)), the understanding of religion (moving to other columns in the scheme) and the understanding of science, which involves discussions about the nature of knowledge (the next row in the scheme).

ii. Separation as a strategy may be a consequence of new knowledge, say biological explanations for the apparent design of organisms and organs. However, if the strategy is separation, the discussion is not so much about details of new knowledge, but rather about the nature and scope of scientific understanding (the next row). An example of such a position is the distinction between primary and secondary causes (see especially [13.3, 31]).

iii. Examples of a partial adaptation of religious views to new knowledge are attempts to find a model for divine action in the context of quantum physics, chaotic processes or via top-down causation [13].

iv. Among attempts to develop an integrated world view have been Pierre Teilhard de Chardin's evolutionary theology, and process theology drawing on the metaphysical notions of Alfred N. Whitehead and Charles Hartshorne [30]. One might also think of views which dismiss religion as a cognitive mistake which is intelligible on the basis of our psychological constitution and our evolutionary past [Chapter 4].

1b. Cognitive claims in religion and the nature of knowledge
The idea that theology should adopt the methodology of the sciences, or that recent insights in epistemology and semantics

provide a fruitful perspective for religion has been defended by various philosophers of religion. As one of them claims, and more seem to believe, 'Methodology, not subject matter, has kept theology trailing behind in the age of science' (Murphy 1990, 127). According to Nancey Murphy, relevant parts of theology could be structured as a Lakatosian research programme, including features such as a hard core, auxiliary hypotheses, and novel data. Hence, the cognitive claims of theology deserve as much credibility as the cognitive claims of science. We will come back to her position and to other attempts to assimilate science and theology along such methodological lines [17.2]. A weaker assimilation in methodological and epistemological respects has been defended by Ian Barbour, when he listed simila-rities *and* dissimilarities between science and religious belief (Barbour 1974, 69; 1990, 65–92; see also Peacocke 1984, 41–4). Thus, some argue that every theological model or metaphor drawing on the sciences has an 'is' and an 'is-not' component. I will argue that this qualification is important but insufficient [17.3].

1c. Cognitive claims about the meaning of the universe
In their popular book on self-organisation, *Order out of Chaos*, Ilya Prigogine and Isabelle Stengers wrote of a 'new covenant' between man and nature [14]. The physicist Freeman Dyson saw in the fundamental characteristics of the universe an indication of purpose, as if the universe in some sense knew that we were going to arrive on the scene; 'the universe is an unexpectedly hospitable place' (Dyson 1979, 251; see [31] on the anthropic principles). In writing thus, they opposed other scientists who had come to the opposite conclusion. The biologist Jacques Monod, for instance, described everything as the result of pure chance: there is no objective foundation for meaning or purpose. And near the end of his popular book, *The First Three Minutes* the cosmologist Steven Weinberg wrote: 'The more the universe seems comprehen-sible, the more it also seems pointless' (1977, 155). This debate is not so much about the possibility or plausibility of any concept of a transcen-dent God, or even an active God, but rather about the way we understand the universe, our place in it, and its future.

2a. Religious interpretations of experience and changing knowledge
Some see new opportunities for an experiential religion. These include 'religious empiricists' who seek continuity with the Christian tradition as well as authors who represent 'New Age' ideas [30]. Among the

sciences, quantum physics and ecology attract most interest among those who seek to develop religion with an experiential emphasis. Such approaches typically aim at integration, either partial or complete.

Research on the differences between the functioning of the left and right hemispheres of the human cortex has led some to claim that ordinary perception and analysis may be located in the left hemisphere whereas the capacity for experiences of the Absolute is located in the right hemisphere (e.g., D'Aquili, Ashbrook). In this way, a separation of scientific knowing and religious knowing can help their integration within a larger framework, which is itself linked with the neurosciences. In the end it is an attempt at integration to understand 'intense religious and spiritual experience in a more scientific form' (D'Aquili and Newberg 1993, 178). However, the same neurosciences have led some to another conclusion: religious experience is not a special kind of experience, but rather an interpretation given to certain experiences. Explaining religious experiences almost amounts to explaining them away [20, 22].

2b. Religious experience and the nature of knowledge
We will consider some philosophers of religion, especially Richard Swinburne and William P. Alston, who argue for the legitimacy of religious experiences as data for theology [19]. Another proponent of the same viewpoint is Nancey Murphy, who appeals to communal discernment as novel data for theology ([17.2], *cf.* also area 1b).

2c. An experiential view of religion and the appreciation of the world
Some American 'religious naturalists' [30], such as Bernard Loomer and William Dean, want to avoid reference to anything inaccessible. There is no relief from the ambiguities of life and death in some realm beyond space and time. Thus, in order to maintain their self-imposed restriction to the experiential realm they prefer to accept ambiguity in God rather than a resolution of evil through a notion of ultimacy beyond history.[16]

3a. New knowledge and religion as a tradition
On the naturalist view that will be presented here, religious traditions are products of evolution. As evolved traditions, they have been closely intertwined with the evolution of morality, and more widely with the evolution of humanity. This view of religion and morality will be

---

[16] Another discussion of this kind is (Stone 1992) with a preface, critical on this issue, by Langdon Gilkey.

presented below, drawing on Richard Alexander's *Biology of Moral Systems* and Ralph Burhoe's view of the role of religion in the evolution of the human species [24].

3b. Religion as a tradition and new views of knowledge

Drawing on the later work of Ludwig Wittgenstein, some defend that religious traditions should be seen as 'language games' or, drawing on Michael Polanyi, as implicit, personal, background knowledge. This seems to grant such traditions a kind of immunity: How could one consider such a framework or background without leaving it, and thereby claiming a detached point of view which does not exist? I will argue against this immunity that the observation that understanding is always relative to a framework does not exclude further analysis [27].

3c. Traditions and appreciation of the world

The few theologians who take the evolutionary, functional view of religion (as a position in area 3a) very seriously, seek to move beyond a functional view of religious traditions as adaptations which have structured societies. They make claims which transcend any local context, and thereby move from function to truth. The theologian Philip Hefner writes that the locus of the God-question has become 'the trustworthiness of the processes of evolution upon which man depends'. Thus, he asks '*whether there is ultimately a resonance between man and his world or a dissonance – whether man is fundamentally at home in his world or out of phase with it*' (Hefner 1970, 10 and 11f.). And the theologian Gerd Theissen seeks to defend that reality is, ultimately, tolerant and graceful. We will return to these authors [26]. I agree with them that religious traditions are to be seen in an evolutionary perspective. However, their shift from functional adaptations in local contexts to ontological claims of universal scope does not seem successful. It is more promising, in my opinion, to accept religious traditions within an integrated, naturalist understanding of reality as rich, functional adaptations to certain historical contexts in combination with a religious appreciation of naturalism, since reality and its intelligibility do not explain themselves [32].

6. ISSUES FOR FURTHER CONSIDERATION AND PREVIEW

In the introduction I contrasted my own position with two other approaches, namely the approach of those who play down science and that of those who overestimate science in a romantic or metaphysical interpretation [1].

With respect to those who play down science, I need to argue about the domain and the status of science. Reflections on our 'inner life', including religious experiences, on human consciousness, and on the evolutionary origins of religion and morality, support the conviction that no phenomena in the world fall outside the domain of the natural sciences [chapter 4]. With respect to the status of scientific knowledge, I will offer arguments against attempts to dismiss or evade the implications of science with the help of philosophical moves, for instance with an appeal to 'post-modern' pluralism (e.g., Allen, see [18]), or via the argument that science needs a foundation in some form of supernaturalism (e.g., Trigg, Plantinga; see also [18]). The reflections on 'scientific realism' [17] and on a naturalist view of science [27] also serve to make it clear why I hold that one should not underestimate the significance of the sciences. This needs to be supplemented by an analysis of the possibility of similar arguments for the status of theology; I will conclude that such a transfer of arguments from scientific to theological realism does not work [17.2].

Against those who overestimate the sciences or include them in a richer metaphysical view of reality, I need to make it clear that recent advances in the sciences do not offer new perspectives for a sense of cosmic meaning [14] and that the provisional character of our knowledge undermines more elaborate metaphysical interpretations [16]. I will also have to argue that this provisional character and the incompleteness of scientific explanations does not count against the naturalist view; even if all phenomena in the world cannot be explained, they can none the less be understood as phenomena in a naturalistically understood world [chapter 4]. In this context, the status of accounts which are not straightforwardly explanatory but present us with an explanation of how things may have happened is to be clarified ([24]; see also, on thought experiments, [15, 18]). The most important competing metaphysical interpretations of the sciences are organic or holistic; they are advocated by process theologians and other 'religious empiricists'. I consider such quite different interpretations to be possible but implausible because of their implications for the disciplinary structuring of the sciences [30].

Against those who believe that science has made all religion futile I will have to argue that religion can be meaningful even if one accepts the explanatory power of physics, evolutionary schemes and the neurosciences [20, 22, 25]. The history of relations between religion and science is not to be seen as one of conflicts between advancing science and retreating religion, but rather may be seen as a history in which the understanding of both religion and science have changed [chapter 2].

Some relate science to theology in an attempt to reformulate theological notions; in the terms of the classification offered above [5; first column], they emphasise the cognitive side of religion. I will argue that attempts to find room for divine action in the natural world are problematic [13], and that the use of science in theological models may be heuristically useful but does not lend credibility to the theological notions [15]. I also will argue that the cognitive claims of theology cannot be defended along the same lines as contemporary defences of scientific realism [17].

Understanding theology primarily in terms of experience and of tradition (second and third columns of the scheme) does not provide safe havens for theology, as I will argue in chapter 4. We will consider what it implies that a believer's point of view can be located within a naturalist view [22]. I also will argue why an argument for a *sui generis* character of religion such as provided by D'Aquili fails [20.4]. Thus, the chapter concerned will contribute to a defence of the viability of a non-religionist approach towards religion, including religious experiences and religious traditions.

The order of the three views of religion used in the classificatory scheme (cognitive, experiential, and cultural) corresponds to a large extent with the order of the chapters (3, 4-A, 4-B). In the final chapters I come to options which I consider most promising, namely the possibility to think about God in terms of transcendence with respect to the natural world [31] – an approach which is in line with my reflections on limit questions (LQ) -- and an understanding of religion as a human phenomenon in which concepts of God have arisen in the course of our evolutionary and (pre-)historical past [26]; I also discuss critically why I do not accept a 'religious naturalism' which offers a view of reality which appears to be more hospitable for religion [30]. Instead, I articulate how I believe that an evolutionary view of religion and the relativising of particular religious views that ensues from a strong sense of transcendence may be held together [32].

Preview

Chapter 2 considers interpretations of the history of the interactions between science and religion. This will show the complexity and context-dependence of these discussions. History has been cast too often in a single mould, whether one of persistent conflict or one of basic harmony between science and religion. I will take issue with some of these stereotypes, especially with the prime myths of conflict, *viz.* the condemnation of Galileo and the responses to Darwin, and with the apologetic arguments which depart from the claim that Christianity formed the matrix in which science could arise. In line with contemporary historians of science we will note that the issue is not just how science and religion related to each other, but also how conceptions of religion and of science were shaped through their interaction. Not only the relation between science and religion, but also the understanding of religion and of science has been shifting over time.

Chapter 3 is for the most part an argument against religious views of reality which emphasise the cognitive and rational character of religion in relation to the natural sciences. In this part we are to a greater or lesser degree comparing like with like, *i.e.* views of theology and of science as cognitive projects, as attempts to understand reality. The first few sections focus on the way the content of science is used to articulate religious views which emphasise some form of ontological transcendence, often joined with belief in activity of that transcendent reality within our empirical reality. In the later sections of this chapter I will challenge the view that science and religion are similar in their general character. I will argue that defences of scientific realism do not carry over to theology, and that cognitive claims in theology have problems in dealing with the provisional character of science, problems which are not solved by moving away from fundamental physics to sciences focusing on 'higher levels' of reality. With these objections to a theological realism modelled after scientific realism and to predominantly cognitivist and rationalist views of the relations between science and religion, the way is cleared for a naturalist view of religion.

In chapter 4 we will pay more attention to differences between religion and science. Here the balance shifts to my articulation and defence of a functional and immanent-ontological, evolutionary view of religion, whereas the preceding chapters were mainly arguments against positions of others. Chapter 4 begins with an exposition of the failure of arguments from experience to a transcendent reality. In some sections I seek to understand religious experience and human identity naturalistically, especially in relation to our brains. We then turn towards religions as traditions which arose in a long evolutionary process and which contributed to that process. The last section [26] of this part considers theological proposals which aim at developing a 'biohistorical' (Kaufman) or 'biocultural' (Burhoe, Hefner) view of human nature and human religion. Without agreeing with such proposals in all details, I argue that they make interesting attempts at a theological appropriation of a naturalist view of religion.

In the final chapter, I defend the significance of the natural sciences without elevating them to a position which would make science itself a phenomenon beyond the naturalist framework. Religion is affected by the naturalist view in two ways: through the naturalist understanding of reality, which challenges religious explanations of or assumptions about reality, and in the understanding of religion that it offers. After reconsidering a naturalist understanding of science and of religion, we will come to some further reflections on naturalism. I will argue that questions concerning the whole of reality do not provide answers or evidence, contrary to some who have claimed otherwise on the basis of the so-called anthropic coincidences. The question of existence, of why there is something rather than nothing, is shown to be intractable; the status of questions concerning the order of the universe is less clear. I shall also consider the possibility of a radically different description of our universe, such as the one offered by process philosophers and theologians who use the conceptual framework of A. N. Whitehead. Such a restructuring of our conceptual framework cannot be excluded; a naturalist view cannot be dogmatically protected. However, currently there seems to be no compelling reason to abandon the materialistic naturalism opted for above, nor do I consider any of the alternatives convincing. Thus, I consider religions as particular traditions that have arisen in our past, but I also consider religion as a response to reflection on the openness highlighted by limit questions about naturalism.

2

Histories of relationships between science and religion

The history of the interactions between science and religion has been described stereotypically as a warfare between two contending powers:

The history of Science is not a mere record of isolated discoveries; it is a narrative of the conflict of two contending powers, the expansive force of the human intellect on one side, and the compression arising from traditionary faith and human interests on the other. (Draper 1875, vi)

In the following sections I will argue that this is an inadequate view of the relationship between science and religion, especially since it portrays the history of this relationship as one in which the relative importance of both sides is at stake. More balanced studies reveal that confrontations were not only about the relative importance of two given enterprises, but also about the natures of science and of religion. Another mould in which the history has been cast is that of a fruitful interaction between Christianity and science. The claim has been made that Christianity has been essential to the rise of modern science. This too is a stereotype which is still operative today. By considering episodes in the history of the interactions between science and religion I intend to show the inadequacy of such stereotypes. Each episode is different, both with respect to the social context and with respect to the understanding of the nature of science and of religion. Thus, this part is meant to contribute to the overall argument of the book's sensitivity to the diversity of, and changes in, conceptions of religion and of science, and to take into account insights from contemporary historians of science who have studied interactions between science and religion.

We will begin with interpretations of two well-known conflicts, the Galileo affair [7] and the theological responses to Darwin [8]. The conclusion will be that these conflicts were as much conflicts within science and within religion as between them. Portraying the history of

54

the relationship of science and religion as one of conflict along a single line of division is neither correct nor helpful [9].

We will then take up the argument that Christianity was the matrix in which science arose. As a general claim, this is as inadequate as the claim that conflicts have always developed along the same lines [10]. Some authors criticise both the conflict-interpretation and the co-operation-interpretation for the incorrect understanding of religion assumed in them, which gives insufficient attention to the differences between science and Christian faith. Viewing the entire history in terms of a loss of faith makes this correct insight into another inadequate stereotype, itself fuelled by apologetic interests [11]. The history of the interaction is one in which the meanings of 'science' and of 'religion' are diverse and shifting. There is a wide variety of activities going under the headings of 'science' and 'religion'. The issue treated in this study is not just the relation between two existing entities, each in itself understood very well, but also ways of thinking about these two clusters of human concerns. In the final section, we will consider what lessons can be learned from recent historical studies [12].

7. THE GALILEO AFFAIR AS THE FOUNDING MYTH OF CONFLICT

Stephen Hawking, a cosmologist, recalls an audience with Pope John Paul II at the close of a study week in 1981 organised by the Vatican Observatory. The pope told the scientists

that we should not inquire into the big bang itself because that was the moment of Creation and therefore the work of God. I was glad then that he did not know the subject of the talk I had just given at the conference – the possibility that space-time was finite but had no boundary, which means that it had no beginning, no moment of Creation. I had no desire to share the fate of Galileo. (Hawking 1988, 116)

Actually, the pope did not object to research into the Big Bang. He made a philosophical point: whatever theories scientists come up with, they will always leave open metaphysical questions about the beginning and existence of reality, since one can always raise further questions (John Paul II 1982, xxviii). Hawking apparently fails to appreciate this central element in the papal statement.

It is remarkable that Hawking invokes 'Galileo's fate'. It would, of course, be in no way in the power nor in the interest of John Paul II to force Hawking to revoke views and to put him under house arrest in

Hawking's own villa. The opposite was actually the case: in 1985 Hawking became a member of the Pontifical Academy of Science (Marini-Bettòlo 1986, 23a). How Hawking reconciled accepting this membership with his expressed fear and felt need to keep silent about his scientific work is not clear to me; perhaps the reference to the papal statement was merely to enliven his book.

By referring to Galileo, Hawking appeals to the most well known example of a conflict between science and religion. To assess the adequacy of this view, we will have to consider what the intellectual issues were, what actually happened, and who the contending parties were.[1]

Problems of the Copernican view

Though the heliocentric view developed by Nicholas Copernicus (1543) is fairly obvious from our perspective, we should avoid the bias coming with hindsight if we want to understand the Galileo affair. There were various reasons for resistance against a heliocentric view. Apparently, the heliocentric view contradicted sense experience. Nobody feels the rotation of the Earth, even though its speed at the equator is over 1,600 kilometres an hour. We still see the Sun rising and setting. Other *epistemological* issues were the justification of the use of instruments such as the telescope, the role of tradition, especially the Bible, in scientific research, and the relation between physics and astronomy. There were also *religious objections*, as the Copernican view seemed at odds with certain Biblical passages.

There were various *astronomical objections* as well. Terrestrial objects were irregular, solid and changing, whereas celestial ones appeared to be spherical, luminous and unchanging. Besides, as Galileo came to realise in 1610,[2] on the Copernican view Venus would have to show the full range of phases, from full to dark. And if the Sun rather than the Earth was the centre of the system of the fixed stars, the apparent position of stars should show annual variation (parallax), which was not observed. Apart from the astronomical objections, the Copernican model did not fit the *physics* of the time, especially the understanding of motion.

---

[1]   The following list of problems with Copernicanism follows Finocchiaro (1989, 7f., and 17f.). Quotations from documents of the Galileo affair have been taken from the translation by Finocchiaro (1989) unless noted otherwise. The order of questions has been inspired by Pedersen (1983 and 1991).

[2]   Galileo's friend Castelli wrote to Galileo about the phases which Venus would have to show in the late summer of 1610 (Gingerich 1982, 136; 1986, 116); whether Galileo was aware of this before Castelli's letter, is unknown to me.

Galileo's research on motion addressed the physical objections; they were definitively resolved through Newton's work at the end of the same century. Galileo's observations with the telescope dealt with most of the astronomical objections. Heavenly bodies such as the Moon turned out to be far from perfect and the phases of Venus were observed. These discoveries, together with the discovery of four moons circling Jupiter, were published in *The Starry Messenger* (1610) and *The Sunspot Letters* (1613). The absence of observed stellar parallax remained a valid objection (though this could be interpreted as an indication of huge interstellar distances), until instances of stellar parallax were established observationally in 1838.

Epistemological problems such as the conflict with sense experience and the nature of knowledge were a continuing source of debate. While, for instance, the observed phases of Venus falsified the Ptolemaic system, it did not follow that they proved the heliocentric system. Tycho Brahe's system, which had the Sun circling the Earth and all the (other) planets circling the Sun, would do equally well. Without referring to this specific system, Cardinal Bellarmine made the epistemological point in his letter written in 1615 to a Carmelite priest, Foscarini, who had defended the compatibility of the Copernican view with Scripture:

I say that if there were a true demonstration that the sun is at the center of the world and the earth in the third heaven, and that the sun does not circle the earth but the earth circles the sun, then one would have to proceed with great care in explaining the Scriptures that appear contrary, and say rather that we do not understand them than that what is demonstrated is false. But I will not believe that there is such a demonstration, until it is shown to me. Nor is it the same to demonstrate that by supposing the sun to be at the center and the earth in heaven one can save the appearances, and to demonstrate that in truth the sun is at the center and the earth in heaven; for I believe the first demonstration may be available, but I have very great doubts about the second. (Bellarmine, in Finocchiaro (1989, 68))

What happened?

On 24 February 1616 the Holy Office headed by Cardinal Bellarmine condemned two theses regarding the position of the Sun and the movement of the Earth. A few days later, on 5 March, the Congregation of the Index issued a decree which prohibited various books by Protestants, and suspended Copernicus' book and a commentary on

Job 'until corrected'. Foscarini's defence of the compatibility of the heliocentric view and the Bible was completely prohibited and condemned. There is no reference to Galileo in this decree.

It was decided by the pope on 25 February 1616, that Galileo would be invited in private by Cardinal Bellarmine to 'warn him to abandon these opinions', and if Galileo would refuse to obey, he would receive a formal injunction in the presence of witnesses. The next day Galileo was received by Bellarmine. It is not completely clear what happened on this occasion. There is a document, lacking proper signatures, reporting that Bellarmine warned Galileo that the heliocentric view was erroneous, and that – without any suggestion that Galileo had refused to obey – immediately thereafter in the presence of witnesses the Commissary General of the Inquisition, a Dominican, ordered Galileo 'not to hold, teach, or defend in any way whatever, either orally or in writing' the heliocentric view. However, the official report by Bellarmine states that Galileo 'had acquiesced when warned' and did not refer to the more specific instruction which the document says Galileo had received from the head of the Inquisition.[3]

A few months later, Galileo was granted an audience with the pope, who affirmed that Galileo was highly respected. As there were rumours circulating about him, Galileo requested and received a certificate from Bellarmine. This explicitly denies that Galileo has been condemned. 'On the contrary, he has only been notified of the declaration made by the Holy Father and published by the Sacred Congregation of the Index' (Finocchiaro 1989, 153; Baldini and Coyne 1984). In 1620 the corrections of Copernicus' book were published. The book went through unchanged, except that the heliocentric view was not asserted but treated hypothetically (Finocchiaro 1989, 200–2).

In 1623 Cardinal Maffeo Barberini, a patron of the arts and the sciences, was elected Pope Urban VIII. He had once written a poem to honour Galileo's work. Galileo was received by him in six private audiences in 1624; the impression is that a discussion of the heliocentric view was considered acceptable if it were treated as a hypothesis. Probably against Galileo's claim that he could prove the truth of the

---

[3]   See for the interpretation of the document, for instance, the discussion between Drake (1965) and De Santillana (1965). It might be that the document was made in advance in case Galileo refused to obey, while no such further injunction, was served, and that therefore the document was left unsigned; it has also been speculated that the Commissary General served the injunction though this was not according to the papal decision and Bellarmine's intentions, and hence that Bellarmine did not report it since officially it had not happened.

heliocentric view on the basis of his theory of the tides, the pope argued that one could never prove the heliocentric view to be true. It would always be within God's infinite power to create the world in such a way that the phenomena which were taken to prove the Copernican view, were brought about by other means.

Galileo began to work on the book that became *The Dialogue Concerning the Two Chief World Systems – Ptolemaic and Copernican*. The pope's argument is brought forward at the end by the defender of the geostatic view. The book was finished in April 1630, but not printed until February 1632. Obtaining a licence to print took time, partly due to external circumstances such as an outbreak of the plague, which inhibited travel, and partly due to hesitations on the side of the officials.

Despite the *imprimatur* and the changes which had been made at the request of the licensers, the book was taken out of circulation in Rome. In September 1632 the Holy Office (Inquisition) summoned Galileo to Rome. In February 1633 Galileo arrived in Rome, where he stayed at the Embassy of Tuscany (Florence). On 12 April Galileo was interrogated, and subsequently detained in the apartment of the chief prosecutor. At the end of April it seemed as if the case would be settled extrajudicially, with Galileo admitting vanity in presenting the heliocentric view too strongly. Galileo was allowed to return to the Embassy. Shortly thereafter, Galileo presented his defence along the lines of the expected extrajudicial settlement.

The pope received a very critical report of the proceedings; the report did not match with the moderating attempt (documented in letters) to settle extrajudicially. At a meeting of the Inquisition on 16 June, presided over by Pope Urban VIII, it was decided that Galileo was to be interrogated 'under threat of torture'. This was the legal term for formal interrogation, and should, according to contemporary scholarship, not be understood as if Galileo was really threatened with torture. On 22 June Galileo abjured, with only seven of the ten cardinals present actually signing the sentence. Galileo was put under house arrest, first at the residence of a friend, the archbishop of Siena, and subsequently, until his death in 1642, in his own villa near Florence.

Who had a conflict about what?
1. Traditionally, the Galileo affair is seen as a conflict between science and theology over the heliocentric view of the universe. As such, it is seen as a conflict about scientific facts and theories.

2. Recalling Bellarmine's letter to Foscarini (quoted above), Finocchiaro holds that the 'key epistemological issue in the Galileo Affair was the *provability* of the earth's motion, that is, whether the earth's motion was something *capable* of being proved true, not whether it had (already) been proved true' (1986a, 200). This emphasis leads to various issues for research, such as the way in which Galileo spoke of proofs, the pope's argument based on divine omnipotence, and the patterns of reasoning involved (Finocchiaro 1980). Seen thus, the conflict has to do with the aims of science. It still is a conflict about intellectual authority, but such an approach gives more credit to the ecclesiastical authorities. They may have been factually wrong about the movement of the earth but philosophically sound in resisting the premature adoption of a new view.

3. The Galileo affair, and especially the events of the first episode (1616), can be seen as a conflict about *hermeneutical principles* and authority in exegesis (Pedersen 1983, 1991). Heliocentric views had been espoused before, even by the high-ranking Cardinal Nicholas of Cusa (1401–64). However, the Catholic Church had defined its position more strictly in response to the Protestant Reformation. The Council of Trent had decided in its Fourth Session, on 8 April 1546, that no one should interpret the Holy Scriptures contrary to the sense that the Holy Mother Church has held and holds, or contrary to the consensus of the Fathers, the recognized theologians of the early church (e.g., Blackwell 1991, 11f., 183). Galileo's letter to Castelli (1613) and his subsequent letter to Grand Duchess Christina in 1615 dealt at length with the hermeneutical issue.

Galileo argues that where science is certain, one has to adapt one's interpretation of Scripture. If science offers merely 'plausible opinion and probable conjecture' in place of sure and demonstrated knowledge, one should give priority to Scripture and the view of the Fathers, and shape one's scientific view accordingly. While he argues that science might correct our interpretation of Scripture in physical matters, Galileo also argues for mutual neutrality of Scripture and science. Galileo quotes a cardinal to the effect that Scripture does not intend to teach us how the heavens go, but how to go to heaven. The Bible is only relevant in matters 'which concern our salvation and the establishment of our faith'.[4]

4. The affair can also be seen as the outcome of *internal conflicts within*

---

[4]   Quotes from Galileo's Letter to Grand Duchess Christina (Drake 1957, 197, 188f.). McMullin (1967, 33; 1981, 18–25) sees a tension between relevance and neutrality; Finocchiaro (1986, 261–8) defends the coherence of Galileo's letter.

the scientific community and within the Catholic Church. The first opposition to Galileo came from colleagues at the university, philosophers steeped in the Aristotelian-scholastic tradition such as Lodovice delle Colombe. In his treatise *Against the Earth's motion* (1610 or 1611), Colombe introduced religious objections in the confrontation over the nature of science. Galileo's letter to Grand Duchess Christina is especially critical of such philosophers. What started as an internal conflict within the academy was transferred to the domain of the church. The emphasis on alliances and struggles over power, including those within the Catholic Church between Dominicans and Jesuits, is central to the account given by Giorgio de Santillana (1955), who pointed out analogies with the use of power and repression by communist regimes of his time.

5. Piedro Redondi has argued that the condemnation of Galileo for his defence of a heliocentric view was a *cover* for a quite different charge, one of heresy with respect to the Eucharist. Redondi has discovered a complaint against Galileo in the files of the Holy Office, filed in 1624 or 1625. The charge in the document was that Galileo's view of matter was at odds with the proper understanding of the Eucharist. The Council of Trent had affirmed that in the Eucharist, the bread and wine are no longer bread and wine in substance, even though they are so in external appearance. An atomistic view of matter which tied secondary qualities, appearance, to primary qualities, substance, was a challenge to this Catholic doctrine. Redondi interprets the condemnation of Galileo in 1633 for Copernicanism as an attempt by Pope Urban VIII to cover up the far more dangerous accusation of heresy with respect to the Eucharist. On this interpretation, Urban remained a friend of Galileo, though appearing to have changed his attitude. However, Redondi is then challenged to explain why Urban had to remain apparently hostile towards Galileo in private correspondence in later years. Though original and drawing upon a wider perspective of that period, Redondi's reconstruction does not seem to be tenable.[5]

6. *Personal animosities* and the characters of the persons involved may well have aggravated the affair. Galileo was involved in various disputes. Psychology might also explain to some extent the position of Pope Urban in 1632 and 1633. At the end of Galileo's *Dialogue* the argument from divine omnipotence is presented by Simplicio. Urban seems to have felt that he was thereby ridiculed. Wider issues, such as

---

[5] See detailed criticisms by Westfall (1989: 84–103; this essay also in *History of Science* 26 (1988): 399–415) and by Mayaud (1992); further references in Finocchiaro (1989, 351, note 16).

his status as a patron of the arts and sciences may also have been involved.[6]

7. The *political situation* may have influenced the course of events as well. The second phase of the affair took place during the Thirty Years War in Europe. Spain, Germany, and Austria, ruled by the Catholic Habsburgs, fought against a Protestant alliance headed by the Swedish king Gustavus Adolphus. Both Catholic France and the papacy allied to some extent with the Swedes against the Habsburgs. Pope Urban was accused by some Spanish cardinals of helping the Protestant cause. It may have been that Urban needed to be strong on doctrinal challenges in order to diminish internal Catholic tensions. The tension between the various Catholic nationalities might explain why some of the cardinals present did not sign the condemnation of Galileo (Redondi 1987, 260f).

The Galileo affair is not a conflict between 'the church' and 'science'. Clergymen, Catholic institutions, and academics can be found on both sides. The conflict had various intellectual dimensions, which had to do with facts as well as with issues of method and authority in science and in theology. Social and psychological aspects were also relevant, and were partly connected with the epistemological issues, as the church was drawn into a conflict amongst scientists and philosophers.

Looking back upon the Galileo affair
Part of the myth of the Galileo affair is that the Catholic Church is assumed to have held the same position for a long time. In the autumn of 1992 newspapers reported on a speech made by Pope John Paul II as if the Catholic Church had now rehabilitated Galileo and finally acknowledged the heliocentric view. This is mistaken with respect to the intervening ages and with respect to the speech of John Paul II.[7] In 1734 the Holy Office allowed the erection of a mausoleum to Galileo in the church in Florence where he had been buried. In 1741 permission was given to print the first edition of Galileo's complete works, including the *Dialogue*. In 1757 the general condemnation of books favouring the heliocentric view was taken off the Index. In 1822 it was

---

6   As pointed out in Westfall (1989, 58–83). The issue of patronage is considered in detail in Biagioli (1993). In a Postscript to the third edition of his book, Langford also points out that contacts between Galileo and various 'subversive' persons may have contributed to Urban's anger towards Galileo (Langford 1966 (1992, 203ff.)).

7   The following data have been taken from (Jacqueline 1987; Finocchiaro 1989, 307; Poupard 1992).

allowed to present the Copernican system as a thesis, a fact, and not only as an hypothesis (Brandmüller *et al.* 1992, Poupard 1992, 375). In the late nineteenth century, but in continuity with earlier activities, the Astronomical Observatory of the Vatican was founded so 'that everyone might see that the Church and its Pastors are not opposed to true and solid science, whether human or divine, but that they embrace it, encourage it, and promote it with the fullest possible dedication' (Pope Leo XIII, *Motu Proprio, Ut Mysticam* (1891), quoted in Maffeo 1991, 34). This observatory participates fully in up-to-date scientific research.

A solemn meeting of the Pontifical Academy of Sciences took place on 31 October 1992. Ambassadors and members of the Curie were present. The pope spoke positively about Galileo, affirming his epistemological and his hermeneutical insights. However, the papal address was not a rehabilitation of Galileo. It lacked the formal setting of a legal rehabilitation. Besides, the address can also be heard as a justification of Galileo's judges; they had made mistakes, but these were intelligible in the context of their times. In recent, more or less official, Catholic writings on the Galileo affair (Poupard 1987; John Paul II 1979, 1992) there is a genuine longing for truth about the historical facts. But there is also the expectation that a better understanding of the affair will support the thesis that science and religion are compatible. However, this latter claim is beyond historical research, and in danger of distorting it (Finocchiaro 1986a, 191). Historical research can falsify the view of the Galileo affair as an instance of plain incompatibility of scientific truth and theological truth. It was a conflict between different persons within the scientific community and within the Catholic Church, with different views of science, of theology, and of the role of authority in these enterprises.

8. POST-DARWINIAN CONFLICTS IN BRITAIN AND AMERICA

The Galileo affair has become the prime myth of conflict between science and the Catholic Church. Controversies over evolution in the late nineteenth century have become the archetype of conflicts between science and Protestantism in the United Kingdom and the USA. In *A History of the Warfare of Science with Theology in Christendom*, Andrew D. White wrote that 'Darwin's *Origin of Species* had come into the theological world like a plough into an ant-hill. Everywhere those thus rudely awakened from their old comfort and repose had swarmed forth angry and confused' (White 1896, 70). A review of Charles Darwin's *Origin of Species* by Samuel Wilberforce, Bishop of Oxford, is White's prime example of the theological response to evolution.

Nor did the bishop's efforts end here: at the meeting of the British Association for the Advancement of Science he again disported himself in the tide of popular applause. Referring to the ideas of Darwin, who was absent on account of illness, he congratulated himself in a public speech that he was not descended from a monkey. The reply came from Huxley, who said in substance: 'If I had to choose, I would prefer to be a descendant of a humble monkey rather than of a man who employs his knowledge and eloquence in misrepresenting those who are wearing out their lives in the search for truth.'
    This shot reverberated through England, and indeed through other countries. (White 1896, vol. 1, 70f.)

We will begin with a brief presentation of the confrontation between Wilberforce and Thomas Huxley. I also will come back to the polemic characteristics of White's book. In both cases, the social context, the professionalisation of science in Britain and in the USA was important. In the last part of this section I will present and criticise the claim that orthodox Calvinists rather than religious liberals were in the best position to incorporate Darwin's theory into their views, partly because Darwin's theory had its roots in their views.

The debate between Huxley and Wilberforce
The confrontation took place during the annual meeting of the British Association for the Advancement of Science, 27 June to 4 July 1860.[8] Since its publication at the end of 1859, Darwin's *Origin of Species* had been reviewed positively, for instance by Huxley in *The Times*, and negatively, for instance by Richard Owen, leading anatomist of the Natural History Department of the British Museum, who had, many years before, collaborated with Darwin on some of the specimens from his voyage on the Beagle. In a discussion at a meeting of the section for botany and zoology of the British Association, on Thursday, 28 June, Owen had asserted an 'impassable gulf' between humans and apes, as human brains contained posterior lobes which apes lacked. Huxley 'denied altogether that the difference between the brain of the gorilla and man was so great as represented by Prof. Owen' (*The Athenaeum* 7 July 1860, 26).
    Two days later, on Saturday 30 June, there was another meeting of

[8]   *The Athenaeum* 1706 of 7 July 1860, 18–27, and 1707 of 14 July, pp. 64–6; reconstruction in Jensen (1988); see also Jensen (1991).

the section for botany and zoology. Between 400 and 700 people were present: scientists, theologians, students, 'and women' (Jensen 1988, 165). The meeting was not set up as a debate between Wilberforce and Huxley. Huxley had intended to visit relatives that day; in his diary were the departure times for the train (Jensen 1988, 173). John William Draper from New York – who many years later published a *History of the Conflict Between Religion and Science* – lectured for well over an hour 'On the intellectual development of Europe, considered with reference to the views of Mr. Darwin and others, that the progression of organisms is determined by law'.[9] Whether the British Darwinians present appreciated this broad sweep of evolutionary thinking, rather than a more limited and technical argument, may be doubted.

During the discussion Bishop Wilberforce was called upon to give his view. He spoke for about half an hour. Wilberforce argued that Darwin's theory was an hypothesis which 'when tried by the principles of inductive science, broke down' (*The Athenaeum* 14 July 1860, 65). According to some accounts, he asked Huxley a question about his descendence from the apes. This may have been related to the discussion in the same section two days earlier; the question and Huxley's answer are not mentioned in the report in *The Athenaeum*.

Huxley rose to defend Darwin's theory as the best explanation of the facts, without asserting that all details were correct or confirmed. He replied to Wilberforce's rhetorical question, according to a letter two months later, as follows:

If then, said I, the question is put to me 'would I rather have a miserable ape for a grandfather or a man highly endowed by nature and possessed of great means and influence, and yet who employs those faculties and that influence for the mere purpose of introducing ridicule into a grave scientific discussion' – I unhesitatingly affirm my preference for the ape.[10]

After Huxley a few anti-Darwinians spoke, and two more supporters of Darwin, including the botanist Joseph D. Hooker. Letters from both sides claim victory among those whom each considers most competent to judge. Press reports gave mixed impressions (Jensen 1988, 172).

Wilberforce's question should be understood in the context of the playfulness of English debate, and of a crowded room after a fairly dull lecture. Though this may be said to Wilberforce's credit, questioning evolutionists as heirs of apes, tadpoles, or mushrooms had already been

[9]   *The Athenaeum* 14 July 1860, 64f.; see also Fleming (1950, 67–73).
[10] Letter of T. H. Huxley to Dr Dyster, 9 September 1860, *Huxley Papers*, vol. 15, fols. 117f. (Jensen 1988, 168; De Beer 1964, 166f.; *Nature* 172 (14 November 1953): 920).

dealt with by Huxley in an essay, and was perhaps not a very appropriate joke for the occasion.[11]

The professionalisation of science in Britain[12]

White's *History of the Warfare* described the exchange between Wilberforce and Huxley as a confrontation between science and theology. However, the exchange was not only a confrontation of ideas; the social and professional context, and thereby the understanding of the nature of science, is important for a proper understanding of this exchange.

Wilberforce, vice-president of the British Association for the Advancement of Science, represented the scientific establishment as much as he represented the church. Huxley, twenty years his junior, was a career scientist (Jensen 1988, 175). If the opponents are seen in this way, the exchange reflects a general change in British science. 'During the first half of the nineteenth century the major characteristics of British science were amateurism, aristocratic patronage, minuscule government support, limited employment opportunities, and peripheral inclusion within the clerically dominated universities and secondary schools' (Turner 1978, 360). Although the utility of science for industry and agriculture received some attention, many 'scientists considered the moral and metaphysical imperatives of natural theology as a proper and integral part of their vocation' (Turner 1978, 360). Around the middle of the century science developed into a profession which sets its own terms for evaluating results and selecting prospective scientists. Rather than seeking aristocratic and clerical patronage, the support of the public was sought by arguing for the relevance of science for the welfare of the nation and hence for the inclusion of science in curricula. The change can be illustrated by the observation that forty-one Anglican clergymen presided over sections of the British Association for the Advancement of Science between 1831 and 1865, while only three held such chairs between 1866 and 1900 (Turner 1978, 367).

---

[11]   (Jensen 1988, 176f.; 1991, 82). Lucas (1979, 327) argues that Wilberforce did not ask about Huxley's descent, but rather spoke in the first person of his own descent, or in the third person of our common descent. On Lucas' reading, he may have challenged Huxley with respect to the place where in a series of progenitors he would locate the shift from one species to another one.

[12]   Developments in other countries have been different. For instance, it has been argued that science became a profession in France with the French Revolution (Crosland 1975, 140); members of the French Academy of Sciences before the Revolution had a professional attitude, for example, disciplinary self-correction, but did not yet form an occupational group (Hahn 1975, 135).

The shift from the gentleman-naturalist to the professional scientist led to conflicts with leaders of organised religion who wanted to maintain their influence on educational institutions. And attempts at reconciling science and religion by religiously minded scientists, both clergy and lay, came under attack due to the naturalist and critical bent of the new scientific generation. The botanist Joseph Hooker, a friend of Thomas Huxley and Charles Darwin, wrote in 1860 that the worst 'scientifical-geological-theologians ... are like asses between bundles of hay, distorting their consciences to meet the double call on their public profession' (L. Huxley 1918, 520).

The decreasing role of clergy in science was not only sought by scientists. It also reflected developments in the churches. There was an increasing emphasis on devotional and theological issues rather than on participation in general culture. This is explicit in the various revivalist movements during the nineteenth century, the Oxford movement, the Salvation Army, and in Catholic circles the revival in Ireland and the attention given to the miracle of Lourdes.

It was not only the social position of scientists that changed, but also their ideology. Whereas they had been 'tracing the presence of the Creator in creation', the ideology of professional scientists of the second half of the century became 'the glorification and strengthening of the nation and its wealth', i.e. the service of the common weal (Turner 1978, 375).

White's Warfare and Cornell University

In England a dominant church was giving way to an independent professionalised science. The American context was different, as there was not a single dominant denomination. But Andrew D. White's *History of the Warfare of Science with Theology in Christendom* (1896) also has a context which explains some of the polemic characteristics of this book.

White was the first president of Cornell University. This institute, the first non-denominational private university, was created in 1865 by the State of New York with the help of funds from Ezra Cornell and from White. The classical disciplines and the industrial sciences were taught, though during his Senior year in college White had regarded the latter 'with contempt – with wonder that human beings possessed of immortal souls should waste their time in work with blow pipes and test tubes' (Altschuler 1979, 61).

Though not denominational, Cornell was set up as a Christian university, with compulsory attendance at chapel (Altschuler 1979,

68, 81). And, even though White claimed that denominational backgrounds were irrelevant, he took great care to create a denominationally balanced faculty (Altschuler 1979, 81). Though Christian, the focus was not to serve religion, but to serve the nation by educating its future leaders. White himself served the country in various diplomatic positions; he was close to running for vice-president in 1900 (Altschuler 1979, 258). As first president of the American Historical Association, he told his audience in 1884 that the historian must use historical facts to drive home a particular lesson (Altschuler 1979, 155). In his *History of the Warfare of Science with Theology* a lesson is driven home chapter after chapter: theological resistance was futile as science always turned out victorious.

Frustrations about the ecclesiastical opposition he met, both in Cornell and elsewhere, may well have influenced the articulation of 'the warfare between science and theology'. White responded strongly to all charges of atheism and infidelity (Altschuler 1979, 95). Earlier in his career, White was not appointed to a position in Yale since the members of the board were not sure enough about his personal religious convictions (Altschuler 1979, 36). And by the standards of the board, which consisted almost entirely of orthodox Congregationalists, they were probably right. Despite his mother's wishes, Andrew White had refused confirmation in the Episcopal (Anglican) Church because he resisted the minister's view that unbaptised children and members of other churches (including his own grandmother) are eternally punished (Altschuler 1979, 25). White took religion seriously, but quarrelled with dogmatic theology and sectarianism. 'Religion, as seen in the recognition of "a Power in the Universe, not ourselves, which makes for righteousness", and in the love of God and of our neighbour, will steadily grow stronger and stronger' (White 1896, vol. 1, xii). Such a religion was in harmony with science and could only benefit from science. As White saw it, conflicts were between science and dogmatic theology.[13]

Both in Britain and in America, conflicts about religion and science were part of the struggle for the establishment of science as an independent profession. However, there was also the content of Darwin's theory, which had to be dealt with intellectually.

[13]   Lindberg and Numbers (1986a, 339) consider White's focus in his *History of the Warfare of Science with Theology in Christendom* (1896) on dogmatic theology rather than religion 'more of an afterthought' as he had spoken in 1869 of 'religion'. However, the evidence given by Altschuler on White's younger years seems to warrant the claim that his appreciation for religion and his resistance against denominationalism and theology, were fairly constant over his life, and already well in place in 1869.

Some British responses to Darwin's theory[14]

Wilberforce was not the only voice from the Anglican clergy at the meeting. The next day Frederick Temple, who became Archbishop of Canterbury in 1896, delivered a sermon on 'the present relations of science to religion' which claimed that God's finger was to be discerned in the laws of nature; Temple recognised a deep identity of 'tone, character, and spirit' between the Book of God and the Book of Nature, God's words and God's works.[15] The list of positive responses from clergy, theologians, and Christian leaders to Darwin's theory can easily be extended. Friendly relations despite disagreements also undermine the adequacy of the 'warfare metaphor'. As the historian Moore (1979, 100) wrote, 'Henceforth interpretations of the post-Darwinian controversies must be non-violent and humane.'

Not only were others open-minded, but Wilberforce himself was not as narrow-minded as legend has taken him to be. In his presentation at the meeting of the British Association, he seems to have emphasized scientific and philosophical problems, as he did in his forty page review of Darwin's book:

and if Mr. Darwin can with the same correctness of reasoning [as Newton] demonstrate to us our fungular descent, we shall dismiss our pride, and avow, with the characteristic humility of philosophy, our unsuspected cousinship with the mushrooms ... only we shall ask leave to scrutinise carefully every step of the argument which has such an ending, and demur if at any point of it we are invited to substitute unlimited hypothesis for patient observation, or the spasmodic fluttering flight of fancy for the severe conclusions to which logical accuracy of reasoning has led the way.

And, after an extensive discussion of various facts and arguments from *The Origin of Species*, skilfully focusing on its weaker points and grander extrapolations, Wilberforce continues:

Our readers will not have failed to notice that we have objected to the views with which we have been dealing solely on scientific grounds. We have done

---

[14] The spectrum of responses varies by country; for theological responses in German-speaking countries, see Hübner (1966), for Catholic reactions in general see Paul (1974, 1979); for a comparative study of the reception of Darwinism, not focused on religion, see Glick (1974). Some differences between responses in England and the United States correlate with differences in theological and philosophical background; in the United States a liberal theology in the tradition of Schleiermacher collided with orthodoxy, whereas English theology had been shaped by a natural theology which was much more threatened by an alternative explanation of biological adaptedness (R. Hensen, private communication).

[15] F. Temple, *The Present Relations of Science to Religion: A Sermon Preached on Act Sunday, July 1, 1860, before the University of Oxford, during the Meeting of the British Association* (Oxford: J. H. & Jas. Parker, 1860) (Brooke 1991, 41, 274; Moore 1979, 89).

so from our fixed conviction that it is thus that the truth or falsehood of such arguments should be tried. We have no sympathy with those who object to any facts or alleged facts in nature, or to any inference logically deduced from them, because they believe them to contradict what it appears to them is taught by Revelation ... There may be to man difficulty in reconciling all the utterances of the two voices. But what of that? He has learned already that here he knows only in part ... This is as truly the spirit of Christianity as it is that of philosophy.[16]

Opposition to Darwin's theory was not restricted to theologians. It came also from scientists such as the anatomist Sir Richard Owen, and the physicists George Stokes, William Thomson (Lord Kelvin), and James Clerk Maxwell. Owen was not opposed to the general idea of evolution, but he was more interested in the order of nature, the pattern of organic diversity, than in the way it had come into being. Homologies, for instance between the wings of birds, the forelegs of tigers and the arms of humans were there, as 'all animals within each major group were variations on a single theme, modifications of a single Ideal Type' (Rudwick 1972, 210). Similarities were not traced to common ancestry but to a common Archetype. The fossil sequence through time shows the gradual embodiment of the pre-existent Ideas. This was a scientific explanation as well as a world view for Owen, as we may glean from a lecture in 1849, *On the Nature of Limbs*.

I have used therefore the word 'Nature' in the sense of the German 'Bedeutung', as signifying that essential character of a part which belongs to it in its relation to a predetermined pattern, answering to the 'idea' of the Archetypal World in the Platonic cosmogony, which archetype or primal pattern is the basis supporting all the modifications of such part for specific powers and actions in all animals possessing it. (2f)

To what natural or secondary causes the orderly succession and progression of such organic phenomena may have been committed, we are as yet ignorant. But if, without derogation to the Divine Power, we may conceive the existence of such ministers and personify them by the term '*Nature*', we learn from the past history of our globe, that she has advanced with slow and stately steps, guided by the archetypal light amidst the wreck of worlds, from the first embodiment of the Vertebrate idea, under its old Ichtyic vestment [that is, as fish], until it became arranged in the glorious garb of Human form. (86)

Owen's Platonism was not 'a naive creationism' but an explanation 'with intellectual credentials quite as high as Darwin's, and with

---

[16] *The Quarterly Review* 108 (July 1860): 225–64, 231 and 256f.; *The London Quarterly Review* (American edition) 108 (July 1860): 118–38, 121, 134.

considerably more credibility to the mind of the time' (Rudwick 1972, 207). Belief in 'design' had at least two faces: the emphasis on functional adaptations which has been typical of William Paley's *Natural Theology* of 1802, and a more idealistic tradition represented by Owen, which emphasised not so much efficiency of adaptation as coherence of an overall plan (Bowler 1977). Owen's approach was not a traditional Platonism with a perfect reality of Ideas of which we perceive mere shadows; 'the vertebrate archetype represented the opposite: the simplest and least perfected conception of a vertebrate' (Rupke 1993, 243). Despite the apparent Platonism, there was a major sense of potentiality, of organic evolution by means of secondary causes. Owen's position was conducive to scientific work, for instance in comparative anatomy. The scientific debate between Darwinians and a man like Owen was intertwined with debates about the aims of science, about metaphysical issues, and about their role in science, as well as with rhetorical moves which sought to build supportive alliances.

Against what he considered to be metaphysical intrusions into science, Huxley coined the term 'agnosticism'. In philosophy it meant that we cannot claim knowledge beyond the limitations of reason, while in science it implied that nothing was to be regarded as true unless based upon reason and experience. It was this agnosticism, 'philosophy, not science, that blocked the path to God in one direction, while suggesting the way forward in philosophy in another' (Gilley and Loades 1981, 301). There was also a moral dimension to Huxley's agnosticism. A detached spectator of the evolutionary process may well be filled with the *Amor Intellectualis Dei*, and see the world as the creation of a good God. However, 'the vision of illimitable sufferings ... mars the prospect for us poor mortals' (Huxley 1894b, 74). Though rejecting metaphysics and theology, Huxley appreciated the Bible, especially the social and religious criticisms by the prophets. In seeking election to the London School Board he pleaded for the inclusion of Bible reading in the curriculum, but without having it controlled by theology, by the churches (Huxley 1894a, 396–9, 401f.).

Calvinist roots of Darwinism?

White held that Darwinian evolution was in conflict with Christian theology. As we have seen, responses of clergy and of Christian lay scientists were more varied than that. Besides, not all opposition was fuelled by Christian theology. An even stronger claim, about a positive correlation, has been made by James Moore in his study of the post-Darwinian controversies.

By considering the views of twenty-eight Christian controversialists in Great Britain and America, it is argued that Darwin's theory of evolution could be accepted in substance only by those whose theology was distinctly orthodox; that this was so because the theory itself presupposed a cosmology and causality which, owing to orthodox doctrines of creation and providence, could be made consonant *a priori* with orthodox theistic beliefs; and that, conversely, other theories of evolution were embraced by those whose theology was notably liberal. (Moore 1979, ix)

Christians who rejected Darwin's theory based themselves 'on philosophical premises to which the name "Christian" cannot distinctively apply' (Moore 1979, 214). Belief in the fixity of species was a remnant from the static world of antiquity.

Liberal Christians seemed to accept Darwinian evolution, but they did not really do so. According to Moore, religious liberals incorporated non-Darwinian views of evolution; they 'could only discern God's purposes in nature if they were ascribed primarily to causes other than natural selection' (Moore 1979, 250).

Orthodox Christian Darwinians 'could see God's purposes being realised through natural selection' and could thus account for divine omnipotence and beneficence without conflicting with Darwinism (Moore 1979, 250). As they saw it, Darwin's theory removed some objections to understanding nature as designed, as the product of God's providence. If one assumed special creation of all species, it was hard to understand the numerous phenomena which seemed without purpose, such as rudimentary organs. However, in an evolutionary perspective, these organs are understandable since they have been useful in the past (Moore 1979, 273). A major issue for orthodox Christian Darwinians was the nature of variation, which Darwin saw as random, but was taken by the botanist Asa Gray and the minister and geologist George F. Wright to be guided by God.

The existence of Christian Darwinians of fairly orthodox, and mostly Calvinist, adherence is beyond doubt. However, Moore claims more than the existence of persons who reconciled their faith and a Darwinian view of evolution. Moore argues (i) that these orthodox Christian Darwinians were the only ones able to accept Darwinism and retain their Christian faith, and (ii) that this was due to the affinity between their understanding of creation and of providence and the assumptions about causality underlying Darwinism, and (iii) that the affinity was not accidental, but a historical necessity, as their Christian convictions were relevant to the development of Darwinism.

In defence of the genetic claim (iii), Moore refers to the influence on Darwin of the English tradition of natural theology, especially the works of the Reverend William Paley. In addition, Darwin gained ideas from the Reverend Malthus about population sizes and selection, which undermined optimistic, liberal views of evolution. For support of both (ii) and (iii), Moore appeals to the argument that the Christian understanding of the world as created had encouraged experimental science; a thesis which will be criticised below [10]. As for (i), liberal Christian evolutionists made the mistake of moving away from a Christian understanding of creation and from the perspective of natural science by adopting a non-Darwinian view of evolution, either investing nature with an innate tendency towards progress or blurring the distinction between God and nature. Darwin's ' "liberalism" was incidental to the development of his theory. The orthodoxy of Darwinism was that, not of its author, but of the theology of nature which his theory presupposed' (Moore 1979, 345).

Moore treats with respect, and some pastoral concern, those who abandoned orthodox faith and became atheists (e.g., Moore 1979, 114f.). However, in the study discussed here, Moore takes it that liberals betrayed Christianity. Basically, there are two parties: liberalism and orthodoxy; a middle ground is not taken into consideration. Nor does he pay attention to changes in the understanding of religion and in ideas about the nature of science. In this respect, this book by Moore still stood in the tradition of conflict-historiography.[17] The difference with authors such as A. D. White is that Moore does not describe the episode as a conflict between religion and science, but as one between atheistic Darwinians and orthodox theistic Darwinians on the one hand, and Christian anti-Darwinians and liberal non-Darwinian evolutionists on the other. The former have been right, the latter have been wrong.

Though the existence of 'Darwin's Forgotten Defenders' (Livingstone 1987), such as Asa Gray and G. F. Wright, rightly challenges the idea that there is an irreconcilable conflict between Christian faith and evolutionary theory, the uncovering of this history does not achieve the wider apologetic purposes which it seems to have for authors such as

---

[17] His more recent biography of Darwin, co-authored with A. Desmond (1991), is quite different in this respect, as is his account of personal factors such as the death of a beloved daughter in the development of Darwin's religious views (Moore 1989).

Moore and Livingstone. Nor does the criticism of particular liberal responses as scientifically inadequate show the inadequacy of any liberal response. However, problems similar to the liberal nineteenth-century optimistic belief in progress also arise for theologies which apply the evolutionary and historical perspective not only to the world, but also to religion (see [26]).

9. CONFLICT-VIEWS

We have considered two historical episodes which have been used as prime examples for the thesis that there has been a persistent conflict between science and religion. As may be clear by now, it is inadequate to treat these episodes as exemplifying a single conflict, with clear and stable demarcation lines.

(i) In each episode, *religious affinities can be found in persons considered to be on opposite sides*. And openness to new scientific insights is not always the privilege of one party; neither Bellarmine nor Wilberforce were scientific nitwits or conservatives at all costs.

(ii) *Facts* are only one component of the conflicts. The Jesuits of the Collegio Romano in Rome had confirmed Galileo's observations with the telescope in 1611. And though there were issues of fact involved in the confrontation at the British Association for the Advancement of Science meeting in 1860, such as the differences between skulls of humans and of apes, the tenser part of each conflict went beyond the facts.

(iii) *Theories*, such as Darwin's explanation of the origin of biological species and Galileo's heliocentric view were a significant part of the disputes. In each case, alternative views which were able to account for the observed facts were available. Tycho's system (which had all the other planets circling the sun, but the sun and the moon circling the earth) was consistent with Galileo's observations (though at odds with later physical theories of motion). Part of the debate was about the choice of theories.

The choice of theories is, of course, partly to be decided on the basis of facts, observations. However, there are also other criteria involved, such as judgements of the relative simplicity of the theories. The coherence with other knowledge is another issue. The debates over evolution also involved a dispute about the length of time available. The physicist Kelvin, who was 'on the same side' as Richard Owen and Samuel Wilberforce, argued on the basis of what was known about energy that there had not been enough time for the process as described by Darwin's theory. This opposition was finally refuted when nuclear fusion was discovered as the source of the Sun's energy. In the choice of theories, and of questions about which theories were formulated, metaphysical commitments were also involved. Owen resisted Darwin's theory on the basis of an underlying 'Platonic' assumption of species as variations on certain ideal types.

(iv) *The hypothetical character of theories* has been an issue as well. In his letter to Foscarini Cardinal Bellarmine emphasised that even if the heliocentric view could account for all observations, this would not prove its truth. In a somewhat similar vein, George F. Wright emphasised the role of induction in Darwinism and in Christianity.[18] Whereas Bellarmine requested certainty, and thus kept unwelcome views at bay, Wright was happy to live with the uncertainty of induction.

The status of theories has also been an important element in the controversies over the teaching of evolution in American public schools in the 1980s. On various occasions 'scientific creationists' have stressed the hypothetical nature of evolutionary theory. Thus, one of the issues has been the question 'What constitutes science?' Is 'scientific creationism' pseudo-science (Kitcher 1982), or is it (incorrect) science (Laudan 1982, 1983)? Or is it religion, as the philosopher Ruse argued as a witness in a trial in Arkansas (Ruse 1982, 1982a)? There was also a pragmatic side to Ruse's defence of this view of 'creationism': the other views would not have worked equally well in the legal context as did the view of 'creationism' as religion disguised as science; American law prohibits the promotion of religion through public schools, but not the teaching of bad science (but see Quinn (1984)).

(v) Conflict views are dependent upon a clear-cut distinction between a *limited number of options.* A recurring assumption in arguments in favour of 'scientific creationism' has been that one has to choose between two options, either evolution or the flood-geology of the creationists (e.g., Gish 1982). If one accepts the dichotomy, everything that counts against current evolutionary theory is evidence in favour of the alternative. This either-or pattern is a rhetorical strategy which is seriously misguided. In the cross-examination at the trial in Arkansas (1981), the geneticist Francis Ayala replied to such

---

[18]   G. F. Wright, Recent books bearing upon the relation of science to religion: No. I – The nature and degree of scientific proof. *Bibliotheca Sacra* 32 (July 1875): 537–55.

an argument by one of the lawyers acting on behalf of the creationists, Mr. Williams, as follows: 'Surely you realize that *not* being Mr. Williams in no way entails *being* Mr. Ayala' (quoted in Gilkey 1985, 141).

(vi) Apart from the choice of theories, the conflicts also deal with *criteria for choosing a religious view*. In the Galileo case, the discussion was whether the Bible tells us only 'how to go to heaven' (salvation) or whether the Bible also bears upon our view of 'how the heavens go' (cosmology). And in the controversies over evolution, the orthodox Christian Darwinians considered by Moore are very much preoccupied with God's sovereignty and all-determining, providential role. Huxley's agnosticism could not allow for these beliefs, nor for his own dualism of ethical and cosmic nature. He none the less held on to such a dualism: 'the ethical progress of society depends, not on imitating the cosmic process, still less in running away from it, but in combating it' (Huxley 1893, 34; 1894c, 83). Andrew White's definition of religion as the recognition of a power in the universe which makes for righteousness is again another view, perhaps more akin to the evolutionary optimism of Herbert Spencer and others (Moore 1985, 80f.), and it thus results in a different agenda for dealing with scientific insights. And in the trial in Arkansas over the teaching of scientific creationism, theologians could be found as witnesses on both sides. Langdon Gilkey, an expert witness, discussed differences between science and religion, but he also argued that the view defended by the creationists was one view of creation which existed alongside many other religious views (Gilkey 1985, 99f., 107f., 119).

(vii) Conflicts were also shaped by the *social situation of science*. Patronage was an important factor in the Galileo affair (Westfall 1989). The conflicts over evolution took place when science was establishing itself as an independent profession. The revival of creationism in the United States of America and the emphasis on the scientific character of creationism can be traced back to the Cold War. In 1957 the Soviet Union was the first to launch an unmanned satellite, the Sputnik; in 1961 the Russians were the first to embark on manned spaceflight. Worried that the USA was lagging behind, the National Science Foundation sponsored development of better curricula and textbooks. Evolutionary theory was given a more prominent place in biology education. Organisations of creationists are in part responses to the new textbooks; the first major project of the Creation Research Society was the development of an alternative high-school biology textbook.[19] As public education became the context of the debate, there was a strong incentive to present creationism as a scientific alternative to evolutionary biology, rather than as a religious position.

The conclusion must be that even some of the best-known conflicts of the past do not exemplify a single stereotype, 'conflict'. Continuing our consideration of historiographies, we will consider a less antagonistic view. Did science arise in the West due to its Christian heritage, and in particular due to the Reformation?

10. CHRISTIANITY AS THE MATRIX IN WHICH SCIENCE AROSE

The sciences would not have advanced to their present state if Linnaeus, Hartsoeker, Euler, Jenner, Wollaston, Olbers, Blumenbach, Robert Brown, Berzelius, Encke, Mitscherlich, Agassiz, etc., had not been born. Happily their fathers, who were clergymen, were not committed to celibacy ... The number of people who can raise their families in the path of morality, simplicity, and hard work, along with the desire to be useful to others and the wish to occupy themselves with intellectual matters in a disinterested fashion is never very great. One is sorry to see that number decreased by a vow of celibacy imposed on those very men who have more education and character than the average. I am speaking here of the Catholic clergy. (De Candolle, 1885, 333f.; transl. Cohen 1990a)

Alphonse de Candolle was one of the first to use quantitative methods in studying the development of science. Using the election to membership of academic societies such as the Royal Society of London and the Academie Française of Paris as an indicator of scientific eminence, he argued that, among foreign members, Protestants were proportionally overrepresented. De Candolle suggests that this might be a consequence of the greater role of authority in Catholicism, which thereby discourages curiosity, and of the celibacy imposed on Catholic clergy.

De Candolle's emphasis on celibacy seems questionable. As most Catholic clergy have no children, they are left with more time to teach,

[19] J. N. Moore, H. S. Slusher, eds., *Biology: A Search for Order in Complexity* (Grand Rapids: Zondervan, 1970). 'This book was approved by many state textbook committees, but was declared unconstitutional by Indiana Supreme Court in 1977' (McIver 1988, 176). Connections between the launch of the Sputnik, the biology curriculum project, and the revival of creationism are discussed in Nelkin (1977; Larson (1989, 4, 86, 91f.); Eve and Harrold (1991, 28f.); Numbers (1992, 240); the creationist Henry Morris stresses also the 'propaganda' for evolution around the centennial of Darwin's *Origin of Species* (Morris 1984, 75, 190f., 194f.).

to control education, and hence to pass on intellectual culture.[20] Leaving aside this particular explanation, we will focus on the contribution of Christianity, and of Protestantism in particular, to the rise of modern science. We will come back to the claim that Protestantism provided the cultural values which were important to the development of science, but we will begin with the claim that it was the Christian understanding of creation which stimulated experimental science.

Christianity versus Greek philosophy

The mathematician and philosopher Alfred N. Whitehead (1925, 18) traced the rise of science in Europe to:

the medieval insistence on the rationality of God, conceived as with the personal energy of Jehovah and with the rationality of a Greek philosopher.

Other cultures with a highly developed sense of learning did not develop science to any significant extent. If God was a despot, why look for regularities? And if God was seen as rational, understanding is expected to come through thinking (as in mathematics) rather than through observation. M. B. Foster is another philosopher who argued that Greek rationalism had negative consequences for science. If God is neither a demiurge nor merely rational, but personal and creative, as Christianity holds, then there is a particular contingency in nature, which is 'only knowable by sensuous experience' (Foster 1934, 464). To allow for empirical science, Greek, rationalist philosophy of nature had to be changed, and this came about through modification of the doctrine of God.

Foster assumes that there is a one-to-one correspondence between theologies and philosophies of nature (Foster 1936, 11), and that there is a unique philosophy of nature which made modern science possible (Foster 1935, 439f.). These assumptions simplify the argument at the expense of adequacy. He bypasses the more empirically based contributions of Archimedes and Greek astronomy, resulting in Ptolemy's detailed system. He thus relies more on Aristotle's Logic than on the actual practice of Greek science (Foster 1934, 454). Relying on global pictures and on propaganda in defending the role of Christianity as the mother of modern science promotes the

---

[20] A similar point about celibacy is made by Richard Dawkins in his *The Selfish Gene*, when discussing the transmission of memes (ideas) in analogy with the transmission of genes. To be fair, it should be noted that De Candolle did not restrict himself to celibacy; he also considered explanatory factors such as socio-economic structure, immigration, educational system, scientific societies, etc.

treatment of 'science', 'Christianity', and 'Greek philosophy' as monolithic entities.[21] If one acknowledges greater diversity, the rise of
science might be traced to various philosophies of nature, each
partially adequate and partially inadequate, and each at some
moment creating certain opportunities for progress. This would also
allow for a more complete understanding of the intermediate states,
the development of science and theology in Arabic and medieval
European culture.

Another 'monolithic', and thereby too simplistic, analysis of the rise
of modern science is to be found in the work of Stanley Jaki. According
to him, either the world is cyclical and meaningless, a 'treadmill', or
time is linear and nature lawful, a created order. As for most authors in
these debates, the role of belief in creation is not merely of historical
interest. To the belief in creation, 'science owes its very birth and life.
Its future and mankind's future rest with the same faith' (Jaki 1974, viii).

This scheme is black-and-white. It is 'a choice between two ultimate
alternatives: faith in the Creator and in creation once-and-for-all, or
surrender to the treadmill of eternal cycles' (Jaki 1974, 357). To uphold
this view, he claims that there is a single and unique biblical view (Jaki
1974, 139). In addition, all successes in the development of science are
ascribed to this biblical tradition. An explanation is needed of how
Maimonides' *Guide for the Perplexed* 'could be written in the Muslim
milieu and yet evince a mentality far superior to it. This is all the more
remarkable as Maimonides showed no condescendence toward Muslim
and Greek scholars' (Jaki 1974, 213). However, as befits Jaki's position,
the superior contribution of Maimonides is due to 'the overriding role
that was played in Maimonides' thinking by the concept of the Creator
and of the *creatio ex nihilo*, as contained in the Bible' (Jaki 1974, 214).[22]

Reformed superiority

Other discussions of intellectual history have more accurately acknowledged the diversity of traditions, both biblical and otherwise. In his
Religious Origins of Modern Science Eugene M. Klaaren pays serious
attention to spiritualist views of creation, as found among enthusiasts of
the radical reformation, in Renaissance Platonism, and among those

---

[21] A criticism of the reliance on 'subjective, propagandist and programmatic sources' can be
found in Hall (1963, 15), against Merton's sociological link of the rise of science and
Puritanism (see below).

[22] In my view, *creatio ex nihilo* is not biblical, but a philosophical conviction which arose in the
second century in the interaction between Christianity and Greek philosophy (May 1978;
Drees 1990, 264–7).

interested in the alleged writings of Hermes Trismegistus.[23] A major representative of this view was Johan Baptist van Helmont, a disciple of Paracelsus. His works received attention from Boyle and others in England in the middle of the seventeenth century. Van Helmont opens a major work, *Oriatrike*, with a prayer to God, 'All', of All, Father of Lights (Klaaren 1977, 58f.; 'Father of Lights' can be found in the New Testament, James 1: 17). As the Spirit is an all-inclusive and all-pervading reality, Van Helmont's '"mysticism" called for penetration into, rather than flight from, the world' (Klaaren 1977, 61). He and others preferred spiritualist, organic motifs, rather than legal or mechanistic ones. Van Helmont's views were heavily criticised in Boyle's *Skeptical Chymist* (1661). For Van Helmont, chemistry was more than knowledge; in his *Oriatrike* (LX: 66) he wrote:

Finally, and finally, Chymistry, as for its perfection doth prepare an universal Solver, whereby all things do return into their first Being, and do afford their native endowments, the original blemishes of Bodies are cleansed, and that their inhumane cruelty being forsaken, there is opportunity for them to obtain great and undeclarable restoration and purification.

As Klaaren, from whose work this quote has been taken, summarises it, Van Helmont sees chemistry as an attempt 'to realize God's own work of restoration and new creation, for purification and perfection are one' (Klaaren 1977, 80). This spiritualism was conducive to the emergence of modern science as it supported interest in particular observations and distanced itself from Aristotelian natural philosophy. However, according to Klaaren, voluntarism had a definite advantage over spiritualism, as it was less holistic and therefore more capable of making discriminating judgements. It differentiated between the various works of God, and hence between the Book of Nature and the Book of Scripture. This differentiation was institutionalised in the Royal Society of London and became characteristic of modernity.

The contribution of spiritualism is also acknowledged in recent studies by Nebelsick and Kaiser. However, these theologians, too, argue for the greater importance of the Reformed view, the emphasis on God as transcendent lawgiver (and therefore provider of order, though a contingent order) rather than as spirit. Esoteric and plato-nising ideas 'fail to maintain the biblical understanding of God as

---

[23]   The hermetic tradition in relation to the rise of science has been discussed at length by Frances Yates, for instance in her book on Giordano Bruno (Yates 1964). For a critical review of later research on the importance of the hermetic sources, non-hermetic occultist traditions, and – in different ways – the label 'hermetic', see Copenhaver (1990).

transcendent over and separate from nature', and had 'to be set aside before the world could become the world of nature and science could become the study of nature proper' (Nebelsick 1992, 65f.). Even if one finds it difficult to identify with spiritualist and Platonist approaches, one needs to recognise their importance to the rise of science. The importance of the voluntarism of the Calvinist tradition and its precursors in nominalist thought should not be overemphasised.

Kaiser credits the spiritualist tradition, especially in Van Helmont and Leibniz, with 'its ability to generate powerful organizing principles like gas, matter and force' (energy) and to give them empirical meaning in quantifiable form (Kaiser 1991, 161). Besides, through persons like Comenius and Samuel Hartlib, it contributed significantly 'to the formation of social and moral values of the emerging scientific community' (Kaiser 1991, 161). However, the central contribution of Christianity was the belief 'that God had created all things in accordance with laws of his own devising, laws which made the world comprehensible to humans and gave the world a degree of unity and relative autonomy, and that God had sent his Son and poured out his Spirit to initiate a worldwide ministry of healing and restoration' (Kaiser 1991, 300). This creationist tradition 'was to last for sixteen hundred years and gave birth to modern Western science and technology before it degenerated into pure naturalism in the eighteenth and nineteenth centuries' (Kaiser 1991, 6). The word 'degenerated' is telling for Kaiser's own stake in the discussion, as he could equally well have written that it 'gave birth to' pure naturalism just as before it 'gave birth' to natural science.

The Puritan attitude and the rise of science
In contrast with the emphasis on ideas, it has been argued that it is:

to the religious ethos, not the theology, that we must turn if we are to understand the integration of science and religion in seventeenth century England. (Merton 1938, 461; 102)[24]

The major origin of social views of the role of religion with respect to modern culture is considered to be Max Weber's *The Protestant Ethic and the Spirit of Capitalism* (1930, which goes back to earlier German essays; Marshall 1982). With respect to the rise of the sciences this theme was

[24]   References to Merton's *Science, Technology and Society* use the page-numbers of the 1938 edition and of the reprint, separated by a colon. Similar ideas, argued differently, were put forward by Stimson (1935) and Jones (1936); extracts and a survey of subsequent discussions in Cohen (1990a).

developed by Robert Merton. One-third of his major study deals with the role of Protestantism in the rise of science; about as much space is devoted to economic and military influences, while the initial chapters focus on shifts in interests, ranging from painting and poetry to medicine, science, and politics, and on shifts in the relative proportions of work done in various sciences.

The argument that Puritanism created the ethos which supported the rise of modern science has become known as 'the Merton Thesis'. The Puritan complex of values consisted 'of a scarcely disguised utilitarianism; of intramundane interests; methodical, unremitting action; thoroughgoing empiricism; of the right and even the duty of *libre examen* [free inquiry]; of anti-traditionalism – all this was congenial to the same values in science' (Merton 1938, 495; 136; similarly 1936, 29).

Merton remains within a sociological framework when he allows that 'it may well be argued that ascetic Protestantism itself is a product of more pervasive cultural changes' (Merton 1938, 495; 136). He does not take the content of scientific theories to be determined by social factors. Rather, the point is that social changes made science a recognised and accepted enterprise, and that there were social aspects in the choice of topics dealt with.

The discussion on the relation between Puritanism and the development of science has not come to a conclusion, more than fifty years after Merton's initial article and dissertation. This may be due to some extent to personal stakes with respect to apparent implications for the status of religion in the twentieth century. The fact that no conclusion has been reached may also be a consequence of factors more intrinsic to the thesis.

(i) A source of confusion has been the use of categories such as 'Puritan'. Puritanism does not refer to a well-defined institutional entity. It refers to a reform movement which arose in the late sixteenth century. The seventeenth century in England saw changing fortunes of kings, queens, and parliaments. 'Puritan' was not a stable concept, nor were people who lived through the various changes consistent in the way that they presented their religious affiliations. This produces problems when one assesses the role of Puritans with respect to science. For instance, 'John Wilkins was brought up as a Puritan, married Cromwell's sister, and during the Commonwealth served as Warden of Wadham College. But after the Restoration, he joined the established church, was formally ordained, and became bishop of Chester. Was the mature Wilkins a Puritan because of his upbringing and early career? Merton would say yes, his critics no' (Cohen 1990a, 62f.; see Shapiro 1969, 5–11).

(ii) The political and cultural changes occurring within the seventeenth century have also made the debate very complex. Charles Webster (1975) argued that science in the 1640s and 1650s was motivated by millennialist expectations. After the restoration of the monarchy and of the established church in 1660 little sympathy was felt for puritanist priorities and achievements. But 'it may turn out that in the scale of values of a future age the utopianism and humanitarianism of puritan science may come to be held in high esteem' (Webster 1975, 520). Again, a personal agenda shines through, this time an agenda in social ethics 'in the most recent crisis in science and technology' (Webster 1975, 517).

Whereas Webster emphasises discontinuity in English political history, others stress continuity. Boyle and others 'did not cease to be reformers, but couched their reforming sentiments in vague terms of improving man's health and estate through science' (Jacob and Jacob 1980, 253). These 'conservative reformers' carried science forward after the revolutionary period. They retreated from millennialism and interest in occult sciences to a view of nature as consisting of atoms guided by God's providence.

(iii) The various ways of viewing religion, ranging from doctrine to social attitude, have not contributed to the clarity of discussion either. Merton sees religion as an embodiment of dominant cultural values; this is to some extent independent of particular theological claims. The incentive to be useful could be derived, and actually was derived, from understanding good works as a sign of grace in a predestinarian theology, but also from treating good works as a means towards grace; 'there is substantial uniformity in the *social* implications of the various Protestant dogmas' (Merton 1938, 422; 63). Other historians and theologians have been less sensitive to the sociological perspective of the history of ideas, understanding religion 'more narrowly, as a body of explicit espousals of intentions in doctrinal form' (Abraham 1983, 373; see also Cohen 1990, 314, 339 and note 21).

(iv) There are two phenomena to be explained: (a) the shift of values that moved scientists to the top of the intellectual hierarchy and made science a recognised public concern, and (b) the greater propensity of Puritans to be engaged in science (Ben-David 1985, 209f.). Chapter six of Merton's book, 'Puritanism, Pietism and Science: Testing an Hypothesis', dealt with the second phenomenon. This counting of participants has been the subject of most criticism; as argued above (i), the meanings of the various labels change over time. However, the more viable part of the thesis has to do with the rise of science as a culturally acceptable practice, rather than with scientific theories and explanations themselves.

(v) One might counter the claim that ascetic Protestantism was specifically conducive to the emergence of modern science by pointing out the limitations of the focus on seventeenth-century England, for instance by presenting the contributions of Catholics elsewhere in Europe (e.g., Ashworth 1986) or by attacking the way numbers of participants from various backgrounds are established and the ways in which labels are attributed. Even if Protestants were overrepresented among early scientists, an apologetic use of the thesis is misguided, even if understood in the more general sense that Protestantism supported the values that made science a highly respected enterprise. Once science had acquired social recognition, the mechanism which had brought about this recognition became something of the past. To some extent external influences have given way to internal systems of evaluation. Besides, an account of the early phase of this process of institutionalisation is incomplete if it deals only with the appeal to the affinity of science with religion; distancing science from religion was another part of the rhetorical expression of the same agenda (Gieryn 1988, 583).

Continuity and discontinuity

It is true that the results of our dominion over nature have been unhealthy in many cases; the powerful river of modern science and technology has often caused disastrous inundations. But by comparison the contemplative, almost medieval vision that is offered as an alternative would be a stagnant pool.

Thus wrote the historian of science Hooykaas (1972, 74) in his book on the importance of Protestantism to the rise of modern science. Discontinuity between medieval and modern science is an important element in this argument.

Even if there were discontinuities in methodology and in metaphysics, we should not judge the medievals on the wrong grounds. 'Their aim was not to anticipate future worldviews' (Lindberg 1992, 363). Their contributions were conducive to the subsequent development of science. They 'created an intellectual tradition. They worked through Greek and Islamic materials. They created the institutional setting of schools and universities. And they created a critical climate in which Aristotelian doctrine was regularly and carefully scrutinized, and which in its fate depended on its explanatory power rather than on any authoritative status it might possess' (Lindberg 1992, 366). With this last observation, Lindberg deviates from the popular view that medieval science and philosophy were strongly dependent upon authority.

Developments at different disciplinary levels were not all concurrent. Focus on global change biases historical judgement towards discontinuity, towards treating historical change as a shift from one monolithic outlook to another. More detailed analysis, however, uncovers the manifold connections between medieval and modern science. This undermines the claim that there was a discontinuity, in which the rise of modern science was correlated with the Protestant Reformation.

The notion of a 'Scientific Revolution' for a radical transformation in which philosophical insights were of major importance is itself a product of the polemic against the positivist emphasis on observation, and is thus to be understood in the context of the development of philosophy and history of science in the twentieth century. Recent detailed studies have challenged the global claims in many ways. The notion of a 'Scientific Revolution' may still be the dominant interpretation, and it serves 'heuristic functions, even if it no longer commands universal assent' (Lindberg 1990, 20). The emergence of modern science was a complex phenomenon. Social attitudes and metaphysical positions generated by religious views were certainly effective in that process.[25] 'To single out any specific religious view seems unwarranted as it neglects the wide variety of religious, philosophical and scientific views that interacted with each other. It would also suggest a kind of necessity which is hard to sustain in historical affairs.

Various studies on the importance of Christianity to the rise of modern science have an apologetic interest, an interest in supporting Christianity today (e.g., Foster, Hooykaas, Jaki, Kaiser, Nebelsick). However, as apologetics for Christianity in our time, such arguments exaggerate differences between Christian views and Greek views that

---

[25] For broad and balanced studies, see Brooke (1991, 52–116), the essays in Lindberg and Westman (1990) and Lindberg and Numbers (1986, 49–237), and H. F. Cohen's study of historiographies of the Scientific Revolution (1994), which I came across only after completing the book.

failed to give rise to science, while they belittle differences between the religious views of the early modern period and contemporary perspectives on the world (Gruner 1975, 79).

Whereas in this section we have considered the contribution of Christianity to the rise of modern science, there is also a contribution of modern science to the development of theology. In the manifold interactions of the seventeenth century, we see the rise of 'a veritable secular theology such as never existed before or after' (Funkenstein 1986, ix). This theology was secular in a double sense, carried out by laymen for laymen, and oriented towards the world, *ad seculum*. This shift in theology will be considered in the next chapter.

II. NON-APOLOGETICAL APOLOGETICS

Nobody doubted the existence of the Deity until the Boyle lecturers had undertaken to prove it. (Remark from the deist and freethinker Anthony Collins, eighteenth century.)[26]

Michael Buckley begins his narrative in *At the Origins of Modern Atheism* with the Catholics Leonard Lessius and Marin Mersenne in the early seventeenth century. They both argued against atheism on the basis of 'a wide-ranging knowledge of natural philosophy' without assigning a position to 'Christology or religious experience' (Buckley 1987, 65). Such a style of philosophical apologetics continued through Descartes and Newton. It was assimilated into theology by Nicolas Malebranche and Samuel Clarke. And in the eighteenth century it resulted in the self-conscious atheism of Denis Diderot and Baron Paul Henri d'Holbach. Remarkable, according to Buckley, is that which is absent from such Christian apologies:

Religious experience of whatever dimension or character counts for nothing, neither the interior claims of an absolute, nor the disclosures of 'limit experiences', nor the movements and attractions towards the transcendent. Or, if one looks not for the witness of subjectivity but for the historical or external witness within human tradition, one will look in vain for the history of holiness as a perpetual manifestation of mystery, the testimony of the mystics, the depths of human religious practice over thousands of years, and

---

[26]   L. Stephen, *History of English Thought in the Eighteenth Century*, vol. 1 (London: Smith, Elder & Co., 1881², 80); see also under 'Deism' in *The Encyclopedia of Philosophy*, vol. 2, ed. P. Edwards (New York: Macmillan, 1967), 331. Van Fraassen (1980, 229) refers to the eighteenth-century witticism that 'Everybody believed in the existence of God until the Boyle-lectures proved it.'

– even more remarkably for a Christian culture – anything of the reality and meaning of Jesus of Nazareth. (Buckley 1988, 94)

Without becoming atheists themselves, natural philosophers (scientists) such as Newton and Boyle shifted the terms of the debate. 'The origin of atheism in the intellectual culture of the West lies thus with the self-alienation of religion itself' (Buckley 1987, 363). 'Inference cannot substitute for experience, and the most compelling witness to a personal God must itself be personal' (Buckley 1988, 99).

John Dillenberger makes a similar case in his *Protestant Thought and Natural Science* (1960). Apologetics in the eighteenth century appealed to evidence from miracles and prophecies and to the wisdom of God as discernable in nature, as it had been done before. However, the role of such arguments from miracles and prophecy had become rather different from the way that they functioned in earlier centuries. Then, miracles and fulfilled prophecies were confirmation for a belief held independently, whereas in the eighteenth century belief had become dependent upon miracles and fulfilled prophecies. 'Confirmation for the revelation of God in Christ was of the same order as that in the natural sciences. The Messiah had Himself become an object of ordinary knowledge and demonstration' (Dillenberger 1960, 146).

A similar shift occurred in relation to the appreciation of God's wisdom in creation, the so-called 'argument from design'. One of its proponents was John Ray. His book was entitled *The Wisdom of God Manifested in the Works of Creation, in Two Parts, viz. The Heavenly Bodies, Elements, Meteors, Fossils, Vegetables, Animals, (Beasts, Birds, Fishes, and Insects) more particularly in the Body of the Earth, its Figure, Motion, and Consistency; and in the admirable Structure of the Bodies of Man and other Animals; as also in their Generation, etc. With Answers to some Objections.* Listing topics in the title was a common practice. Here it gives an impression of the scope of this book. Examples of divine wisdom are abundant throughout nature. One example, quoted from the eleventh edition (1743, 239f):

The great Wisdom of the divine Creator appears, in that there is Pleasure annex'd to those Actions that are necessary for the Support and Preservation of the *Individuum*, and the Continuation and Propagation of the *Species*; and not only so, but Pain to the Neglect or Forbearance of them. For the Support of the Person, it hath annex'd pleasure to eating and drinking, which else, out of Laziness or Multiplicity of Business, a Man would be apt to neglect, or sometimes forget; indeed to be oblig'd to chew and swallow meat daily for two Hours Space, and to find no Relish or Pleasure in it, would be one of the most burdensom and ungrateful Tasks of a Man's whole life; but because this Action is absolutely necessary, for abundant Security Nature hath inserted in us a painful Sense of Hunger, to put us in mind of it; and to reward our Performance hath adjoin'd pleasure to it; and as for the continuation of Kind, I need not tell you that the Enjoyment which attend those Actions are the highest Gratifications of Sense.

These writers claimed to follow the tradition of the early Church, but 'they had inverted the original apologetic'. Christology was separated from the domain of nature. 'Reflection on this period raises the question whether a conscious apologetic is not usually a boomerang' (Dillenberger 1960, 153), as the distinctive grounds of religion are lost from sight.

Moving beyond history to an assessment of the situation of his time, Dillenberger sees new opportunities in the theology of the twentieth century, especially in the contributions of Karl Barth, Paul Tillich, and Rudolf Bultmann; 'they restored the Christian drama of redemption to central importance' (Dillenberger 1960, 263); through existentialism the dimension of depth was recovered (265). The *naïveté* which we are to overcome is reductionism, both in biology and in analytical philosophy (Dillenberger 1960, 279 and 282n.).

Dillenberger and Buckley present a different view of theology than we encountered in the preceding sections. However, to the extent that Buckley and Dillenberger emphasise a single issue throughout the history of theology and science, their position resembles views discussed in earlier sections. A difference is that arguments about conflicts or affinities between Christian religion and science [7–10] are mostly based on a cognitive view of religion in line with the understanding of the natural sciences, whereas their argument focuses more on differences, assuming rather an experiential view of religion.

In emphasising 'religious experience', either as 'the witness of subjectivity' or as 'the historical or external witness within human tradition' (as Buckley does in the text quoted), the debate is quite different from most discussions on the relationship between science and religion, but this emphasis does not imply that there are no issues to be considered. When one builds upon particulars in human experiences and in human history, the area of debate shifts from debates about the world 'out there' (see chapter 3) to debates about our understanding of human nature, human experiences and human traditions, and thus to 'reductionism in biology' (see chapter 4).

12. LESSONS TO BE LEARNED FROM HISTORY

Contemporary historians of science have objected to the emphasis on unity. In presentations which argue for a persistent conflict [7–9], affinity [10], or betrayed distinctiveness [11]:

> it is almost always assumed that there are lessons to be learned from history. The object of this study is not to deny that assumption but to show that the lessons are far from simple ... The real lesson turns out to be the complexity. (Brooke 1991, 4f.)

Contemporary historians of science are more neutral than their predecessors; a historian of science who used the warfare-style of Draper or White would not receive much recognition from her academic peers today. Current historians are not only, in general, more accurate with respect to their sources, they have also come to the conclusion that there is an enormous richness, diversity, and complexity in the interactions between science and religion in various episodes. Even a single individual may entertain different views in different periods of his life or in front of different audiences. Streamlining the historical account of science in its relation to religion is a temptation which should be avoided. Counter-examples to any stereotype can always be found.

Historians have shifted the agenda from an analysis of the interaction between science and theology to an analysis of the way religion and science developed and changed in the course of the processes. The historian cannot define in a strict way 'science' and 'religion' before embarking upon her research. Otherwise, she would be unable to understand authors such as Newton who did not live by that distinction. It is of special interest to understand shifts in the meanings of the terms 'science' and 'religion', and hence of the boundaries between what was considered science and what was considered religion. Taking science and religion as clearly defined entities involves the danger of neglecting the variety of activities covered by these terms and of isolating both from their common cultural and social context (Rudwick 1981, 243; Brooke 1991, 7f.).

As an example of shifting meanings, one might even consider the evolution of creationism, as there have been 'substantial changes in creationist thought during the twentieth century' (Numbers 1992, xiv). In the late nineteenth century the issue was God's creative role and the

understanding of the world as designed, whereas contemporary creationism takes a strong stance on the literal meaning of the first chapters
of Genesis. As the concepts 'science' and 'religion' are subject to
change, 'we must not ask "Who was the aggressor?" but "How were
Christianity and science affected by their encounter?" ' (Lindberg and
Numbers 1986a, 354).

Not only do meanings change over time, but they are also diverse
and used eclectically at any moment, since the style and strategy
pursued by an individual often reflect the rhetorical situation in relation
to the audience and the aims of the moment.

Methodologically historians opt for an intrinsic, local understanding of
the various episodes, in relation to the social and intellectual setting of
the participants. An encompassing view of the history of science (and
thus of science's relation to religion) seems to be lacking; 'there is a
danger that the important revisions of recent years will simply be
slotted into conventional large-scale narratives that drain the analysis
of any real edge ... As a result, a construct founded on the primacy of
method, genius and heroic discovery continues (albeit awkwardly) to
organize a body of specialist literature devoted to criticizing the
coherence of such concepts' (Secord 1993, 388).[27] Attempts at thinking
through relationships between science and religion can go awry in
similar ways, either by overemphasising methodological issues or by
focusing narrowly on a few heroic individuals, for instance on the faith
of a major scientist.

With respect to the contemporary situation, strategies may be
pursued which are similar to those of the historians, and similar
conclusions can be reached. Positions of various contemporary authors
can be understood better when attention is given to the understanding
of religion and of science involved and to the audiences to which
certain ideas are addressed (see, for instance, [4, 5, 23]). I intend to
operate in a similar way as the historians of science considered here, in
following a contextual and non-religionist approach (see [3.1]). In doing
so, I seek to avoid simple conflict-interpretations [7, 8, 9] as well as
apologetic attempts which seek to claim support from the history of

---

[27] C. Hakfoort discusses 'the missing syntheses in the historiography of science' in a similar way,
and argues that historians of science might attempt to write synthetic surveys on 'the historical
background to the present uncertainty about what science is' (Hakfoort 1991, 214f.). This
resembles the situation with religion and science, where the argument is – as argued in the
text – not so much one about the relationships between religion and science as one about the
nature and status of science and of religion.

science or from current science for traditional beliefs or which claim room aside from science [10, 11]. Rather, I identify with the assesment by James Secord of the direction in which a new 'big picture' of the history of science might develop: 'Essentialist stories of science as the central actor in a drama of triumph or disaster, will be replaced by a focus on questions, debates and contests for authority' (Secord 1993, 389). As a philosophical interpretation I intend to build upon the work of such historians of science and of science's relations to religion, not so much in detail (since I seek to articulate a general view rather than make very specific claims about particular episodes) as in general style and spirit.

The work of the historians derives its strength from a self-chosen limitation; they attempt to understand each episode in relation to its own context. In doing so, they avoid the issue of the intellectual credibility of religion in our time. Though a thorough historical tour is fascinating, studies of particular historical cases cannot be transposed to our time, especially since each episode is embedded in its own wider context. This study aims at an exploration of the avenues that are open to us in an intellectually honest way, given the resources of our time. Hence, we have to move on from historical studies to reflections on contemporary science. The historical explorations may alert us, however, to the diversity of views of religion, of agendas in relating religion to science, and of meanings of religion; a diversity which is very probably not smaller now than at any time in the past.

3

Theology and knowledge of the world

Religion is about reality, that is about creation and about God. Science informs us about reality. If the central concerns of each enterprise are seen thus, how do science and religion interact? We will consider in chapter 3 two areas of interaction, namely in relation to *the discoveries of science*, the insights about the world, and to *the discovery of science*, the rise of science to a major, if not the major, position in our attempts to find out about the world. In the terms of the earlier 3 × 3–classification [5], we are dealing with the first column (a cognitive understanding of religion), and especially with areas 1a (new knowledge, the discoveries of science) and 1b (new conceptions of knowledge, the discovery of science).

We will begin with theological responses to the discoveries of science. A major issue is the impact of these discoveries on our understanding of the world as a tightly knit web of processes described by laws. What possibilities are there for an understanding of divine activity within the processes of the world? I will argue that a quest for gaps in natural processes is unsuccessful, given the coherence of scientific insights, but that the denial of such gaps within natural processes does not foreclose all options for a view of divine action, since *divine* action may also be conceived as a unique creative-sustaining (not causal-temporal) action with respect to everything [13]. We will also consider alternative conceptions of the divine which do not involve anything that resembles divine activity in the world. Rather, they emphasise a cosmic sense of meaning or mystery [14].

After considering these examples of religious views in relation to our understanding of the world, we will come to the general theme of using scientific insights for theological purposes. First, I will argue that the use of science in theological models may be heuristically fruitful as well as helpful for communicative purposes, but that it does not contribute much to the credibility of the theological ideas thus developed [15]. With respect to the hierarchy of levels, theology may seem to be remote from areas such as fundamental physics and cosmology where consensus on the theories and their interpretations seems lacking. However, I will argue that the provisional character of scientific theories which are relatively remote from human interests challenge an argumentative use of science [16].

In the last sections of this part we will turn towards the discovery of science. We will begin with a survey of contemporary defences of scientific realism. This is done for two purposes. Firstly, as an end in itself, in order to counter attempts to cope with science by playing down its importance. Secondly, in relation to debates on theological realism. For some authors writing on the relationships between science and religion attempt to transfer arguments from the philosophy of science to the philosophy of religion; I will argue that such moves are unsuccessful [17].

In the concluding section I will come to arguments which seek to find room for theology or metaphysics via science by arguing that science rests upon a metaphysical or theological basis (Trigg), or to find room for religion despite the results of science, since science is a cultural practice (Allen), or claim that epistemological naturalism is best understood in the context of metaphysical supernaturalism (Plantinga) [18].

13. DIVINE ACTION [1]

Though themes relating the doctrine of creation to questions of origins often come to mind most readily in discussions of science and religion, a more central theme from a theological perspective is *God's action in the world* (e.g., Russell *et al.* 1993, 1995). Views of divine action are involved in views of divine providence, prayer, miracles, the understanding of the life, death, and resurrection of Jesus, and human freedom and responsibility, to mention just a few issues. Views of divine action in the world have been challenged for various reasons. A major reason has to do with the reality of evil: If God acts in the world, and especially if God acts in response to the needs of individuals, why is there so much evil and suffering in the world? Here I will focus on the other major

[1] After having developed the arguments in this chapter I came across a dissertation by Steven D. Crain (1993), which deals with the same issues at greater length, and which considers William Pollard as well as Polkinghorne and Peacocke.

kind of problem, namely the challenge which arises when one seeks to combine belief in particular divine actions with scientific insights about the lawful behaviour of natural processes. In this section we will briefly consider the idea that an occasional, scientifically unobserved miracle would not be a problem. Then we will discuss more extensively two proposals for understanding divine action in relation to the natural world, focusing on the unpredictability of complex processes, and on the way the behaviour of particular constituents in a system is shaped by the state of the system as a whole (top–down causation). Both proposals turn out to be problematic. Then, I will consider an understanding of divine action which avoids any conflict with and dependence on the natural sciences by emphasising the distinction between divine action (as atemporal creation of the whole) and temporal processes in the world.

An odd miracle and integrity
The philosopher William Alston has written that

> the odd miracle would not seem to violate anything of importance for science. It would be quite a coincidence if a miracle should be among the minute proportion of cases of X that are examined for scientific purposes. (Alston 1991, 244)

It may well be that God has interfered just when and where we did not look. Arguments to that effect are formally strong, just as the ingenious Omphalos argument reconciling evidence for a long evolutionary past with a recent creation: God may have created the world some six to ten thousand years ago with all the traces of a longer past, including Adam and Eve with navels (suggesting a mother, though there was none), trees with rings, the fossils which are mistakenly thought to be remnants of earlier organisms, and the light which appears to come from distant stars, and keeps the astronomers busy [see 15].[2]

There are all kinds of gaps in our knowledge; we have not checked conservation of energy everywhere and we do extrapolate from evidence found now to past events. However, to exploit such limitations in order to avoid unwanted conclusions is to depart from regular scientific practice. By undermining scientific reasoning, this argument for the possibility of occasional miracles does undermine something 'of importance to science', even though it does not conflict with any

---

[2]   The argument was articulated a few years before Darwin's *Origin of Species* (1859) by Philip Henry Gosse in his *Omphalos: An Attempt to Untie the Geological Knot* (1857).

observations. The argument undermines the integrity of science, both that of its methods and that of its results. Integrity has various meanings, including overtones of a moral character. Here it is used in the way it might be used in a legal context: one may have stayed within the formal boundaries of the law, while violating the underlying spirit, the larger web of beliefs, intentions and procedures of which it is a part (e.g., Schüssler Fiorenza 1991, 138f.). Thus, in the following I will not explore theological approaches which use such gaps in our knowledge, but consider approaches which seek to respect and interpret the understanding of reality delivered by the natural sciences.

13.1. Divine action in unpredictable processes

Theories regarding chaotic behaviour introduce an openness into our description of the natural world which was missing in classical Newtonian physics so far. This openness would be a kind of local contingency which might allow for human or divine free will and human or divine agency.[3] This view has been eloquently defended by the Anglican priest and theoretical physicist John Polkinghorne, even though in the end he takes a more pronounced distance from the ordinary interpretation of science, when he argues for an under-standing of the laws of physics as a 'downward' 'approximation to a more subtle (and supple) whole' (Polkinghorne 1993, 439). In this way he takes exception to the disciplinary order of the sciences; the laws of physics are to be distinguished from the laws of nature. In principle, more fundamental reinterpretations of the sciences such as this one and the further developed one proposed by process philoso-phers are possible, but I consider them unlikely; I will come back to this below [30].

Here the focus is on discussions which relate to the laws of physics. We will first consider Polkinghorne's interpretation of chaotic systems, before arguing on the basis of a more general view of scientific explanations against such a view of divine action.

The 'choice' of path actually followed corresponds, not to the result of some physically causal act (in the sense of an energy input) but rather to a 'selection' from options (in the sense of an information input) ... God is not pictured as an interfering agent among other agencies. (That would correspond to energy

---

[3] R. J. Russell (1988) introduced the concept of local contingency, in contrast to global and nomological contingency, with further differentiations.

input.) Instead, form is given to the possibility that he influences his creation in a non-energetic way. (Polkinghorne 1991, 45)

The laws of nature allow for openness, gaps which might allow for divine and human action. Central to this argument is that there can be information input without energy input, thus without interfering with physical laws regarding energy. In *Science and Providence* Polkinghorne uses the example of a bead at the top of an inverted U-shaped wire. In this case, he argues, there would be no energy barrier between different options, i.e. moving the bead to the left or to the right. God could act without input of energy (Polkinghorne 1989, 32).

Polkinghorne proposes a model for divine influence on physical processes which does not violate the conservation of energy. However, this approach has at least two drawbacks. It puts divine information input in competition with energy input from the environment, especially if one takes into account the amplificatory powers of natural systems. Polkinghorne also moves from unpredictability to openness in a way which pays insufficient attention to the scientific theories available. We will deal with these two aspects in turn.

A bead at the top of an inverted U-shaped wire would in due course end on either the left or the right side, as molecules from the surrounding air will have pushed it in one direction or the other. Once one such collision has taken place, one could not without some expenditure of energy make the bead fall the other way. Thus, a God who would like to provide information without energy would have to act quickly, before energetic influences such as those arising from the environment have moved the system out of the state of unstable equilibrium. In this sense, there is a competition between divine input of non-energetic information and the input of energy. This is a general feature of such a model, which seeks a picture for divine action in a physically effective but non-energetic way. Polkinghorne distinguished between energy input and information input, with the latter determining the 'selection' of one of various possible options, but this distinction is not sufficient to avoid competition. Once one allows the system in its environment some time, the 'selection' will be made by the environment. This is a consequence of the way natural systems may amplify the consequences of tiny differences in energy.

We are often not aware of tiny differences in energy input. Take, for instance, two different mental acts corresponding to a choice between two options. We experience them as different in information content, not (*qua* mental acts) as physically different in energy or labour involved. However, the apparent fact that we have information differences without energy differences may well be an illusion, due to the enormous amplificatory powers of the central nervous system (Dennett 1984, 77f.) and the fact that we do not monitor the physiological processes in our brains. Theories of chaos and self-organisation show that the amplificatory powers of physical systems with respect to small initial differences are much more impressive than previously thought. One should avoid confusing zero and close-to-zero in this context; it is essential to Polkinghorne's position that the difference in energy input is zero rather than almost zero, whereas a naturalist description may understand the process as regulated by low-energy events which act as switches modulating processes which expend larger, observable amounts of energy. On a naturalist view, information and energy go together. The alternative, of information-differences without energy-differences, may respect conservation of energy, but it makes God and physical causes compete for temporal priority.

If there were such a competition, and if God were to act first whenever God decided to influence natural processes, the outcome of the act would seem to be the consequence of a natural process, which we would, mistakenly, believe to have happened. In presenting us with an illusion, this position has some similarity to the idea that God might have created the world with the appearances of a long geological and evolutionary past, an illusory past which we study (a kind of 'Omphalos' argument to which we will return [15]); the difference is that here we are mistaken in our understanding of minute effects of the thermal background rather than of effects on a grand scale.

In a slightly different way, the same problem holds for Polkinghorne's interpretation of unpredictability as a sign of ontological openness:

if apparently open behaviour is associated with underlying apparently deterministic equations, which is to be taken to have greater ontological seriousness – the behaviour or the equations? (Polkinghorne 1991, 45)

This preference for the phenomena (unpredictability) rather than the current explanation (*deterministic* chaos) is problematic, given Polkinghorne's defence of critical realism elsewhere. Defences of critical realism conclude from the explanatory power of a theory to its ontology. In this sense, in critical realism 'epistemology models ontology', a slogan Polkinghorne wears on a T-shirt, and which he explains as 'acquired knowledge is a guide to the way things are' (Polkinghorne 1993, 440). Polkinghorne seems to assume that the acquired knowledge which is to be followed is that certain processes are unpredictable; this he sees as an indication of ontological openness. However, the acquired knowledge is much richer than the observation of limited predictability. It includes the theory which explains the processes, including our inability to predict their course; this theory is formulated in non-linear, deterministic equations. In this sense, a comparison with the analysis of quantum uncertainty is mistaken, as there the theory allows, at least according to some major interpretations, the conclusion that there is genuine indeterminacy. The scientific study of self-organising, complex, and chaotic systems has not revealed new gaps, which might be filled by some external actor. Rather, complex systems exhibit behaviour as if they were guided by an external organising principle or an intentional self, but the theories show that such behaviour is explainable without invoking any such actor – whether a self, a life-force, or a divine Informer. As such, chaos theory is the extension of the bottom–up programme to complex systems rather than suggesting the existence of some 'top' from which 'intentional causation' as 'information' proceeds downwards, as Polkinghorne claims.

Polkinghorne acknowledges that the use of openness as the causal joint between God and the world looks like a 'God-of-the-gaps', even though God is not competing as 'an alternative source of energetic causation'. However, Polkinghorne argues that there is a fundamental difference between these gaps and earlier gaps, which 'were epistemic, and thus extrinsic to nature, mere patches of current scientific ignorance' (Polkinghorne 1993, 446). I agree that there is a fundamental difference, but it works in the other direction. In the case of epistemic gaps that reflect our ignorance, one might maintain an agnostic stance with respect to the possibility of a scientific explanation. However, with respect to the processes described by chaos theories there is no reason for such an open attitude, since we have an underlying theory. To claim the existence of gaps is not merely to remain agnostic where we do not know, but to go against acquired knowledge, the unpredictability of systems which are described by deterministic equations. At this level, we are not confronted with any indications of 'gaps' in the processes, unlike the situation at the quantum level and, perhaps, the cosmological level.

My objections to Polkinghorne's argument are based upon more general reflections on gaps and scientific explanations. There are at least two conceptions of explanation, an epistemic one, which considers phenomena explained when they are located in a wider theoretical framework (e.g., Kitcher 1981), and an ontic one, which considers phenomena explained when underlying causes or mechanisms are discerned (e.g., Boyd 1985). Such ontic and epistemic approaches 'are not mutually exclusive, but, rather, complementary' (Salmon 1990, x).

Chaotic processes have been explained, in both senses. They fit into a wider theoretical framework, parts of which have been around for centuries (differential equations) whereas other elements, for example, fractals, were developed at about the same time as chaos theory was being developed. Chaos theory has not diminished the unity of explanatory accounts, but increased it, as more phenomena are now treated within the framework of mathematical physics. And a causal account of chaotic processes of limited predictability is available. Even though we could not have predicted a specific storm two weeks in advance, since we were unable to observe the then prevailing conditions in sufficient detail (what is colloquially called 'the butterfly effect'), we can think of a possible causal mechanism which generated that storm. We cannot predict the numbers that will come up when we throw a pair of dice, nor are we able to predict which way the bead will fall along an inverted U-shaped wire. But in either case, we can explain how it may have come about the way it actually came about (due to minute influences from the air, the surface, etc.). Predictability is no condition for explainability.

We are not limited to two options, as if a phenomenon is either predictable, or is unexplainable due to some genuine 'gap' in nature. In between are phenomena which are in principle explainable but are currently unexplainable because we do not yet have the correct theory – as was the situation with the discovery of 'high temperature' super-conductivity in ceramic materials. Even without an explanation we assume the phenomenon to be explainable in terms of physics, probably current physics, but otherwise with a modification of current physics. There may also be phenomena which are explainable but will never be predictable – as is the case with chaotic processes. As the events will never be fully predictable, one can never exclude a particular divine action hidden in the unpredictability.[4] However, as I see it, if there is no indication of, or need for, such an assumption of openness and divine action, the assumption is not justified.

Quantum uncertainty may be different. Here we have good grounds to exclude ordinary (local) 'hidden variables', and thus to rule out an explanation of the limited predictability as a consequence of unobserved but real local physical processes. Therefore, quantum physics may be a more appropriate level for envisaging divine action than any process at a higher level of reality. Its 'gaps' are not asserted despite the presence of a competing explanation, *viz.*, deterministic laws and causal mechanisms underlying chaotic processes, but are reflected in the fundamental structure of the theory (which describes reality in terms of a superposition of various states).[5] I am none the less sceptical about the use of quantum physics in an attempt to locate divine action. One reason is that quantum indeterminacy might be resolved either via a modification of quantum physics or via some future reinterpretation. Another reason is that quantum indeterminacy does not require a metaphysical supplement to physical causes, even though it may perhaps allow such a move. There is no need to adhere to a metaphysical principle of sufficient reason, even though a methodological principle of sufficient reason is a good heuristic notion within any naturalist approach.

Unpredictability is very relevant beyond the strictly scientific context, especially in the context of ethics. If we can have only a limited view of the consequences of our actions, this may affect the way in which we assess our responsibilities. But unpredictability does not offer or undergird a specific view of divine action in individual events or a view of a causal joint between God and the world. Unpredictability is metaphysically uninteresting, or at most a necessary but insufficient condition for metaphysical openness.

13.2. Top–down causation as a model for divine action

An alternative to an interventionist view of God's action within unpredictable processes has been presented by Arthur Peacocke in his

---

4   As argued by R. J. Russell in a contribution which will be published in (Russell, Murphy, and Peacocke 1995).

5   As in the contributions by G. F. R. Ellis, N. Murphy, and T. F. Tracy in Russell, Murphy, and Peacocke (1995).

Theology for a Scientific Age. It relies on the notion of top–down causation, a notion originally introduced by D. Campbell (1974). I will briefly present this idea and its application in the context of theology, before coming to some critical comments.

Examples of top–down causation

There are physical and chemical systems in which there is co-ordinated behaviour of myriads of individual molecules. Chemical clocks (mixtures which rhythmically change colour) and Bénard cells (stable convection cells in a fluid between two plates) are examples of this. The system exhibits a global pattern, as long as certain conditions are maintained at the spatial boundaries. Individual molecules behave according to this global pattern, rather than in the manifold possible ways described in the statistics of an ideal gas. As Peacocke formulates it,

the changes at the micro-level, that of the constituent units, are what they are *because* of their incorporation into the system as a whole, which is exerting specific constraints on its units, making them behave otherwise than they would do in isolation. (Peacocke 1993, 53f.)

Bernd-Olaf Küppers has on various occasions presented theories regarding self-organising systems as theories regarding 'boundary conditions' (e.g., Küppers 1990). There are spatial boundary conditions, such as the temperatures at the bottom and the top of the fluid in which Bénard convection cells occur. More relevant to our understanding of reality are DNA-molecules which shape the development of each organism and may be seen as some sort of initial conditions. Boundary conditions are, of course, a traditional feature in physical descriptions, corresponding to the freedom of the experimenter to choose a certain experimental set-up. However, in the case of the DNA of organisms, we are not dealing with such almost totally contingent boundary conditions. The boundary conditions which are initial to one stage are the outcome of the preceding step, and beyond that they are the product of a long sequence of generations that gave rise to complex organisms.

Another example of top–down causation, sometimes mentioned, is the relation between mental phenomena and brain states. According to Peacocke, top–down causation provides a middle ground between an unacceptable Cartesian dualism of two entities and a physicalist reductionism of mental states to brain states. There is a danger of a circularity here: one may invoke top–down causation to understand the relation between mind and brain and invoke our understanding of brain states and mental phenomena in order to present top–down causation. The risk of circularity, and of relying on unclear ideas about the relation between mind and brain, should be a major reason for caution in appealing to this example in theological contexts. I also have the impression that a reductionistic approach, if it includes environment–organism interaction and the difference between a first-person and a third-person account, has a stronger case than is granted by authors who appeal to top–down causation in order to understand the mind–brain relationship (see below, [21]).

A more general concern about the idea of top–down causation is whether it deserves the label 'causation'. There certainly is a place for top–down analysis, but that is an epistemological rather than an ontological notion. For instance, the neuroscientist Roger Sperry who advocates the notion of top–down causation mentions, as an example, 'how a wheel rolling downhill carries its atoms and molecules through a course in time and space to a fate determined by the overall system properties of the wheel as a whole and regardless of the inclination of the individual atoms and molecules' (Sperry 1980, 201, quoted in Arbib and Hesse 1986, 66). Arbib and Hesse agree that to consider the positions and motions of all individual atoms and molecules is not the most expedient way of analysing the course of the wheel. However, as they point out, the wheel makes the movements it makes *because* the atoms and molecules behave in certain ways; the whole is not acting independently, 'regardless' (Sperry) of the constituent particles and their interactions; the example does not make it clear that a level has emerged from which causal action proceeds downwards.

The example of the Bénard cells is a clear instance where the conditions at the boundary, in combination with the properties of the components and their interactions, determine the behaviour of billions of individual molecules; the internal properties are emphasised in arguments about *self*-organization; the boundaries are emphasised in arguments about *top*–down causation, as in this section. However, here one could replace the term 'top–down' causation by 'environment–system' interaction. That environment, which determines the temperature at the boundary plates, is a physical system, just as the system in which the Bénard cells occur. All influences can be traced as local phenomena within the space–time framework. For instance, changing the boundary conditions does not have an immediate impact on the behaviour of molecules at some distance from the boundary; it takes the system some time to settle into a new co-ordinated state. In such cases, there is a sense in which a whole (state at the boundary-plates; DNA) serves as the boundary for the system, while the next stage of the whole, for instance the DNA of the next generation, is shaped by the development of the system (the organism) in its environment. However, there is no sense in which the system-as-a-whole has a specific, 'emergent' causal influence. All causal influences can be traced locally as physical influences within the system or between the system and its immediate environment. Boundaries are local phenomena, rather than global states of the system-as-a-whole.

Top–down causation as model for the God–world interaction

Peacocke emphasises the inadequacy of all human models and metaphors as models or metaphors regarding God (e.g., Peacocke 1993, 14, 167). This, however, does not keep him from an attempt to picture God's relationship with the world with the help of the model of top–down causation. The state of world-as-a-whole 'can be a "top–down" causative factor in, or constraint upon, what goes on at the myriad levels that comprise it' (Peacocke 1993, 158). On this view, divine action could make a difference without violating in any way the regularities and laws of physics.

My suggestion is that a combination of the notion of top–down causation from the integrated, unitive mind/brain state to human bodily action ... with the recognition of the unity of the human mind/brain/body event ... *together* provide a fruitful clue or model for illuminating how we might think of God's interaction with the world. ... In this model, God would be regarded as exerting continuously top–down causative influences on the world-as-a-whole in a way analogous to that whereby we in our thinking can exert effects on our bodies in a 'top–down' manner. (Peacocke 1993, 161)

This is not merely a general influence on the world: 'initiating divine action on the state of the world-as-a-whole can itself have a causative effect upon individual events and entities within that world', without ever being observed as a divine 'intervention' (Peacocke 1993, 163).

Peacocke acknowledges the problem that, in all cases with which we are familiar, transfer of information requires transfer of energy. However, divine action now has been located at the interface between the world-as-a-whole and God, rather than within the natural order. 'This seems to me to be the ultimate level of the "causal joint" conundrum, for it involves the very nature of the divine being in

relation to that of matter/energy and seems to me to be the right place
to locate the problem, rather than at some lower levels in the created
order at which divine "intervention" would then have to be postulated,
with all of its difficulties' (Peacocke 1993, 164).

The issue of energy and information has already been considered
above [13.1]. Here I will consider the application of the notion of top–
down causation to the world-as-a-whole. In taking top–down causation
as the point of departure for describing the relation between God and
particular events in the world, there is a significant extrapolation from
particular environments to the encompassing notion of 'the world-as-a-
whole'. God is introduced as the one who sets the boundary conditions
for the world-as-a-whole, at the global level. This seems to me to be
problematic if not unwarranted with respect to the science at hand. In
the examples which led to the notion of top–down causation, there is
always an important role for the physical environment. One could say
that in the example of the Bénard cells it is the environment which acts
as the 'top' which sets the temperature at the plates, and thereby the
state of the system. And in the DNA example, it is the preceding history
which has resulted in the DNA that serves as a boundary condition for
the organism that is to develop. When we start talking about 'the
world-as-a-whole', the whole notion of a context, of an environment,
becomes a metaphor. In science, we always deal with a context which is
itself also captured in terms of the same laws of physics.
     With Peacocke I agree that the 'world-as-a-whole' may be a more
appropriate location for 'the causal nexus' than any place within the
world of natural processes. However, viewed as a model for understanding the *causal* nexus between the divine and the world, divine
action on the world-as-a-whole still interferes with any assumed
completeness of a naturalist account. An alternative which avoids such
interference is provided by a reflection upon the naturalist account
itself, especially on the themes of the existence, order, and intelligibility
of the world; rather than seeking an understanding of divine action *in*
or on the world, we might interpret the world itself *as* God's action.

13.3. Non-temporal views of divine action

In the preceding sections we considered attempts to understand divine
action in the context of our knowledge of natural processes or in
analogy with natural processes. However, one might also abstain from

such an analogy – the Creator is to be thought of as unique and so different from any creature that God's mode of action would not be like the actions of created entities. Divine action should not be conceived of as an additional causal factor among others. One major way to conceive of such a difference, is to think of divine action as something which is not action in time, as all natural activity is. Rather, God is thought of as the non-temporal ground of all that is.

In the Christian tradition an early advocate of such a view was Augustine of Hippo, one of the early theologians, who in his *Confessiones* argued that we should not ask what God was doing *before* God created the world, since the concept of 'before' does not apply; time was created with material reality, and is not something which is independently applicable. Temporal reality is as a natural and temporal reality the creation of God.

One of the differences between 'temporalists' and 'atemporalists' is in the understanding of God, with emphasis on God's interaction and personal characteristics or on God's transcendence. With respect to divine action, the atemporalist view has been developed with the help of the distinction between primary and secondary causality. Secondary causality is creaturely activity, whereas primary causality is the divine creative act which underlies the whole of natural reality (including natural processes with their secondary causality). This view of divine action in terms of primary causality should not be conflated with a deistic view, which has it that God acted once, in the beginning, with the world continuing on its own. Rather, everything is at all times held to be dependent on the primary cause; without it, nothing would exist.[6]

There is an enormous variety of philosophical and theological literature on this approach to divine action, for instance its compatibility with human freedom as freedom within creation. By emphasising the distinction between divine and natural causality – and thereby avoiding an analysis of divine and human roles as if they are two players competing in a zero-sum game, where one loses when the other gains – one might seek to salvage genuine human freedom and responsibility without detracting from divine freedom and power (e.g., Burrell 1993, 62). I will not enter into such philosophical

[6] See for overviews Thomas (1983) and the introduction by R. J. Russell (1993) in *Quantum Cosmology and the Laws of Nature: Scientific Perspectives on Divine Action*. McMullin (1988) offers a lucid account of the historical background of, and differences between, temporalist and atemporalist construals of God's relationship to nature as understood via the natural sciences. See also references in notes 4 and 5 of chapter 5.

discussions here, but rather focus for a moment on the relation to the natural sciences.

Upon such a view, whatever the natural sciences come up with as the best description of the world, can be accepted as the description of created reality. There is no need to opt for indeterminism or top–down causality to maintain a locus for divine action. This is the advantage of this position, but this aloofness may also be seen as a disadvantage: the irrelevance of our knowledge of the world threatens to make our ideas about 'primary causality' abstract and superfluous, unless belief in primary causality as God's creative activity is rooted in something else. However, if those roots are to be found in particulars of human history or of human experience, where God would have been revealed or disclosed to us, the problem of particular divine action in the created order returns with full force, even though perhaps not so much in relation to the natural sciences as in relation to history and human experience (see, for instance, Buckley's position [11]). When talking about divine action within history, one seems to allow with respect to historical processes something which one would not allow for natural processes, namely the incompleteness of an account in terms of creaturely (natural, including cultural) processes. Hence, the interaction with the natural sciences is not so much direct – in arguments which seek to pin down how God might act within natural processes – but indirect, namely via the question to what extent anthropology (history, experience) may be considered independent from natural processes. I will return to this understanding of God in terms of primary causality which sustains the world at all times in the final sections [31, 32], after explorations into the anthropological domain [chapter 4] and in combination with some reflections on limit questions about reality, since such limit questions may be seen as incentives to an atemporalist understanding of God.

14. COSMIC MEANING AND MYSTERY

Above, we concentrated on divine *action*. However, some have entertained in reflections on science conceptions of the divine which do not so much conceive of God in terms of action, but in terms such as 'meaning' or 'mystery'. After a brief discussion of 'meaning' we will consider some aspects of relations between science, religion, and mystery.

Cosmic meaning

Order out of Chaos by Ilya Prigogine and Isabelle Stengers had as its original title in French *La Nouvelle Alliance: Métamorphose de la Science.* There is a new alliance between man and nature, due to changes in science. As they see it, the classical (Newtonian) physical sciences treated human experiences as illusions, for instance the experience of the passing of time. Changes in science have, in their opinion, paved the way for a new view of the meaningful place of humanity in natural reality. Unlike God's covenant with Moses made on Mount Sinai, this one is not with a God who transcends reality. This covenant is rooted in physical reality itself. Humanity is no longer a stranger in a strange, mechanistic world. Rather, within the universe there is a tendency towards higher complexity and order.

The distance between us and the medieval synthesis can be attributed to changes in the content of our knowledge, changes in our ideas regarding the nature of knowledge, and changes in our appreciation of the world (see above, [5]). Prigogine and Stengers argue that changes in the content of our knowledge have reopened the way for a new synthesis with a positive appreciation of the world.

When Nobel prize-winner Prigogine and his co-author Stengers proclaimed a 'new covenant', they responded to Nobel prize-winner Jacques Monod whose influential book *Chance and Necessity* ended with the following sobering (or liberating?) thought:

The ancient covenant is in pieces; man at last knows that he is alone in the universe's unfeeling immensity, out of which he emerged only by chance. His destiny is nowhere spelled out, nor is his duty. The kingdom above or the darkness below: it is for him to choose. (Monod 1971, 180)

The kingdom above is the kingdom of knowledge, 'within man, where progressively freed both from material constraints and from the deceitful servitudes of animism, he could at last live authentically' (Monod 1971, 180). The 'darkness below' is the variety of animisms, including utopian ideologies such as historical materialism. The ethics of knowledge is based on an ethical choice, an axiom which humans impose on themselves. It 'thereby differs radically from animist ethics, which all claim to be based upon the "knowledge" of immanent laws, religious or "natural", which are supposed to assert themselves over man' (Monod 1971, 176f.). Animisms fail to discriminate properly between judgements of value and those of knowledge. Meaning is not found in the process described by science, but in the human choice for objectivity. Objectivity as the ethical axiom cannot itself be based upon some scientific objective basis. It is this ethical axiom which bars science from becoming a basis for further values.

The issue seems to be whether knowledge and values or meaning may be integrated into a single intellectual scheme, or, even stronger, whether a scheme based upon science can provide a basis for ethics. Prigogine and Stengers have a metaphysical agenda, when they offer a description which at the same time purports to be a prescription. Just as with the models of divine action, it is disputable whether in the quest for meaning and values such approaches do not reach beyond the actual achievements of science with its focus on local, relative contexts, parts of the world. We will come back to an evolutionary explanation of morality below [chapter 4-B]. Such an explanation does not offer a firm foundation for specific values, but rather links the values that arise to the contexts in which they arise. We do not, via science, seem to reach beyond the diverse reality in which we live. Should we not rather pay attention to the limitations of science, instead of over-valuing its results? It is to such an approach that we will turn in the rest of this section.

Mystery: a common awareness of not-knowing?

For the scientist who has lived by his faith in the power of reason, the story ends like a bad dream. He has scaled the mountains of ignorance; he is about to conquer the highest peak; as he pulls himself over the final rock, he is greeted by a band of theologians who have been sitting there for centuries. (Jastrow 1980, 125)

The essence of modern cosmology is, according to Robert Jastrow, that the universe 'began at a certain moment of time, and under circumstances that seem to make it impossible – not just now, but ever – to find out what force or forces brought the world into being at that moment' (1980, 12). Is an awareness of not-knowing, of mystery, common ground for theologians and scientists? We will consider arguments from science to mystery, but first we will take a look at the theological side.

Roots of negative theology and of critique of religion
In his *The Elusive Presence* Samuel Terrien traces the role of hiddenness through the whole Bible. One example is the story of Jacob wrestling with a stranger during the night; the stranger cannot be seen in the

light of the day nor is his name revealed (Genesis 32). 'Thick darkness' characterises the place of God, both at Mount Sinai and in the temple in Jerusalem (Exodus 20: 21, 1 Kings 8: 12, 2 Chronicles 6: 1). The Ten Commandments prohibit the carving of images. According to Isaiah (8: 17, 45: 15), God hides himself. Job is challenged to tell where he was when God laid the foundations of the earth. Job places his hand in front of his mouth and is silent (Job 38–40). Job does not so much acknowledge moral guilt as hubris. In Jesus God's presence is not obvious. Is this not the carpenter? Do we not know his parents, brothers, and sisters? (e.g., Mark 6: 3). And he is not even able to save himself from the cross (Mark 15: 29–32)! But then the centurion recognises this man as the Son of God (Mark 15: 39). Through humiliation comes exaltation (Philippians 2: 5–11).

The life of Jewish and Christian communities is not structured around a holy place, a temple where God would be present. Central to Jewish and Christian life are holy times of remembrance and expectation. The Sabbath recalls the Creation and the Exodus and is a foretaste of fulfilment. The synagogue is a place of memory and hope, recalling God's great deeds in the past for the sake of the future. The hiddenness and absence can be seen mystically, in relation to God's holiness, but also in relation to prophetic engagement: this world is not as God intends the world to be.

Later European negative theology and criticism of religion draws also upon Greek philosophy. Xenophanes (*circa* 470 BCE) criticised anthropomorphic views of the gods; if they could, horses and oxen would make themselves gods in the form of horses and oxen.[7] According to Plato's *Apologia*, Socrates persistently asked critical questions, but these questions do not yet lead to an affirmation, to negative theology. With Plato, we find a further step in that direction, when he considers the *archè*, the origin of everything. The Sun gives light and thereby allows growth (existence) and vision (knowledge). Similarly, existence and knowledge owe their possibility to the idea of the Good (*Politeia* 508 d/e). As the condition for the possibility of existence and of knowledge, this idea of the Good is itself beyond existence and knowledge. Philo of Alexandria, a Jewish thinker around the beginning of our era, identifies such metaphysical notions with the biblical God. With him, emphasis shifts from the history of Israel to philosophical reflection.

---

[7]   H. Diels, *Die Fragmente der Vorsokratiker*, vol. I. Berlin: Weidmannsche Buchhandlung, 1906², 49 (15).

Negative theology receives its most influential articulation at the close of the fifth century by an author referred to as (pseudo-)Dionysius the Areopagite (Hochstaffl 1976, 82–155). Pseudo-Dionysius coined the term *apophatic theology*, negative theology. We do not move upward by extrapolation from the image via the imageless to the divine but by negation, by relinquishing form. Negation has a mystagogic function in a hierarchical framework. The masses need symbols, images. However, with respect to the divine, negations are true whereas affirmations are inadequate.[8] Through negation of all positions the road winds towards a position beyond all negations.

With the loss of a hierarchical understanding of the world such a mystagogic method lost its context. It was no longer clear that the negation at one level propelled one upward to a higher level. What are the possibilities for the emphasis on an unknowable, on mystery in relation to contemporary science? We will take a look at two proposals, focusing on the provisional character of scientific theories and on the hiddenness of quantum reality.

Provisionality and hiddenness
In his *Cosmic Understanding* (1986) Milton K. Munitz gives a philosophical analysis of scientific cosmology. The universe as it is known, as an intelligible unit, results from the application of a conceptual scheme. The point is epistemological: One cannot escape being bound to concepts if one wants to achieve intelligibility. One transcends the conceptual limitations of a theory by entering another conceptual scheme, which has its own boundaries. Each understanding of the universe is a mask which is held in front of the real, but in itself unknowable, universe (Harrison 1985).

Munitz defends more than a view of knowledge; he suggests 'a dimension of reality "beyond" any account of the known universe (or any of its contents), of which we can have a mode of awareness that is not hemmed in by the constraints and ever-present horizons of cosmological knowledge' (Munitz 1986, 229). This reality would not be conceptually bounded, and thus could never be captured adequately in language.

We shall be driven, consequently, and at the end, to silence, although the 'talk' on the way, if at all helpful, will have had its value in making the silence

---

[8]   *De Coelesti hierarchia* 2,3 in J. P. Migne, *Patrologia cursus completus, series graeca* 3, 141 A.

a pregnant one, and indeed the occasion for having an overridingly important type of human experience. (Munitz 1986, 231f)

Munitz attempts to point to something which is at the heart of reality, but transcends all our knowledge.

A similar position has been argued by the physicist Bernard d'Espagnat in the context of quantum physics. As he sees it, 'present-day physics calls for a clear-cut distinction between two notions both designated in the past by the word "reality"': independent reality which is distant, 'veiled', and empirical reality, the totality of phenomena. As he sees it, 'in our time science itself has provided us with pressing reasons for accepting the (philosophical) duality of Being and of phenomena' (D'Espagnat 1989, 7). These reasons are supposed to come from quantum physics, since quantum physics is not merely a theory about the nature of reality, but also about the possibilities of acquiring knowledge of reality.

Various comments can be made about these arguments for mystery in the context of science. To summarise them in advance: Firstly, even if we do not know certain things, there are other things which we know not to be the case. Secondly, the specific claims about cosmology and quantum physics are disputable. And thirdly, would such an unknown or veiled reality be religiously significant?

(1) In looking for mystery, the emphasis is on what we do not know. However, in reflecting upon the religious implications of science we should not neglect what we know not to be the case. Ideas previously held to be true have been shown to be incorrect, at least very probably incorrect. As an example, one might think of the age of the universe. It has not been settled whether the universe had a beginning a finite time ago, had an infinite past, or is not adequately captured in either of these expressions. On the basis of Munitz's account one would expect that this will never be settled. However, even then one might say with confidence that the age of the universe is not restricted to a few thousand years – and, thus, does not fit a count of years based on the genealogies in the Bible. Science as knowledge about what is not the case (e.g., no young universe, no universal flood) challenges religious views in as far as they rely upon, or have been expressed, in terms of the knowledge of an earlier age. Even if one holds that science does not provide a grand view of reality, scientific research forces one to reconsider ideas.

(2.a) A more specific objection to Munitz's argument concerns his expectation that theories will continue to be replaced. It would be a fair situation if the world were arranged in such a way that no generation could claim to possess the final truth, or even be nearer to it, than any earlier generation: 'For both of us the slope is the same, and reaches as far ahead and as far behind' (Fowles 1980, 22). And, when we take the lessons from history to heart, it also seems wise to adopt a humble attitude with respect to the completeness of our current knowledge. None the less, some scientists are more pretentious about our knowledge. Nobel prize-winner Steven Weinberg entitles his book *Dreams of a Final Theory* (Weinberg 1992), and Steven Hawking predicted in his inaugural lecture in 1980 that we might have the fundamental theory by the end of the twentieth century.

In what sense could our scientific knowledge become complete? This topic deserves a more elaborate treatment than can be given here (e.g., Barrow 1991, Drees 1990, 89–94). It seems reasonable to expect that within the next few decades, centuries, or millennia physicists will come up with a theory which integrates all known particles and interactions in a single mathematical scheme. This would not imply that all phenomena could be derived from these fundamental equations. The mathematics could be too complicated to handle. Besides, the theory may allow various solutions, without deciding between them. As an analogy, one might think of a theory about traffic based upon considerations of safety and efficiency. On such a theory, the situation where everybody drives on the left-hand side of the road would be as good as that where everybody drives on the right, but a choice has to be made. An encompassing theory would also not imply that there could be no other theory that would do justice to the phenomena. Nor would the theory explain why reality behaves in accordance with the theory. If one accepts such restrictions, a fundamental and complete theory of physics is imaginable. There would be no reason to expect that such a theory would be replaced by another, as there would be no intrinsic reasons to assume that science could do a better job at describing and explaining the phenomena. However, even then Munitz's position could be defended, since uniqueness would not be settled; one would not be able to exclude an alternative theory, using a different conceptual framework.

(2.b) Just as the persistent provisionality of theories may be disputed and qualified, d'Espagnat's claim about the duality of Being and phenomena in quantum physics is by no means trivial. Quantum physics might be replaced by some other theory, based upon a different conceptual framework even though the new theory would need to reproduce the successes of quantum physics. This is not a mere theoretical possibility, as quantum physics and general relativity, the theory about gravity, space, and time are incompatible without fundamental changes in at least one of them. And even if one does not appeal to future theories, quantum physics can be (and actually is) interpreted differently, without the duality of Being and phenomena considered by d'Espagnat (see also note 13).

(3) Is *mystery* an appropriate term in relation to the provisional character of our knowledge? Scientists do not stop in front of an ill-understood phenomenon in respectful contemplation, but consider such a phenomenon as a problem to tackle. For instance, Jastrow said that it would be impossible to know what happened before the Big Bang, and hence that cosmologists have to acknowledge their defeat after scaling the highest peak. In this form the claim is already outdated by the development of quantum cosmologies. There is no accepted theory, but explorations show that new theories might result in radical changes in the concept of time. As a consequence, the question of whether there was a 'before' might be no longer adequate (e.g., Isham 1988, 1991, 1993; Drees 1990, 41–75; 1993). Current answers resemble in this respect the answer given by Augustine when asked what God was doing before God created the world. According to Augustine, time is created with the created order (*creatio cum tempore*), whereas the question assumes creation in time, and thus is ill posed (*Confessiones*, Book 11). Similar ideas can be found a few centuries earlier in Philo of Alexandria's *On the Account of the World's Creation by Moses* (section 26). The Aristotelian understanding of time as the measure of movement implies that in a state without material creation, or without movement of material creation, there would be no time. Contemporary research in cosmology, resulting perhaps in another understanding of time, shows that cosmologists are not outdone by reaching the limit of the Big Bang theory. It may be a problem rather than a mystery.

Theologians are hesitant to make too much out of apparently mysterious aspects of reality as described by the sciences. The catchword is 'God-of-the-gaps'. Gaps in scientific accounts have often been seen as possible *loci* of special divine intervention. This resulted in religious retreats when science filled such gaps. Could there be gaps which do not disappear? I do not see any such gaps *within* the scientific account. However, limit-questions *about* the scientific approach to reality may allow for a more acceptable 'God-of-the gaps'. Two fundamental candidates worth considering might be the existence of the world and human subjectivity.

Persistent mysteries of existence and subjectivity?

Though the natural sciences reach out to the chemical composition of stars and to the emergence of time, two issues might be considered as candidates for escaping the omnicompetence of the natural sciences: the mystery of the existence of the world and the mystery of subjectivity (Durant 1990, 167–70).

Even if there were a complete theory of all fundamental interactions, such a theory would not by itself explain why there is a reality which behaves accordingly. This is a modern version of a traditional philosophical question: Why is there something rather than nothing? Answers which are given within the terms of the natural sciences, for instance referring to a quantum fluctuation in a vacuum, always assume certain givens, say laws of nature and a reality which behaves accordingly. Hence, the mystery of existence seems scientifically unassailable. Even if one agrees that science is unable to provide an answer, theology may not be able to do much better. As the physicist Charles Misner (1977, 96) wrote

Saying that God created the universe does not explain either God or the Universe, but it keeps our consciousness alive to the mysteries of awesome majesty that we might otherwise ignore, and that deserve our respect.

Whether subjectivity will escape the omnicompetence of the natural sciences seems more disputable. There is, of course, a difference between the experience from within and a description from the outside. While I experience love, hate, or boredom, the scan shows electrical and chemical processes. Can scientific insights and philosophical analysis explicate how the experience from within has come into existence and how a 'self' functions in relation to its environment and its constitution? We will return to subjectivity in chapter 4; other potential limit-questions are considered in chapter 5.

Even if one envisages a mystery beyond science, one may wonder what its significance for religion can be. Constructive use of the limitations of science is risky. Only in the context of a broader view of reality which would itself be above uncertainties, as the Neoplatonic theologians still held, does it seem possible to ascend through the critical questioning of science on a mystagogic way. As such a framework beyond dispute seems unavailable to us, science does not contribute to a negative theology which results in an affirmation of God. But awareness of the limitations of scientific theories may help to keep alive a sense of wonder, of the non-triviality of reality.

15. USING SCIENTIFIC DISCOVERIES IN THEOLOGY (1): MODALITIES OF MODELS

There are differences not only in the concept of ultimacy (an active God, meaning, mystery) considered in relation to the sciences, but also with respect to what is considered achievable. Can strong claims be made about the relationship of science and religion, for instance that science proves or disproves a certain religious view, or at least that it contributes to its (im)plausibility? Or should we speak of science as providing models for religious thought? We will first consider the farther-reaching claims (proof), before turning to three ways in which the notion of *model* is used in these discussions.

Proof and argument

Knock-down proofs are few and far between. Arguments which are not logically compelling, but make a claim to plausibility, are much more abundant. There is even a book by an Anglican bishop of Birmingham, Hugh Montefiore, with the title *The Probability of God* (1985). One area for such arguments for religion on the basis of science is cosmology, for instance in relation to the origin and the order of the universe. The initial singularity as envisaged in the Big Bang model of the universe could be claimed as evidence of a creator; the anthropic coincidences have been read as evidence of design.

A closer consideration of cosmology shows that such claims reach beyond the framework of the scientific theories at hand. In historical or archaeological research it is assumed that in certain respects past human behaviour resembles current human behaviour; our ancestors also needed food. The Big Bang theory is comparable to historical analysis in relying on assumptions about the validity in the past of the laws of physics as we know them today. Since current physics works well in interpreting observations from stars and galaxies far away in space and in time, we have sufficient warrant to rely on those laws in reconstructing the history of the universe. This results in the Big Bang model of the universe. However, there is less reason to believe that our physics (and with it the model) is adequate for the earliest stages of the model, during the first fraction of the first second of the model. On the contrary, there are good grounds to believe that current physics is inadequate when we calculate backwards to a fraction of a second from the apparent 't=o'. In this way we see that the Big Bang theory is not about the origin of the universe, but about its subsequent evolution.

This limitation of the theory is not too relevant in relation to current observations on the background radiation and the abundances of the elements, but it seriously affects the use of the theory in the context of an argument about an absolute beginning. The Big Bang model is not final. Some speculations about future theories imply that the notion of time loses its meaning for those 'earliest' stages. Other proposals envisage a much larger or perhaps even infinite universe like a boiling liquid; our Big Bang universe would be one expanding bubble. The absoluteness of the beginning would be an artifact, a consequence of the fact that we look at a bubble from the inside. Such speculations are different with respect to the understanding of the beginning of the universe and of the nature of time. The provisional character of scientific theories, especially with respect to such issues as an absolute beginning, should be respected in arguments based on science.

Similar problems arise when the order of the universe is considered. Some see the fact that the universe has the right conditions for the emergence of life as supporting a belief in design, in purpose (the so called 'anthropic principles'). However, here too arguments reach way beyond the scientific evidence. Even if there are characteristics of the universe which make it seem 'fine-tuned' for life, there might be a future theory which explains these features. It might also be that the features are only typical of our neighbourhood, the currently observable part of the universe. The observation that we happen to be in a corner of the wider universe where the conditions are right would not be too amazing; we could not have been elsewhere reflecting on those properties (see on anthropic interpretations also [31]).

Issues of design, necessity, or randomness may be philosophically interesting. However, science does not offer a basis for a clear argument. Theories may change, and they do allow for different interpretations. Thus, one cannot claim proofs, whether for or against design or with respect to other metaphysical or religious convictions. Probabilities are also hard to assess, since one would be assessing probabilities on future developments of scientific theories. And to have a clear view of such future theories would be to have these theories already – prediction of scientific theories, or more generally prediction of new ideas, is quite different from predicting the weather. The provisional character of theories, together with the underdetermination of theories by current data, prohibits any strong metaphysical claims. We therefore will turn to more modest claims which do not attempt to ascribe numerical probabilities to competing theses, but rather speak of *models* in different ways (e.g., Hesse 1967, Barbour 1974); in the next section, we will come to the question of how to deal with areas of science where there is marked disagreement.

Models in a logical approach
In formal logic, one can consider a collection of symbols, axioms and rules, without ascribing any meaning to them. However, one can also interpret the symbols and rules in a model. A certain abstract set of terms ('point', 'line') and of axioms ('through two "points" there is one and only one "line" ') may be represented by geometrical figures in a plane. The model is an interpretation of the original axioms and symbols. Models are 'possible worlds' with respect to these axioms.

Models serve as a test for *consistency*. If there is a consistent model which interprets the axioms, they are consistent. If there is no model, the axioms are inconsistent. Though this rule is simple, its application need not be, for how would one know that a model itself is consistent? Such models have also a *semantic* function – a model offers a context in which the symbols acquire an interpretation, a meaning. There may be more than one model for a given axiomatic system, and each of those models could be richer in different ways than the system it models. Thus, interpretation through a model offers a possible meaning, not 'the meaning' of the terms involved.

In theology, some proposals can be characterised as models, understood as interpretations of a given system of axioms. Thus, a model can be invoked to show the *consistency* of various assumptions. An example is the Omphalos-argument in relation to evolution. The issue is whether one can maintain that God created the Earth a few thousand years ago, even though the evidence from paleontology and geology seems to teach us otherwise. A consistent articulation of this possibility, a 'model' for the theological conviction together with the scientific evidence such as geological strata and their fossils, was given by Philip H. Gosse in his book *Omphalos* (navel) in 1857, two years before the publication of Darwin's *Origin of Species*. A few thousand years ago God may have created all the evidence of a longer past, including Adam's navel (suggesting a mother), the fossils in the geological strata, and the light which we (upon this view mistakenly) assume to come from distant stars. Hence, there is no formal inconsistency between accepting the discoveries about fossils and geological strata and believing in a fairly recent creation. However, the consistency achieved in this model has a price; God becomes a deceiver, and sciences such as geology and astronomy are not so much studies of events in a distant past or at distant places, but studies of the extent to which we have been fooled.

A more recent example of an argument for consistency by envisaging possible worlds, is Alvin Plantinga's treatment of natural evil in combination with God's omnipotence, omniscience, and goodness. Rather than explaining why God would allow for such evil, Plantinga restricts his aim to a defence of the consistency of certain beliefs about God and the presence of evil. The consistency of the fact of moral evil with God's omnipotence, omniscience, and goodness is argued on the basis of the freedom to make wrong choices. Plantinga then turns to natural evil, disasters such as earthquakes and floods. Such evil is shown to be compatible with his beliefs about God by finding a 'model'. Plantinga finds one by assuming that natural evil might be due to one or more non-human agents, say Satan and his cohort. This reduces the issue of natural evil to one of moral evil, which he had already solved (Plantinga 1974, 58f.; similarly Plantinga 1985, 42ff.).

Plantinga does not assert that earthquakes are actually caused by Satan, but rather that it is logically possible to understand apparently natural evil as evil caused by free persons. By finding a possible world with evil and an omnipotent and morally good God, Plantinga claims to have offered a philosophically (though not thereby pastorally or emotionally) adequate defence of the consistency of the theistic position. As in formal logic, the problem of consistency returns at the level of the model, the consistency of the proposed understanding of free will, possible worlds, Satan, and so on.

To get a clearer view of differences in the purposes of such arguments, it may be helpful to contrast Plantinga's defence with the free-process theodicy as John Polkinghorne has defended it. God allows the world to be itself, in an exploration of its potentialities through chance and necessity. 'God no more expressly wills the growth of a cancer than he expressly wills the act of a murderer, but he allows both to happen' (Polkinghorne 1989, 67). Whereas Plantinga deliberately restricts himself to an argument which proves the consistency of his beliefs with natural evil, a 'possible world', Polkinghorne attempts to offer more: an imperfect but none the less real understanding of the actual world.

The Omphalos view of creation and the Satan free-will defence of natural evil are both examples of a rather formal approach. The concern is with possibility, understood as logical consistency, rather than with plausibility. A disadvantage of the use of such models in philosophy, unlike the use of models in science, is in the role of the background assumptions. In a thought experiment in the physical sciences, one can describe the imaginary situation and the empirical consequences that would result if the situation occurred. One treats these consequences then as informative, in the sense that they could be the outcome of actual experiments. Such thought experiments carry with them a major *ceteris paribus* clause: it is assumed that other aspects of reality are unchanged. A clear example is provided by a dispute between Albert Einstein and Niels Bohr about quantum physics. Einstein had conceived of a way of determining both the time and the position of an event, in violation of the Heisenberg uncertainty relation. Bohr subsequently showed that the thought-experiment did not actually yield the alleged result, since not all effects had been taken into account; Einstein's own theory of general relativity should have been included in the considerations.

Wilkes (1988: 1–48) has compared thought experiments as they occur in the natural sciences and in philosophical arguments. Her conclusion, with which I concur, is that much of the burden of proof lies in the *ceteris paribus* conditions. It is there that thought experiments in the natural sciences perform well, whereas thought experiments in a philosophical context perform poorly. In science the consequences of a theory are developed against a well-defined background (and as far as it is left unspecified, it is assumed that the background is our world in all respects relevant to the thought-experiment). 'Put in another way, the "possible world" is *our* world, the world described by our sciences, except for one distinguishing difference' (Wilkes 1988, 8). If the background is left unspecific or incomprehensible, the conclusions from a thought experiment are left inconclusive. We might, in a thought experiment, think of the logical possibility that gold does not have atomic number 79, that water is not H_2O, that whales are fish, or that iron bars can float on water, but such a world would not be in relevant respects similar to our world. Such possible worlds may be fine in literary fantasy, but they do not thereby establish the possibility of the imagined state of affairs. 'It is of course true that if things *had* been radically different, then so would be our concepts' (Wilkes 1988, 47), but a flight of the imagination does not thereby provide a better understanding of our world or our concepts.[9]

Models in logic not only serve to show consistency, but also offer possible *meanings* of the terms involved. For instance, Luco van den Brom (1982, 1984, 1993) has proposed to understand divine omnipresence and transcendence by envisaging physical reality as embedded in a reality which has at least two dimensions more than the dimensions of natural reality. (With only one additional dimension God's space would be divided by physical reality; a line divides a plane and a plane divides a three dimensional space.) Such an approach may be especially helpful in understanding a possible meaning of philosophical terms used in theology, such as contingency and necessity, transcendence and immanence, or time and eternity. Such models may draw upon the natural sciences and the philosophy of the natural sciences; Van den Brom considers disputes about relational and other views of time. But the usefulness of the exercise is more dependent upon the ingenuity of the model than upon the natural sciences. The issue is not so much whether the model is an adequate model of reality as whether it offers a consistent proposal for understanding the concepts involved.

In these examples of formal approaches, consistency was important. In the natural sciences the issue is not so much consistency (as most models and theories are known to be inconsistent in some respects), but rather whether the model approximately depicts reality or, less realistically understood, whether the model is heuristically fruitful. It is to such ways of understanding models that we will now turn.

Models as approximately depicting reality
Perhaps we cannot attain certainty, but we may none the less aim at a plausible view of reality, for instance when we depict a gas as a box of billiard-balls, or when we think of God as acting in reality in a way analogous to top–down causation in physical systems [13.2]. Can the natural sciences contribute to models for understanding theological ideas, such as divine action? The aim would be to develop a model that is plausible though not perfect. For instance, with respect to divine action the authors considered above do not claim that chaos theory is

---

[9]   Similar to this hesitation about thought experiments in philosophy is the warning by Dennett against *intuition pumps* (Dennett 1984, 12); they may be useful pedagogical devices, but they can also be misleading due to inadequate simplifications and analogies.

the final theory science will come up with, nor do they think that it is the basis for a perfectly adequate model of the way God acts. Rather, they claim that it is a good model for conceiving of divine action, a good approximation to the way divine action in the world actually is. The looseness of terms like 'approximation' has a natural appeal to working scientists, as their models also have a positive and a negative analogy.

The classic example of a theoretical model is a gas modelled as a collection of billiard-balls. By identifying notions such as mass, velocity, and kinetic energy for billiard-balls and molecules and by correlating certain phenomena such as temperature with microscopic properties such as mean kinetic energy, the Law of Boyle and Gay-Lussac about the relation between pressure, volume, and temperature can be derived. We thus have a model of a gas which explains features such as pressure (by analogy with collisions between the balls and the walls). In considering the analogy we are selective. We hold that the size of molecules is incorrectly represented, and we do not pay attention to aspects such as colour or the non-zero volume of the balls. Thus, there is a positive analogy (the elements taken seriously, such as velocity), a negative analogy (actual size), and a neutral area (colour, non-zero size). It is this latter area which allows for the development of the theory (Hesse 1963, 1967). For instance, if one starts taking the non-zero size into account, one might come up with a slight modification of the Law of Boyle and Gay-Lussac, a modification which can be corroborated in experiments.

The negative part of analogies and models is explicitly appreciated by some theologians. It would be idolatry to take any model as adequately representing God or God's relation to the world; the negative analogy reminds us of the qualification that in certain respects God *is not* as depicted in any model (e.g., McFague 1982, 13; see [17.3]).

Models as communicatively and heuristically fruitful
There is at least one more way of thinking about theological models drawing on science. Rather than seeing them as attempts to present underlying mechanisms and offer explanations, their heuristic and communicative function can be emphasised (e.g., Hesse 1981, 287).[10] For instance, the notion of 'complementarity' as it has arisen in relation

[10]   A single author might, of course, do both; for example, Russell (1988a).

to quantum physics has been claimed in various ways for theology. There are two ways to read such proposals. One way is that complementarity as it occurs in physics tells us something about reality which is relevant for theology, for instance about the relation between observers and the reality observed. A claim might be that the structure of reality as described in theology is analogous to the structure of reality as described by physics. Another way of reading proposals about complementarity is less controversial: the analogy is not so much a claim about reality, as it is used as a heuristic tool which may help to produce new insights.[11]

The two ways of using models work out very differently with respect to the justification of claims. In the case of a theoretical model such as the gas-billiard-balls model, new insights, such as the modifications of the Law of Boyle and Gay-Lussac, can be justified on the basis of the model (though, of course, there is still a need for empirical corroboration). In the case of a model or analogy which serves a heuristic function, the model does not contribute plausibility (and hence does not justify), as the model is not supposed to reflect the underlying structure. When physics is supposed to show something relevant to theology, one is apparently moving within the first realm of discussion (theoretical models as approximately matching reality); when a theology has to stand on its own, theologians may adopt models for heuristic and communicative purposes.

The difference between a justificatory and a communicative use of models corresponds to the distinction between natural theology and theology of nature. *Natural theology* has two distinctive connotations in the tradition of European theology. It is associated with the English tradition of arguments from design; the intricacies of the natural world would lead one to conclude to its creator. Natural theology is theology based on experience and reason, without appeal to revelation, Scripture, or similar source of authority. I will follow this usage. The term has acquired a somewhat different connotation in German theology, where it was used for theology which based itself on social and historical realities and fictions such as nation and race. *Theology of nature* is used for theologically based reflection on the natural world. It

---

[11]   The issue is here the heuristic and communicative use of models and metaphors from the sciences in theology; this is to be distinguished from the use of scientific models in the natural sciences, where McMullin (1984, 30–5) has argued that heuristic fertility is a reason for confidence in the entities involved in the model; see for the discussion on realism and theological realism [17].

has become 'politically correct' in theological circles to present oneself as doing theology of nature rather than natural theology. Thus, belief in divine action is not itself taken to follow from scientific knowledge, though divine action may be described in a model drawn from the natural sciences. The style of 'natural theology' is more explicitly present when scientists or philosophers are finding meaning or mystery through their scientific knowledge [14]. John Polkinghorne also presents himself as reviving natural theology, which he sees 'as the completion of the task, instinctive to the scientist, of seeking the deepest possible explanation of what is going on, the most comprehensive available account of the one world of experience' (Polkinghorne 1990, 87). Whereas he sometimes argues from science to claims about God, for instance when considering the intelligibility of the universe or the anthropic coincidences [31], Polkinghorne's treatment of divine action [13.1] and of natural evil (above) is more in the tradition of theology of nature.

In this section, we have considered expectations one might have about the use of theological models which are partially derived from science. Formal models were found unsatisfactory. Models may serve a heuristic function within theology, and they might perhaps also be used to justify theological claims. However, this is dependent upon the way one handles the provisional character of scientific theories, a topic to which we will return in the next chapter.

16. USING SCIENTIFIC DISCOVERIES IN THEOLOGY (2): LEVELS AND LACK OF CONSENSUS

Scientific knowledge is diverse in status and character. Some theories are part of a widely shared consensus; others are strongly disputed. I accept atomistic views of ordinary matter and evolutionary views of living organisms as part of the consensus. In this section, we will concentrate on areas of science where there is no such consensus. This is not merely relevant to opinions on the status of scientific insights, since areas where there are various competing theories have often attracted thinkers interested in metaphysical or religious speculations, and such thinkers have often operated eclectically. Before turning to general remarks, we will first consider one area where disagreements are persistent, namely cosmology.

Limitations of the consensus in cosmology

The Big Bang theory is a successful scientific theory about the development of the universe over, approximately, the last fifteen billion years. It can with good reason be accepted as the current scientific consensus, though there is some debate. Part of the theory is a sudden beginning of the universe, a 'Big Bang'. However, this initial moment is not part of the consensus. Somewhere in the first fraction of a second we end up in a fog which makes it impossible to look farther back; the accepted theories of matter and of space and time become unreliable or break down. We thus cannot reliably reach back to the apparent beginning. There is no consensus on the very early stages of the universe, the history of the universe during the first fraction of a second. There may have been a phase preceding the (apparent) beginning. It might also be that the fog covers a reality which is quite different from anything we have imagined so far.

Cautious writers about science and theology have explicitly abstained from attaching theological significance to the apparent beginning of the universe. They have restricted themselves to the scientific consensus, claiming that the Big Bang theory shows us the dynamic nature of the universe, the essential role of time. As Barbour (1989, 143) expresses it, 'astrophysics adds its testimony to that of evolutionary biology and other fields of science ... It is a dynamic world with a long story of change and development.' This conclusion rests upon a methodological decision, namely that:

> we should consider only the broadest and most well-established features of the world disclosed by science, not its narrower or more speculative theories. (Barbour 1989, 143; similarly 1990, 60f.)

Such authors intentionally restrict themselves to the more general, apparently safer, features of the model. Thus, it seems as if they do not need to pay attention to speculations in quantum cosmology and quantum gravity, such as those of Hawking, which would affect only our ideas about the very early universe.

A problem is that this view only considers one type of future development of cosmology, namely an answer to the question of whether there is an extension of the universe further back in time (or not). However, quantum cosmology would not necessarily be restricted to the choice between a finite past with an absolute beginning and an extension further back in time. Rather, an integration of quantum and space-time theories may lead to a revision of our understanding of space, time, and matter, and therefore affect the entire interpretation of the Big Bang theory, including the part about which there is consensus, and thus including the dynamic nature of the universe, which Barbour took to be a safe part of the consensus. The coexistence of a plurality of serious research programmes which all accept the Big Bang theory in its 'consensus' domain, shows that the Big Bang theory is open to a variety of future developments or interpretations, suggesting different ontologies (e.g., the approaches by Linde, Hawking and Penrose discussed in Drees 1990, 62–9; 1991a). Restricting oneself to the consensus may be a good strategy when one considers specific predictions and explanations, for instance when the Big Bang model is used to discuss the abundances of different elements or the evolution of galaxies. But relying on the consensus is a problematic strategy when one argues for metaphysical claims about the most fundamental structure of reality or about its ultimate origins, since ontologies may change abruptly, even when successful theories develop continuously.

Strategies with respect to scientific disagreements
In general, there seem to be four possibilities with respect to the way that theologians might deal with disagreements within science.

(i) *Cheap dismissal*: As long as the scientists do not reach a consensus, anything goes. Theologians need not pay attention to science, since the scientists themselves are not certain of their claims. Thus, theologians are free to hold whatever position they like. Such an approach neglects the partial consensus among scientists, especially on the alternatives that have been ruled out. Even if we do not know the answers, we do know that certain answers are wrong. Hence, to dismiss science completely because of a lack of consensus is not warranted.

(ii) *Cautiously wait and see* what will become the consensus; theologians need not consider theories which are still controversial. I agree that there is no need for theologians to be consistent with all speculative scientific theories. However, the scientific consensus is not that clear and safe either. In active areas of research there are always competing research programmes. Waiting for a final consensus may take quite long, if not forever. 'If our strategy is to wait for agreement, I fear we will be limited to historical studies. Moreover, agreement is seldom univocal: when will it really been reached? what about reversals after a theory was considered settled?' (Russell 1988a, 370).

(iii) *Eclecticism*: one takes whatever fits best. This attitude is present in the religious use of more speculative and disputed scientific statements, such as those of David Bohm, John Wheeler, or Rupert Sheldrake. Taking one's pick from science in such a manner may be a contribution to the development of an intelligible and coherent view. However, it makes no contribution to the credibility of the position under consideration, except by showing that it is a possible position given the current state of science, at most as likely as the specific scientific theory that has been chosen. If the selection is made in an arbitrary and dubious manner, an eclectic strategy will backfire upon the credibility of the position constructed. Scientists are also critical when they spot eclecticism with respect to whole disciplines, for instance when Pope John Paul II emphasises cosmology but ignores biology (Eaves 1990; John Paul II 1988) or when the theologian Pannenberg prefers to consider life in the context of non-linear thermodynamics and human behaviour in terms of anthropologies shaped by the humanities, while passing over behavioural genetics (Eaves 1989, 203f.; Pannenberg 1989, 260–3).

(iv) *Reverse eclecticism*: taking the worst possible case. If one is able to show how what initially seem to be for theology the most problematic results of science can be incorporated into a certain religious-metaphysical scheme, one can claim real progress. Taking science 'where it hurts most' (Eaves 1989, 203) offers the greatest challenge, but is also capable of producing the greatest profit with respect to credibility. In this spirit, I have argued that one should not appeal to unpredictability when one seeks to articulate a possible locus for divine action, since such unpredictability might well be the consequence of deterministic laws or of purely random processes [13]. Similarly, I prefer to analyse in chapter 4 the consequences of naturalist approaches to human experience and human traditions rather than playing down these sciences.

In my view, in as far as there is a clear consensus among competent scientists (and on who is competent to judge the issues under consideration), theologians or others who seek to interpret or use scientific insights should rely on the experts. However, no consensus is without its limitations; there are always domains in space and time where, and conditions under which, the theory has not been tested; there are disagreements which fuel further research; and there is a variety of interpretations of the current consensus. Thus, in building upon scientific insights, even if part of the current consensus, one should note their provisional character, and ways in which they may have to be modified or reinterpreted as a consequence of further research. As for disagreements, one may be eclectic when the sole purpose is to develop one's ideas. However, if one intends to test a position, it is most fruitful to respond to insights which challenge the position most strongly.

Disputes about quantum cosmology and the very early universe may seem far removed from most questions theologians are interested in, which concern human beings who are situated squarely within the epoch which is well described by Big Bang cosmology. However, changes in quantum gravity may have implications for our understanding of time and space at all times and at all places. This has to do with the coherence among the variety of disciplines, an issue to which we will turn now.

Levels and reductions

Chemistry can be done without paying attention to the quark structure of atomic nuclei. More generally, there seems to be a hierarchy of levels of complexity in reality and a hierarchy of scientific disciplines.[12] A strict ontological or disciplinary hierarchy is an inadequate view of the sciences. One cannot locate plasma physics and solid state physics with respect to each other as 'higher' or 'lower', though both are secondary with respect to quantum theories of matter. There are 'horizontal' links, for instance when nuclear physics is applied in the astrophysics of stars, as well as 'vertical' ones, say between physics and chemistry. Besides, structural sciences such as physics and biochemistry, and historical sciences such as cosmology and evolutionary biology do not neatly fit into a single ordering. In addition, one might ask what kind of entities or disciplines are to be ranked highest. Should it be the most encompassing entities, and thus disciplines such as ecology and cosmology? Or should one rather place at the top tightly knit complex systems which exhibit the richest known behaviour, i.e. humans? A further objection to hierarchies is that some disciplines do not belong to a single level; 'the most important fields are often those that do not have a clear place on the scale' but rather serve to integrate different levels (Juengst 1988, 77). Genetics in biology serves to integrate ecology and ethology as higher levels with histology and molecular biology at lower levels.

A strict hierarchy seems too simple. A network might appear to be a

[12] Bechtel and Abrahamsen (1991, 257); similarly Peacocke (1993, 217; 1994). A. F. Sanders (1988, 232f.; 1992, 48), following C. Sanders and H. van Rappard (1985), speaks of various ways of cognitive structuring.

more suitable image. However, presenting the sciences as a network does less justice to the intuition that some sciences are more basic than others. Therefore, I will continue to use in this section the image of higher and lower levels.

One might ask how one could fit theology into such a hierarchical view of disciplines. One proposal is to go up the hierarchy:

We can, I would urge, go further. I refer to that most complex and all-embracing of the levels in the hierarchies of 'systems', namely the complex of nature-man-and-God. (Peacocke 1986, 30)

According to Peacocke (1994) one should not attempt to locate God somewhere in such a hierarchy of being, as if God were one emergent entity among others. God is understood to be related to everything. At the top end of the scale one can place the relations between God and the world, and especially with human beings. This would lead one to expect that these relations require special concepts and methods, beyond those of the lower levels. An alternative view would not conceive of theology so much as a discipline related to the highest level, as a discipline which integrates across all levels, in analogy with the role of genetics in biology. I consider such proposals not very informative, for two reasons. One first has to argue that theology is a discipline of a similar kind to the natural sciences, and is related in a suitable way to the other scientific disciplines; just locating some potential cognitive enterprise, whether theology or astrology, somewhere in the network of disciplines does not contribute to greater intelligibility or credibility. Furthermore, once one seeks to relate theology to the other disciplines, one encounters a problem (to be considered in the next chapter) which also inhibits the transfer of defences of scientific realism to theological realism: whereas in scientific realism the existence of an underlying reality is undisputed, and the issue is the adequacy of our knowledge about that reality, in theology the existence of a corresponding realm remains disputed. Locating theology among the sciences, whether structured hierarchically or as a web, is not helpful in articulating a response to a naturalist view of reality, including religion and morality.

If there are various sciences pertaining to different levels of complexity, one might ask how these different sciences are related. The naturalist view [2] has it that ontologically higher levels of complexity consist of the constituents of lower levels. For instance, molecules are made of atoms; humans are made up of molecules. However, this does not imply that reductionism in a methodological sense must be an effective strategy for scientific research: it may well be that the study of higher-level phenomena is best pursued by using concepts which are appropriate at that level (see [22]). Thus, 'reductionism is not a guideline for research programs, but an attitude towards nature itself' (Weinberg 1992, 52). As an attitude towards nature, and a concomitant 'belief in the connectedness of scientific knowledge' (Weinberg 1992, 49), it excludes claims of total independence of one cognitive enterprise from the others; astrology cannot be autonomous.

Reductionism is a challenge to any theology which seeks to restrict itself to the use of insights about 'higher levels' while avoiding problematic aspects of lower levels, either the uncertainty about fundamental theories or the actual insights of our current theories. Reductionism may however, also be seen as an opportunity for theology – where one cannot refer to 'the man in the next office', the physicist in company with the cosmologist (for the ultimate historical issues) may well say 'God knows' (Misner 1977, 97; see [2]). This groping for an ultimate explanation makes popular books on physics and cosmology so attractive to religiously and philosophically minded readers (e.g., Davies 1983, 1992; Hawking 1988). However, it is precisely here that a major challenge to theology lies: the 'God' of the cosmologists and the physicists seems to be a principle of order, a First Cause, or whatever, rather than a God interested in human concerns, providing guidance to our lives.

In order to arrive at a concept of God which is more relevant to humans, some thinkers seek to understand cosmology in a more hospitable way, for instance by understanding the life-allowing features of our universe as a consequence of intentional design. Others retreat from these discussions about science, falling back on experience and tradition. Again other authors, such as Arthur Peacocke and Ian Barbour accept a form of ontological reductionism (there are no separate entities involved in life), but object to epistemological reductionism, the claim that higher-level phenomena can be fully explained in terms of lower levels, and ultimately in terms of physics. However, even then one needs to pay attention to the relations between the various levels; they are not totally autonomous. Higher levels of reality are constrained by lower levels, even if perhaps not fully determined by them. A biological description of reality may not be reducible to one in physical terms, but it cannot contradict the physical laws involved. For example, if energy is conserved, this should hold both in physics and in biology. Changes in our understanding at lower levels of the hierarchy of the sciences have consequences for higher levels in so far as the higher levels use the same concepts and laws.

17. SCIENTIFIC REALISM AND DEFENCES OF THEOLOGICAL REALISM

Theology is supposed to explore reality, both God and creation. Hence, judgements on whether the object of theology is real seem to depend upon views of human knowledge of reality, as discussed under the rubric of 'scientific realism'. 'Realism' has many meanings, in part dependent on what is perceived to be the opposite of realism. Some take the opposite of realism (without making a distinction between realism and scientific realism) to be idealism or solipsism, the denial of a reality 'out there'. For example, Roger Trigg sees a battle 'between realists who believe that there is a world to be investigated which exists independently of human belief and language, and anti-realists' (Trigg 1993, 6). I consider this a misleading view of discussions on scientific realism, as if the central issue is the *existence* of reality. Most non-realists do not deny the existence of a reality independent of our beliefs and language. The central issue in debates about scientific realism is not the existence of reality, but to what extent our ideas about reality represent what reality out there is like (semantic), to what extent our methods are adequate for finding out which entities there are (ontological), or on what grounds we base our belief in our ideas about reality (epistemological). Thus, the discussion about *scientific* realism in this chapter is not so much on the existence of a reality 'out there' as it is about *the nature and quality of our investigations, and thus of our scientific knowledge, and thus about whether to ascribe existence to certain theoretical entities*.

The debate about scientific realism, as a debate about the results of science, is not in itself a debate about naturalism, in the ontological sense in which it is defined above [2], or about its implications for theology. Both scientific realists and scientific anti- or non-realists might deny or affirm the existence of particular realities out there, such as a divine being, the Absolute, values, or whatever. Indirectly, however, the understanding of scientific realism may be relevant to the understanding of theology, and thereby of importance to the reflections on the implications of naturalism. The presence of a naturalistic view of reality (including religion) would carry much less weight if scientific claims are not interpreted realistically or if the cognitive status of theological claims can be argued for as similar to the status of scientific statements. This approach will be considered critically below, when we come to philosophical arguments for similarity *qua* status [17.2] and to motives for realism in theology [17.3]. Before coming to arguments about views of knowledge in theology, we will consider some aspects of contemporary debates on scientific realism [17.1].

17.1. Scientific realism

Realism seems to be the common-sense view of science. Scientists are not making up a story, but they are finding out about the real world. The far side of the moon was the same before and after human astronauts first saw it, and, whether we like it or not, tectonic plates are causing earthquakes and mountain formation by their slow motions. If the results of science were fiction rather than fact, why would taxpayers spend money on it? Santa Claus, God, the ego, the United Nations and paper money may perhaps be human constructions, and some of them are none the less very real, but how could anybody in his right mind doubt realism with respect to the natural sciences? Scientists do not construct quarks, do they?

They do, if judged by the title *Constructing Quarks: A Sociological History of Particle Physics* (Pickering 1984). Even if one does not follow Pickering in all respects, he seems to be obviously right in two ways: (a) the concept 'quark' – the word and the theories in which it functions – is not found, but made by scientists, in this case by picking up a meaningless word from a novel; (b) 'high-tech science is highly *artificial*. We do not simply go out and look at unadulterated nature. The events we detect are so highly contrived and constrained as to be "man-made"' (Nickles 1992, 101). Artificial need not mean fictitious; the recent ceramic materials which exhibit superconductivity at higher temperatures than previously known are not less real than iron or water, even though they, perhaps, never existed before in the Solar System or maybe even in the observable universe. Though man-made, their existence tells us about a possibility of material reality.

We will begin with some challenges to realist views of scientific theories, before turning to contemporary defences of scientific realism. It will be shown that such defences move beyond a narrow focus on theories. Furthermore, contemporary defences of scientific realism are rather modest in their metaphysical claims. In the next section [17.2], I will argue that this modesty impedes the transfer of arguments for scientific realism to the defence of theological realism. Hence, even if theologians, or philosophers of religion, are right in arguing that scientific realism can be defended, they are mistaken when they assume that this is helpful for a defence of theological realism. I will also argue that it may be attractive for theology if its claims are not understood in a strongly realist way [17.3].

Challenges to a realist view of scientific theories
Do our best theories correspond to what the world is like? And if so, how do we evaluate which theories do and which do not? This is problematic, and even more so if 'correspondence' is construed as 'depicting' in a one-to-one relation, for how could we ever know that our theories are adequate? We can compare a painted portrait or a photograph with the original, and thus assess whether it is adequate, but we cannot compare our theories with naked reality, only with reality as it is caught in human theories (or in human common-sense language).

In experiments we seem to test theories against the real world. However, a sceptic might continue the debate by pointing out that in experiments reality presents itself in a restricted way. High-tech science relies on instruments. To interpret the results of the experiments we have to take into account what the instruments do, and hence we have to rely on theories about these instruments. *Data are theory laden*; we seem to be caught in circularity, as we rely on theories in order to test theories. Against this circularity due to the theory-ladenness of data a realist might argue that none the less experiments do inform us about reality, or at least, more modestly, may inform us about the inadequacy of our theories. In many cases, the theories used in an experiment are different from, and better established than, the theory tested in the experiment. In using a microscope one relies on optics while studying bacteria.

The problem of the theory-laden character of data is more serious when the theory to be tested is also used in understanding the measuring device. A clear example of such an unavoidable circularity is the detection of neutrinos produced by the Sun (Shapere 1982). Neutrinos are extremely elusive particles: zillions pass through the entire Earth every second. In detecting some neutrinos produced by nuclear fusion in the Sun we observe the interior of the Sun rather than the outer layers from whence we receive light. To avoid unwanted influences from other particles, neutrino-observations have been set up in tunnels, deep inside mountains, a very unusual location for astronomical observations. Huge tanks of specially prepared fluids are there to catch some of the neutrinos produced by the Sun. Now comes the same-theory-ladenness: we cannot avoid using the same theory of weak interactions in the theory of the source for calculating the expected production of neutrinos in the Sun; in the theory of the receptor for calculating from the observed phenomena how many neutrinos are believed to have passed through the detector; and in the theory of the transmission between the Sun and the detector. However, this does not diminish the value of these experiments. They were informative: fewer neutrinos were detected than expected. There was something wrong, either with the theory or with other assumptions such as those about the temperature in the interior of the Sun. If differences with alternative theories had been cancelled by the fact that the theory to be tested was involved in the interpretation of the data, the experiment would have been uninformative. However, the differences showed up in a more pronounced way. The theory-ladenness of data is not necessarily fatal for testing scientific theories.

Another challenge to a realist view of theories is the observation that theories are *underdetermined* by the available data. We face the possibility of a plurality of theories which are all empirically adequate but different in their view of the world. One can imagine theories which are different but not (or not yet) distinguishable. One might, for instance, add to an equation a term with effects so minute as to escape all feasible observations. Seen thus, any theory seems to have an infinite number of close neighbours – though these neighbours may be mathematically far less simple, because the additional terms spoil the mathematical symmetries of the original theory.

A different kind of underdetermination can be found in theories of motion, where we have different formulations which are not only equivalent with respect to current observations, but also theoretically equivalent. Newton assumed an absolute reference frame for rest and motion. However, in calculations only relative motions are relevant. Hence, one can envisage a whole set of equivalent theories which differ only in the absolute frame of reference they assume. Leaving aside Einstein's corrections to Newton's theory, a realist might assume that precisely one of this set of theories is the correct one, even though we cannot know which one. We do not know which frame of reference is absolute; our knowledge is limited. Van Fraassen has argued for a more radical agnosticism; accepting the empirical adequacy of these equivalent theories does not depend on holding any of these theories to be true. This is what we do when we reject the notion of an absolute frame of reference (Van Fraassen 1976; 1980, 44–7). Arguments for significant underdetermination draw mostly on mechanics and quantum physics, but quantum and classical mechanics are exceptional in allowing for theoretically equivalent theories.[13] In these few cases, 'no decision can be made in this case as to what the theory, on a realist reading, commits us to' (McMullin 1984, 11). But that should not keep us from a moderate realist understanding of other theories, such as evolutionary biology or plate tectonics.

Another challenge to realism with respect to our scientific theories has come from the awareness of discontinuities in the *history of science.* Changes in theories are often refinements, but occasionally they have been 'revolutions', more radical changes in the ontology, i.e. in our ideas about the entities constituting the world. Larry Laudan has presented a list of theories which were 'once successful and well confirmed, but which contained central terms that (we now believe) were nonreferring' (Laudan 1984, 121; see also Laudan 1981). This is the basis for the 'inductive argument against induction', the suggestion that 'since we have failed so often we are likely to be failing right now' (Levin 1984, 134).

[13] *Quantum physics* has figured prominently in discussions on realism, independently from reflections on 'underdetermination'. Quantum physics has features which are strange if considered from the classical (pre-quantum) perspective. Measurements seem to be not so much observations as interactions, shaping the determinate outcome out of the indeterminate state preceding measurement. A few authors have suggested that the indeterminate character continues until the level of consciousness is reached – thus making reality to some extent dependent on the mind. Another feature of quantum physics is the presence of aspects which do not seem to lend themselves to treatment as localisable properties. Besides, there is a plurality of interpretations of this highly successful type of physical theories. The strangeness of the world as described by quantum physics, including non-locality and the superposition of different states, is not thereby anti-realist, even though it is quite unlike common-sense views. On the contrary, the fact that we have developed such a theory suggests that reality has forced upon us views that would not have occurred to us without external pressure. However, an empiricist can reply that what has been forced upon us are certain phenomena; whether one should commit oneself to the strange ontology of the theory or keep an agnostic attitude with respect to it is not thereby decided. Even within a single type of interpretation such as the modal interpretation, one may find authors inspired by a realist view (Dieks 1989) and by an empiricist view (Van Fraassen 1991). Whatever the outcome of debates about the interpretation of quantum physics, the case for scientific realism would still be open. A determinate character of unobserved reality is not necessarily part of realism. Perhaps reality is foggy to some extent, and perhaps the physical interactions involved in observation provide determinateness.

One response open to a realist is to deny the link between realism and steady progress. A realist need not hold that we only refine beliefs without ever abandoning any beliefs. He can especially grant, without much reason for concern, radical changes in sciences which were, by criteria we would currently apply, not well developed. Furthermore, the observation that many theories of the past have been discarded is not enough for the anti-realist argument from history. 'What the anti-Realist needs to establish is that the history of unobservable posits has been thoroughly *erratic*; for example, T' jettisons most of the ontology of T; T'' jettisons most of that of T' and does not retain what T' saved from T; and so on' (DeVitt 1984, 147). Furthermore, Kitcher has also argued that in many instances the reason why the theory failed and was abandoned concerned other elements of the theory than those that contributed to its success, which were retained (Kitcher 1993, 143; see, for a similar argument also Psillos 1994). One may also grant discontinuities with respect to theories but deny that this challenges our sense of the advancement of science. Thus, Philip Kitcher argues that scientific practices, which consist of more than theories, can be considered progressive in some respects even when theories that were once believed to be true, subsequently failed (Kitcher 1993, 140–9, 272–90). Thus, one can perhaps reject the apparent lesson from the history of science that since we failed so often, we are likely to be be always equally wrong.

This has been a brief tour of some challenges to scientific realism. One conclusion, beyond the dispute about scientific realism as such, is that none of these challenges imply such a limited status for the sciences that other human practices which purport to yield cognitive claims, such as astrology or folk-medicine, can claim equal status without offering serious credentials.

Underdetermination, theory-ladenness, and our history of failures as well as successes show the need for caution. We should avoid overstatement, especially when considering the implied ontology of our current theories; it may well be that some future theory will prolong the empirical successes of our current theory (and add some more) while jettisoning some of the main elements of the apparent ontology of the theory. But the challenges do not refute the possibility of a modestly realist attitude towards scientific theories. That theories and observations are intertwined, as in the example of neutrino astronomy, does not imply that we can make up theories the way we want;

experimental results, even if not acquired independently of a specific theory, can challenge that theory.

Defences of modest scientific realism

It seems easier to object to specific attacks on and defences of realism than to offer a positive case for realism or anti-realism. Let me continue this brief tour with the two kinds of arguments in favour of scientific realism that seem to have most support amongst contemporary philosophers of science. They both take off from, and stay close to the instrumental success of science in our interaction with the world (technical manipulation, prediction, control, exploration). The modesty of scientific realism is a feature which will be important when we come to consider the relevance of scientific realism for theology.

That these major defences of realism argue from instrumental success to realism is not too amazing. How else could one defend realism in a non-circular way? Pointing to the success of science in understanding or depicting reality or in referring to it, would assume what defenders of realism are seeking to defend.

(1) One argument in favour of realism has been made by shifting from theories to the practice of science. As long as electrons were only theoretical entities introduced in theories, one could remain agnostic about their existence. However, for current experimentalists, electrons are not theoretical entities. They manipulate electrons; they use them as tools to achieve something else. 'Experimental physics provides the strongest evidence for scientific realism. Entities that in principle cannot be observed are regularly manipulated to produce new phenomena and to investigate other aspects of nature. They are tools, instruments not for thinking but for doing' (Hacking 1982 (1984, 154); similarly Giere 1988, 125f.). This is a realism which is not about theories and truth but about entities used as tools, on the basis of their causal powers. In such a realism reference is more important than representation or correspondence (Radder 1984, 91; 1989, 309).

(2) The other argument takes realism as 'the only acceptable explanation for the current instrumental reliability of scientific methodology in mature sciences' (Boyd 1983, 88). The datum here is the *instrumental* success of the *methodology* that generates these theories. 'Scientific realism ... is a quite limited claim that purports to explain why certain ways of proceeding in science have worked out as well as

they (contingently) have' (McMullin 1984, 30). A realist and an empiricist would agree that empirical adequacy, 'saving the phenomena', is an important criterion in evaluating scientific theories. However, in the selection of theories other criteria, aside of empirical adequacy, may be important. Such other, complementary, virtues may be coherence, consonance with other parts of science, or perhaps even with broader world-views, fertility and unifying power, and uniqueness, the absence of credible theoretical alternatives (McMullin 1994, 103); as vices one might think of various forms of *ad hoc*ness or artificiality. It is a contingent fact of history that such complementary virtues support success in the quest for empirically adequate theories. The effectiveness of such strategies is intelligible upon a realist attitude, since a realist would expect our theories to match the coherence of reality and would expect a positive contribution to fertility from avoiding *ad hoc*ness; if theories would not bring us in touch with reality beyond what is observed, there would be no reason to honour virtues and shun vices. Hence, these 'complementary virtues make sense only in a realistic perspective' (McMullin 1994, 104). Such a defence is not beyond dispute. For instance, one might also attribute the fruitfulness of various complementary virtues to the economy of thought they support.[14]

It may be noted that both defences deal with more than just theories; the first emphasises empirical practice, while the second concentrates on scientific methodology. Avoiding overstatement, and objecting to overstatements which ease refutations of realism, is one of the strategies explicitly espoused by contemporary defenders of realism (e.g., McMullin 1994).[15] If one accepts the successful character of science as an argument for realism, there is the further issue of how far such

---

[14] I owe this argument in the present context to Hans Radder (private communication).

[15] Another example of someone avoiding overstatement is Rom Harré (1986), who seeks to articulate a modest form of realism rather than 'truth realism' which he considers dependent upon an 'over-demanding principle of bi-valence' (Harré 1986, 58f.; similarly 65ff.). Incidentally, Harré, who misspells Van Fraassen's name consistently, also misrepresents him when he criticises him for a neo-Berkeleyan ontology which would deny existence to the back of the moon until observed (1986, 56f.). Van Fraassen does not endorse such an ontology, but pleads for the legitimacy of an agnostic attitude. Besides, Van Fraassen distinguishes between entities that are in principle observable and those that are not; the far side of the moon being clearly something that is in principle observable just as are the moons of Jupiter – 'as astronauts will no doubt be able to see them as well from close up', while 'the purported observation of micro-particles in a cloud chamber seems to me a clearly different case' (Van Fraassen 1980, 16f.). The meaning of 'observable' as 'observable to us' is not a restriction on existence (contrary to what Harré seems to take Van Fraassen to say). The restriction is 'too anthropocentric for that', but it has 'to do with the proper epistemic attitude to science' (Van Fraassen 1980, 19).

realism extends: when should one take which theories seriously with respect to the entities they assume and the properties and relations they ascribe to these entities? Avoiding overstatement also implies a cautious attitude in this respect. Once the debate about realism has moved away from the overstatement of metaphysical realism and the understatement which denies the existence of unobservable entities, the debate about realism continues in a more refined form over the criteria to be used in theory evaluation.[16]

From modest to metaphysical realism?
On both sides in debates about realism and anti-realism, authors defend their own view against their reconstruction of the opponent's view. If one links scientific realism with the attempt to give a metaphysical answer to all 'Why?' questions, 'achieving a world-picture, something that purports to be the "One True Story of the World"' (Van Fraassen 1994, 116), it becomes quite vulnerable. If one takes anti-realism in the very radical sense of viewing knowledge as nothing but a summary of observations, or nothing but a mental or social construct, it too can be refuted easily.

It is remarkable how, in contemporary debates among philosophers of science, realists and empiricists to a large extent have come to take a similar stance with respect to the extremes. At the 'low end', they all agree on the presence of regularities in empirical reality and on the instrumental success of science. Both arguments in defence of realism considered above were geared to the instrumental success of science, either manipulation in experimentation (Hacking, Giere, Radder) or predictive reliability (Boyd, McMullin). The claims of most scientific realists are moderate. Even though theories may change, the instrumental success of theories and related practices justifies committing ourselves provisionally to the existence of the entities described in these theories or assumed to be used in these practices. A strong claim, a metaphysical realism that assumes that science offers access to the one true, unchangeable view is avoided by the defenders of realism as much as it is objected to by empiricists rejecting realism.

For example, both Ernan McMullin, a defender of scientific realism, and Bas van Fraassen, an empiricist, agree on the inappropriateness of metaphysical extensions of scientific conclusions. McMullin

---

[16] Or one might say that the debate on realism and anti-realism is abandoned, as some advocates of a metaphysically minimal 'non-realism' propose (e.g., Fine 1984; Rouse 1987, 127–65; Radder 1989, 304ff.); a more interesting and relevant debate then takes its place.

rejects the link between scientific realism and metaphysical realism; scientific realism 'is not immediately undermined by the rejection of metaphysical realism' (McMullin 1984, 25). Current theories need not be true or approximately true, and theoretical explanations are open-ended, allowing for metaphorical extensions (McMullin 1984, 36). Explanatory success allows us, 'in favorable cases, to make a truth claim *of a limited sort* for the theory' (McMullin 1987, 52; emphasis added). And Van Fraassen resists answers that pretend too much; 'the restraint to acceptance delivers us from metaphysics' (Van Fraassen 1980, 69). Van Fraassen is interested in knowledge about the world, but concerned about claiming too much. He identifies the following question as one that he and realists might have in common: 'How could the world *possibly* be the way physical theory says it is?' (Van Fraassen 1984, 171).[17]

This is not the place to sort out all genuine disagreements among philosophers of science on realism and criteria for the evaluation of theories. However, many seem to agree to a large extent that actual science is of limited value for metaphysics. We now turn to the defence of theological realism in discussions about theology in the context of scientific knowledge, where *prima facie* one might expect a stronger interest in metaphysical claims.

17.2. Transfer from philosophy of science to philosophy of theology?

In the less metaphysical and more empiricist tradition of English-speaking philosophy, however, there has been a tendency to analyze religious belief by borrowing models from contemporary philosophy of science (usually a decade or so behind). (Arbib and Hesse 1986, 19)

In the preceding section we considered disputes about scientific realism. As pointed out at the beginning of this chapter, a major assumption was not disputed, since it is shared by realists and most anti-realists, namely the existence of a reality 'out there', to some

[17] Similarly in his book on the interpretation of quantum mechanics (Van Fraassen 1991, 4 and 9), and in a quote from René Descartes' *Principes* (iv. 204) on its front page, of which the second half reads 'il suffit d'expliquer comment elles (les choses) peuvent être'. In private conversation Van Fraassen told me that he encountered the question posed in the text in a lecture in Pittsburgh by a Jesuit philosopher of science. This could be Joseph T. Clark, who argued that the philosopher attempts to explain 'how things can consistently be as they are observably known to be by science; the speculative theologian seeks to explain how things can consistently *be* as some God is reliably reported to say that they actually are' (Clark 1966, 307).

extent independent of the mind of the knower (even though the existence of many phenomena, such as social facts and ceramic superconductors is dependent upon human activities). Thus, debates about scientific realism were seen as debates about our knowledge, our access to reality.

When we turn to theological realism, such an assumption can no longer be taken for granted. One might define theological realists as those who hold that theological claims are about an external reality and that their claims are in some sense adequate with respect to that reality. If we assume that theological claims are about a Being who transcends the natural realm and is active within natural processes, such a theological realism is at odds with naturalism as defined in this study ([2]).

We can now distinguish between two kinds of theological anti-realists: those who challenge *existence* and those who challenge *access*.

(1) Some may object to the existence of a divine being or a divine reality, or at least see no reasons to accept any claims about divine existence. Some of them may hold, for instance, that we have naturalist accounts which should replace the theological view of reality. Thus, they may be scientific realists who deny a similar cognitive status to theology because the reality to which it purports to refer is non-existent, or at least substantially different from the way it is claimed to be; where a claim seems to be about a transcendent reality, it might be taken to refer to intrapsychic and cultural processes.

Within the context of science, there may also be disagreements over the adequacy of ascribing existence to particular entities. However, the existence of a reality behind the phenomena is not disputed in the reflections considered here. One might say that in the case of a naturalist account of religion too, some reality behind the phenomena is not disputed, but only the character of that reality, whether it is natural or supernatural. However, this challenge is of such major importance to theology that I treat it as distinct from the second challenge.

(2) Others may deny the adequacy of cognitive claims in theology, not because they deny a corresponding reality but because they consider our cognitive capabilities for knowledge inadequate. One might also defend this kind of anti-realism for theological reasons, say due to the ineffable nature of God.

In this section, I will first focus on attempts to transfer defences of scientific realism to theological realism. Then I will consider another example of the transfer of an approach in the philosophy of science to the philosophy of theology, namely Nancey Murphy's defence of the usefulness of a Lakatosian view of theological research programmes.

In arguing for realism in theology by analogy with realist views of the sciences one needs to consider whether the nature and quality of theological 'theories' or 'experiments' is such that they *justify on their own grounds a similar move* as Hacking and Radder make for scientific experimentation and manipulation and McMullin and Boyd make for scientific theorising. Can a similar success be claimed, and can it be made the basis for an argument for realism along similar lines?

There are obvious differences in success between the sciences and theology, if success is judged at a fairly common-sense level. Success may become manifest in a consensus about beliefs and practices, but theology does not exhibit the amount of convergence and consensus found in the natural sciences. Success may also show up as fertility, when current findings are an effective basis for further work (one of McMullin's complementary virtues). However, we seem to lack in theology a cumulative argument preserving previous results or practices, or some other indication of such fertility. Another measure of success appealed to in defence of scientific realism was found in experimental practices, our ability to manipulate entities and to produce new phenomena on the basis of current knowledge. However, a similar manipulative or constructive virtue seems to be absent from theology. Whenever control over reality on the basis of a specific theology is claimed, for instance in the ability to heal illnesses, most outsiders tend to become very critical, considering it quite plausible that psychological mechanisms are involved. Incidentally, many Christian theologians are also critical of claims about direct effects of religious practices; God's grace is not thought of as if it were under human control.

Thus, with respect to measures of success which could be appealed to in defence of theological realism, there is a fundamental difference. As Ernan McMullin wrote with respect to science:

There is something here to be *explained*, namely the success of scientific models not only in prediction but in handling anomalies, in suggesting imaginative extensions, and the like. This is a contingent fact about the history of science since Galileo's day, and especially in the structural sciences since around 1800.

Whereas for theology,

there is no corresponding argument, alas. (McMullin 1985, 43)

Given the differences in success, we cannot defend theological realism in the same way that scientific realism is defended. Hence, we cannot co-opt the prestige of science for theology in this way.

One might object to this negative view of the success record of theology. Polkinghorne considers differences between science and theology, for instance, with respect to the ability to achieve some consensus or to manipulate reality, to be a matter of degree rather than of principle. 'I believe the answer to lie in the recognition that science is easy and theology hard, because of the greatly differing degrees of control and power to interrogate that each exercises over the object of its inquiry ... The successes of science are purchased by the modesty of its ambition' (Polkinghorne 1991, 8f.).

I side with McMullin in judging that the different success records of theology and science reflect genuine differences between these enter-prises; differences which are significant for the debates on theological and scientific realism. In the remainder of this section we will come across additional philosophical and theological reasons for emphasizing the differences. This is not to deny that it may be fruitful to analyse theologies in schemes borrowed from philosophers of science, or for that matter, philosophers of language, by reconstructing theological developments in terms of research programmes, paradigms, or what-ever. Such a reconstruction may be heuristically fruitful, but it does not support a realist understanding of the theological claims thus recon-structed. The strength of defences of critical realism with respect to science and to theology is in the

insistence that the objects of science lie beyond the range of literal description just as the objects of religious belief do ... But it would be unwise to push the parallels any further, or suggest that what enables the realism of science to be self-critical and progressive may somehow be transferred to the domain of religious belief. (McMullin 1985, 47)

Problems similar to those considered with respect to the transfer of defences of realism arise when other discussions are transferred from the philosophy of science to the philosophy of theology.[18] If claims about methodological parallels between science and theology are not merely claims about parallels, but are assumed to allow cross-traffic, then those elements that guarantee reference of claims, or rationality of inferences, or whatever aspect is considered central to the comparison, need to be established on the theological side as well.

For instance, Nancey Murphy (1990) has argued that one might reconstruct good theological research in the form of research pro- grammes as described for the natural sciences by Imre Lakatos. Thus she presents theological approaches in terms of a hard core, auxiliary hypotheses, and a positive heuristic. Such a reconstruction may clarify the structure of the programme, but is in itself not enough to justify pursuing a theological programme in the way one is rationally justified in pursuing a progressive scientific research programme. Thus, she rightly sees the need to argue that both theoretical progress and novel facts can be found in theology. Theologically relevant novel facts are specially found, according to her, in communal discernment on religious, theological and ethical issues, a discernment guided by the Holy Spirit. While I appreciate her reconstruction of the development of theological ideas in terms of research programmes, I doubt whether this view of novel facts in theology works. The evaluation of communal discernment, or, for that matter, of other varieties of religious experi- ence, is far more problematic than the evaluation of novel facts in astronomy or geophysics. Are such experiences to be understood as psychological and social phenomena, or are they data about God? If they are understood as data about God, one might compare them to data in the sciences, such as data which are relevant to belief in tectonic plates. However, such a comparison fails. Apart from differences in precision and in fertility, which may be played down as differences of degree rather than of kind, there is the fundamental difference that the tectonic plates are within the realm of the natural, fitting into the wider

---

[18] Arbib and Hesse (1986, 19f.) and Van Huyssteen (1989) describe some earlier examples of defences of religion following changes in the philosophy of science. Barbour (1974) defends the rationality of religion on the basis of insights about the role of models and paradigms in science; Banner (1990) uses Kuhn's understanding of scientific revolutions in combination with ideas about 'inference to the best explanation'; Murphy (1990), treated as an example in the text, bases her account on Lakatos' view of research programmes with hard cores kept intact by commitment and justified by theoretical and empirical progress; Clayton (1989) adds Habermas' view of the social sciences to Lakatos' view of the natural sciences, seeking a mediation between formalist and historicist views; Sanders (1988) reconstructs Polanyi's epistemology, and Van Huyssteen (1993) argues for a holist post-foundationalist epistemology in theology.

pattern of the physical sciences, whereas God is taken to be of a different order. The possibility of understanding communal discernment and religious experience in naturalist terms, which will be considered in chapter 4, does not undermine their novelty, but it does undermine their relevance to the theological programme they are supposed to support. In terms of the two varieties of theological anti-realism distinguished above, the issue is that the justification of theological claims has to overcome both the ineffability of God (2) and the difference between ordinary and divine reality (1), whereas a similar justification in the sciences is restricted to the ineffability of reality 'as such', and thus only to problems related to an assessment of the match between theories and reality, rather than between theories and two realms of reality.

So far, I have argued that defences of positions in the philosophy of science cannot be transferred to defences of similar positions in the philosophy of theology. Another issue is that philosophical literature which models theology on science with respect to method, rationality, or realism, is in danger of missing a major part of what science is about. Debates about rationality, realism, and epistemology risk becoming a separate, almost autonomous kind of literature, neglecting substantive insights about the world and their implications for theology. A strong concentration on the epistemological side of the debate involves the fallacy of assuming that science is defined by its method.[19] Yet, science is neither defined by its method alone nor by its content alone. Nor is theology challenged only in its epistemology; the content of its claims is problematic as well (and this includes eschatological expectations, claims about the human soul and life beyond death, divine action, and divine existence). This is, in other terms, the wider import of the challenge to 'existence' claims, a challenge which is not in a comparable way present in disputes in philosophy of science where we deal only with arguments about our access to (and thus our claims about) particular existents.

17.3. Theological realism

A narrow focus on analogies between the philosophy of science and the philosophy of theology is not only in danger of misconstruing science. It is also in danger of misconstruing theology. It is to this concern that

---

[19] That this is indeed a fallacy is corroborated by the historical studies in Schuster and Yeo (1986), a reference I owe to John H. Brooke.

we will now turn. I will consider why some theologians or philosophers defend realism in science and in theology, and I will argue that these motives do not require such a defence of theological realism.

Motives for theological realism

A *natural theology* which defends the truth of faith, or its plausibility, on the basis of features of the universe such as its intelligibility and order, assumes that scientific knowledge is knowledge about the world. The argument could not take off if the order or intelligibility were imposed by us. The conclusion natural theology aims at is of a similar realist kind: God is an objective, supernatural reality. Our knowledge may be imperfect, but the intention is to be realist in theology and in science.

Not all who opt for scientific and theological realism do so because they intend to argue from science to theology, as in natural theology. Others seek to bring together scientific insights and theological convictions in a wider scheme of things, for instance a *theology of nature* which integrates knowledge about reality (assuming scientific realism) with ideas about God (assuming some form of theological realism, but not necessarily indebted to a defence along the same lines as scientific realism). We considered the use of the sciences in such an integration above [15, 16]. Such an integration may be deemed desirable because it would enhance the credibility of theology. If scientific knowledge and theological claims could be brought together in a single scheme, the suggestion that they are inconsistent would have been dispelled. A mediating, integrative approach can also be seen as an attempt to communicate religious views to humans who see their world in terms provided by the sciences (e.g., Hesse 1981, 287).

Even if the knowledge content of science and that of theology are not brought into relation with each other, there still is a theological interest in scientific realism. If science were not knowledge of reality, how much more would we have to fear that this is the case in theology, where the symbolic nature of language is much more persistent and the interaction with the reality hoped for is far less tangible.[20] For instance, Peacocke (1993, 19) has it that if one would accept a social constructivist view of science, one would have to 'adopt *a fortiori* a similar view of the cognitive claims of theology'. However, defending scientific realism for this

---

[20]   The inference *a minore ad majus*, or in Rabbinic writings *qal wahomer*, ('if ... , how much more ...') has been formalised by H. G. Hubbeling (1987, 222–4). It does not seem to be logically compelling without substantial assumptions about the minor and the major compared, *viz.* science and theology.

reason seems to me to be misguided. One cannot avoid the problematic defence of theological realism by turning towards the easier, but for the purpose at hand irrelevant, defence of scientific realism. Whichever view on the complex character of science with its success and its persistent openness to development and change is to prevail, theological realism would still have to be justified on its own terms.

A positive theological motive to defend theological realism has to do with a major function of the symbol of God, that of providing trust and hope. If God were not real, our hope would be in vain. Though this is convincing, it does not follow that 'If God were not real, belief in God would not fulfil this function.' More important in our context, the statement does not require theological realism to be analogous to scientific realism. God might be totally different from the way God is believed to be, and beliefs about God might be untestable, while none the less the hope expressed in the beliefs might not be vain. This motive is at odds with eliminative anti-realism; one cannot maintain the functions of hope and trust provided by the symbol while eliminating any reality with which it might be linked. However, it does not conflict with a modest assessment of our epistemic capacities, as, for instance, in an agnostic empiricism as advocated by Van Fraassen. Nor does it conflict with a major human role in constructing our theories and practices.

Part of the drive for a theological variant of scientific realism is abhorrence of the alternative. If theology were not about a reality, the reality of God, would it not be a mere instrument, a tale which may serve social and psychological functions but which has no basis in reality? Is God going the way of Santa Claus and the Easter bunny: a nice story for kids, but not for grown-ups?

There may be various responses to this abhorrence of the alternative. Firstly, the alternative need not be seen in such dark terms. Some non-realists or anti-realists in theology, for example D. Z. Phillips, paint their approach in more positive terms, as the attempt to preserve genuine faith in the form of an attitude of existential trust rather than of assent to certain cognitive claims. Thus, one might rebut that realists distort faith by modelling it too closely after science. A theological realism which affirms truth and meaning out there 'is politically conservative, and pictures the universe as being rather like an English boarding school. You should accommodate yourself or fit yourself into a pre-established order of things' (Cupitt 1990, 56).

Secondly, other theologians do not so much present themselves in opposition to realism, but rather seek to enter a dialogue with science along different lines, in concentrating on experience and on tradition. We will come back to such approaches in later chapters.

And thirdly, one might stick to theological realism without seeking to defend theological realism along the same lines as scientific realism. That seems to be the position taken by Ernan McMullin. As he sees it, the issue in the area of theology and science is to develop broader world views. Such world views do not exhibit the convergence and success which would warrant a defence of theological realism along the same lines as the defence of scientific realism. Such a position accepts the integrity of science without burdening science with the task of providing support for theology; the theological debate is at the level of world views rather than directly at the level of science. This distinction between the debate within science and the debate about world views is central to McMullin's resistance against Plantinga's proposal for a theistic science (McMullin 1991; 1993, 304; on Plantinga, see [18]). World views are a proper area of disagreement; science, by weeding out errors in a persistent testing process, is a distinct area of consensus building. World views are tied to the place where one stands, here and now, in a cultural context with certain values and interests.

Some authors grant a particular world view or metaphysical scheme priority in shaping their science (or their interpretation of science) and their theology. Some prefer the philosophical conceptual framework of Hegel or Heidegger, and in the context of discussions on the relations between science and religion, the conceptual framework of Alfred North Whitehead has gained some followers. Some of the more prominent authors, such as Barbour, Birch, and Cobb, have not so much assumed and imposed this scheme as argued for it, developing their insights in extensive dialogue with the natural sciences and with religious traditions. If one wants to give priority to some metaphysical scheme, one has to face at least two problems, that of choice and that of justification: Which metaphysical scheme and why? The need to justify a choice is felt more strongly with respect to theological or metaphysical positions than with respect to science. In philosophy, discussions are persistent. It is almost a tautology to say that unresolved issues are metaphysical; issues that allow for resolution tend to be classified as scientific.

Whatever conclusion one comes to with respect to scientific realism, the instrumental success of science is a major phenomenon of our time. It may not be sufficient to extend the credibility of scientific insights to the answers to philosophical questions about the existence and structure of the universe, but it does force us to take science very seriously, even though its answers are provisional, and consensus is sometimes lacking and, on other occasions, of limited value [16]. I appreciate the engagement of theological realists with scientific insights, but I do not believe that attempts to formulate theological views in continuity with scientific insights will succeed. This is not merely a negative conclusion. If there were too much continuity and similarity between science and theology, we would have a theology which could not provide us with a sense of contrast, whether a contrast that could be understood evolutionarily or one that has to be undergirded by an understanding of God as transcending natural reality.

Is-not is not enough contrast

Amongst those who defend a modest (often called 'critical') realism in science and in theology, many have stressed that an important qualification has to be added to all their theological models, metaphors, theories and arguments. There is to any model a positive analogy, the way the model *is* like the item modelled, as well as a negative analogy, the way the model *is not* like the item modelled. Quite a few refer to Sally McFague's theological justification of such an is/is-not distinction in *Metaphorical Theology*. She suggests 'that one of the distinctive characteristics of Protestant thought is its insistence on the "and it is not". It is the iconoclastic tendency in Protestantism, what Paul Tillich calls "the Protestant Principle", the fear of idolatry, the concern lest the finite ever be imagined to be capable over the infinite.'[21] The 'is-not' which is whispered with each metaphor saves us from worshipping an idol, which would happen if we mistook our images for God.

Thus, in the emphasis on the 'is not' of our models and metaphors, including theological models which draw on science, there is a positive analogy, namely one between our cognitive limitations in science and in theology. This makes it 'perfectly respectable to use models of a God who "cannot be named"' (Soskice 1988, 182). Both in physics and in theology we do not know what the underlying reality is in itself; in both cases our models and language are limited. For instance, Peacocke (1985, 22; similarly 1984, 46) argues that:

---

[21]   (McFague 1982, 13); see also 134f., where she refers to Ricoeur for the distinction.

referring successfully to an entity, say an electron, can be achieved by affirming that one is referring to that which causes (say) this cloud chamber track to take such and such a path. And this can be achieved without knowing what electrons are 'in themselves'. Given the parallel between the use of models and metaphors in scientific and theological language, it seems to me to be equally legitimate to affirm that God can be 'that which causes this particular experience now (or in the past) in me (or others)'.

In my opinion, the claim that there is a similarity in limitations of our language in science and in theology, should itself be accompanied by a major 'and it is not'. The is-not character of theoretical models, the underdetermination of theories by data, or the difficulty of referring to theoretical entities such as 'electrons' is quite different from the inaccessibility of the Holy. The 'is not' of our models in science is purely a reflection of our limited knowledge of particular processes, whereas the 'is-not' in theology also reflects the sense that God is an existent (if so) of a totally different kind. We again encounter the difference pointed out when we embarked upon reflections about theological realism [17.2], the difference between concerns about the adequacy of our knowledge, which applies to scientific and to theological cognitive claims, and concerns about the existence of a corresponding reality, which arise especially with respect to theological claims.

For a 'mystical' theology, which reflects a desire for unity, for a divine presence in continuity with our lives and our knowledge, awareness of the limitations of our models may do sufficient justice to its understanding of the otherness of the divine. However, the 'is not' is insufficient as an expression of the distinction between our models of the divine and the divine reality itself for a 'prophetic' theology, which is characterised by a sense of difference and contrast, of divine absence rather than presence, of contrast between what is and what should have been. On a 'prophetic' understanding of theology, there is a sense of 'and it is not' for which there is no analogy in science. In a prophetic theology, people also seek to articulate a sense of contrast between God and the world, between how humans behave and how God intended them to behave (e.g. Isaiah 55: 8), or, more naturalistically, between ideas about 'what ought to be' and 'what is', as such ideas have evolved within reality. An 'is not' meant as a form of modesty about our language and knowledge is not enough to articulate such a sense of contrast.

18. FROM THE DISCOVERY OF SCIENCE TO THEOLOGY?

There are the discoveries of science and there is the discovery of science, of a complex of approaches which is successful in coping with and finding out about various aspects of the world. Some authors argue that this discovery is itself relevant for theology or metaphysics. We will consider two examples of arguments to this effect. Roger Trigg has defended the claim that science depends on metaphysics; otherwise, science would be nothing more than one cultural practice among others, and thus one would end up in nihilism. And Alvin Plantinga has defended epistemological naturalism, but argued that such an episte-mological naturalism is best explained in the context of an ontological supernaturalism, and at odds with ontological naturalism. Plantinga has also defended the claim that methodological naturalism is unac-ceptable for Christians, and that science as pursued in that way should be replaced by something else, a 'theistic science'. Even though this latter plea for a non-naturalist science is not an argument from the discovery of science to theology or metaphysics, I will none the less consider both arguments of Plantinga in this chapter.

Either metaphysics, or science is just one practice among others.
The philosopher Roger Trigg believes that: 'Science has to depend on metaphysics if it is not itself to be discredited' (1993, 225). Without metaphysics, science might be nothing but a social practice, the conceptual scheme of a particular period and group in human history. Without foundation in and orientation on metaphysics, science lacks grounds, standards, and direction.

> The idea, however, that there is no target for our beliefs, no purpose for our scientific investigation, no genuine object on which faith, whether scientific or whatever, can be fixed, suggests that all our reasoning is going to be unconstrained. There will be no difference between good or bad reasoning, justified or unjustified belief, or pseudo-science and the genuine article. (Trigg 1993, 225)

Trigg considers the spectre of relativism a threat to science as well as to religion. However, other philosophers and theologians have welcomed such a pluralism as providing room for religion in granting it leave from science.

> A massive intellectual revolution is taking place that is perhaps as great as that which marked off the modern world from the Middle Ages. The foundations

of the modern world are collapsing, and we are entering a postmodern world. (Diogenes Allen 1989, 2)

In the post-modern[22] world we are now entering, Diogenes Allen maintains, we can have 'the full wealth of conviction' (subtitle of Allen 1989). Post-modernism has made us aware that all forms of reflection are located within particular traditions; objective knowledge, free of an historical and cultural context, does not exist. If everything is bound up in traditions, the Christian tradition (or any other particular tradition) can claim a cognitive status on an equal footing with other world views, including secular ones such as the natural sciences and historical criticism, another major force in the modern period which has contributed to the declining credibility of the truth of historical religions.

It seems to me to be a mistake to treat science and critical historical scholarship as traditions on an equal footing with others. In principle, a basic tenet of historical criticism is 'that any belief or conclusion may be challenged, and so the boundaries of the conversation may have to be expanded', as the New Testament scholar John Collins (1993, 747) argued. Scholars and scientists do not always live up to such an ideal, but the ideal none the less implies that such scholarship is not intrinsically tied to a particular tradition. In principle all particular beliefs are open to reconsideration. In historical criticism and in the natural sciences, one should be willing to abandon any conclusion if new empirical evidence becomes available – a methodological attitude of openness – but one lives with the results achieved so far.

The post-modernist seems to adhere to a different principle of openness: the principle that traditions are wholes, which all deserve equal status as wholes. Conclusions reached in the context of one tradition, or framework or whatever, may not be challenged because of insights in another tradition. Thus, according to such a quite different methodological attitude, boundaries between various discourses are closed, and beliefs are shielded from interaction.

[22] 'Post-modern' is a term with many connotations. Here it will be used to refer to the position taken by Diogenes Allen, who is quoted in the text: whereas the 'modern' period emphasised the priority of Western science, we have now become aware of the unavoidable role of cultural contexts with their presuppositions; different cultural traditions deserve equal respect; the cognitive conclusions from historical and scientific studies within the Western modern tradition are merely one view amongst others. A different 'post-modernism' (e.g., Hensen 1990, 53ff.), namely as a critical attitude with respect to universal claims which do no justice to particulars, and especially to those who are powerless and speechless, those who suffer, those who are different, etcetera, is not disputed here. Such an engagement need not distance itself from reason and from science, but questions forms of moral discourse which lack sensitivity to diversity among individuals and within and among cultures.

Insights originate in particular traditions. However, acknowledging the unavoidable role of a particular tradition does not justify that tradition. A positive case for the status of science can be made by observing that we do not have to justify science as a whole as a single tradition, but can rather understand science as the unfinished accumulation of many piecemeal changes and developments in theories, criteria, and the like. Insights about the unavoidable role of a particular historical context are carried too far when applied sweepingly. This has been expressed well by Linell E. Cady, criticising theologians such as Diogenes Allen, to whom she refers here:

Even without saying anything more in support of substantive specificities, theologians can enjoy the borrowed status that comes from rubbing methodological shoulders with science. As one theologian has put it, 'In a postmodern world Christianity is intellectually relevant.' This strikes me as a bit too convenient. A blanket endorsement of intellectual relevance too easily allows a general reprieve of nonscientific inquiry to substitute for piecemeal defenses. (Cady 1991, 88f.)

I agree with Cady and Trigg that science deserves to be taken seriously. A facile pluralism is to be avoided. However, unlike Trigg, I do not accept the dichotomy: either an easy pluralism which diminishes the significance of science or a strong metaphysical basis. Rather, whether any particular 'metaphysical' assumptions are needed is to be explored in a more piecemeal fashion, through reflections on science and scientific insights about the world. In the final chapter of this study I will argue that science can be understood and accepted as a human practice guided by certain regulative ideals; such a naturalist view of science does not need a great deal of metaphysics [27]. I will also argue that our understanding of reality raises some questions, questions which are not themselves answered by science and thus may be considered as pointing beyond science to metaphysical issues, without, however, pointing to one particular metaphysical view [31]. I would like to leave this issue here for the moment. However, there is another claim about science which would point to something beyond science, namely Plantinga's claim that scientific epistemological naturalism requires ontological supernaturalism.

Plantinga-1: epistemological naturalism requires a supernaturalist ontology
Plantinga argues in his *Warrant and Proper Function* that 'a belief is warranted if it is produced by cognitive faculties functioning properly

(subject to no malfunctioning) in a cognitive environment congenial for those faculties, according to a design plan successfully aimed at truth' (Plantinga 1993, viiif.). He considers this a naturalist position, with naturalism taken in an epistemological (and definitely not an ontological) sense, since 'the only kind of normativity it invokes figures in such sciences as biology and psychology' (Plantinga 1993, 194). I consider his proposal on warrants for belief well-argued in his book. But in the last two chapters of his book (Plantinga 1993; references in this section are to this book) he argues that this epistemological naturalism requires metaphysical supernaturalism rather than naturalism. I distinguish three arguments, namely (a) ontological naturalism cannot give a satisfactory definition of the notion of 'proper function'; (b) it is unable to explain the occurrence of proper functioning faculties; and (c) 'metaphysical naturalism when combined with contemporary evolutionary accounts of the origin and provenance of human life is an irrational stance' (ix).

(a) Plantinga argues that there is no satisfactory naturalist analysis of the notion 'proper function'. He points to weaknesses of some contemporary proposals, especially by invoking (often somewhat artificial) counter-examples. For example, the claim that an organ functions properly cannot be logically equivalent with the claim that this is the way it functions most frequently; even if most older carpenters have lost a finger or a thumb, the lucky few with all ten digits would not be dysfunctional, and the fact that most baby turtles do not reach maturity does not make those that do dysfunctional (200f.). The contribution to reproduction is not a good criterion either; if in a certain culture broken legs are necessary to attract a mate, broken legs would contribute to reproductive success, but one would not ordinarily say that these broken legs function properly (204). Another potential definition overlooks systems which function properly only when the organism of which it is part is disrupted, such as a scab-forming mechanism (207).

If I grant for the sake of the argument that there is currently no completely satisfactory definition of proper function – though I think that an evolutionary understanding of proper function as advocated by Ruth G. Millikan (1984, 1993) is able to deal with the alleged counter-examples and objections – Plantinga's conclusion to the falsehood of naturalism does not follow. The absence of a satisfactory general naturalist definition of proper functioning is not evidence that there can be no such a definition. The definition may have eluded us so far. However, it is more likely that the request for a strict definition is too demanding. Biology is more piecemeal than physics, with fewer interesting general laws and the like; definitions which are interesting and have no exceptions are rare. However, the lack of a strict definition and the impossibility of assigning or denying proper functioning in all borderline cases and contrived examples need not inhibit the adequate use of the notion. Rather, some vagueness is typical of most (or perhaps of all) our notions. The main issue is not whether there is a satisfactory general definition of proper function – general in the sense of holding in all conceptually possible worlds – but *whether all actual instances can be understood in a naturalist way.*[23]

(b) Plantinga also argues that an evolutionary view is unable to explain the occurrence of proper functioning satisfactorily (in contrast to analysing or defining the notion), whereas a theistic view has no such problem: 'From a theistic perspective there is no problem in applying these notions to natural organisms, for (from that perspective) natural organisms have indeed been designed' (197). On the evolutionary view, you either cannot properly employ the notion of proper function, or you are challenged to give 'a satisfactory *naturalistic* explanation or analysis of the notion of proper function' (198).

The theistic position is not as satisfactory as Plantinga claims. While the evolutionist can explain rudimentary organs, inefficient design (by technical standards) and undesirable limitations to cognitive and other capacities as indications of a history of tinkering with available designs, Plantinga appeals to the unavoidability of trade-offs (38ff.). Such an explanation works well if there is a trade-off between two desirable features of a design. However, the appeal to 'trade-offs' does not answer cases where the apparent designer could have done better without, to the best of our knowledge, losing out elsewhere. In many cases, we are stuck with certain undesirable features which could have been remedied if the organism had been designed, but which, on an evolutionary view, could not yet disappear without a trace, and may even be unlikely ever to disappear except when the species and its descendants become extinct.

[23] Millikan (1989 (1993, 17–19)) discusses similar objections to her notion of 'proper functions'; according to her, such conceptual analysis is 'the misconceived child of a mistaken view of the nature of language and thought' (Millikan 1989 (1993, 15)).

Plantinga argues that there could be functions of natural organs or organisms which are beyond evolutionary explanation.

More generally, from a theistic perspective it could be true that many subsystems of our cognitive and affective systems have functions, and function properly, not because their functioning in that way promotes survival, but because it serves other ends: the possibility of a certain sort of knowledge, or of morality, or loyalty, or love, or a grasp of beauty, or something else. It is therefore obviously possible that such a system have a function that confers no survival-enhancing propensity at all. Indeed, it could be that its functioning properly should put its owners at something of a *disadvantage* with respect to survival. Since this state is clearly possible, it is possible that a thing have a function (and function properly) even if that way of functioning confers no sep [survival-enhancing propensity] upon its owner. This proposal therefore fails as a naturalistic analysis of proper function, and fails resoundingly. (209)

Given the possibility of a theistic perspective, there could be properly functioning systems which do not confer evolutionary advantage. However, evolution would only fail as a naturalist explanation of epistemic proper functioning in our world if there were *actual* cases where we have features which cannot be understood within an evolutionary perspective. Plantinga points to the ability to do higher mathematics and appreciation of beauty in art and nature. Below [24, 25] we will come to an evolutionary understanding of morality and religion; it seems that such 'higher' forms of behaviour can be understood in an evolutionary perspective, even if they do not always contribute to survival, as long as culture and the plasticity of human brains are taken into account. The ability to do advanced mathematics can be understood evolutionarily as the use of cognitive capacities which evolved for other purposes (plasticity), just as the ability to read evolved and spread in a relatively short span of time, probably without a corresponding change in the structure of the brain. Evolutionary theory may be wrong and there could be phenomena which are inexplicable, but that possibility does not count against an evolutionary view. The presence of capacities which in their current form do not contribute to survival, is not a sufficient argument.

The power of evolutionary explanations should not be underestimated; a more realistic analogue for the society where broken legs would confer an advantage in attracting a mate (see above, a) is the peacock's tail, which is probably much longer than is optimal for flying and walking. Male peacocks who are able to grow a long tail, and furthermore are able to do well despite the burden of such a long tail, may be attractive mates – and once tail-length has become a criterion for attractiveness, they become even more attractive since their sons are likely to have long tails as well, and thus to be attractive too.

The mere possibility that inexplicable features logically could have existed does not count against the possibility of a naturalist understanding of our world. The issue is to some extent empirical: are there any features which are evolutionarily unintelligible? Candidates, such as social behaviour from which non-relatives benefit, or examples of unpractical display such as the peacock's tail, may be explicable within an evolutionary scheme (see below, [24]).

(c) Plantinga also argues that a naturalist, evolutionary view is irrational. An evolutionist would have to see as the ultimate purpose of our cognitive faculties 'something like *survival* (of individual, species, gene, or genotype); but then it seems initially unlikely that among their functions – ultimate, proximate, or otherwise – would be the production of true beliefs' (218).

On an evolutionary view, there is no need to oppose these two ways of proper functioning. One can well understand why legs (or hands, wings, or fins) are good for locomotion in the relevant environment and why they contribute to survival; there is no need to oppose these. Similarly, the ability to acquire true beliefs about our environment ('there is an apple in that tree') is as intelligible as having the ability to climb and get hold of the apple.

There is, of course, a further disagreement about the extent to which our beliefs are true, especially in the representational sense, or effective in a more pragmatic sense. Plantinga claims that an evolutionist should, on his view of our cognitive faculties, be sceptical with respect to the truth of our beliefs. If our cognitive faculties arose to promote survival, they could do so in various ways – by endowing us with the possibility of having beliefs which are true (or approximately true and only so in circumstances relevant to survival) or by endowing us with false beliefs which none the less generate adequate behaviour. We could do the right things on the basis of wrong beliefs. Plantinga gives the example of running away from a tiger. Paul could do so because he desires to pet that big pussy-cat, and he thinks that running away is the best way to get that nice pussy-cat to be petted by him. Or he could confuse running away from, and running towards, a tiger. Or he could have formed the resolution to run a mile at top speed whenever presented with the illusion of a tiger. Or he may believe that the appearance of the tiger is the starting signal of a race he wants to win. And so on (225f.). Since our beliefs need not be true to be survival-enhancing, Plantinga argues that on a naturalist view the reliability of our beliefs might be less than 50 per cent. Since we take our beliefs to be reliable, this counts against the naturalist view. On a theistic view there is no such problem. In that case, we should ascribe a high reliability to our cognitive faculties, since upon that view we are created in God's image, and thus may have cognitive faculties which correspond imperfectly to God's epistemic faculties.

The thought-experiment which establishes the low probability has a clause which I consider to be of major importance (as clauses about the background are in general decisive when the relevance of any thought experiment is assessed; see [15] and Wilkes (1988, ch.1)): '(Of course we must postulate other changes in Paul's ways of reasoning, including how he changes belief in response to experience, to maintain coherence)' (225). This clause reveals the strange character of Plantinga's thought experiment. He has to assume that Paul modifies his beliefs in response to his experiences in a way which does not improve the quality of his beliefs, not even in the long run. Rather, Paul modifies false beliefs about the environment into other equally false beliefs which are coherent and which generate appropriate behaviour given the true state of affairs in the environment. Plantinga seems to exclude piecemeal improvement, both of our belief-forming mechanisms and of our beliefs, in continuous interaction with the environment. We would rather expect that since our environment is causally involved in the formation of our beliefs and concepts, we may expect these concepts to match that environment. It is reported that the Innuit developed words for different kinds of snow, whereas one would not expect an adequate language about snow near the equator (except for words for snow on high mountains).

Plantinga argues that the case against evolution is even stronger for those areas of knowledge which are (and have been) irrelevant to survival and reproduction, such as the more theoretical parts of science (Plantinga 1993, 232f). This is also unwarranted. The point is that structures and faculties previously selected for other purposes may be applied to new ones. For example, reading is (evolutionarily speaking) a fairly recent invention, and therefore not likely to have become hardwired in the structure of the brain. However, most humans are able to learn to read, using structures which were adaptive for some other purpose, perhaps reading animal tracks. This plasticity (and capacity for learning) is more pronounced when humans are young.

Plantinga claims: 'Naturalistic epistemology conjoined with naturalistic metaphysics leads *via* evolution to scepticism or to violation of canons of rationality; conjoined with theism it does not' (237). In this section I have argued that this is mistaken with respect to the implications of evolutionary theory and that it requires too strict canons of rationality, in definitions and in the demands of dealing with logically possible but fictitious counter-examples. There could be such counter-examples; evolution could be a false belief about the world. However, one has to come up with actual counter-examples to show that it is a false belief. I have also argued that the theistic position is not as simple and safe as Plantinga suggests, especially when one considers examples of imperfect apparent design.

Plantinga-2: Methodological naturalism is wrong; we need theistic science
In the preceding section, we considered epistemological naturalism. Plantinga argued that metaphysical naturalism is unable to offer an analysis of, and explanation for proper functioning epistemic faculties. However, he also holds that our belief-forming mechanisms have led us seriously astray in science: we need a quite different kind of science than that which is most commonly practised. We need to abandon 'methodological naturalism'. The two terms need to be distinguished. Whereas 'epistemological naturalism' refers to canons of rationality, namely that the same normativity that is accepted in biology and psychology is to be invoked when we consider other epistemic projects (Plantinga 1993, 194), 'methodological naturalism' refers to approaches to the world that seek to understand processes exclusively in terms of natural causes without drawing on information from the Bible (Plantinga 1991). Thus, 'methodological naturalism' is close to metaphysical or ontological naturalism, which he considers to be the adversary of theism, whereas epistemological naturalism is a different issue, actually – according to him – resulting in a defeater of ontological naturalism.

    Plantinga writes that the difference between the kind of science which he proposes, which he calls 'Augustinian science' or 'theistic science', and contemporary modern science is more pronounced in human and social sciences than in the natural sciences, but he has also taken a very critical stance with respect to evolutionary biology. We will discuss evolution in some sections in chapter 4, but here I will comment briefly on this other discussion Plantinga is involved in (with, apparently, for him the same purpose as in the arguments developed on the basis of epistemic naturalism, namely in order to refute ontological naturalisms informed by evolutionary biology).

The biological realm provides examples of adaptations more wonderful than the intricate design of watches. The complex coherence of organisms suggested design to William Paley (*Natural Theology*, 1802). Richard Dawkins agrees, in his *The Blind Watchmaker*, that biological complexity is impressive. He thus considers theism to have been appealing until there was a naturalist explanation: 'although atheism might have been *logically* tenable before Darwin, Darwin made it possible to be an intellectually fulfilled atheist' (Dawkins 1986, 6).

   To Alvin Plantinga, Dawkins' claim confirms that secular science is part of the battleground in the struggle 'between the Christian community and the forces of unbelief' (Plantinga 1991, 30), or, referring to Augustine, between the City of God and the City of Man (Plantinga 1993a). Christians need to develop their own science, resisting the methodological atheism assumed by secular scientists.

'Unnatural Science', 'Creation Science,' 'Theistic Science' – call it what you will: what we need when we want to know how to think about the origin and development of contemporary life is what is most plausible from a Christian point of view. What we need is a scientific account of life that isn't restricted by that methodological naturalism. (Plantinga 1991, 29)

Plantinga accepts as plausible that the age of the Earth might be billions of years, but he objects to the common ancestry of all life, to the Darwinian explanation of evolution, and to naturalist theories of the origin of life. Just like Dawkins, Plantinga also assumes a similarity with respect to the issues addressed by science and by theology: special creation and evolution are competing and conflicting claims, and the Bible offers knowledge relevant to theories of biological history (see also [9, 23]).

   The atheist Dawkins and the Christian philosopher Plantinga are allies in presenting us with a choice between two conflicting options. Their common adversaries are those who try to have both secular science and genuine religion. The attempt to have both has been developed in various ways, both orthodox and liberal, both through separation and through integration and modification. In response to Plantinga, Ernan McMullin argued that evolution reflects our best available understanding of the way living organisms came into being in God's creation, which is the whole natural world (McMullin 1991, 77, see also [31]; for an extensive critique of Plantinga's position see also McMullin 1993), while the astronomer Howard van Till argued for 'categorical complementarity' of the issues pursued by science and those pursued by religion (Van Till 1991, 39–42; see also Van Till 1986).

Even if one considers Plantinga's objections to the modern evolutionary explanation of the origin of species and to the empirical evidence in favour of it to be completely mistaken, as I do (see [24]), this does not do away with his general thesis about the presence of religious elements in science. This thesis resembles our earlier observation about the role of metaphysical issues in the controversies surrounding Darwin's theory of evolution (above, [8]). Speaking of 'Bauplans', 'Ur forms', and 'typology' (Plantinga 1991a, 104) is similar to Owen's invocation of archetypes. It expresses a metaphysical perspective which does not fit Darwin's theory. Similarly, one might point out that metaphysical disagreements about time, contingency, and necessity underlie the variety of research programmes in contemporary cosmology (Drees 1990, 62–7; 1991a, 384–7). However, even if one accepts the presence of such metaphysical elements in scientific research programmes, Plantinga's plea for theistic science is still unsatisfactory for at least two reasons.

Plantinga's plea for theistic science conflates religious and metaphysical convictions. The view of special creation corresponding to archetypes is Neoplatonic, not necessarily Christian. There is genuine diversity among Christians with respect to such metaphysical issues. Portraying the interaction as a struggle between two contending parties ignores the diversity among Christians, locating all those who have another opinion on the metaphysical issues in the camp of the enemy, rather than treating them as fellow Christians. Explicitly addressing metaphysical issues would have had the disadvantage (for Plantinga's case) to grant more room to other elements than Scripture, and thus to introduce more plurality into the debate, which he presents as a struggle between two parties.

Another objection concerns the level at which one considers the competition, if any, between religious views and secular science. Though not espousing a completely literalist reading of Scripture, Plantinga confronts Scripture with elements of Darwinian evolutionary theory. In taking the Bible as basic, he still has to explicate how to interpret Scripture. Furthermore, such an approach is in danger of *ad hoc*ness with respect to criticisms of scientific theories, criticising a few steps rather than dealing with the theory as a whole. It would be more adequate to discuss the theory as a whole, focusing for instance on the exhaustiveness of evolutionary explanations, the notion of explanation involved, and its compatibility with an understanding of the evolutionary world as God's creation. 'Secular science versus theistic science' seems the wrong level of discussion, as the discussions are about world views in which scientific insights are embedded. Disagreements about world views may be reflected in disagreements in science, and about the scope and aims of science. However, this is not a direct contribution from religion to science, but an indirect one, via the dispute about world views.

4

Theology and knowledge of human nature

In the preceding chapters we considered ideas on issues such as divine action in the world, ways of using science in theology, and realism in science and in theology. Someone who is uncomfortable with my conclusions may argue for a different outcome on one or more of these issues. Another option, however, is to argue that the discussion was misconceived since the character of religion was wrongly construed.

One way to question the relevance of knowledge of the world to religion could be to emphasise the distinction between God and the world, and argue that therefore God's mode of creative action is not to be understood along lines similar to our understanding of natural processes in the world. Such a distinction may be articulated as one between temporal processes and an a-temporal divine creative and sustaining act [13.3]. If the difference between God and the natural world is strongly emphasised, it seems less relevant to consider implications of the natural sciences for theology. However, such an advantage is also a liability: due to the strong claim that divine and natural action are different, it may become totally unclear how to think of God's relation to the world, or, if the imagination is fertile enough to propose some models, any model may appear to be totally irrelevant, at best a mere option which might be attached to one's view of the world and one's way of life [31.3]. In order to avoid irrelevance, a 'transcendentalising' move, where God is understood as the atemporal ground of being or in some other abstract way which avoids direct confrontation with the natural sciences, is often supplemented with belief that we have come to intimate this divine reality, either through particular experiences of ourselves or via a tradition which relates us back to predecessors considered authoritative.

Another way to distance ourselves from the discussion with the natural sciences is to opt for a non-cognitive view of religion. In earlier sections [3.2, 5] I adopted distinctions made by G. Lindbeck in distinguishing three different emphases in the understanding of religion, namely on cognitive, propositional claims, on experience and expression, and on religion as a guiding, culture-shaping tradition. The last two views of religion surfaced also in the analysis of historiographies when we discussed authors such as John Dillenberger and Michael Buckley who argued that theology has surrendered itself too much to a certain kind of interaction with the natural sciences, and thereby has become alienated from its genuine basis [11]. Thus, one might attempt to stay aloof from discussions on the theological implications of scientific knowledge about the world with the claim that – on the view of religion one holds – cognitive claims are irrelevant.

Such strategies do not deliver religion from engagement with the sciences. When the emphasis is on experience and tradition, either in an attempt to supplement an abstract philosophical theology or as the primary basis of theology, the encounter with the natural sciences is not primarily to be found in physics, but rather in those areas of the natural sciences that most directly influence ideas about human nature, such as the neurosciences and evolutionary biology. The neurosciences relate most intimately to our understanding of experience, consciousness, etc., whereas an evolutionary perspective relates more directly to religions as traditions which shape human lives. There will first be some sections on human experience (chapter 4-A), thereafter some sections on evolution and religion (chapter 4-B); each group of sections begins with a more specific introduction of its own.

A. EXPERIENCES NATURALISTICALLY REINTERPRETED

> Whenever theology touches science, it gets burned. In the sixteenth century astronomy, in the seventeenth microbiology, in the eighteenth geology and paleontology, in the nineteenth Darwin's biology all grotesquely extended the world-frame and sent churchmen scurrying for cover in ever smaller, more shadowy nooks, little gloomy ambiguous caves in the psyche, where even now neurology is cruelly harrying them, gouging them out of the multifolded brain like wood lice from under the lumber pile.   (Updike 1986, 32)

A 'Rediscovery of Inner Experience', to paraphrase the title of a book by Bregman (1982), appears to be widespread in Western cultures. Advocates of inner experience deal with dreams, often with references to C. G. Jung, with day-dreaming and fantasy, mystical experience and peak experiences (A. Maslow), with madness (R. D. Laing), with sexuality (e.g., the female orgasm as 'a genuine way of restoring to ourselves a more primordial harmony with the cosmos', Bregman 1982, 102), and with dying as *the* ultimate experience of one's life (e.g., Elisabeth Kübler-Ross). The 'psychological religiousness' has developed mostly outside the churches though to some extent it has been integrated with the pastoral and theological work of the churches. The limits of this market are not yet in sight:

Inner experiences could also be promoted by airlines; the mystical potential of above-the-clouds flight is real enough, and might be publicized as a way to get the most out of flying. By stressing the extraordinariness of flight, passengers would have the chance to transcend their usual preoccupations and participate in a new awareness of nature's immensity. Airlines could offer brief training classes for passengers. (Bregman 1982, 137)

Christianity too has been called to return from doctrine, metaphysics, and biblicism to experience. 'Inference cannot substitute for experience, and the most compelling witness to a personal God must itself be personal' (Buckley 1988, 99; see also [11]). Granting priority to experience is not new in Christianity; one might think of pietism and revivals during the eighteenth and nineteenth century, Friedrich Schleiermacher's emphasis on the feeling of absolute dependence in the early nineteenth century, and the interest in William James' *Varieties of Religious Experience* (1902) and Rudolf Otto's *The Holy* (1917).

The turn towards experience may seem to relate positively to science, which from its beginning has been marked by a move from authority and metaphysics to empirical adequacy. However, whereas a theology which builds cognitive claims upon science is in danger of asking more from science than it is able to deliver [chapter 3], I will argue that approaches emphasising experience run the risk of taking less from science than it might have to offer. There are links between feelings of love and hormones, and some explain ethical behaviour as indirect reciprocal altruism [24] and voices of the gods as communication between the right and the left hemisphere of the brain [20.3]. When we come to experience, there is less reason to emphasise grand cosmological themes about the origin and explanation of everything. There is the temptation to take extraordinary claims as attractive for religion. However, the nature of science is more clearly exhibited in a critical attitude towards the extraordinary than in an easy acceptance of such claims. In my opinion, one should seek a 'reverse eclecticism' [16] when one attempts to understand the prospects for religion in our time. If we face the most challenging, most naturalist understanding of human nature, the results may be limited, but they will carry more intellectual weight. One has to consider the way the natural sciences, and the cognitive sciences building upon them, cover human behaviour and human experiences in naturalist terms. Can one say, with the vivid image of Updike quoted above, that believers have been 'scurrying for cover in ever smaller, more shadowy nooks, little gloomy ambiguous caves in the psyche, where even now neurology is cruelly harrying them, gouging them out of the multifolded brain like wood lice from under the lumber pile'?

In this section, 4-A, I seek to explore the possibility of a naturalist understanding of religious experiences and our mental life. The aim is not to discuss in detail current knowledge to be found in the neurosciences and psychology, but to understand how religion and its relation to the sciences may be approached in this kind of discussion. This part concludes with a more general reflection on relations between various descriptions, and thus on reduction and elimination. We will have to note that science *accounts for our experiences differently* than we would do otherwise. This aspect of science is often labelled reductionism, though it might perhaps be perceived better as a shift in understanding, and could even be labelled a form of holism – as it seeks to fit the understanding of all phenomena into a single scheme. Central to the position here is the fourth element in my initial definition of naturalism, that is its *conceptual and explanatory non-reductionism* (CEN), namely that 'the description and explanation of phenomena may require concepts which do not belong to the vocabulary of fundamental physics, especially if such phenomena involve complex arrangements of constituent particles or extensive interactions with a specific environment'.

19. EXPERIENCE AS EVIDENCE OF GOD?

Do we perceive God? What is the evidential force of religious experience? Some have argued for a positive answer to such questions on the basis of similarities between religious experience and experience of worldly objects. We will consider two arguments to this effect. The philosopher of religion Richard Swinburne has argued that the credulity with which we accept experiences of natural objects should also be applied to religious experiences. Another philosopher, William

Alston, has argued that believers are justified in taking religious experiences as experiences of God, despite the inherent circularity, since we accept a similar circularity with respect to ordinary sense perception and other belief-forming practices. I will argue that neither approach is satisfactory.

Before coming to the arguments, let me indicate very briefly some of 'the varieties of religious experience', to quote William James's title. Six broad categories may be used (Davis 1989, 32–65). Sometimes events are *interpreted as* religiously significant, and the interpretation is based on an existing religious framework, rather than due to any unusual features of the experience. There are *quasi-sensory* experiences, such as visions and dreams, voices, or the sensation of being touched. Flashes of insight, moments of inspiration, sudden convictions, and perhaps even mystical visions may be called *revelatory*. Perhaps most common are *regenerative* experiences, such as finding oneself with new hope and strength, experiences of comfort, healing, forgiveness, and joy, especially if obtained in a religious context, such as during prayer. More dramatic are *numinous* experiences, experiences of the divine with its terrifying glory and unapproachable holiness, accompanied by enhanced creature consciousness (Otto 1917). In *mystical* experiences one apprehends an ultimate reality, with a sense of freedom from limitations of space, time, and the individual ego.

This is quite a mixed collection. The existence of such experiences – as described by the individuals who had them – is not disputed here. The Religious Experience Research Unit in Oxford, founded in 1969 by the zoologist Sir Alister Hardy, has collected a wide variety of specimens of such experiences, in anecdotes and accounts (Hardy 1979, Hay 1990). Their conclusion is that 'religious or transcendent experience in contemporary Western society ... is widespread and that, in a word, it is normal' (Hay 1990, vii). Anti-religionists who dismiss religious experience as non-existent are not fair with respect to genuine experiences of honest and able persons (see below, [20]).

Once their existence as experiences is granted, the question arises of how the experiences should be evaluated, what they imply about God or about human nature. In general, the most satisfactory interpretation of widespread experiences need not be the one most obvious to common sense. As an analogy from physics, we may recall that for millennia it was considered natural that terrestrial objects spontaneously came to a halt; sustained motion required a persistent force. This is still one of the many common-sense insights that a physics teacher needs to overcome. Physics since Newton has interpreted sustained motion as natural; coming to a halt implies friction, a resisting force. Without denying the experiences as experienced subjectively, we need to consider whether we should take them credulously as experiences of God.

Swinburne's Principle of Credulity

If it seems to me that there is a table there, I assume that there is a table there. If it seems to a subject that an object is present, then probably that object is present. Perception is *prima facie* evidence for existence. The English philosopher of religion Swinburne considers such a Principle of Credulity a fundamental principle of rationality.[1]

From this it would follow that, in the absence of special considerations, all religious experiences ought to be taken by their subjects as genuine, and hence as substantial grounds for belief in the existence of their apparent object – God, or Mary, or Ultimate Reality, or Poseidon. (Swinburne 1979, 254; 1981, 186)

Swinburne holds that there is a specific reason to be credulous about experiences of God, compared with credulity about experiences of Poseidon or Mary: 'if there is a God, any experience which seems to be of God, will be genuine – will be of God', as 'any causal processes at all which bring about my experience will have God among their causes' (Swinburne 1979, 270, taking up an argument from Wainwright 1973; 1981, 70ff.).

The claim that, if there is a God, *any* experience of God will be genuine, is too generous; 'it would mean experiences such as the Yorkshire Ripper's [who acted, allegedly, in response to a divine voice] must be considered veridical perceptions of God' (Davis 1989, 226). It is not sufficient to count as a perception of God that God is involved somewhere, say in upholding the laws of nature. I do not, while looking at a wooden chair, perceive the early history of the universe, nor even the tree out of which the chair was made, even though both are causally involved in the chair's existence. I will leave this problem aside here, and focus on Swinburne's principle of credulity.

In my view, the principle of credulity is either uninformative or wrong. If one stresses the *prima facie* which qualifies the principle, the principle of credulity is uninformative, since all the work still has to be done.

---

[1] Plantinga (1993, 33) traces this 'principle of credulity' back to the eighteenth-century originator of Scottish common-sense philosophy, Thomas Reid.

One still needs to understand when which experiences are to be trusted. More relevant in the present context is the claim that perception of an object counts as evidence for its existence, a claim which, I will argue, is wrong when it is applied without discrimination.

Swinburne opposes such credulity to scepticism. 'Initial scepticism about perceptual claims – regarding them as guilty until proved innocent – will give you no knowledge at all. Initial credulity is the only attitude a rational man can take; there is no half-way house' (Swinburne 1981, 195). Swinburne opposes two extremes to be applied across the board, denying any discrimination. However, credulity is developed as an infant explores her world, and the child learns to apply credulity with discrimination – not to jokes, not to dreams, not to promises made under certain conditions, etc. We do not live by a general principle of credulity, nor by a general principle of scepticism. Nor does science assume one of these principles. Quite often one accepts a theory provisionally, thus living in 'a half-way house' between credulity and scepticism; the precise attitude often depends on the relation between a particular claim and the background of explicit and implicit knowledge, including judgements about the reliability of various sources.

The Principle of Credulity is not an ultimate principle of rationality, but an *inference* justified on the basis of past experience. We do accept it for tables, since almost each time when it seemed there was a table, we were able to put things on it. We are less credulous about the content of dreams or about the convergence of railroad tracks towards the horizon, as our past experiences have not confirmed the reality of what seemed to us to be the case. If the inference from 'what seems to me to be the case' to 'what is the case' is based upon past success, it is dubious whether such inferences can be made in the religious realm. Unlike our past experiences with tables, corroboration of religious experience is not as straightforward as putting plates on a table or knocking on it. Earlier, we considered problems in the transfer of various strategies for the defence of realism from science to theology, due to the fact that they did not have a similar record of instrumental success [17]. The same problems arise when we go from credulity with respect to sense experience to credulity about religious experience.

An apparently more modest version of Swinburne's argument has been developed by the philosopher Caroline Franks Davis (1989). Rather than defending general credulity in all instances, she has argued that Swinburne's principle of credulity is helpful if there are two competing explanations. On her interpretation of the Principle of Credulity, a reductionist account must not just be shown to be plausible, 'but to be *more* probable than an explanation which preserves the veridicality of religious experiences' (Davis 1989, 228). If a naturalist and a religious explanation fare equally well, then one should prefer the credulous, *i.e.* religious one, because (by the principle of credulity) 'an explanation which preserves a perceptual experience's veridicality is always *prima facie* more probable than an explanation which does not' (Davis 1989, 228).

This interpretation of the principle of credulity is unfair. If the two explanations are equally probable (if one could ever make such a quantitative claim sufficiently specific) since they both account equally well for the phenomena as they appear to the subjects, the naturalist explanation already has had to account for the experiences of the subjects (and not only for the phenomena 'out there'). If the naturalist explanation accounts equally well for the experiences of the subjects, there is nothing more that it should do, nor is there any further reason to save the veridicality of the experiences.

Alston's defence of circularity

The philosopher William Alston does not seek to justify religious experience as evidence acceptable to a non-believer. He defends the view that people who already believe in God are not irrational when they interpret religious experiences as experiences about God. The circularity involved is not fatal; we accept a similar circularity with respect to ordinary sense perception (Alston 1991, 143f.). In emphasising the rationality of whole practices, he is less 'atomistic' than Swinburne in his use of credulity with respect to individual experiences (Alston 1991, 195).

Alston's main arguments concentrate on non-sensory mystical perception.[2] He accepts the idea 'that every conscious experience is

[2] A special problem with respect to sensory perception is that we are considering the perception of an immaterial being as if it were material. We are used to perceptions which deviate with respect to details from what an object is like: 'a square tower may look round from a distance; a white object may look red under certain lighting; and so on. More fundamentally, there is a long tradition that holds that secondary qualities like colors do not really characterize physical substances. Thus it is not inconceivable that God should appear to us as looking bright or sounding a certain way, even though He does not, in His own nature, possess any sensory qualities' (Alston 1991, 19). The distinction between secondary qualities (as perceived) and primary qualities (as true of the underlying reality) is a variant of the Aristotelian distinction between form and essence. However, perceiving God as a material being while maintaining that God is an immaterial being lacking all sensory qualities, seems to make significantly more of the difference between primary and secondary qualities than is usual for ordinary perception.

proximately caused by neurophysiological happenings in the brain' (Alston 1991, 231). Sense perception is none the less perception of something else, as it is influenced by the light reaching the retina and by sound waves entering the ears. Similarly, a tight link between religious experiences and neurophysiological processes would not count against the validity of the experiences as experiences about something beyond us, since, as he argues in the same way as Swinburne (above), if God exists, 'God figures somewhere among the causal conditions of any occurrence whatsoever' (Alston 1991, 232). He accepts that God's involvement is not a sufficient condition to make something into a mystical perception of God, since that would imply that every experience was an experience of God. But if God were not involved it would certainly be impossible to consider a religious experience to be an experience of God.

With respect to God's involvement, Alston sees no contradictions between established scientific results and central Christian doctrines. Miracles would not be a problem either; 'the odd miracle would not seem to violate anything of importance for science. It would be quite a remarkable coincidence if a miracle should be among the minute proportion of the cases of X that are examined for scientific purposes' (Alston 1991, 244). The genuine conflict for Alston is a conflict with a 'naturalistic metaphysics'. However, both a naturalist and a theistic understanding of mystical experiences have their place in the context of world views. Thus, both are to some extent caught in a circularity with respect to the question of whether they include or exclude any realm beyond the material. If we accept sensory perception (with its circularity), we cannot deny the legitimacy of mystical perception. '*Any* doxastic [belief-forming] practice that is not grossly internally inconsistent can be strongly supported if epistemic circularity is allowed. We just use the practice to determine the facts reported by the practice; since it will all agree with itself, it will turn out that it is inevitably correct' (Alston 1991, 143). If we impose restrictions upon religious practices which we do not impose upon science or common-sense perception, we illegitimately use a 'double standard'.

I have already argued that an 'odd miracle' would violate something 'of importance for science' [13]. Later [22] I will consider the way reductionistic explanations in the sciences challenge references to non-natural, transcendent factors [22]. Here I will concentrate on the core of Alston's argument, which seems to me to be the claim that mystical perceptions are dependent upon doxastic (belief-forming) practices (such as the Christian Mystical Perceptual Doxastic Practice), which cannot be defended in a non-circular way, but which none the less can be considered rational and reliable, since we also accept such forms of circularity for practices such as sense-perception and natural science which we consider reliable.

Even though, on Alston's view, there is no non-circular justification of practices, there may still be some justification for a practice, namely 'significant self-support'. Alston mentions two forms of self-support for sense-perception [SP]. (1) The practice is fruitful; we can make predictions, many of which turn out to be correct, and we can to some extent control events. (2) 'By relying on SP and associated practices we are able to establish facts about the operation of sense perception that show both that it is a reliable source of knowledge and why it is reliable' (Alston 1991, 173). Other practices may not have, and need not have the same forms of self-support. Beliefs about God do not result in predictive efficacy, but they provide 'effective guidance to spiritual development' (174).

According to Alston, significant self-support is always circular. He therefore refrains 'from taking it to be an independent reason for supposing the doxastic practice in question to be reliable' (174). Rather, Alston defends a holist stance towards justification of practices: '*a firmly established doxastic practice is rationally engaged in provided it and its output cohere sufficiently with other firmly established doxastic practices and their output*' (175). Apart from the coherence with other practices, there is no way to evaluate a practice; 'there is no appeal beyond the doxastic practices to which we find ourselves firmly committed' (177).

I agree with Alston that there is no appeal beyond the collection of practices, but I consider his emphasis on practices as wholes mistaken. In science we have differential epistemic justification, rather than justification of a whole practice at once. Science can be understood as a collection of a wide variety of interacting individual cognitive practices, each consisting of various components such as concepts, theories, techniques, questions (e.g., Kitcher 1993; see [27]). Justification is the collective result of all the justificatory efforts directed at specific insights, procedures, questions, concepts, etc. Piecemeal change makes it possible to justify the various elements of science, despite the presence of a global circularity in justification, namely the dependence of any justification of science on current science. Defending another practice despite circularity requires a detailed analysis of the justification of piecemeal changes within such a practice, rather than a global argument about the circularity of science and sense-perception. Such an analysis would not provide a general justification of a practice, but rather result in differential justification of its claims.

Differential justification arises when we study the sense organs, as Alston notes when considering 'self-support' of our ordinary sense perception practice (Alston 1991, 173, 250). We can study the ears, and thereby learn about limitations to the sound frequencies accessible to humans. Similarly, we can study the eyes, and learn that they may lead us astray when images are flashed in front of us many times a second, a phenomenon which allows us to make movies from sequences of static images. We do not have to take the information provided by our sense organs for granted, but can rather study the possibilities and limitations of these organs. In the case of religious experience, we seem to lack knowledge corresponding to the knowledge of the sense organs (Donovan 1979, 51). It could be that the analogy between religious experience and sense perception is mistaken. Another possible interpretation of this dissimilarity between religious and scientific experiences, may be that we are ignorant about these processes, an ignorance which some might defend theologically. However, such ignorance would inhibit one from building up confidence in the mystical perceptual doxastic practice on the basis of increased knowledge about the relevant ways the perceptual beliefs were generated.

20. A NATURALIST VIEW OF RELIGION: RELIGION AND THE BRAIN

The heart has its reasons which reason does not know. (Blaise Pascal)

Religion is often seen as a matter of 'the heart', not of reason. The heart symbolises love, desire, and passion. The heart is uncontrollable and sometimes contradictory. One does not decide to fall in love; one falls in love – it simply happens. At least, that is how falling in love is often thought of. In the Christian tradition the heart has a similar symbolic value, even though the mind is called upon as well in the command to love God (Matthew 22: 37).

Since 1967, human hearts have been transplanted into other humans. During surgery, machines may take over the functions of heart and lungs. The associations attached to the 'heart' have no root in the plain reality of this muscle which pumps the blood through the body. Even though the rhythm of the heart is affected by emotions, it is not the seat of all that has been attached to the symbol. The passions of 'the heart' mainly have to do with the brain, and to a lesser extent also with the spinal cord and the hormonal glands. The brain is not a cool calculator; all the confusing and contradictory feelings of 'the heart' originate there. We will briefly describe its complexity before turning to some ideas about religious rituals (and non-conscious functions of the brain) and about the neurophysiological basis for religious experiences. Before developing along such lines the view that religious experiences are rooted in our constitution, I will consider (and reject) the suggestion that religious experiences should be understood as pathological.

20.1. Pathological explanations

Only oedipal apes can have religion. (La Barre 1991, 146)

There is a variety of explanations of religious experiences as pathological phenomena. An otherwise healthy body and mind may have been set off-track by drugs. Sensory deprivation, which occurs when people are in deserts, on mountain peaks or in other isolated places, or by sitting in a quiet and dimly-lit chapel, may act similarly in inducing mystical experiences. It is thus not too amazing that a large proportion of seers have been drawn from the shepherd class all over Europe and Asia (Chadwick 1942, 59; Staal 1975, xii). Isolation, concentration, fasting, monotonous recitation, dancing or singing to the point of exhaustion, breathing exercises and other preparatory techniques have physiological consequences. Such 'explanations' of religious experiences are far from complete; they may explain why one person is more susceptible than others, but they do not come near to explaining the specific experience. Concepts and symbols, beliefs and traditions in a culture may explain more of the specifics, but even then, the combination of cultural symbols and physiological consequences of preparations do not thereby falsify the experience as an experience of something; one might hold that the preparations induce greater receptivity rather than 'cause' the experience.

Explanations may also refer to social factors, such as pressure from peers or parents, or effects of upbringing and indoctrination. Without entering into the debate on the status of psychoanalytical psychology in general, we will briefly consider here one Freudian explanation of a religious phenomenon. A survey of appearances of the Virgin Mary between 1100 and 1896 found that they occurred in about 80 per cent of the cases to sexually mature individuals without obvious sexual partners (Carroll 1983, 210). They also occur significantly more often in Italy than elsewhere.

The distribution of claimed appearances of Mary has been explained on the basis of family structures. In Italy, adult males spend more time away from their family than elsewhere, but the father regularly comes home to the family. Hence, according to Carroll, the bond between a son and his mother will be stronger than in Northern Europe (due to the father's absence), but it will be equally strongly suppressed (due to his regular presence). Therefore, Oedipal conflicts will be more prominent among Italian males than among males elsewhere. A religious sublimation oriented towards Mary, perpetually Virgin and hence not associated with sexual intercourse, will not activate the fear of the father (castration anxiety). Since the problem is more prominent in Italy than elsewhere, the solution will be more common in Italy than elsewhere. The argument for Marian apparitions to females resembles this argument, with minor differences since patterns of identification and sublimation are not the same in girls as in boys. Carroll concludes that:

> Marian apparitions derive from an especially strong sexual desire for the opposite-sex parent forming during the Oedipal period, and that such apparitions are most likely to occur when sexual outlets are blocked in later life. (Carroll 1983, 216)

The conclusion is an overstatement; the appearances need not 'derive from' the sexual desire, even though that may be one of the factors which contribute to a greater propensity towards such experiences. The explanation explains, at best, a greater frequency of such occurrences in Italy, not any actual occurrence.

The prospects for explaining all religious experiences as pathological are weak. The phenomenon of religion in all its variety is so widespread that more structural explanations seem to be called for, both evolutionary explanations – it has to serve some function or to be linked with something which was advantageous – and psychological explanations, in the structure of humans, for instance in the prolonged infancy and consequent dependency which distinguishes them from other animals (La Barre 1991). I will not focus on developmental psychology, though this is an interesting angle worth exploring, nor on the role of interaction with the environment, though that may be quite important to the understanding of religion (e.g., Arbib and Hesse 1986). Here, the attention is focused on the way spiritual life might be connected to the constitution of the normal, adult human brain.

20.2. The complexity of the brain

The brain is the most complex organ we have; scientific understanding of the brain is incomplete, though our knowledge has increased enormously during the last few decades. Since the brain is complex, it is hard to understand. However, if the brain were simpler, we would probably be too simple to understand much of it. The following is a little tour of this rich structure inside our skulls.

Nerve cells in the brain have many connections to each other. Ordinary building-blocks have six sides, and hence mostly six to fourteen neighbours. The hundred billion cells of the brain each have connections with thousands of other cells. Furthermore, these connections are not permanent; they can develop or disappear. This flexibility could be the basis for learning and memory.

Within the brain various subsystems can be distinguished. The oldest structures, evolutionarily speaking, are located close to the spinal cord. The medulla (brainstem) regulates involuntary functions such as respiration, circulation, and digestion. The cerebellum regulates movement and balance. The hypothalamus has to do with the production of hormones. Hunger and satisfaction are regulated here; uncontrollable eating disorders can be seen as a disturbance at this level. Even though full-fledged emotions are more closely connected to the next level (the limbic system), this deeper level regulates the expression of many emotions, for example blushing (even if you do not want to), compulsive laughing or crying, and blind anger. These structures evolved approximately 500 million years ago – long before the mammals became prominent.

Approximately 200 million years ago the limbic system evolved in our mammalian ancestors. Six structures located around the medulla and part of the cortex have to do with long-term memory, olfaction, and emotions. Many of these processes are not controlled by higher levels in the brain; sometimes one feels sad or angry even when one knows that this is not reasonable; you like someone even though you know he might be cheating you. Sometimes the older part is referred to as the reptilian brain, while this level is called the mammalian brain: the tears belong to the crocodile while the emotion itself is part of our horse-like nature.[3] The terminology should not be taken too seriously; crocodiles and horses are not ancestors of humans, but modern stages of other evolutionary lineages. And, more importantly for the understanding of humans, functions of lower parts of the human brain have changed with the development of further structures.

A third layer of structures is the neocortex, well developed in dolphins, apes, and especially in humans. Here various forms of perception and action are integrated; here too is the neurological correlate for our capacity to handle symbolic information such as language. The cortex consists of a left and a right hemisphere, which are connected at three places. The most prominent of these connections consists of hundreds of millions of links between cells on the two sides. Although the cortex appears to be fairly symmetric, the two hemispheres have different functions. The left hemisphere co-ordinates movements of most of the right side of the body, and vice versa. In most right-handed individuals, speech is located on the left side; spatial orientation is mostly located in the right hemisphere. In some severe cases of epilepsy, surgeons have cut some of the connections between the two hemispheres. Most tasks are performed adequately by these patients, but in some well-devised experiments remarkable examples of independent functioning of the two hemispheres have been recorded. For instance, a person was instructed to pick up with his hands pictures related to images displayed to him. The left hemisphere was shown a chicken's leg; the right hemisphere a snow scene. The right hand (left hemisphere) picked an image of a chicken; the left hand a shovel (for the snow). Both hemispheres properly identified the visual information, and made adequate associations. But asked to tell what he had seen and done, the subject reported that he had seen the chicken's leg, and therefore pointed out the chicken, and that the shovel was needed to clean the chicken-house. Apparently, the left hemisphere noticed that the left hand picked the shovel, and without hesitation made up a story to account for the actions (Kylstra 1983, 17; similar examples in Jaynes 1976, 114f.).

Tight links of chemical and structural aspects to emotional and mental aspects have been demonstrated in many ways. Remarkably specific effects of various localised disorders have been documented.

[3] The division into three structures became popular through Paul MacLean; I have taken examples from Vroon (1989).

Chemicals may have significant influences on our mental life. A classic example is the treatment with L-Dopa of patients who had been 'frozen' in decades-long periods of absentmindedness as a consequence of sleeping sickness (Sacks 1990).

In brief, the brain is a complex organ, which performs many functions. It is the organ of most major aspects of personality, both conscious and non-conscious.

20.3. Brains and religious rituals

Most religious rituals address our brains not only at the level of the cortex. Burning incense or a candle, with its specific smell and light, may well evoke memories of a 'world past'; smells reach into the limbic system. The regular pattern of liturgy with the repetition of well-known words may also appeal to deeper structures in our brains. Preaching may also affect us there, especially when it evokes feelings of guilt and sin, of powerlessness or acceptance. Stories are memorable; they are not dispensable vehicles for a cognitive argument, as there is more than the neocortex. Silence, meditation, and prayer affect the brain in different ways. When we close our eyes for a moment of silence, while we are awake, certain dominant processes are temporarily suspended, and other processes may become more prominent. What these will be depends on the environment, on our preparation, on our personal biography, and on our culture with its symbols and concepts.

Some aspects of liturgy may also relate to the differences between the dominant (mostly left) hemisphere and the less dominant one. Music is dealt with mostly in the right hemisphere, whereas spoken and written words speak to the left hemisphere. Songs may have an emotional meaning which surpasses a cool (left hemisphere) analysis of their words; upon analysis the words may well turn out to be outmoded and unacceptable. That liturgy often takes place in a special place – large, high, dimly lit – may well affect us also in less rational ways, and thus elicit a different response than the same words would elicit in a well-lit classroom.

Julian Jaynes has offered further speculations on potential connections between the left–right differentiation of the cortex and religion. He has argued that the modern understanding of ourselves as a conscious unity arose approximately three millennia ago in the period between Homer's *Iliad* and the later Greek philosophers, between the patriarchs of Israel and the time of the prophets. In fact, before the development of that unity of consciousness, 'the gods take the place of consciousness' (Jaynes 1976, 72). Voices of the gods, both as described in writings preceding the origin of a unitary consciousness and as heard by epileptics and schizophrenics or by a Joan of Arc, are signals from the right hemisphere received by the dominant, left one; they are received as if they come from elsewhere, rather than from another part of the same brain. Whatever the view of the religious implications, Jaynes' questioning of the unity of consciousness is supported by research on 'split-brain' patients (better, 'split-cortex', as other parts of the brain are left intact) and by analysis of the philosophical implications of various personality disorders (Wilkes 1988, 100–67).

What I seek to argue for here is simple: we do not know precisely what is happening inside our heads, for instance when participating in religious practices, but it is clear that meditation, singing, silence, burning candles or incense, and many other religious practices affect us in ways which are not entirely under our control. Dismissing rituals as useless and ineffective practices would be a mistake based upon too narrow an understanding of ourselves.

This does not imply that all rituals are good; whatever has power has potentials and risks. Horrible examples of mass psychology and of individuals suffering from their religious upbringing make it clear that a critical evaluation is also important. Nor does the reach of ritual into deeper layers of our brains imply that all practices need to be kept unchanged. Renewal is necessary in a changing culture, especially if the messages of religious practices in the deeper layers of the brain are to match with the information in the cortex. Otherwise they would not contribute to integration but to disintegration. Renewal need not be a reduction to cool argument and abstract ideal – the richness of traditions with stories and rituals and music correlates with the complexity of the brain.

Not just ritual is psychologically effective; religion in general relates to psychological needs, such as the need to cope with the challenges of life, with contingencies. As one could say in German, religion is a *Kontingenzbewältigungspraxis*. For instance, the theologian and psychotherapist Dietrich Ritschl (1986, 9f.) notes that the rise of the major religions concurred more or less with the transition from humans living as hunter-gatherers to a sedentary life-style, and the subsequent development of villages and cities. In the demanding new style of life, religion was a way of shaping the lives of individuals and communities, bridling aggression and stress. This is in a sense complementary to Jaynes' claim about the origin of consciousness during a later stage of human pre-history. On Ritschl's view, new demands on humans, individually and socially, which arose when agriculture developed, resulted in stress which was resolved in religion by introducing 'external', religious authorities (see also Jaynes 1976, 137), whereas, upon Jaynes' view, with the subsequent rise of integrated consciousness such an external authority was replaced by an increased sense of autonomy.

We will come back to the origin and function of religion when we consider evolutionary perspectives [24]. If one accepts that human nature, including human religious experiences, is tightly linked with the structure of our brains, how does this knowledge affect religion? One option is to seek to articulate important aspects of theology such as God's relation to us, in a way which is consistent with contemporary neuroscience. In the next section, we will consider one attempt to do so.

20.4. Neuroscience and experiences of the Absolute

Earlier we considered ideas about divine action in the openness of processes or as top–down causation [13]. A variant of such arguments is the idea that divine action is to be found in the processes going on in the brain. This idea has various attractive aspects. It will not be falsified easily, as the system is complex. The system is very sensitive; different outcomes of quantum processes may be amplified to macroscopically different states of the brain, and thereby to different mental states. The cosmologist and Quaker G. F. R. Ellis (1993, 396) uses the hiddenness of quantum processes in the brain and the brain's sensitivity to minor differences to argue that God may illuminate and guide us with an inner light, while at the same time allowing for a free response. He believes that such a view may be compatible both with human freedom and responsibility and with a recognition of the autonomy of the world; a view of divine action which would exclude human freedom would exacerbate problems about God's acceptance of and responsibility for evil. A problem with Ellis' view, apart from the questionable theological use of the superposition in quantum physics, is, in my opinion, that it seems indebted to the idea of an 'inner cinema' somewhere in the brain where 'I' see images – generated elsewhere in the brain in a process which at the quantum level is influenced by God – and where I freely respond, whereas I will argue in the next section that there is no such centre.

More specific about the detailed structure of the brain in relation to God has been Eugene d'Aquili, who seeks to understand 'the neuroepistemological status of the experience of the Absolute' (D'Aquili 1987, 375).[4] D'Aquili speaks about the experience of 'absolute unitary being', in which reality is viewed as a whole. This experience 'arises from the total functioning of the parietal lobe on the non-dominant side (or at least certain parts of that area)' (D'Aquili 1987, 377). The dominant hemisphere deals primarily with our perception of the external world in all its variety; the non-dominant one delivers – occasionally, when the dominant one is not dominant – 'the perception of absolute, unitary, atemporal being' (D'Aquili 1987, 378). More specifically, D'Aquili and Newberg focus on 'tertiary association areas', where we find 'the highest integration of sensory information ... We postulate that these areas, under certain conditions, may be involved in the genesis of various mystical states, the sense of the divine, and the subjective experience of God' (D'Aquili and Newberg 1993, 179). Among the conditions is a 'de-afferentation', which means that neural input into certain structures is 'cut off' (185), a situation which can be approached through meditation which intends to clear the mind of thoughts and words. As a consequence, a 'reverberating circuit' may be formed in the right hemisphere, increasing electrical activity until it spills over and stimulates certain other systems, 'resulting in ecstatic and blissful feelings' (187). 'We believe that this results in the subject's attainment of a state of rapturous transcendence and absolute wholeness which carries such overwhelming power and strength with it that the subject has the sense of experiencing absolute reality' (189). As an integral part of this process, including the de-afferentation, the role of the senses and also that of words and concepts is diminished. One comes to 'an absolute subjective sensation of pure space' (189) and obliteration of 'the self–other dichotomy' (193).

I abstain from an evaluation of the specific neurological mechanisms these authors have proposed above and, other writings on ritual, the shaman's journey, mature contemplation, and void

---

[4]   See also essays by Eugene d'Aquili, James Ashbrook, Roger W. Sperry, and Colwyn Trevarthen in Ashbrook (1993), and the essays in *Zygon* 28 (2 June 1993) dedicated to D'Aquili's contributions.

consciousness.[5] Which neurological processes in the brain are related to which experiences seems to me, in principle, an issue for empirical research, especially since the advent of non-invasive scanning techniques. Whatever the details, some mechanisms which inhibit certain pathways, and thereby inhibit certain forms of sensory input and of conceptual analysis, may well turn out to correlate with mystical states or other experiences considered religious. Of prime relevance in the context of this study is a different issue: if we can describe such neurological processes, does this support or undermine a naturalist view of religious experiences?

D'Aquili and his co-workers argue that their analysis should not be seen as reductionistic, as 'explaining away' either the phenomenon or the external referent. Doing so would be 'equivalent to maintaining that the person's experience of the "objective" reality of the sun, the earth, and the air we breathe is reducible to neurochemical flux' (D'Aquili, Newberg 1993, 197). We see two major modes of operation of the brain; the 'ordinary' one of perception and linguistic cognition, and the other one corresponding to some experience of absolute unitary being; the first is ruled primarily by the dominant hemisphere, the other by the non-dominant one. If we trust that we are in touch with reality via the dominant hemisphere, why would we not trust, so the argument goes, experiences governed by the other side? Hence:

it is possible to conclude that 'something out there' is being manifested in two modes. One mode is the everyday world that all people experience; the other is the world of ultimate wholeness often interpreted as God. I conclude further that each mode has equal reality since neither mode can be systematically reduced to the other. (D'Aquili 1987, 378)

The primacy of ordinary experience holds only from within that perspective; from within the other perspective there is no question about the reality of what is experienced thus.

The argument resembles defences of religious experience considered above [19]: if we take sense perception by the dominant hemisphere seriously as perception of the external world, then we should also take religious experience by the non-dominant hemisphere seriously as perception of reality. The argument faces similar problems (see also

[5] On ritual: D'Aquili, Laughlin, McManus (1979); on the shaman's journey, mature contemplation, and void consciousness: Laughlin, McManus, D'Aquili (1992). A criticism of the neurological circuits referred to by D'Aquili *et al.* has been given by Rodney Holmes (1993).

[17.2, 22]). In this case, the two hemispheres have co-evolved, but there is no need to say that they function in similar ways. In many respects, they function in complementary ways; certain structures are more involved in the perception of the world, others more in emotions or in creating (rather than perceiving) an encompassing perspective which allows for balanced action. It is not clear what external input this second type of experience would have; it may well be seen as an integration of earlier experiences of the individual and sense-experience (including the effects of position, smell, and the like). The more we understand how the brain is able to make up stories (such as in the example of the split-brain patient, explaining the acts of both his hands), the less reason there seems to be to assume any additional input.

The position of another neuroscientist illustrates this well. Roger Sperry won a Nobel prize for his work on split-brain patients. He has argued more recently that there is a new mentalist paradigm in psychology, which considers subjective mental states as 'legitimate, ineliminable explanatory constructs' (1988, 607). Since subjective phenomena such as purpose, value, and morality 'are vital to religion', this opens a way to overcome the contrast between science and religion as mutually exclusive world views. No longer do we have 'a value-devoid, physically driven cosmos, ultimately lacking in those humanistic attributes with which religion is most concerned' (608). However, this new understanding comes at a price: the new, mentalist approach in psychology 'opens the way for a consistent naturalistic foundation for both scientific and religious belief' (607).

I agree with Sperry that an increased understanding of processes in our brains has its 'price' (even though I do not therefore agree with other elements of his position). The view that some mental notions are 'ineliminable explanatory constructs' in no way supports a claim to the effect that religious experiences require any non-natural input. On the contrary, the more successful we are in understanding the richness of behaviour and experience that can be generated on the basis of natural processes, the less reason there is to invoke further elements in our understanding of reality. In the terms of the definition of naturalism presented in the beginning [2], conceptual and explanatory non-reductionism (CEN) does not conflict with ontological naturalism (ON) and constitutive reductionism (CR). We will come back on reduction below [22], but first, we will briefly consider contemporary discussions on consciousness. I will conclude that this too might be an ineliminable construct which none the less can perhaps be understood naturalistically.

21. A NATURALIST VIEW OF CONSCIOUSNESS

Humans are not only objects, whose behaviour can be described and studied by others (a third-person approach). They are also subjects, who have experiences and make decisions. In religious terms, they may be seen as persons who relate to God as an 'I' to a 'thou'. Is it possible to explain our sense of being a self-conscious person in a naturalist perspective? Subjectivity seems to be a major challenge to a naturalist view of reality. In this section, I point to philosophical literature which attempts to answer that challenge. This is not directly relevant to the understanding of religion, but it does away with one of the last ways of conceiving an ontological dualism in reality, namely a distinction between the mental and the material, just as earlier advances in knowledge removed other dualist models, such as the one relying on the distinction between heaven and earth. This supports the idea that a theological dualism of God and the natural world either has to stand on its own or is to be relinquished.

Who is the 'I' that sees and hears, that listens and speaks? How am I to think about the mind in relation to the brain? I first want to clear away a potential misunderstanding, namely that we are dealing with a small entity somewhere in our heads. This can be illustrated with a sketch of human vision. One may be tempted to think of vision as a process analogous to the way films are made. The eyes are the camera that collects light from the external world; the pictures they make are processed from the retina via the optical nerves to the brain, where I look at it, and respond to it with certain feelings and decisions to act. In my private cinema I am looking at the film of the outside world. But if one distinguishes the seeing of my eyes (seeing$_1$) from the seeing which happens inside (seeing$_2$), where 'I' look at the film, what would this second process of seeing be? Is there a minute 'I' in there, with eyes to see$_2$? If so, what would this seeing$_2$ of the 'I' in my head mean? Is it again processing of information until it is displayed somewhere to be seen$_3$? Such an understanding of vision results in an infinite regress, a set of Russian dolls inside my head; each time the 'I' retreats further as information is processed and displayed. The solution is that there is no such inner cinema or 'Cartesian theater' (Dennett 1991). There is no single place within the brain where all the information of the senses comes together, is evaluated by someone, and where the decisions for future action are taken. Our mental life is distributed throughout the brain. I am not somewhere inside the brain; in some way, I am my brain – though I need not be identified equally with all parts of the brain. There does not seem to be a subject of the experiences once one looks at a scale smaller than an individual skull.[6]

In what way mental phenomena are related to the brain is highly contested; an accurate account would have to do justice to our subjective experiences, the physiological processes in the brain, and our interactions with the environment. An extensive discussion of the literature on consciousness and other aspects of our mental life is far beyond the scope of this book. It is not the task of this study to make a choice among various competing approaches, but rather to indicate some of the ways in which a naturalist view of the mind might be developed, and to contrast it to two other approaches, namely a dual aspect view as advocated by Thomas Nagel (which is at odds with my constitutive reductionism (CR), certainly when combined with the emphasis on physics (PP)), and the view advocated by Paul Churchland that constitutive reductionism with respect to the brain should result in the replacement of mentalist language by a different vocabulary, and thus in the elimination of mental notions (which is at odds with my conceptual and explanatory non-reductionism (CEN)).[7]

According to Churchland, notions such as beliefs, desires, and intentions are part of a folk-psychology which will be explained away and

---

6   There are individuals, such as the split-cortex patients mentioned above [20.2] or persons suffering from a 'multiple personality' syndrome, who might be said to have more than one centre of subjectivity. However, in all these cases there are links between the various 'persons'; the two hemispheres of 'split-brain' patients always share the various undivided 'lower' structures of the brain (Wilkes 1988, 100–67).

7   In the *Scientific American* 271 (1 July 1994): 72–8, John Horgan offers an overview of various schools on the prospects for a scientific explanation of consciousness. I will be brief about approaches which emphasise the interaction of an organism with its environment. They square well with an evolutionary view, which states that transmissible traits, organs, and behavioural patterns which allow for a fruitful interaction with the environment are likely to become more prominent in a population. Thus, I agree with Looren de Jong (1992, 7), that 'ecological psychology is a branch of *naturalism*, which takes organism–environment relations as the central issue in psychology'. Arbib and Hesse (1986) also emphasise the interaction between an organism and its environment. A move from reflection on 'mental life' to interactions with the environment is also characteristic of 'connectionism' (Bechtel and Abrahamsen 1991). I consider such environment-oriented approaches as being within the range that fits the naturalism considered here, and will not discuss them any further here.

replaced by neuroscience. Folk-psychology will disappear. 'Its intentional categories stand magnificently alone, without visible prospect of reduction to that larger corpus' of physics, chemistry, biology, and neuroscience (Churchland 1981 (1991, 620)). If Churchland is right, we will come to have a naturalist understanding of ourselves, and in due time we will modify our language so as to reflect this view.

His expectation that the vocabulary of folk-psychology will be eliminated in due course seems exaggerated to me. I think that folk-psychology offers a vocabulary that might still be a useful vehicle for expressing complex mental (and, upon this view, therefore neurophysiological) processes. And even more, the case for the explanatory usefulness of notions from folk-psychology seems to me to be stronger than Churchland allows. Hence, I would expect that a neuroscientific understanding of the brain will retain notions such as 'beliefs' and 'desires' in a *moderate revisionist reduction* (see below, [22]), rather than that such notions would be eliminated. However, whatever conclusion is reached on the elimination of folk-psychology (and the implications for religion of such an elimination), if the approach of Churchland is successful, mental language is no challenge to a naturalist view of reality.

Dennett seeks to respect folk-psychology and thus to maintain a place for beliefs and intentions as part of our self-description. When I see the cat sitting near the fridge, I report 'the cat wants food'. This is a first-order belief about a cat. When I report 'I want food', this is a second-order report, a belief about one of my beliefs, namely a belief about myself, rather than a first-order report about some 'I'. However, since 'I want food' appears similar to the first-order report 'the cat wants food', we take reports about our own mental states as if they are reports having a clear referent (such as 'the cat'), and hence as if there is an 'I' inside (Dennett 1991, 305ff.). A conscious state is distinct from a non-conscious state due to the fact that it has 'a higher-order accompanying thought that is about the state in question'; the higher-order belief is reported, and the content of the report is taken as referring to an inner unit, the 'I' about whom the report seems to be.

According to Dennett, there need not be a centre where everything comes together. There is a pandemonium of events – Dennett speaks of the Multiple Drafts model – in which coalitions form and other events disappear without leaving many traces. Some coalitions may result in the utterance of sentences in natural language, creating a text, which creates the benign illusion 'of there being an Author' (365). Dennett sees the Self as an abstraction, but one which is none the less real, just as the centre of gravity of an object is an abstraction (where we assume all mass to be concentrated) but still a useful one, referring to a specific place. The Self is the Center of Narrative Gravity (410). Once this view of the self is in place, the 'higher order thoughts' need not be understood as reports about beliefs preceding the report; rather, while being reported they are constituted; 'The emergence of the expression is precisely what creates or fixes the content of the higher-order thought expressed' (315).

Experiences of colours (and tastes, etc.) are in the reports, the text created by the brain, as ways of accounting for reflective properties of surfaces out there. However, this is not a way of accounting for their objective properties as uncovered by the natural sciences (wavelengths), but rather for their significance. That we enjoy certain colours and dislike others is part of the evolutionary context; warning and luring is their life, not just informing. And similarly for taste. 'What we want when we sip a great wine is not, indeed, the information about its chemical contents; what we want is *to be informed* about its chemical contents in our favorite way. And our preference is *ultimately* based on the biases that are still wired into our nervous systems though their ecological significance may have lapsed eons ago' (384).

Dennett acknowledges that his view is eliminative; 'there has to be some "leaving out" otherwise we wouldn't have begun to explain' (454; see [22]). Explaining life 'doesn't leave living things lifeless' (455), but we tend to fail to understand this when it comes to explaining consciousness. However, even though this view is eliminative at the level of understanding, it is not (as Churchland's proposal is) eliminative at the level of language; we still like or dislike the wine, and we will continue to say that we drank water 'because we were thirsty'.

John Searle, another philosopher, also accepts that 'the *mental* state of consciousness is just an ordinary biological, that is, *physical*, feature of the brain' (Searle 1992, 13). However, he considers Dennett's work among 'several recent attacks on consciousness' (149). According to Searle, Dennett is one of those who redefine consciousness in a way that denies 'the central feature of consciousness, namely, its subjective character' (55). Searle's point is epistemological: consciousness or intelligence is not exhausted by third-person descriptions and criteria (57).

On his view, consciousness is causally emergent. However, it differs from other causally emergent properties, such as heat or colour, in a way which is relevant to the separate status of mental phenomena. We can redefine the notion of heat, by defining temperature as mean kinetic energy, and we can redefine red as light with a wavelength of 600 nanometres. Such a redefinition eliminates reference to the subjective appearances, the way heat or colour appears to individuals. 'But where the phenomena that interest us most are the subjective experiences themselves, there is no way to carve anything off' (121). Conscious states are always someone's; 'to be a pain, it must be *somebody's* pain' (94). Thus, consciousness cannot be redefined in physical, third-person terms.[8] This irreducibility is merely a consequence of the way we define terms. If one accepts the existence of (subjective, qualitative) consciousness, 'there is nothing strange, wonderful, or mysterious about its *irreducibility*. Given its existence, its irreducibility is a trivial consequence of our definitional practices' (Searle 1992, 124; *contra* Nagel 1986). But then, its (epistemological) irreducibility is not an argument against its ontological naturalness, nor does irreducibility imply that it is not biological, and beyond that chemical and physical.

Thomas Nagel differs from Searle with respect to the physical and biological basis of consciousness. He has argued that a unified conception of life and the world is impossible; we are left with the interplay of an objective view of the world and the perspective of a particular person inside the world. In physics 'we have achieved our greatest detachment from a specifically human perspective on the world', but we could only achieve this by leaving 'undescribed the irreducibly subjective character of conscious mental processes, whatever may be their intimate relation to the physical operation of the brain' (Nagel 1986, 7). Thus, unlike Searle and Dennett, Nagel challenges the fundamental place given to physics: 'The subjectivity of consciousness is an irreducible feature of reality – without which we couldn't do physics or anything else – and it must occupy as fundamental a place in

---

8 Searle also has it that with respect to consciousness 'we cannot perform the ontological reduction' (1992, 116), but this is a different, more epistemological notion of reduction than the constitutive reductionism (CR) as used in this study [2]. However, as pointed out there, my conceptual and explanatory non-reductionism (CEN) does allow for the possibility of taking entities picked out by terms at 'higher' levels in an ontological sense, for example, a belief as the cause of an action, or money as the means by which a person acquires goods. With Searle, I take it that such notions need not ascribe to higher levels causal powers which cannot be explained by causal interactions of the features of which it is composed, their interactions, and their relations to the environment (Searle 1992, 111f.).

any credible world view as matter, energy, space, time, and numbers' (1986, 7f.). Any 'correct theory of the relation between mind and body would radically transform our overall conception of the world and would require a new understanding of the phenomena now thought of as physical. Even though the manifestations of mind evident to us are local – they depend on our brains and similar organic structures – the general basis of this aspect of reality is not local, but must be presumed to inhere in the general constituents of the universe and the laws that govern them' (1986, 8). A dualism of matter and non-physical mental substances is unlikely, since the relation between the mental and the physical is very intimate. Nagel opts for a 'dual-aspect theory'; the same entities can have physical and mental properties. He argues for more than epistemic non-reducibility. He rejects the combination of constitutive reductionism (CR) and the belief that physics is the science of the fundamental aspects of natural reality (PP).

I consider this position unlikely. The main motivation seems to be negative, a rejection of the possibility of ever acquiring an objective view; we cannot know the subjective experiences of others, and especially not of other species. 'We will not know exactly how scrambled eggs taste to a cockroach even if we develop a detailed objective phenomenology of the cockroach sense of taste' (1986, 25). Such an argument is very much dependent upon future theorising, both about a physicalist or functionalist view and about the 'dual-aspect' alternative, which, as Nagel admits, is currently 'largely hand waving' (1986, 30). I will later criticise arguments which consider the absence of evidence as evidence of absence [28]; here we are in danger of making a similar move from not knowing an objective view to its impossibility. Furthermore, Nagel moves on from epistemological impossibility to ontological claims, whereas the first person perspective could also be salvaged by a form of epistemological non-reducibility, as defended for instance by Searle.[9]

In a later section [30] we will consider the possibility of views of reality which comply with ontological naturalism, but not with the emphasis on physics and ontological reductionism; an understanding of the ontology of mental life along the lines suggested by Nagel might be an example. However, it is too early to give up. I consider it likely that somewhere in the realm indicated by Churchland, Dennett, and Searle – to which various other proposals could have been added – there is a

---

[9] For other criticisms of Nagel's position, see, among others, Dennett (1991, 441–8, 457f.); Searle (1991, 100ff., 116–24).

possibility for a future theory of mental life which is naturalist in my sense (see [2]). There is a further reason why this is appropriate in the context of a study of challenges to religion: such naturalist views are more challenging to most religious positions than a dual-aspect theory – and I have argued above for the intellectual virtues of a 'reverse eclectic' rather than an 'eclectic' attitude towards competing scientific approaches [16].

One of the concerns which have been raised against naturalist theories of consciousness is that they explain by leaving essential characteristics out of the picture. A similar issue has arisen with respect to the understanding of religious experiences. It is to this more general issue that we will now turn.

22. EXPLANATION AND ELIMINATION

If you want us to *believe* everything you say about your phenomenology, you are asking not just to be taken seriously but to be granted papal infallibility, and that is asking too much. You are *not* authoritative about what is happening in you, but only about what *seems* to be happening in you. (Dennett 1991, 96)

Explanation and elimination have been recurrent notions throughout these sections. Does the presence of naturalist explanations eliminate a transcendental reference of religious experiences? And does a naturalist view eliminate mental concepts? I will begin with an attempt to clarify some central notions. I then argue that explanation does not imply elimination as long as we operate within the natural world. In the final part, I will argue that a non-eliminative view of our mental life cannot be transferred to claims about non-natural, divine factors.

Describing, explaining, and explaining away

'I experienced a tree' can be said in two ways, descriptively and as a judgement. It can be a description about how something seems to me, without regard to the accuracy of that seeming. I may say 'I experienced a tree, but then I realised I was mistaken.' But experience is also used as an achievement word; 'I experienced a tree' if it not only appeared to me that there was a tree, but that I was awake in the presence of a real tree which I saw or felt. 'This second sense includes a judgment on the part of the observer about the accuracy of the subject's understanding of his or her experience' (Proudfoot 1985, 229).

We cannot explain away experiences as they appear to the subjects. The self-description should not be reduced or denied, unless one has reason to believe that the description is intentionally dishonest. However, it is a fair game of science to explain the experiences as they appeared to the subject in a different way than the subject himself does. '*Explanatory reduction* consists in offering an explanation of an experience in terms that are not those of the subject and that might not meet with his approval. This is perfectly justifiable and is, in fact, normal procedure' (Proudfoot 1985, 197). Accepting a subject's experience in the descriptive sense as authentic need not imply the judgement that the self-description is correct.

This combination, of accepting the experience descriptively while suspending judgement, is likely to irritate. It deviates from 'normal interpersonal relations' (Dennett 1991, 83). The visiting anthropologist accepts all the accounts of a tribe, but at the same time adopts an attitude of distance and neutrality – whereas the natives do not just want to be taken as sincere; they want to have their beliefs shared. It may be a paternalism which irritates, just as when a father says he understands how the child feels, while at the same time signalling to the child that she will outgrow those feelings.

If one accepts first person accounts as genuine (in the first sense), is it possible that science might explain religious experiences or other important human experiences, and even explain them *away*?

After an explanation some experiences are gone. Once I know that what seemed to me to be a snake in a dark corner was actually a rope, the original experience with its emotional components, such as fear, is gone. 'It is only . . .' An explanation may liberate from unnecessary fear. It may also be a loss of the innocence of childhood, which diminishes joy and spontaneity, as in the explanation of Santa Claus. This kind of 'explaining away' is effective only if the explanation is communicated to, and accepted by the subject.

'Explaining away' is sometimes taken in a more paternalist way: the subject may still entertain her experiences, but the investigator knows better. While we experience the Earth to be stable, the astronomer knows that we are actually moving with a speed of a few hundred meters per second around the Earth's axis. What needs explanation in this case is also the delusion, why we do not feel the speed. Only a few are bothered by the loss of the static Earth, but if an explanation is offered for inner experiences, say of the fact that someone is prone to be irritated ('hormones; it is your period'), we are much more likely to be offended. It seems as if the explanation takes away the genuine character of the feelings by changing the terms.

Changing the terms is part of what it is to be an explanation. 'If your model of how pain is a product of brain activity still has a box in it labelled "pain", you haven't yet begun to explain what pain is' (Dennett 1991, 455). Explaining why opium puts people to sleep by saying that it has a *virtus dormativa*, a sleep inducing power – as happens in Molière's play *Le Malade Imaginaire* is no explanation at all, nor is calling someone 'photogenic' an explanation of the fact that she looks good in pictures (Dennett 1991, 63). An explanation explains in other terms, explains to some extent 'away'. However, this need not be accompanied by the disappearance of the experience. Opium still puts people to sleep, even if one does not consider the statement that opium has a 'sleep-inducing power' an explanation.

When we deal with explanations of religion, part of the discussion should be about the nature of the explanation. Does the explanation undermine the experience, or does it offer an understanding without undermining it? The same question can be posed about other explanations, for instance of explanations of mental phenomena in terms of physiological processes or of biological phenomena in terms of physics and chemistry. We will consider the issue in that context before returning to the specific issue of explanations of *religious* claims, especially in as far as they purport to refer to something beyond the natural realm.

Explanation need not be elimination

One of the worries that is evoked by reductionistic explanations is the fear that successful reduction would eliminate the phenomena considered, or more accurately, that it would eliminate our common-sense ideas about them. This is especially a worry expressed in relation to reductionistic explanations of human mental capacities.

The opposite view of reductionistic explanations is also encountered sometimes. A physiological basis for a trait can also be understood as an affirmation of its reality. Genes are not less real for being understood as strands of DNA, and pain is not less real if physiologically understood. Rather the opposite: if the doctor can locate the physiological process underlying my pain, my friends will take my complaints with more seriousness.

'Reduction' is, of course, a notion which needs to be considered with some care. One view is that all empirical consequences of the first theory, T_1, can be derived from a more encompassing second theory, T_2, which is at least equally specific in its predictions and explanations. Hence, to explain the phenomena (which were understood as empirical consequences of T_1) one does not need T_1. Thus, the phenomena can be understood differently. For instance, the idea might be that 'reduction would eliminate psychology because it would be a dispensable middleman between physical theory and observational statements about behaviour (including neural behaviour)' (Schwartz 1991, 205). Psychology and economics would still be useful disciplines and theories, as we are, for all practical purposes, unable to replace them by applied physics, but that would, on this view, only be a reflection of our limitations. And classical mechanics would still be a useful theory for many problems, but it would in principle be dispensable – as it does not explain any observations which would not be explained by the more fundamental theory.

If a theory is superfluous, it is not thereby wrong. Rather, if one could derive the superfluous theory T_1 from the more fundamental theory T_2 the first theory would not be autonomous, but it would still be a good theory for the domain with which it deals. Such a form of reduction is conservative with respect to reference; it identifies entities, properties, relations, and questions rather than eliminating them (Schwartz 1991, 210).

Most scientific reductions do not reproduce the earlier theory but some theory which resembles the original theory in certain aspects – classical mechanics is not reproduced by relativistic mechanics; there is no such thing as classical mass. The reduction is corrective, and so, presumably, would be a reduction of psychology to, perhaps, neurophysiology. But a corrected psychology 'would be a psychology still. Insofar as correction and improvement "threaten" our current folk psychology, we should welcome such threats' (Schwartz 1991, 212).

Even in cases where there is no scientific reduction between functional sciences such as biology and psychology and non-functional sciences such as physics, there still may be a relevant form of co-operation between different kinds of explanations, in which one science results in modifications in another science. A. R. Mackor (1994, 555) points to one such possibility when she writes: 'Functional explantions tell disciplines that deal with the causal or computational explanation what it is that they have to explain, but the findings of the latter might lead to adjustments in the classification of the phenomena in question.'

A worry may be that revisions are not ontologically conservative. If there are inconsistencies between scientific chemistry (with the concept of H_2O) and folk-chemistry (with the concept of water), the folk notion should be dropped. Similarly, it has been argued by Paul Churchland (1981, 67) that 'our commonsense conception of psychological phenomena constitutes a radically false theory, a theory so fundamentally defective that both the principles and the ontology of that theory will eventually be displaced, rather than smoothly reduced, by completed neuroscience'. It will disappear; we shall have to choose between our naive views and a better view. If we have to choose, we are not dealing with an example of reduction, but with competing theories. The suggestion seems to be that we have to choose between a common-sense view and a scientific one, which Sellars (1963, 5) called the 'manifest image' and the 'scientific image', as if they are incompatible. Philipse (1994, 11) argues that such an 'incompatibility thesis' underlies a wide variety of philosophical problems. However, the thesis that common-sense ontology and ontologies as they are implicit in scientific theories, are incompatible, can be disputed.

The compatibility of a common-sense ontology and a scientific one can be defended in the case of 'Eddington's two tables'. The physicist Sir Arthur Eddington distinguished between 'two' tables in his room, the ordinary one, a substantial thing, and the 'scientific table', which is 'mostly emptiness'. The argument is that these 'two tables differ in properties, indeed in essential properties, so they cannot be identical' (Schwartz 1991, 213). The fallacy with the argument about the two tables, according to Schwartz, is in the understanding of substance – which is both a common-sense notion (I can lean on it, I cannot put my hand through it, etc.) and a notion which carries various philosophical commitments, for instance that the presence of substance excludes empty space all the way down to the smallest microlevel. The common-sense notion of substance, say solidity, is underwritten by, explained by, and somewhat modified by the scientific account. We might have to give up some, or perhaps even all philosophical notions attached to substance, but we do not eliminate common-sense solids, including Eddington's 'first' table. Any scientific description of the table will have to incorporate the fact that I cannot put my hand through the table (unless with considerable force and with major consequences for the table and for my hand). 'If all we mean by commonsense solidity is the functional notion, we have a reduction of solidity which preserves the main features of the folk notion by identifying it with its physical microstructure, or showing how it is constituted' (Schwartz 1991, 217). Both tables are equally real; they are the same table. Such a reduction is moderately conservative rather than radically eliminative.

One can distinguish a range of cases of 'reductionism', ranging from *identification* (water and H_2O), where elimination would be incoherent; *constitutive*, as when genes are discovered to consist of DNA, where the reduction embeds the original notions more strongly in our understanding of reality; *approximative*, where the uncorrected science remains useful and relevant; and *moderately revisionist*, where the effect is not so much elimination as revision (of our ideas about solidity). 'In all these, reduction is an alternative to, not a form of, elimination' (Schwartz 1991, 218). Just as quantum physics does not eliminate solid tables, but leads us to a different conception of them, so too would a different conception of mental states in some future psychological theory, for instance in terms of neurology, not thereby eliminate the states. 'More plausibly, reduction would be a way to vindicate psychology as part of a unified science' (Schwartz 1991, 219).

Elimination of transcendent factors
The argument that reduction does not imply elimination works less well for religious experience interpreted as an experience of God. The point is that any identification or constitutive reduction is at odds with the transcendence of God. Understanding the notion of 'God' as approximately valid, introduces the further question as to what it would approximate. If there could be an explanation of religious experiences in naturalist terms, as considered above [20], such an explanation would eliminate any reference to a transcendent being, to God. Whereas the table is there, though our description is revised, in this case the revision would eliminate the need for a concept of God. The parallel is not between the common-sense table and God, but between the table and the religious experiences – they might still be there after a moderate revisionist reduction, though perhaps understood somewhat differently. But God is one of the causes which was supposed to be behind the religious experiences, just as the non-emptiness of substance was one of the aspects of the philosophical notion of substance behind the common-sense notion of solidity – and at that level, the revision hits most strongly. The same problem arises with respect to a reduction of psychology to physiology for someone who is interested not only in resisting the elimination of mental states, but preserving a separate referent for mental states, say the soul or the self.

If the scientific understanding of the table is able to account for our common-sense experiences with respect to the table (such as its solidity), we may accept that we have one table described in different vocabularies, rather than two tables. We may have to modify our vocabularies to some extent, for instance our understanding of substance, but both accounts would refer to the same table. The situation is somewhat different with respect to religious experiences that are considered experiences of God. If the experiences are understood as the consequence of complex physiological states, they would still be the same experiences, but the two accounts would no longer refer to the same entities. We would have to revise our view of the reality related to the religious beliefs in a much more radical way.

B. EVOLVED TRADITIONS

The sensuous hues [of art] and dark tones [of religious experience] have been produced by the genetic evolution of our nervous and sensory tissues; to treat them as other than objects of biological inquiry is simply to aim too low. (E. O. Wilson, *On Human Nature*, 1978, 11)

One might attempt to treat human cultures, including human morality, art, and religion as objects of biological inquiry, and seek to understand them all in terms of reproductive advantages. The opposite extreme is the claim that culture, morality and religion go against or beyond the evolutionary developments in such a way as to undermine a naturalist view which draws primarily upon evolutionary biology. Below, I will defend the view that culture (etc.) arose as an element in an evolutionary successful way of life, but that it is not exhaustively understandable in terms of reproductive advantages. Religion and morality fit into an evolutionary perspective, though some crude variants of evolutionary views of ethics and religion need to be rejected as inadequate in their understanding of human culture and/or evolutionary processes [24].

Subsequently, I will reflect on the consequences of an evolutionary view of morality and religion for morality and religion. It will be argued that the consequences for morality are moderate, as a procedural understanding of ethical justification avoids reference to nonnatural entities, whereas the same kind of explanation has more radical implications for theology [25]. In the last section, we will consider how one might incorporate an evolutionary perspective into a theological view of reality which purports to be relevant for us today [26].

Before coming to an evolutionary view of religion, and to reflections on its consequences for theology, I locate the approaches considered here in the wider field of discussions about religion and evolution. This will also explain why some debates which have received much public attention, such as the debates on 'scientific creationism', are left aside [23].

Another preliminary issue is methodological. If religions are seen as cultural traditions, they function as a framework in the context of which events are understood. Every understanding seems to be relative to a particular framework of 'tacit knowledge' (Polanyi). Why should one give one particular framework, that of the natural sciences, a prominent role in understanding traditions? Does a scientific approach to traditions not thereby elevate science to a position outside the naturalist framework?

Before arriving at an answer, we should understand that the role of science is restricted. Science is not elevated to the prime enterprise in all respects. The assumption is that science as an epistemic enterprise deserves more credit than earlier ways of acquiring knowledge about reality, or than contemporary alternatives, including 'common sense' or folk wisdom – even though there may be a great deal of practical knowledge embodied in these. This does not make science into an a-historical entity. Rather, it can be seen as the current level of an iterative process in which knowledge, methods, and criteria 'have been refined and improved over centuries' (Kitcher 1993, 390). In chapter 5 we will come back to the understanding of science and its legitimacy [27]. In the following four sections, we will focus on the understanding of religious and moral traditions within an evolutionary perspective.

23. SIX DEBATES ON EVOLUTION AND RELIGION

There are at least six different discussions concerning religion and evolution. Three deal with the evolutionary perspective on the world; the other three extend the evolutionary approach to religion itself. I will not develop the first three discussions beyond the following brief survey; the last three form the main focus of the next sections.

1. Most resounding has been the clash between Christians who claim the literal truth of the Bible, in this case especially the first few chapters of Genesis, and the teaching of evolution in American schools (see also

[9]). One leading 'creationist' expressed the clash as follows in a title: 'It is either "In the beginning, God ..." – or "... Hydrogen"' (Gish 1982). 'Creationists' see two mutually exclusive positions: acceptance of the Bible or acceptance of evolutionary theory. Disputes concern not only the evidence for or against evolutionary theory, but also the nature of Biblical statements and the nature of theories. Most contemporary theologians distance themselves from creationists. Theologians have been very critical of the way the Bible is treated by creationists, namely, as a source of propositional and a-historical truths. As theological opponents of creationism see it, Christians do not believe in the Bible as such; they believe in God, the Creator of heaven and earth – a belief to which the Bible testifies in the language of its time. That modern science speaks of millions and billions of years whereas the Bible counted in generations (adding up to a few thousand years) is not necessarily a problem for such theologians.[10]

Among believers more open to scientific insights into evolution and a less literalistic understanding of the Bible, two approaches may be distinguished.

2. Natural order has been seen as evidence for design (see also [8, 11]). Arguments in the British natural theology of the eighteenth and nineteenth century were mostly based on the structure of organisms, either by stressing functional adaptedness or coherence and unity of type (Bowler 1977); more recent variants have taken up the argument at the level of the universe as a whole (anthropic principles, see below [31]). A classic exposition of of arguments from functional adaptedness is William Paley's *Natural Theology* (1802), which was part of Darwin's intellectual background. Before turning to a wealth of information on the natural world, Paley considers a watch. If we should find a watch in the fields, we would conclude that someone had designed this marvellously complex and effective instrument. As organisms are endowed with an even more intricate and effective structure, we should conclude to a 'cosmic watchmaker'. In his *The Blind Watchmaker* (1986), Richard Dawkins agrees that natural complexity – and hence the appearance of design – is impressive. Dawkins claims, however, that natural, effective complexity can be fully explained as the product of a long evolutionary

---

[10] There is an extensive literature written by scientists, philosophers, and theologians, which analyses and responds to contemporary creationism (e.g., Frye 1983; Gilkey 1985; Kitcher 1982; Montagu 1984; Ruse 1982, 1982a). For a history of the evolution of anti-evolutionism, see Numbers (1992).

process. The 'watchmaker' is blind, without purpose, foresight or intention. As with the debate over creationism, the options are presented as mutually exclusive: either order is the product of purposeful design or of natural selection operating on variety due to random mutations.

3. Whereas the preceding two discussions tend to be formulated as an opposition, other believers have been seeking a mediatory approach. Rather than looking for evidence of design, they have argued that Christian beliefs were not necessarily inconsistent with the evolutionary origin of species. Or, engaging more intensely with the sciences, they have been looking for constructive opportunities, reformulating convictions in so far as they are needed. Such reformulations concern such questions as: If one accepts what the sciences tell us about our world, how can we think of divine action (e.g., Russell *et al.* 1993, 1995)? Is evolution God's way of creating the world? If so, what does this imply for our ideas about God? There is a whole spectrum of proposals. Some consider the possibility that specific divine action is hidden in what in science is called chance (e.g. Polkinghorne, see [13.1]). Others argue that chance might really be chance, also from God's perspective; this would not preclude the possibility that God achieves God's purposes through chance processes (e.g., Bartholomew 1984). Again others opt for a view of God as the 'Primary Cause' of the evolutionary process, the laws of nature and the initial conditions, while holding the evolutionary account to be complete in itself, without requiring any special divine action within the realm of (secondary) causality. In taking scientific insights about evolution into account in theology, the issue is not just creation. Every theological topic, including the doctrines of God, Christology, and eschatology, is up for reconsideration in an evolving world (e.g., Peacocke 1979, 1993). Reformulation may be sought for various reasons, such as the wish to defend the consistency of scientific knowledge and religious convictions, or the desire to formulate an approximately adequate view of reality, or the wish to develop images and metaphors which communicate the religious message to persons whose views of reality and of methods have been shaped by science (see above, [15]).

So far, we have considered three areas of discussion in relation to an evolutionary understanding *of the world*; they oppose or combine a theological and a scientific view of the world, including the apparent design in organisms.

Humans, with their nature and culture, are part of the evolved world. Thus, rather than considering science and theology as competing explanations, or at least as interacting with respect to insights about the world (as above), one might also consider the possibility of a scientific, evolutionary explanation of religion. This will be the issue considered here. If one reflects upon evolutionary approaches to religion and morality, three discussions may be distinguished.

4. One issue is the history and evolution of Christianity, and of other religions. Discussions about this are prominent in the writings of various great theologians of the nineteenth century such as F. C. Baur, Albrecht Ritschl, Adolf von Harnack, and Ernst Troeltsch, and in comparative studies on the histories of religions (e.g., Platvoet 1993).

5. Another approach 'seeks to identify just what significance Christian faith itself *has for* the evolutionary process' (Hefner 1989, 214; here Hefner also distinguishes the options 3 and 4). In principle, this is a project that is of interest not only to theologians or believers, but also to scientists as such since it seeks to uncover the role of one factor, religious faith, amongst others in the evolution of our species. We will consider the evolutionary role of religion and morality in combination with the possibility of an evolutionary explanation (discussion 4) in the next section.

6. Theology is more than an analysis of the functions and histories of religions. A proposal for a theological view of reality seeks to be relevant, say as a true claim about important features of reality or as an ideal guiding us in the manifold decisions we have to make individually and socially. Thus, the challenge arises whether one can formulate theological proposals which are relevant for us, as well as adequate with respect to our knowledge about the evolved character of the world, of morality, and of religion. Some proposals of this kind will be considered [26].

24. THE EVOLUTION OF MORAL AND RELIGIOUS TRADITIONS

In this section we will move from evolutionary approaches in biology to evolutionary approaches to morality, culture, and religion. Along this trajectory theories become more speculative; there is less consensus and more diversity of opinion. For two reasons, morality and social behaviour will be discussed before we turn to religion. Firstly, the literature on morality is more extensive and of higher quality than that on religion (e.g. Kitcher 1985, Alexander 1987, Irons 1991, Nitecki and Nitecki 1993). Secondly, religion and morality have been, and on many occasions still are, closely intertwined and many of the problems for evolutionary approaches to morality and religion appear to be similar. However, despite similarities, I will argue in the next section [25], that an evolutionary view of religion has more radical consequences for religion than an evolutionary view of morality has for morality.

Evolutionary biology

Evolution is central to biology. Studies of anatomy and fossils, the biogeographical distribution (such as Darwin's observations on the finches of the Galapagos islands), and the biochemical structure of organisms, *viz.* their proteins and DNA-molecules, all converge on a single tree of descent of all living beings on Earth, a reconstruction of the history of life. Evolutionary theory is more than such a reconstruction. Beginning with Darwin's *Origin of Species* (1859) and greatly expanded in molecular biology, an increasingly detailed understanding of the causal mechanisms underlying the development of life has arisen. Conditions for such a development by natural selection are threefold.

(i) Traits are passed on to future generations (*heredity*). Thus, nature builds upon achieved successes. The material basis for continuity is in the genes,[11] parts of the DNA-molecules which are mostly in the nuclei of cells.

(ii) Small changes (*mutations*) may occur in complexes of genes governing traits. In sexually reproducing species mixing of genes from parents also contributes to *variation*. Thus, new traits may arise.

(iii) Not all individuals, as carriers of genes, are equally successful. Some are more effective than others in finding food, escaping predators, attracting mates, conceiving offspring, and raising offspring so as to become attractive partners (and thus more effective in producing grand-offspring). Due to differences in reproductive success (*differential reproduction*), some traits will be more common in later generations, other traits less so.

Darwin's theory of evolution, and its later development, is not merely a claim that these three principles are at work (as most opponents in the nineteenth and twentieth century would have

---

[11] Evolutionary explanations consider different variants of a gene – say of a gene for eye-colour (if due to a single gene). There may be a variant resulting in blue eyes and another variant resulting in brown eyes. Such variants are called 'alleles'. In the following I will stick to the more popular usage of 'gene' as a word which refers both to alleles, *i.e.* variants which may 'compete' with each other, and to the locus where one of several variants may be found.

accepted as well), nor that they, in the course of generations, result in a higher prevalence, within a species, of characteristics which enable their bearers to survive and reproduce. The claim is that these principles provide a basis for explaining an extremely wide range of biological phenomena (Kitcher 1993, 19f.).

Heredity, variation, and differential reproduction characterise the general pattern of evolutionary explanations. However, differences in success need to be determined in more detail in each situation – whether they are due to resistance against drought or to an ability to run at high speed in order to escape predators. Similarly, the sources of variation and the mechanism of passing on traits have only been hinted at; more detailed insights into these issues have been acquired during what is almost a century and a half since the publication of Darwin's book. Even with such more recent insights the theory is a scheme which needs to be fleshed out in each particular context. Thus, if empirical results seem to challenge the evolutionary scheme, the first option is to reconsider the way the scheme is converted into a specific theory for the particular circumstances to which the empirical results apply. As most evolutionary explanations concern historical processes rather than controlled experiments, this gives evolutionary explanations the flavour of a 'just so' story, a story which explains how things could have happened rather than an account of how things did happen. Underdetermination (of histories in view of available evidence and the general scheme) is quite common; the biochemical processes within the organisms and the ecological and geophysical processes which shape the environment are varied, complex, and not known in every detail.

Therefore, there may at a certain time be more than one Darwinian history explaining a certain phenomenon, say the presence of marsupials in Australia. Independent evidence acquired at some later time, for instance from geology and palaeontology, may result in choosing one in preference to the other. A conclusion might be that marsupials came from Antarctica rather than from Indonesia, as fossils were found in the Antarctic (Kitcher 1985, 65). A *possible Darwinian history* is satisfactory (in the context of this study, and more generally speaking in the context of arguments about the adequacy of an evolutionary view of reality) if it explains a feature in way which is consistent with currently available knowledge. The claim that one can describe a possible course of evolution is less ambitious than the claim to have the *actual Darwinian history* which resulted in the features of an organism; the latter requires a more elaborate process of investigation (Kitcher 1985, 72, 74). The distinction between possible and actual Darwinian histories is relevant with respect to more pretentious expectations about sociobiology. Making predictions on the basis of evolutionary models and giving advice on such a basis about individual behaviour or social policies requires more than a possible history; it assumes that one knows all the relevant factors in the actual situation (and for the relevant future).

Not everything needs to be completely determined genetically. There is a species of lice which develop wings if there are too many of them on a single leaf, but not otherwise. Thus, they develop the capacity to migrate to other plants if necessary, but avoid the investment when wings are superfluous. Genes need not fix a single pattern of behaviour, but can create the structure which allows for variability in behaviour, depending on circumstances. In humans this *plasticity* has become very pronounced.

One might even say that nothing is determined genetically. If a seed does not fall in good soil, none of its potential traits will come to expression. A proper *environment* is essential to the development of all organisms – the genotype (as the collection of genes) is not enough to generate a phenotype (an individual as it appears). The cytoplasm of the initial cell is part of this environment, and for each gene the other genes are as well, but the environment also extends to the ecological system and climatic conditions. Though no traits are genetically determined in an absolute sense, biologists may come to the conclusion that, in a given environment, differences between organisms are genetically determined if differences between organisms are due to differences in genetic constitution (e.g., Van der Steen 1993, 2f.).

There are various complications in the evolutionary picture. For instance, most genes have multiple effects and most effects are consequences of more than one gene. The selection of mates in sexually reproducing species affects the distribution of genes. Genes may be linked to a greater or lesser extent by being more or less close to each other on a chromosome. The frequency of genetic mutations due to cut-and-paste work in genetic material may increase due to environmental factors. Selection can be dependent on the frequency of a trait in the population. An environment may change, perhaps also due to the organisms themselves. The first organisms released oxygen, thus creating the conditions to which later organisms adapted. Humans live in environments such as cities which are to a large extent shaped by humans themselves.

Evolutionary success – defined as an increased frequency of certain genes – is not to be identified with the largest number of offspring. One needs offspring which produces further offspring. This can be achieved by mass production or by intensive care of a few, as in birds and mammals. Concentration of parental care on a few is attractive when an environment is fairly reliable and the difference parents can make is significant; the more unpredictable and unstable a situation is, or the less power the parents have, the more attractive it becomes to have more offspring and to invest less in each individually. That families tend to be larger in poorer countries, and smaller in countries with good medical care, is thus quite intelligible. This is also an example of plasticity: there need not be a genetic basis for preferences about family size. What may have evolved is an unconscious tendency to have the size of one's family in accord with perceived risks and opportunities.

As far as genetics is concerned, nephews and nieces are also relevant; they carry copies of some of one's own genes. Thus, instead of investing in one's own offspring, it can be a good strategy to support nephews and nieces. The *inclusive fitness* of an organism includes all contributions to the continuation of one's genes, whether via one's own children and grandchildren or via the extended family. The notion of inclusive fitness has become important in the understanding of social insects. Worker bees invest in the offspring of their queen (mother), and hence in sisters rather than in their own offspring. This is evolutionarily intelligible, since due to a peculiarity in the genetic constitution of males, workers share 75 per cent of their genes with their sisters (daughters of the queen), whereas they would share only 50 per cent of their genes with their own offspring (Dawkins 1976, 186ff.).

We have our own view of the causes of our behaviour. Since heat is painful, I withdraw my hand from a fire. I see a green tree, since the retina of my eye receives light of certain wavelengths. Such currently present causes are called *proximate causes*.

Why are we structured in such a way that these causes work the way they do? Why has our nervous system developed in such a way that we experience pain? How did the eye come to be? Evolutionary theories consider *more remote, so called 'ultimate' causes* behind the proximate causes.[12] Bodies, including nervous systems, and behavioural patterns have evolved since they contributed to the survival and continuation of the genes involved. Organisms with less adequate (proximate) mechanisms for interacting with their immediate environment did less well in the long run ('ultimate' cause). To put it crudely, we owe our relatively good sight to the fact that individuals in our ancestral population who had inadequate eyes missed the branches they jumped for, and thus dropped dead.

The preceding paragraphs have presented a brief sketch of evolutionary theory, as it applies to yeasts, elephants, roses, and humans. Most of it is uncontroversial, though its application is not, and a few fundamental issues continue to be subjects of debate. For instance, there are alternative views of the units of selection; some consider not only the gene or the individual organism but also groups or species as units of selection (see Ruse 1988, 32–4). And some have argued that the evolutionary process is not so much one of gradual change as one of periods of stasis and relatively swift changes (Ruse 1988, 35–9). The appearance of discontinuity may arise when an area with a certain population is invaded by individuals from another population which had been geographically isolated for some time.

For the purposes of this study I assume that such controversies among biologists do not generate challenges to the main fruit of evolutionary theory: apparent design in organisms can be understood as the outcome of a natural process of random change and selection due to the interaction with the environment. We will now turn to the idea of an evolutionary understanding of culture and morality.

Human culture and morality

Humans have arisen in the course of a long evolutionary process, which we shared until a few million years ago with some of the great apes. Thus, it seems a natural enterprise to understand our constitution and behaviour in analogy with other species, especially other primates; a popular example of such an attempt is the bestseller *The Naked Ape* by Desmond Morris (1967). Going beyond arguments which rest upon analogies, sociobiologists have developed arguments about social beha-

---

12   The terms 'proximate' and 'ultimate' are commonly used in evolutionary biology, and I will use them thus in the chapters in this part. In other parts of this study, the quest for an 'ultimate' explanation is not focused on evolutionary origins, but on an explanation of properties of natural reality as a whole.

viour and social institutions; arguments which draw upon notions in evolutionary theory, such as inclusive fitness, and upon reconstructions of past environmental conditions. Such theorizing has led to various claims about human nature and behaviour, such as claims about differences between the roles of males and females, incest, aggression, and racism.

Many of these arguments focus on behaviour with obvious reproductive consequences. For instance, Wilson (1978, 142–146) explains homosexuality on the basis of kin-selection; a homosexual may support his sister's children. Since it can be explained biologically, homosexuality cannot be rejected as unnatural. Wilson remains cautious about this kind of argument; it would be illogical and unfortunate 'to make past genetic adaptedness a necessary criterion for current acceptance' (1978, 147). Wilson does not claim that we are completely determined by our genetic heritage. However, the more we attempt to deviate from our heritage, the greater the price in terms of human happiness.

Critics have pointed out that actual studies do not deliver the grand claims made on behalf of human sociobiology. 'People have unparalleled abilities for assessing both their own situation and the strategies that are being pursued by those around them. Hence, we can hardly expect to represent our own behaviour by restricting ourselves to the simple, unconditional strategies often singled out in studies of animal behaviour. Nor do we yet understand how to represent the interactions between the behaviour of individuals and the surrounding culture' (Kitcher 1985, 436). Two aspects of human behaviour complicate a biological analysis: our cognitive capacities and the cultural traditions in which we operate.

The position I will argue for is the following: the emergence of human nature, including human cognitive abilities and human culture, is intelligible in an evolutionary perspective, but explanations of human behaviour which bypass or underestimate culture and cognitive capacities, and the behavioural plasticity thus generated, are inadequate.

In *The Biology of Moral Systems* Richard Alexander (1987) presents a modern evolutionary account of the origins and function of morality, especially of altruistic behaviour. I will follow his arguments here. A first step is to consider altruistic behaviour with respect to *relatives*. Parents invest in their children and grandchildren; they 'sacrifice themselves'. Though this is altruistic at the level of the individual person, it does not constitute a problem at the level of genes, since the genes of the parents are also embodied in the children. If persons carry variants of genes which contribute to active parental care, they will, on average, take good care of their children, and thus these genes will be continued in the next generation. Nepotism is evolutionarily intelligible.

Partners need not be close relatives. But partners combine their genes in their children, and thus have *shared interests*, though only to some extent; if the husband[13] can have offspring elsewhere without significant 'costs', for instance without being found out by his wife and without taking away resources from his legitimate children, this might be attractive, genetically speaking. But the value of mutual trust and self-esteem is not to be underestimated; the potential costs of adultery may be significant.

'Shared interests' can be relevant also at a larger scale, say that of a village, a tribe, or a neighbourhood; one can promote one's interests by promoting those of the larger group to which one belongs. *Group cohesion* in the competition with other groups may well have been significant in human evolution. In the evolutionary past of humans, other groups of hominids were a major threat if not the major threat. Culture provides characteristics which distinguish a group from other groups. Individuals will serve the interests of the group to which they belong, as their own interests and those of their descendants are tied up with the prospects for the group as a whole, at least to some extent (see below, on deception).

Among partners and neighbours there is, in addition to shared interests, another mechanism which promotes co-operative behaviour: *reciprocity*. It is advantageous to do something for another even if that takes time (or money, or whatever), if you may expect the other to help you on some other occasion. The return need not be immediate, nor has it to be a benefit of the same kind. It is not even necessary that there is an actual return: 'Whenever you might need help, please call me' is (if it is a reliable promise) a valuable asset, whether you ever need to appeal for help or not. The favour need not be returned to the same person; it can also benefit your children or relatives rather than yourself. Essential to such more or less direct forms of reciprocity is that

---

[13] A woman can also be involved in adultery, but the perspective is different. The minimal investment for a male is semen (and some courting); he could increase his number of offspring by relating to various women in the same year. A woman's costs begins with at least a year of physical investment (pregnancy); she is less likely to gain from adultery as far as the number of children produced and raised during her lifetime. However, there may be benefits to a female as well, for instance as a safeguard against the male's sterility (Williams 1989, 200, and references therein).

individuals see each other more than once – as is the case for people in a village or neighbourhood, or among colleagues at work.

In some countries, people voluntarily donate blood, without receiving money for it. It is not specifically given to one's own family. Nor need the recipient be someone who will return the favour whenever necessary. Nor do donors receive a preferential treatment whenever they need blood. Direct benefits or direct reciprocity are not involved. Behaviour such as donating blood or risking one's life to save an unknown person in danger of drowning, is evolutionarily intelligible if we take *indirect reciprocity* into account. A blood donation may induce in others a positive view of the donor. Someone who is considered to be a socially responsible person may be considered an attractive partner for various transactions. Indirectly, this can be advantageous. The return does not come from the person who benefitted in the first place, but indirectly, via the culture in which one participates. War heroes may be dead, but the social costs of opting out may have been significant, whereas the honour of the dead hero may benefit the relatives at home. And even if nobody notices one's altruistic actions, it may contribute to one's own self-esteem. Indirect reciprocity is important for cultural beings who live in networks of relations, where elements of status and solidarity are very important. These processes need in no way be conscious, as if they were directly based on calculation. Characters and codes of behaviour are mostly implicit, and probably at least as much culturally as genetically determined, but none the less real. In an evolutionary perspective one might view the rise of moral systems as a way of promoting personal interests by means of indirect reciprocity.

If a certain level of moral behaviour is considered customary, you cannot fall far behind. Otherwise you might get excluded from the community, and your children might have more difficulty in finding a job or a partner. It is advantageous to have social status, to be a respected person. Thus, moral codes may develop over time, even without external pressure. A culture might become more demanding as the expectations shift, for better or for worse. For example, when, in a group of teenagers, the standard for boys is macho-behaviour towards girls, or the possession of knives or guns, it will be attractive to have an above average macho-status. Since all seek to be there, the average and the unwritten code will change.

To summarise Alexander's proposal: the evolution of cultures with moral codes may have been driven by two major factors: group cohesion (for the group as a whole, against other groups) and indirect reciprocity (as a mechanism serving individual interests within a group).

Everybody has to be moral, for instance by paying taxes. In the meantime, as long as it goes undetected, it is attractive for me to get away with paying slightly less than my fair share. It is attractive to appear to be nicer, more socially responsible than I am. For my social investment will be lower, whereas the returns I get from the system remain the same. It is also to my advantage if I can get others to do more than their fair share, even if I do not live up to the norm myself. It might also be attractive to appear to be more naive or dependent than I am. The other will underestimate me, and thus be tempted to think that there will be more to be gained by dealing with me than is really the case. Deception, both consciously and unconsciously, is a natural companion to morality. This does not only apply to serious forms of deception; one could also think of make-up and fitness exercises as attempts to disguise one's age.

Not only is it attractive for me to deceive others. It is also important to be able to notice when others attempt to deceive me. However, if others have the ability to spot attempts at deception, it becomes attractive to hide one's deception even more. And thus it becomes attractive to spot deception more accurately. This is a self-enhancing process. One of the ways deceptive behaviour has become less notice-able is by suppressing it, making it unknown even to oneself. Alexander (1987, 114–26) holds that the evolution of the brain, with consciousness and unconsciousness, is part of this arms race of covering up one's weaker sides and spotting those of others. One's conscience is 'the still small voice that tells us how far we can go without incurring intolerable risks' (Alexander 1979; 1987, 253).

It may appear cynical to consider morality in such an evolutionary perspective. It is understood as rooted in one's own interests (or those of one's offspring and relatives, or even those of one's variants of the genes, if genes may be said to have interests). For that matter, the resistance against an evolutionary view is itself evolutionarily intelligible too; acknowledging these origins seems to imply that one acknowledges that one is selfish (in the genetic, offspring-including sense); this would not be a good strategy in a culture which praises altruism, or at least mutual solidarity (e.g., Ruse 1993, 152f.; Alexander 1993, 187).

Although morality is rooted in our evolutionary past, it is not adequate to interpret all moral behaviour in terms of the consequences it has for one's inclusive fitness. Rather, the evolutionary process has generated the proximate mechanisms (our psychological constitution and our cultural codes) which operate within the complexities and uncertainties of cultures. Moral motives may well be genuine, as proximate mechanisms, even though culture and character have their roots in the biological process described in evolutionary theory.

In the evolutionary perspective one could say that we are all 'selfish', as far as the ultimate causes of culture are concerned. This does not carry over to considerations about proximate causes, where the term 'selfish' has discriminative value. It is normally used to point out certain forms of behaviour which are depreciated, while other forms are appreciated by calling them altruistic, generous, or whatever. In that context, the terms 'selfishness' and 'altruism' continue to mean what they have always meant. 'Altruistic' is a label for behaviour which promotes the well-being of others (or of the group as a whole); this is not less altruistic for being an action in the context of a culture which on average indirectly allows for one's own well-being or inclusive fitness. In paying attention to motives, the discourse moves beyond the evolutionary explanation (ultimate causes) of cultural mechanisms to an evaluation within a certain cultural pattern (proximate causes). If someone would say that pain is not pain because it serves organisms to increase their inclusive fitness, he would mistakenly confuse the actual mechanism (pain) and the evolutionary processes which created the mechanism. Similarly, there is no reason to deny human culture in the name of an evolutionary explanation. The genetic background is not necessarily at odds with altruistic cultural codes. On the contrary, it has made us into beings who may have altruistic motives:

Kin-selection ... can make it extremely adaptive to be nice to others ... Because these tendencies do *not* spring from calculation, but from inherited dispositions, they cannot be regularly switched off when someone less closely related heaves in sight. They are not strictly proportioned to blood relationship, but respond to many other cues, such as familiarity, admiration, liking, and the special needs of others. And in human beings, the complexities of culture can give them a much wider range of channels than is possible for other species ... Virtue is as real a fact in the world as vice is, and the variety of genuine human motives is also real. (Midgley 1985, 127)

To conclude this section: A move from 'selfish genes' (Dawkins 1976) to selfish individuals neglects the way we are embedded in wider networks of culture and ecology. We have evolved as moral and cultural beings, who can be altruistic or egoistic in character and behaviour. Edward O. Wilson, author of *Sociobiology: The New Synthesis* (1975), which concluded with a controversial chapter on human social behaviour, a few years later co-authored a book on the co-evolution of genes, mind and culture, emphasizing the need to take the diversity of cultures and the development of individual minds into account (Lumsden and Wilson 1981).[14] Cultural and psychological factors are to be taken into account in any attempt which seeks to understand any specific human behaviour or make claims about the possibility for changing human behaviour. We should be suspicious of short-cuts from genes or from analogies with the behaviour of other animal species to recommendations about our behaviour. However, a critical stance towards a naive sociobiological approach to self-understanding and social policy need not result in the rejection of the ontological naturalist assumption underlying sociobiology: humans, including human cognitive capacities and cultural patterns, have come into being through a long evolutionary process.

Religion in an evolutionary perspective

We now come to the role of religion in evolution, to the fifth of the six approaches listed above [23].

In *The Biology of Religion*, Reynolds and Tanner focus on the question 'How does membership of a religious group, or belief in a religious faith, affect individuals' chances of survival and their reproductive success?' (1983, 2). Rules about marriage may close or open the gene pool. Religious rules may allow or disallow premarital pregnancies. Rules about divorce, widowhood, and remarriage affect reproduction, as do rules about intercourse and contraception, nursing and infanticide, male and female circumcision, legitimacy and illegitimacy of children, food preparation and cleanliness, and child care. All of these are relevant to the survival of children and thus to the inclusive fitness of the parents concerned. Reynolds and Tanner link the differences between religious traditions on these issues to differences in environments; as would be expected (see above, the paragraphs on 'offspring'),

---

14   Lumsden and Wilson (1981) shows that even persons coming from sociobiology as developed for animals without elaborate cultures see the need to introduce culture and mind. I do not by this illustration intend to endorse their vies of gene-culture co-evolution. The views of mind and culture may be inadequate, especially too atomistic; for a critical discussion, see Kitcher (1985, chapter 10), and references therein.

religious rules promote more care in stable cultural circumstances, while they promote a larger number of children in less stable ones.

Their view is not sociobiological in a restricted sense, viz., that all behavioural patterns are genetically determined. It is sociobiological in the wider sense in that they attempt 'to find a theory that can link up the characteristics of human cultures with human evolution in the organic sense (differential reproductive success of individuals, etc.)' (Reynolds and Tanner 1983, 259); they aim at a theory of culture which draws upon the explanatory schemes of evolutionary theory. It is in this broad sense that I will use the term 'sociobiology' here.

Although Reynolds and Tanner widen their considerations beyond reproductive mores by including care, they still restrict their scope too much. The biology of moral and religious systems is intimately intertwined with the whole creation of culture. Or, to express it differently, sociobiological considerations do not only apply to sexual morality, but to all spheres of life. To some extent, this liberates the discussion from a too-narrowly conceived context, from proceeding as if culture (including morality and religion) is to be understood as immediately concerned with reproduction. However, it also enhances the challenge, since religion and morality are not only considered in relation to reproductive mores but in all other aspects.

Above, human altruism was linked with human culture as the context for cooperation among unrelated individuals. Ralph Burhoe has argued that it is in the creation of culture that religion plays an important role. One of his essays carries the title: 'Religion's role in human evolution: The missing link between ape-man's selfish genes and civilized altruism' (Burhoe 1979; see also Burhoe 1981; Breed 1992).

As Burhoe sees it, in humans genetic information is joined with non-genetic, cultural information, which is transferred by language and example. These two kinds of information are fairly independent: it is our environment which determines our mother tongue, and it is our genetic heritage which determines our eye-colour and our brain size (as long as environmental conditions, such as food, are sufficient). Because of their relative independence the two kinds of information can strengthen each other in a co-evolutionary process.

The constitution of modern humans is different from the constitution of our ancestors a few million years ago; the underlying genetic information has changed. What has most markedly evolved is the brain, and thus the capacity to use, memorise, and transfer cultural information. This fits well a co-evolution of culture and genes. To ask what came first, the genetically determined capacities (brain, possibility of speech) or the cultural information, such as language, is misguided; they co-evolved. Humans would not be humans without culture and culture would not be what it is without the human brain, though, of course, less richly developed forms of transfer of information by behavioural rather than genetic means can be found among animals as well (Bonner 1980, 4).

Burhoe's point is that religions are systems which embody the fundamental values of a culture. Through ritual and story, religions mediate between the genetic and the cultural level, as they transfer cultural information to the brains, the steering mechanisms of individuals. The first proto-religions may have evolved a million years ago. Over time, religions have made larger societies possible, even when genetic kinship was not sufficient to sustain cooperation. One way has been to create a strong sense of (pseudo)-relatedness: we are all brothers and sisters. In the Book of Genesis alone we already find three myths to that effect, referring all humans back to a single ancestral pair, Adam and Eve, all nations to the three sons of Noah, and relating more closely the various tribes of Israel by linking them to the twelve sons of Jacob.

Three general claims about religion in an evolutionary perspective can be made.

1. Possible Darwinian evolutionary histories can be sketched. Therefore, humans and their cultures, languages, aesthetic and moral codes, and their religious practices can be seen as results of a natural, evolutionary process, as stated in the quote from E. O. Wilson with which I began these chapters: 'The sensuous hues and dark tones [*i.e.* art and religious experience, WBD] have been produced by the genetic evolution of our nervous and sensory tissues', or at least our capacity to experience these hues and tones in certain environments, under certain cultural conditions has been produced by natural processes. However, the complexity which was pointed out above, makes me disagree with Wilson's next statement: 'to treat them as other than objects of biological inquiry is simply to aim too low'. I agree that it would be too modest for biology to exclude the study of humanity. However, due to the complexity of the issues at hand, we rightly approach human culture, including art and religion, also by various other means such as the social sciences and the humanities, which are part of the richness of our heritage.

2. The actual history of morality and religions and their actual functioning in the web of genes, mind, and culture are very complex, and therefore not clear. The complexities of culture and mind and the lack of complete knowledge of the variety of actual human constitutions (and of the actual Darwinian history that produced that variety) should not be glossed over in short-cuts from genes to explanations of human behaviour and social institutions, and even less in short-cuts from genes to recommendations regarding social policies and individual behaviour.

3. Not only can religions be seen as the product of a natural, evolutionary process, but it may well be the case that they have contributed significantly to that process by fulfilling important functions. However, that they were functional does not imply that they are approximately true descriptions of reality. And what was functional in the past need not be so now; our situation is in many ways different from the environments in which these traditions may have been adaptive. Thus, we come to the topics of the next sections: Can one reach beyond an evolutionary view of religion to a religious view which might be acceptable and relevant for us? How can one integrate an evolutionary view of religion into religion? [26]. And what are the implications of an evolutionary view for morality and for religion? [25].

25. CONSEQUENCES FOR MORALITY AND FOR RELIGION

Before focusing on the implications of an evolutionary view of religion for religion, I would like to consider the following question about morality: How does an evolutionary view of the origins of morality influence our morality? This has been debated ever since (and even before) Darwin, and is one of the recurrent themes in the disputes about sociobiology.

Morality and evolution
Thomas H. Huxley, who had the famous exchange with Bishop Wilberforce (see above, [8]), clearly distinguished the question of whether Darwinian evolution would be able to account for morality from the question of whether it should be adopted as an ethical principle. Huxley's answer concerning the evolutionary origin is positive, but he rejects an evolutionary ethics (Nitecki 1993, 24). In his Romanes lecture (1893), Huxley seeks 'to remove that which seems to have proved a stumbling-block to many – namely, the apparent

paradox that ethical nature, while born of cosmic nature, is necessarily at enmity with it' (Huxley 1894c, viii). The difference between the evolution *of* morality and taking evolution *as* a guide in morality is in itself fairly obvious; no one would confuse an evolutionary account *of* any physical structure, such as our hands or the wings of birds, with a statement about evolution *as* such a physical structure. With respect to evolution and ethics, at least three discussions have been distinguished: (1) the evolution of ethics, (2) the ethics of evolution, that is the question of 'whether trends or patterns can be seen in evolution that can be assessed in terms of their ethical worth or merit', and (3) evolutionary ethics, 'concerned with establishing an ethical or value system on the basis of a scientific understanding of empirical evolutionary events' (Caplan 1978, 312). Here, we will concentrate on implications of the first kind of research, *i.e.* implications of the evolutionary origins of morality, for our assessment of morality, and consider critically proposals for an evolutionary ethics. Some of the theological proposals which will be discussed in the next chapter evaluate the evolutionary process, and are thereby examples of the second kind of discussion, the ethics of evolution.

In debates on human sociobiology, one fear – apart from an unwarranted elevation of evolution to the status of a moral principle – seems to be that an evolutionary understanding of morality would undermine the specific moral character of such behaviour. There are at least four sources for such a fear (Kitcher 1985, 395–434). It can be seen as (1) the fear that our moral language is a screen for hiding amoral motives. It can be understood as (2) the fear that, given their humble ultimate origins, moral considerations are not as worthy as we take them to be. And the fear can be related to 'ontological' issues, such as (3) the apparent denial of human freedom or (4) of objective values.

The first dispute concerns proximate mechanisms, such as the nature of our motives. The suggestion is that we use moral language to serve, and hide, our own interests. We may think that we are driven by moral considerations, but we are mistaken about the mechanisms that drive our behaviour. Instead, our actions are based on (unconscious) calculations about the consequences of the available options for our inclusive fitness, rather than on, for instance, concern for the well-being of others.

In order to evaluate this suggestion, let us briefly consider another phenomenon: the feeling of pain. When I have my hand too close to a flame, I will quickly move my hand away. The proximate mechanism is neurological, partly automatic (reflexes) and partly conscious (feeling pain). An evolutionary account of the origin of these neurological mechanisms does not in any way deny their reality, or the reality of the sensation of pain. Nor is it reasonable to argue that the actions are always in accord with maximising inclusive fitness. The reflex still operates when the doctor comes to inject me, even if that is important for me and my offspring. As has been argued by the philosopher of biology Michael Ruse (1993, 147), the way we have become reasonably good at co-operation (which serves our interests) has been to endow us with a genuine desire to co-operate. Motives and feelings are not covering up a supercomputer which calculates which behaviour is most profitable, but they are the means by which we have come to co-operate. Thus, as proximate mechanisms our motives and moral pronouncements may well be sincere.

The second source of concern about the implications of the evolutionary view for morality is the expectation that the recognition of the evolutionary origins of our motives would undermine 'our normal assessment of their worth' (Kitcher 1985, 404). Kitcher considers the example of a childless couple spending time and energy caring for children with birth defects. To point out that this behaviour derives from the propensity to care for offspring, and thus arose to maximise inclusive fitness, in no way diminishes the personal sacrifices made by the couple and the moral worth of their actions. The remote action of evolutionary forces 'is irrelevant to the assessment of moral worth' (Kitcher 1985, 404).

The argument concerning the childless couple in the example brings us to the third challenge to morality, the absence of freedom. Their care of handicapped children is driven by the innate propensity to care for children, a propensity which is 'merely the means that evolution has employed in shaping humans to maximize their inclusive fitness' (Kitcher 1985, 405). If their behaviour is the consequence of evolution, they were externally or internally coerced to behave the way they did, and thus their actions – though perhaps morally good if judged by the results – are not really moral. Their behaviour is determined by the evolutionary past and/or by the environment in which they live. Such an objection can be raised with any explanation of behaviour, not only an evolutionary one.

There seem to be two ways of responding to the claim that freedom in a morally relevant sense is threatened by an evolutionary view. Firstly, one might object to the image of humans as puppets, unfree because they are steered by others (the evolutionary past and environment), or of humans as robots or simple organisms, unfree as they do not adapt their behaviour in a significant way to their actual environment, but rather move according to simple pre-programmed schemes (e.g., Dennett 1984, 11f.). Rather, in humans, with their highly developed central nervous systems, there is a sense of 'internal coercion' which is not necessarily unreflective and without deliberation. This brings us to the second response: freedom is not the opposite of determination. Rather, freedom is self-determination, that is determination by my character and desires, controlled by my rational reflection on my past actions and potential consequences of various options, by my second order desires with respect to my life plan, and by my values. It is not clear that such a notion of freedom conflicts with an evolutionary understanding of ourselves (Kitcher 1985, 405–17). However, it is at odds with a crude version of an evolutionary understanding of human nature, which does not pay sufficient attention to the complexity of culture and mind which generate the possibility for self-reflection, deliberation, and acting on the results of deliberations – conditions for behaviour being ethical (Williams 1993, 234). Thus, though human morality is not independent of evolved biological structures, human morality has further 'conditions that must be explained and justified in ways that go beyond evolutionary ethics' (Gewirth 1993, 255).

The fourth fear seems to be that sociobiology undermines the possibility of objective values with respect to which we evaluate moral behaviour. It is at odds with an evolutionary perspective to consider human values as revealed or imposed by religious authorities or as entities residing in some timeless realm. Thus, we seem to be left with a subjectivist view of values (rooted in the emotions of the individual) or with an evolutionary view which grants the presence of values which are shared by various organisms, but only in as far as these organisms share a common evolutionary past or have similar interests in similar situations. The sociobiologist E. O. Wilson has it that values are rooted in deeper structures of the brain: 'ethical philosophers intuit the deontological canons of morality by consulting the emotive centers of their own hypothalamic-limbic system' (Wilson 1975, 563; see also

Wilson 1975, 3; 1978, 6). A sociobiological understanding of those emotive centres would, in his view, not so much undermine ethics as offer an explanation *and* foundation for the values we need. Wilson believes that we can thus understand that we need to support human rights and protect biodiversity (Wilson 1978, 198f.; 1992).

There is something odd about the emphasis on the limbic system. Why would a sociobiologist consider the higher structures of the brain, including the capacity to reason about consequences and about principles on the basis of which certain behaviour could be defended, to be superfluous, not affecting the functioning of the limbic system, nor affecting canons of morality? The 'oversight' of the role of higher structures in the explanation of moral behaviour is, as I will argue here, even more problematic when it comes to the justification of moral behaviour.

Whether sociobiology offers an adequate explanation of the evolution of human moralities is not at issue here; it is assumed that it does explain this evolution adequately if cultural phenomena and human faculties, such as the habit of making moral judgements and the capacity to make moral deliberations, are taken into account (see the preceding section). Here we focus on issues of justification.

The claim that scientific insights, and especially insights from sociobiology, deliver the values we need, has been disputed by various philosophers, including philosophers who do not reject sociobiological explanations of human behaviour (e.g., Singer 1981, Kitcher 1985). To take an example, Singer considers a sociobiological explanation for double standards with respect to extramarital sexual activity of humans. The greater proclivity towards sexual promiscuity among males and towards restraint among females is explained in a straightforward way: males may gain considerably in the number of offspring by inseminating many females, whereas females do not, but rather gain from male support with parenting, and thus from luring males into more lasting relationships. However, Singer points out that even if we accept a sociobiological explanation of these differences in behaviour and of traditional moral attitudes with respect to such differences, we still may consider such a double standard an example of sexism which is morally unacceptable; there is room for a considered moral judgement which differs from conventional moral sentiments. And even more, according to Singer, since sociobiological explanations actually allow us to distance ourselves from any innate tendencies: 'by explaining the widespread acceptance of the double standard, we also remove any lingering idea that this standard is some sort of self-evident moral truth. Instead it can be seen as the result of the blind evolutionary process and, as such, something about which we should make a more deliberate decision, now that we have understood it' (Singer 1984, 154). I agree with this argument: a sociobiological explanation does not offer a justification, but rather an opportunity to reconsider the behaviour. But then the question arises by what standards we evaluate our 'natural' moral sentiments.

The committed sociobiologist might say that we do not escape our biology here; we only bring into play further values which are also part of our biology, and we strive for coherence – a coherence which may imply that we have to give in on the double standard referred to above. In this process of evaluating our moral sentiments, we may reach agreement with humans from different cultural backgrounds, since we share a common biological history and structure; rape may be wrong for all humans, and judged to be so by all reasonable ones, and human rights may be universal for humans. However, rape would not necessarily be wrong on Andromeda, in a species with a different biology (Ruse 1989). We have to live with the resources we have: the values which are handed down to us by cultural traditions (which, upon a sociobiological view, are themselves fruits of a selective process) and the capacities we owe to our constitution. The values are not believed to be innate in a full-blown form; sociobiologists have argued that there are 'epigenetic rules' which are innate, and which in the course of a person's development in suitable cultural environments result in certain values and behavioural patterns.

The view that all moral judgements are forged upon us by our past and that they are in a fundamental way species-dependent (as in the example about Andromeda), seems to me to be insufficient for morality; it still identifies the moral justification with an explanation of how we came to have the preferences which we do turn out to have; there is no room for a contrast between 'what is' and 'what ought to be'. However, upon a naturalist view as developed here, there seem to be no other sources for substantial moral judgements than the heritage of our biological and cultural past. There is no room for the justification of ethical decisions in relation to entities in some Platonic realm, as if we come to hold moral principles by intuiting an absolute moral order.

However, there are proposals for ethical justification other than an appeal to moral absolutes or to biologically based sentiments. A procedural view of moral justification such as offered by Rawls (1971) may be compatible with an evolutionary view (Alexander 1993, 180ff.). It does not justify claims about categorical objective moral truth, but such an absolute, 'rational intuitionist notion of objectivity is unnecessary for objectivity', and can be replaced by a social one (Rawls 1980, 570). It is, in my view, a valuable complement to and corrective of our ethical intuitions as rooted in our biology. Ethical objectivity need not be linked to a realm of ethereal entities, such as abstract values. Rather, it 'involves the existence of a standard beyond personal wishes, a standard in which the wishes of others are given their place' (Kitcher 1985, 432). A procedural form of ethical justification may offer us ways to cope with the conflicting interests of individuals.

This emphasis on procedures is not a separate way to morality, as if ethical values could be deduced by thinking alone. The sociobiological dimensions come into play in at least two ways: we owe our moral intuitions (such as conceptions of persons, of suffering, and of a well-ordered society) and our capacity for reflection to our evolutionary past. We do not start as blank minds, who develop moral notions out of nothing. Rather, we reflect upon our moral intuitions, and thus consider whether they have certain general features which we consider desirable. For instance, the 'golden rule' which states that one should not do to someone else what one would not want to happen to oneself, is a general ethical principle which could be brought to bear upon many moral intuitions. In our reflection, we may test our moral judgements by criteria such as generality and disinterestedness, coherence, contribution to happiness and to the reduction of suffering, etc. We owe our intuitions to the evolutionary past, but they can be considered and corrected, since we have the ability to evaluate our primary responses and to act upon such evaluations, though we do not act easily upon them, as the apostle Paul observed (Romans 7: 19). Such difficulties underline that genuine ethical behaviour does not come to us 'by nature', but rather requires moral effort; ethics is not prediction of what is most likely to happen.

The ability to engage in abstract forms of reflection, which allow us to distance ourselves from our 'natural' inclinations, is itself a natural capacity. It may have served other functions in our evolutionary past; thinking allows for flexible responses to changing circumstances and thinking ahead may considerably diminish risks. Whatever the origin of the human capacity for reflection on one's own behaviour and the behaviour of others, we now have this capacity and can use it for new purposes, such as a reconsideration of our moralities. This human capacity for reasoning and the patterns of reasoning which we are able to pursue are subject to change themselves. Thus it may seem as if there is a higher norm by which we would adjudicate whether we can improve our thinking. However, this need not be the case: in the complex interplay of intuitions and sentiments, procedures and results of reflections, and criteria used in such reflections, we may well come to the conclusion that we could change some aspect in our procedures. (A similar argument can be made with respect to scientific methods, see [27]).

The criteria which we use in moral evaluations, such as the requirement of disinterestedness, may also be seen as the product of our evolutionary past. At some moment in the past one of our hominid ancestors asked a fellow hominid the equivalent of the question 'Why did you do that?' in the presence of a third party, and the answer was couched not in terms of emotions (I like to do that) or in terms of self-interest, but in terms which were sufficiently general to be recognisable and acceptable to all bystanders, and thus, perhaps, brought the others to similar behaviour (Singer 1981, 92ff.). Perhaps, as Singer grants, before such explicit moral deliberations arose, customs were there as embodiments of collective reason. The point is that we developed the habit of evaluating and justifying behaviour in terms which were sufficiently general to be acceptable to the whole group. As for the ability to reason considered in the preceding paragraph, the criteria delineating the relevant group are not necessarily beyond change.

Formal analysis, the application of criteria such as disinterestedness and coherence, and the moral deliberation of many people together are important for the credibility of morality, precisely because they surpass and may correct the conclusions of our ordinary biological and psychological mechanisms. One might include all these elements in a sociobiological description, but then ethical considerations would not so much have been eliminated, but they rather would have been included in a modified sociobiology which includes consideration of the mechanisms by which we override the psychological processes explained by traditional sociobiology. Or one could say that our moral intuitions are explained by sociobiology, but that these intuitions need not be our best ethical conclusions, since we can reconsider them. A similar conclusion will be defended with respect to the status of epistemology [27]: either we expand psychology by including scientific procedures, such as double-blind experiments, etc., by which we correct our ordinary belief-forming processes, or we acknowledge the difference between psychology and epistemology: there is no need to say that epistemology, or, in the present context, morality is eliminated in a naturalist view.

Religion and evolution

So far, I have argued that an evolutionary view of moral behaviour need not be in conflict with the 'moral character of morality'. Could one make a similar claim for the consequences of an evolutionary view of religion?

The philosopher of religion Vincent Brümmer has argued that, whatever understanding there would be of the way faith arose in me – whether pathologically or naturally, as a psychological projection or as an evolutionary strategy – a believer could always say something to the effect: 'So that was how God brought me to faith?'[15] In a similar vein, in the midst of a discussion on ethics, Kitcher objects to the view that an evolutionary scenario that accounts for the emergence of religious ideas would undercut the view that religious doctrines are true. 'Even if Wilson's scenario were correct, the devout could reasonably reply that, like our arithmetical ideas and practices, our religious claims have become more accurate as we have learned more about the world' (Kitcher 1985, 419). An account of origins, how we have come to a certain conviction, does not in itself decide on the truth of that conviction. To argue otherwise, conflating issues of origins of beliefs and of their justification, is to commit what is called the 'genetic fallacy'.

However, there are relevant differences between the status of mathematics and ethics, and the status of religious ideas. Mathematics may be seen as a second-order activity, growing out of the analysis of human practices such as counting and trading. Similarly, ethical considerations involve a second-order reflection, upon procedures or standards which may be fruitful in resolving conflicts of interests with reference to an (unavailable) impartial perspective. As second-order activities, they aim at norms of universal validity, but both may be construed without reference to a realm of abstract objects apart from the natural realm with all its particulars. Moral intuitions and judgements may be considered first-order phenomena, but they do

---

[15] In a conversation during the symposium 'Physics and our view of the world' organised by the Praemium Erasmianum Foundation, in May 1992 at Oosterbeek, the Netherlands; papers in Hilgevoord (1994).

not need a 'supernatural' realm for their explanation nor for their justification.

In contrast, religions are first-order phenomena in which there is, in most cases, some form of reference to transcendent realities, denizens of another realm. Whereas such references in morality and mathematics may be reconstructed in terms of procedures for justification (and of some insights about human nature and the world in which we act), religions are much more tied to an ontological view of those realities: gods are either supernatural realities or they are unreal, non-existent. In this sense, an account of the evolutionary origins and adaptive functions of religion is a much stronger challenge to the truth of religious doctrines than is a similar understanding of the origin and function of arithmetic or morality, since mathematical and moral claims are not so much seen here as truth claims about reality, say about causally efficacious entities, whereas religious claims are often taken to be truth claims (though they can also be seen differently, see [3.2]).[16]

If a naturalist account of the way beliefs originated, both in our culture and in individuals, is possible and satisfactory, there is no need to assume that they offer an approximately true view of reality. However, a naturalist explanation does not necessarily exclude their truth: there might be a supernatural reality, God, who conforms to the way people think about God in a particular tradition. Although this solution is logically possible, it has to face various difficulties, such as the fact that there is a wide and incompatible variety of religious claims. More relevant to the arguments developed here is another objection: it would be extremely unlikely that our ideas would correspond to a reality if the origin of these ideas is not shaped by that reality.[17] Thus, in the example given above, Brümmer had to claim (emphasis added): 'that was how God *brought* me to faith'. Some causal contribution of God in the temporal processes that brought someone to faith is essential to the likelihood that claims concerning God's existence may be true. But if there is such a divine causal role, the naturalist account is incomplete, and therefore wrong.

16   Ruse (1993, 155f.) makes a similar case for a disanalogy between epistemology (the existence of a train bearing down on me) and ethics. See also above, [22], on explaining and explaining away.

17   Segal (1989, 79). This argument depends on a philosophical view of reference which gives some place to our interactions with the world, but not necessarily on a causal theory of reference which emphasises the initial dubbing and subsequent use which is supposed to intend to preserve reference (Kripke 1980; emphasis on wider context in Evans 1973; see A. W. Moore 1993, 18).

Thus, there is at least this relevant difference between an evolutionary view of morality and one of religion. Whereas an account of ethics which avoids reference to a non-natural realm may be available, a similar move in theology would have more radical consequences, as it would undermine the referential character of statements which purport to be about a non-natural God. In the next section, we will consider two strategies which have been employed to respond to this challenge for theology.

26. THEOLOGIES OF EVOLVED HUMAN RELIGION

Among those who are not willing to discard evolutionary theory or diminish its scope, and who also seek to maintain an understanding of religions as consisting not only of functional phenomena, but to some extent of true claims about reality, at least two approaches can be found. Some have argued that the evolutionary process itself has certain qualities which make it revelatory of God, or perhaps even represent God. Others, especially Lindon Eaves, have argued that the religious metaphors should not be considered as claims about a non-natural reality or about the process of evolution as a whole, but rather as referring to phenomena within natural reality. We will return to this approach, but first we will consider representatives of the first option with its focus on particular qualitative features of the evolutionary process.

Qualities of the evolutionary process
Various thinkers have emphasised different qualities of the evolutionary process as theologically significant. Here I will consider the views of Ralph Burhoe, Gerd Theissen, and Gordon Kaufman, who have emphasised power, grace, and creativity as theologically relevant major characteristics of the evolutionary process.

Ralph Burhoe has not only offered some ideas about the role religions have played in our evolutionary past [24]. He has moved on from these to a theological proposal about the most adequate view of God.

The scientific pictures join the religious myths in saying that the same system of reality and power that created the earth and life upon it also created, sustains, and judges human life, including our religions. It makes little difference whether we name it natural selection or God, so long as we recognize it as that to which we must bow our heads and adapt. (Burhoe 1981, 21)

God is the Creator, the Lord of History – and that is the evolutionary process. Burhoe sees God as that reality to which one has to bow; in evolution that powerful reality shows itself as natural selection. Humans are not autonomous, nor can they pretend to be the Lords of History. Rather, our salvation lies in adaptation to the majestic reality that created us, and in which we live, move, and have our being (with reminiscences of the Acts of the Apostles 17: 28). Natural selection will crush any individual or group which does not adapt. Thus, science confirms what most traditional religions have always held: there is a power which creates and judges, punishes what is evil and rewards what is good.

Burhoe selects a particular aspect of reality to be regarded as God. With many theologians, both contemporary ones and theologians of previous ages, he emphasises divine power and human dependence; the Lord of History creates and judges by natural selection. In choosing – in company with many others – these elements to identify God, Burhoe reflects, implicitly, his Baptist background (Breed 1992, 1). Even though his sense of the majesty of God expresses an antidote to human anthropocentrism, it risks breathing fatalism – it is the process to which we have to adapt, rather than a process in which we participate, and within which we bear responsibility. It does not offer much guidance; rather than a sense of direction it offers a sense of dependence.

There are other attempts at taking the evolutionary perspective seriously which articulate other views of God. The German Lutheran Gerd Theissen sees grace rather than power as the primary characteristic of God. He argues that in the course of the evolutionary process an enormous variety of organisms has developed. He argues that this rise of variety reflects a major feature of reality: its tolerance for variation. Ultimate reality is tolerant. Thus, whereas Burhoe identifies God with natural selection, Theissen (1985, 72) is convinced that 'Belief in the one God is a protest against the principle of selection.' One reason is that Biblical monotheism gave certain human groups 'a power to survive' which they would have lacked without such a faith. His monotheism is not only rooted in biblical history, but also in a wider view of reality:

where people arrive at the conviction that the decisive 'environment' for them is God, whose resources can be shared among an infinite number of people without losing their value, they have found the Archimedean point from which they can shift the principle of selection which controls all life. They are still subject to this principle of selection, but they know that it does not represent ultimate reality. (Theissen 1985, 73)

Theissen's argument seems to be that evolution displays an increasing tolerance for variation, a tolerance which has become more pronounced with the emergence of culture; the ultimate limit corresponds to a monotheistic view of the deepest reality as God who is inexhaustible, and therefore able to tolerate all variations.

Theissen extrapolates from increasing tolerance for variation to absolute tolerance for variation. If we were to know the central reality completely, the central reality (the ultimate, God) would reveal itself as a reality with unconditional tolerance for variation. If culture reduces selective pressure, religion is the heart of culture. Theissen sees religion, and certainly Biblical monotheism, as a rebellion against selection; it opens humans to a larger reality in relation to which every individual has infinite meaning.

Rather than the stern God of judgement (by selection) which Burhoe envisages, Theissen offers a God who is primarily graceful, tolerant of variation. However, given the historical record of Christianity and Islam it is hard to maintain that monotheism is as closely tied to tolerance as Theissen would like to have it – as he acknowledges (Theissen 1985, 71). Besides, Theissen's emphasis on the inexhaustibility of God as our ultimate environment, which thus takes away the need for competition and striving, may well have adverse consequences for our value-system. Does it help to build up the self-restraint needed in the human use of natural resources?

Apart from such considerations on the historical and ethical adequacy of Theissen's view, it is also disputable whether his view is adequate with respect to evolutionary theory. Theissen moves from observations about beliefs which were functional in specific contexts, *i.e.* those of the historical situations of the Israelites, to an ontological claim with universal scope about the tolerance for variation exhibited by the ultimate, or central reality. However, evolutionary theory always considers adaptation with respect to actual environments, local realities. Some environments allow for a wide variety of organisms of various species to coexist; other environments are more restrictive. Claims about the central reality and unconditional tolerance have no place in such a perspective; evolutionary tolerance is always conditional on a specific environment. With the rise of culture, selection has changed, but it has not disappeared, and one could even make a good case that it has not diminished. In ascribing tolerance to reality as such, as an ontological claim, Theissen seems to me to be in danger of presenting an unwarrantedly optimistic view of reality. A consequence might be that the continuity between culture and non-cultural evolution is stressed too much, projecting back on reality the general regulative ideals which have emerged especially in certain human cultures.

The theologian Gordon Kaufman seems to combine a sense of dependence (Burhoe), a sense of grace as central to Theissen's proposal, and an ethical interest in regulative ideals which are not identified with actual practices. God is a human symbol, which refers to the serendipitous creativity of the biohistorical process (Kaufman 1993, 267), on which we are dependent, and which refers also to regulative ideals which shape human life.

On the one hand, thus, the word 'God' stands for something *objectively there*, a reality over against us that exists whether we are aware of it or not: we did not make it ourselves; we were created by cosmic evolutionary and historical processes on which we depend absolutely for our being. On the other hand, however, the word 'God' functions as a symbol within our minds, in our self-consciousness as beings who are not entirely made from without but who significantly contribute to our own creation, shaping and forming ourselves in accordance with images and symbols to which we are devoted. (Kaufman 1993, 320)

As the symbol 'God' shapes human life, one is justified in evaluating models of God by the functions they perform, especially their ecological and geopolitical consequences in an era when we move towards a history and culture which is global, even though it has many local varieties.

Kaufman objects to 'postulating an "other side" or "other world"', though we need to keep in mind that all our knowledge 'always shades off into ultimate mystery, into an ultimate unknowing' (Kaufman 1993, 325f). Dualism was functional, as it signalled that the normative was not identified with the given. The normative is expressed in a non-dualist way in the concept of 'God' as 'an ultimate point of reference' (Kaufman 1993, 327). Notions such as creator and lord, with their association of purpose, can be poetic expressions symbolising and focusing the vast cosmic movement of which we are aware today; these expressions need not and should not be reified (Kaufman 1993, 329).

I agree with Kaufman's emphasis on the human, constructed nature of all symbols of 'God', and the importance of functional, moral criteria in evaluating theological proposals. By emphasising the constructive character of our ideas, he avoids inferring positive qualities from the evolutionary process. However, this results in a certain ambivalence – a problem which is mine as well. On the one hand, the symbol 'God' is a human invention, a regulative idea beyond the evolutionary processes, which calls humans to lead adequate and fulfilling lives. On the other hand, it refers to the most fundamental character of reality. This problem is not specific to Kaufman; it is an example of the general problem that we create our ideas, as they are useful to us (functional, regulative), and then commit ourselves to them (as if they have an ontological status) – and as such this discussion is similar to the disputes on scientific realism [17.1]. In Isaiah (44: 15ff.) we hear of a man who cuts a tree, uses half of it to cook his food and the other half to carve a statue of God – and then prays to it 'Deliver me, for thou art God.' This is supposed to show the oddity of worshipping a human creation, an idol.

Kaufman accepts that we can never reach beyond human ideas, but none the less 'it will be understood that those who profess "faith in God" in fact mean to be committing themselves not simply to their own ideas of God but rather to that reality *whatever it may be* which draws us on toward full and responsible humanness' (Kaufman 1993, 355f.). Kaufman avoids reification of the dualism of perfection (ideal, God) and reality on earth. Rather, he identifies the evolutionary process with God – suggesting that it draws us toward humanness. If the evolutionary process becomes God, the question becomes: 'how can we fit our actions into God's overarching activity which is their context?' (Kaufman 1993, 358).

Why should we fit into the process? The desire to 'fit' is justified once we have already put a rubber stamp of approval upon the process by identifying it with God. Such a view is in danger of undermining the contrastive role of religion, as an inspiration to more than what is given, and thus as articulations of criticism rather than affirmation. Besides, an identification of the process and the normative ideals is unhelpful. 'To say that God is involved in everything without exception gives us no help at all in making the many quite *particular* choices of which life is made up' (Kaufman 1993, 418).

The way out of the dilemma between committing oneself to the process whatever it may be and the need for moral direction is for Kaufman, and also for Theissen, Christology. That provides a specific content to the values after which one strives, and thereby a means for distinguishing between whatever happens and what one values. Kaufman thus seeks to construct our view of God on the basis of what we know about Jesus and the new order of human relationships surrounding him, as the events related to Jesus are considered to be a revelation of the evolutionary process:

> In and through Christ the serendipitous activity, which underlies the evolutionary-historical trajectory that brought humanity into being, has revealed the direction it is moving with humanity, and what this means for human lif. (Kaufman 1993, 388f.)

Kaufman notes that tying the image of the truly human to specific, particular events increases evocative power, but also increases the potential for serious perversions.

Introducing Christology in this way in an evolutionary approach is problematic, as the emphasis on the evolutionary process tends to treat all stages as equally transient and relative to certain environments. By opting for Christology to introduce particular normative content, Kaufman returns to the particularity of a specific tradition. Any theological view which seeks to avoid dualism by identifying certain qualities of the evolutionary process with God (or ultimate values, or regulative ideals) runs into the problem that such an identification does not offer guidance for decisions to be made within the evolutionary process. And vice versa: emphasising particular norms relates a view to a particular perspective, which is related to a particular environment, and thus lacks the universality which is achieved by the attempt to link theology to the evolutionary process as a whole.

A further problem with such approaches, beyond their lack of particular values which help discriminate within the process, is that the process lacks the qualities assumed here, such as tolerance, concern for humanity, or for Goodness or Beauty. The indifference of nature is to some extent accepted by Kaufman when he points out the anthropo-centric meaning of the word 'evil' (Kaufman 1993, 361ff.), and thus the problematic character of the concept 'natural evil' – such as the earthquake that destroyed Lisbon in 1755 (my example; see above, [5]). A positive valuation of the process is challenged even more once one considers the far future, on a cosmological scale, when the Sun and the Earth will be no more (see Peacocke 1979, 319–29; Drees 1990, 242–53).

Given the problems with approaches which emphasise the evolu-tionary process, and then seek to justify particular values, one might consider the reverse procedure: why not acknowledge that we are in the middle of the process, in the middle of certain traditions as embodied in myths and rituals. It is this point of departure which the Lutheran theologian Philip Hefner seeks to combine with an evolutionary understanding of reality.

Motivated by myths

Both Kaufman and Hefner are seriously concerned about our situation, our failure to deal with the global and ecological challenges. Kaufman seeks to propose more adequate concepts of humanity, nature, and God. However, can concepts motivate people? Hefner does not focus on cognitively adequate concepts. He seeks to begin with existing structures that motivate us.

> I believe we will meet the challenge to our culture-formation from the bottom up, rather than the top down. By that I mean we are more likely to move through and with our existing myth-ritual traditions into new and more adequate myth-ritual formations than to proceed from science-based concepts into new channels. I term the latter a top–down approach, since it tends to abandon the traditions of the last 40,000 years. (Hefner 1993, 214)

I see various advantages to Hefner's emphasis on existing human traditions with their myths and rituals. Just as we do not have a universal language, but only particular ones, so too do we only have particular religious traditions. They provide orientation, whether for better or for worse. In focusing on myth which provides orienting images, and on ritual, which consists in symbolic actions, Hefner is speaking at the level of particular traditions, rather than having to introduce them as a kind of afterthought. His conception of theology is more like a ship which is reconstructed in the open sea with the materials available,[18] whereas Kaufman seeks to take the ship apart in a dock and reconstruct it out of the best available materials.

Emphasis on myth and ritual is also more congenial to the Biblical material, for instance in its reflections on human responses to the life and death of Jesus of Nazareth (e.g., Theissen 1987). It also seems to be more adequate with respect to the role of religion in personal life, which is not so much intellectual, but at a 'deeper' level of our personal life. And the emphasis on myth and ritual is in line with anthropological studies which approach myths and rituals as characteristic

[18] Otto Neurath used this image in another context when he argued against the existence of pure protocol sentences, in A. J. Ayer, ed., *Logical Positivism*. Glencoe, Ill.: Free Press, 1959 (original in *Erkenntnis* III (1932f.)).

elements of cultures. But we do not live by ritual and myth alone; we need, or cannot avoid, systematic reflection. Intellectual culture is the context for Kaufman's quest for clear and adequate concepts as well as for Hefner's intense dialogue with anthropology and biology.

Hefner not only argues for the importance of myth; the theory which he proposes has also some of the characteristics of a myth. To see ourselves as *created co-creators* is a proposal within theoretical discourse, within critical thinking, but also a proposal for a new rendering of our self-understanding, and as such it is a reformulated myth. The notion nicely captures both our dependence upon the processes that created us and our responsibility as co-creators. This mixture of dependence and responsibility is essential to his view of theology: the religious symbols out of which theology works 'embrace within themselves both the *is* and the *ought* and also an expression of how the two are unified' (Hefner 1981, 58). Both aspects are united in the core of his proposal for understanding human nature:

Human beings are God's created co-creators whose purpose is to be the agency, acting in freedom, to birth the future that is most wholesome for the nature that has birthed us. (Hefner 1993, 27)

The strength of the focus on myth and ritual – their hold on motivation and imagination – is also its danger. The idea of an ultimate gracious-ness in the evolutionary process, or any other academic alternative, is pale in comparison with the forces evoked by the image of a personal God up there. Myth and ritual may shape the attitude of masses and individuals in disastrous ways. Thus, critical thinking is a valuable counterpoint to any call for remythologising. However, critical thinking needs to recognise the power and complexity of our genetic heritage and of our brains. To reduce it all to well-articulated concepts, is to miss important aspects of human life.

In relation to the importance of myth and ritual, the role of science can be developed in various ways. Some attempt to develop a new mythology, drawing upon the sciences. Examples of such a scientific remythologising can be found abundantly, both among the popularisa-tions of science and among the literature on the shelves labelled 'science and spirituality' or 'New Age' in many book stores (see also the earlier discussion on models, [15]). To some extent, the emphasis on power, tolerance, or serendipitous creativity as main characteristic of evolutionary reality (as considered in this section), is similar. A problem with such approaches is that the achievements of science are not taken for what they are, but that they are used as a springboard to reach far beyond them in an insufficiently controlled flight of the imagination.

Hefner represents another perception of the task of relating science and theology. He seeks to preserve the wisdom embodied in religious traditions, while scrutinising and testing that wisdom in a critical dialogue with the science at hand. He does not appeal to a mystery at the limits of science. Rather, '*God-talk should be viewed as expressing something about our experience of the world that is scientifically understood*' (Hefner 1993, 81).

However, Hefner's approach reaches beyond that which is scientifically understood in offering a revised mythical image ('we humans are created co-creators') in the context of a positive view of reality. '*The central reality that undergirds all of concrete experience and to which we continually seek to adapt is disposed toward us in a way that we can interpret as graciousness and beneficent support*' (Hefner 1993, 194). Does religious myth, from which the 'graciousness and beneficent support' are taken, portray 'the way things really are', a term which Hefner uses in an attempt 'to clarify what is meant by the terms *God* and *ultimacy*'? (Hefner 1993, 287) Hefner needs a positive view of 'the way things really are', since he identifies the normative proposal of a way of living with an hypothesis about reality. 'The only persuasive ground for this commitment is the possibility that the hypothesis is a true, declarative picture of the nature of things' (Hefner 1993, 187).

I doubt whether this link between commitment and truth is as close as Hefner has it. Myths and ritual address deeper layers of human existence. To be effective at those deeper levels the explicit, consciously communicated words need not match with the unconsciously received message. Even within science, an adequate picture need not be true; the Newtonian view of gravity as a force acting at a distance is not true, but it has been and still is very adequate for almost all practical purposes. It is obvious that effective moral behaviour requires proper knowledge of our situation and of the possible ways to change it, but is the moral input in the choice itself dependent upon cognitive insights about the ontology of the world? I fail to see that the moral commands are dependent upon the 'way things really are'. Hefner writes: 'Christian theology interprets this behaviour [altruism, love] as expression of basic cosmological and ontological principles' (1993, 197). An evolutionary view does not deliver such cosmological principles; love and altruism are phenomena which have arisen in certain contexts.

The command to love is not wrong if reality is indifferent rather than loving; love would still exist as a real phenomenon within reality even if one could not consider reality as a whole to be loving.

This brings me to the next author, Lindon Eaves. He does not seek to discern certain qualities of the evolutionary process as a whole, but rather considers the nature of religious language as a language used within particular environments.

Nature and nature's God (Eaves)

Lindon Eaves, geneticist and Episcopalian priest, agrees with the other authors considered here in treating religion as speaking in and about this reality, rather than about 'another world'. 'Reality shapes itself' (Eaves 1991, 501). None the less, it is useful to distinguish 'nature' from 'nature's God'. Why can there be such a distinction?

The glimmer of a biological answer to that question is that we cannot live simply in a world of 'is'. The process of natural selection also produces an 'ought' within nature, in the form of the DNA-coded history of many past experiments with nature. The capacity to 'dream', however fragmentary the dreams, and to conceive of an alternative world, may also be DNA's solution to potentially inhospitable environments. The 'ought' and the 'dream' are experienced as 'nature's God', that is, as the existential pole of an evolutionary adaptive 'is' embedded in nature. (Eaves 1991, 501)

In making a distinction between 'nature' and 'nature's God', Eaves avoids the problem of affirming qualities of the evolutionary process such as power, tolerance of variation, or creativity; our God-language refers to a segment of our experiences with reality, especially some which are unconscious and intractable for us:

At least part of the human consciousness of transcendence may stem from the fact that we bear in our genes non-cognitive ways of functioning that have been adaptive in the past ... humans are puzzled by their awareness of the divine and feel compelled to give a name and coherence to its basis in reality beyond immediate experience. (Eaves and Gross 1992, 272)

The claim is not that specific myths are coded in the DNA, but rather that 'the processes of encoding and ontogenetic decoding of adaptive responses characteristic of the continuity of the germ line represent a material foundation to the basic elements' of the idea that we grasp transcendent Ideas by *anamnesis*, or that we have a 'collective unconscious' which harbours archetypes (Eaves and Gross 1992, 272).

Eaves and the theologian Gross go on to consider the biological basis of religious notions such as grace and evil, community and diversity, sin and death, transformation and fulfilment. However, developing new ways of thinking about traditional religious concepts is only part of the job. More challenging is another question:

How does a geneticist maintain his or her integrity while standing at the altar on Sunday talking *to* (not merely *about*) God? (Eaves 1991, 495)

Why continue using personal language? Eaves considers the personal language to be metaphorical. However, in metaphors it does speak about important aspects of reality which would be less adequately addressed in non-personal language.

Clearly, the 'thou' is metaphoric. But the puzzle for biology is accounting for the power of the 'thou' compared with the 'it'. That is, even if the 'thou' is metaphoric, something is lost when we attempt to translate the religious reality to the language of 'it', much as the joy of sex is not always enhanced by understanding the neurobiology of orgasm. (Eaves 1991, 502)

I do not think that 'the puzzle for biology' is to account for the power of personal over impersonal metaphors. In our evolutionary past (and in our present), people, and to a large extent also animals, have always evoked stronger responses of fear and affinity than inanimate objects. Whenever inanimate processes were experienced as unpredictable, a personal metaphor became quite prominent – spirits, demons, or gods of winds and water, for instance. Animism is a 'natural' way of experiencing the whims of nature, our 'manifest image'; many people even speak in such a way about cars or computers.

The problem is not the power of personal metaphors, but whether we can justify continuing to use such personal metaphors, even when we have become aware of their metaphorical character. Eaves makes the analogy with the joy of sex and the neurobiology of orgasm. There we use both kinds of language, whenever appropriate. The personal and affective dimensions can be there, and be communicated to the other, and thus have genuine meaning and consequences, whatever further analysis the neurobiologist offers. The demise of dualism between matter and spirit, between the chemical basis of life and the affective and cognitive features in humans and their cultures, may undermine the last analogy for a dualism between God and the world. However, it need not deprive us of a rich language which, in different ways, makes sense of higher and lower levels of analysis – a language in which the metaphor of a 'thou' to which we speak and sing may be appropriate for certain purposes, especially in our responses to phenomena which we do not control or understand, for which we feel grateful or which we are unwilling to accept. Eaves's approach avoids an absolute ontological claim about 'the way things really are', 'ultimate reality', or the overall direction of the evolutionary process.

Concluding remarks: functional and immanent ontological religion
We have considered two tendencies in theological proposals which seek to take an evolutionary view of everything very seriously. On the one hand, there is the tendency to focus on the evolutionary process as a whole, and to argue that it has certain features (power, tolerance, creativity), which justify a religious view of evolutionary reality. On the other hand, there is the proposal to consider different aspects within reality, such as the wisdom from the past which is encoded in our genes and articulated in religious metaphors, or the regulative ideals which humans construct.

In my opinion, the second approach has two major advantages. It is more in line with an evolutionary understanding of reality, which focuses on particular contexts rather than on the whole and which does not seem to justify an evaluation of the evolutionary process in positive religious terms, such as grace. And it allows for a contrastive role of religions, as systems which confront us with a sense of distance between what is and what should be, a prophetic role for religion, whereas the first approach aligns more with a mystical religious view which gives primacy to the sense of belonging to a harmonious whole. I do agree that there is a genuine role for reflections upon the whole, but they do not so much support answers (such as 'ultimate reality is tolerant') as provide an awareness of limitations, questions which remain open, as I will argue in the next and final chapter of this study.

I see particular religious traditions, which propose answers or responses to such limitations, as phenomena within reality, which have a certain role and reflect certain features of natural reality in a metaphorical way. As Eaves (1991, 499) formulated it, religions provide 'a symbolic and metaphorical framework for speaking (inadequately) of an overwhelmingly powerful and mysterious prevenient biological reality whose origins are lost in the mists of evolution and hidden from language and logic in the genetic code' (Eaves 1991, 499). Hence, religion is neither about a supernatural reality, transcending the evolutionary process, nor is it purely functional, merely *clothed* with a fictional aura of facticity (as in Geertz 1973, 90f., see [3.1]). There is an ontological aspect to the position articulated by Eaves and Gross:

religious language reflects the rich reality of our genes and cultures with all the adaptive wisdom thus encoded, wisdom which is not exhaustively accessible to analysis.

To some extent this is a return to the God-of-the-gaps. We do not use religious language to account for lightning, since we understand lightning and are able to manipulate it by putting up lightning rods. However, we do use religious metaphors in dealing with aspects of reality which are 'hidden from language and logic in the genetic code'. However, the discredited strategy of postulating a God-of-the-gaps has tried to fill apparent holes in natural processes as described by the sciences with the action of a supernatural being. Here, there is no similar ontological claim, as if the absence of evidence (of a naturalist explanation) is the evidence of absence (impossibility of a natural process by which the aspects which are 'hidden from language and logic' could have arisen).

The wisdom in our genes and our traditions stems from our tribal past; it need not be the wisdom for today or tomorrow. Thus, whereas we should not and cannot deny our evolutionary heritage, critical analysis and normative reflection, as they arose in our heritage, remain called for.

5

Science, religion, and naturalism

In the preceding two chapters we considered the impact of knowledge of the world and of knowledge of humans on various arguments about the relationship between religion and science. In this final part I move on from discussions on particular issues to a general articulation of my own position on science, reality, and religion. I also intend to present arguments against the two alternatives which I consider most challenging. Some dismiss all forms of religion by opting for a more radical naturalism which conflicts with those elements in my naturalism that provide minimal room for religion, *i.e.* conceptual and explanatory non-reductionism (CEN) and limit questions (LQ). Others opt for a richer naturalism which seeks to salvage religion in a realist way by giving a less prominent place to the natural sciences, and in particular to physics and functional, evolutionary explanations (thus *contra* CR, PP, EEP; see also [2]). In addition to opposing other views, I will also indicate how one can articulate some form of personal faith and theology in the context of the naturalism defended here.

To achieve these ends, I will draw together the various elements of the naturalist view in three sections dealing with science, reality, and religion. Firstly, in the naturalist view developed here the natural sciences play a major role. I will argue that the significance of science for our view of the world does not elevate science to a position beyond the naturalist view. The main contributor to a naturalist view can be understood and justified naturalistically [27]. Secondly, we will consider a naturalist understanding of reality and the consequences this has for religious views [28]. Thirdly, we consider a naturalist understanding of religion [29].

Then I will consider three major options for theology in relation to such a naturalist perspective.

We begin with the possibility of a different naturalism, which accepts science but seeks to offer another view of reality than the naturalist one presented here [30].

Then we come to an understanding of God which emphasises God's transcendence with respect to natural processes in such a way that there can be no conflict with a naturalist view. Such a view interacts with the sciences with respect to the understanding of time. It can also be seen as a response to limit-questions as they arise in relation to a naturalist view [31].

In the final section [32] I draw upon this non-temporal understanding of God's transcendence and upon theologies which build upon an evolutionary understanding of religion, relating their concept of God to 'the way things really are', as discussed above [26]. However, such ideas are not so much affirmed as realist claims, but rather accepted as speculations and regulative ideals. Religion can be accepted as a particular human articulation of a way of life, an articulation which is qualified and relativised by a sense of transcendence which may be nourished by reflections on limit-questions [32].

27. SCIENCE IN A NATURALIST PERSPECTIVE [1]

We need a view of science which avoids understatement as well as overstatement. If we have a too modest view of science, it ceases to be relevant. And if I have offered a too pretentious view of science, science itself will become something supernatural – which would make naturalism self-contradictory, as it would be unable to accommodate its most important contributing source, the natural sciences. The demise of the 'Legend' that science delivers truth in some a-historical way (see [2]) saves us from such an inconsistency. However, once one has avoided overstatement, one runs the risk of understatement. If science can be understood in naturalist terms as a phenomenon which arose and developed through a natural process,

---

[1] This section mainly follows Kitcher (1993), from whence the term 'Legend' has been taken. Giere offers another example of a naturalist view of science as a cognitive practice, 'requiring no special type of rationality beyond the effective use of available means to achieve desired goals' (1988, xvii), an approach which fits well with a naturalist emphasis on evolution. A label for such naturalist approaches to knowledge is also 'evolutionary epistemology' or 'naturalist epistemology', as referring to approaches which link the study of how people actually form beliefs, theories, etc., to ideas about the justification of beliefs, theories, etc.; see essays in Kornblith, ed. (1994).

and in which judgements arise through social interactions, interactions with nature, and individual, natural, cognitive processes, without reference to some absolute rational principles, we then need to argue for its special status in comparison with other practices.

An analogy may be the development of precision tools. Can one understand that one can make a precision tool for measuring lengths in microns (a thousandth of a millimetre), even if one has to start with a shed which contains only large and imprecise tools? The answer is: Yes. We can trace the history of technology, and thus come to see how new instruments have been made by means of a preceding generation of instruments. One could not construct a precision instrument at the level of microns in one step from scratch, say with only plain hammers and screwdrivers. Our current generation of tools is the fruit of a long chain of technological achievements. Rather than a jump from the bottom to the present level, the history of technology resembles an ascending spiral.

Similarly, the development of science is characterised by a long and convoluted road of perpetual modification. However, there is one relevant difference between science and technology: whereas technology may be judged by non-epistemic, namely practical goals, science is, in the present context, defended for its epistemic success. Thus, the norm for science is more abstract and elusive than the norm for technology, though the norm for technology might turn out to be hard to agree upon once one passes beyond the instrumental success to its contribution to human flourishing.

A naturalist view of science can be challenged in various ways. For instance, a naturalist view presents humans with all their capacities as biological beings, with limited memories and limited capacities for rational reflection. If humans are markedly limited in these ways, one could argue, science as a successful rational enterprise cannot be what it is. Hence, humans must be more than merely biological beings; their capacities as they are evidenced in science, and perhaps also in other activities, reach beyond what can be understood naturalistically (see [18]). One might also focus not so much on human capacities as on the norms by which science is evaluated. How could one ever evaluate these norms, if not by reference to some higher standard?

A naturalist answer can be envisaged with the help of an analogy. Science may be the legal system in a science-based naturalist view, but judges (individual scientists) are fallible and laws are not always just. Judges are not beyond judgement by their peers. And the laws can be reconsidered and modified. Speaking loosely, one might say that the legal system is evaluated and modified by the legal system. However, behind such a general statement one can discern an intricate network of persons and rules, parts of which are momentarily stable while other parts may be in flux.

Similarly, a more adequate view of science would need to pay attention to the variety of persons and procedures within science, rather than sticking to a general statement that science is judged by science, and is thus apparently caught in a circularity. Some scientists evaluate claims of others via procedures that are currently part of the accepted consensus, other scientists propose new instruments, again others propose a modification of accepted procedures since they do not account properly for results obtained and accepted as part of the current consensus, etcetera. Science is an interplay of various aspects, such as theories, concepts, and criteria of credibility, instruments, sets of questions considered significant, and sets of explanatory schemata. All these aspects have their place in practices of individual scientists and in the (often not articulated) consensus of the moment. When a theory is replaced by a different one, one can ask by which standard we have evaluated them, and preferred the one over the other. Apparently, the norm which is applied to both theories is supposed to be stable during that evaluation. On some other occasion, major concepts may change, or the division of labour, or the set of questions deemed significant, or the norms for credibility. Such processes occur at the level of individual scientists with their individual practices. Such changes affect the consensus practice of any given moment. The process, with all the variety of work within individual practices, which shape a temporary consensus, which shapes subsequent work in individual practices, which shape a new consensus, is iterated again and again. All the work is done at the level of individuals, interacting with each other and with nature. There is no need to invoke an abstract notion of knowledge or rationality beyond the knowledge and rationality as exhibited by human individuals with a wide (and in many cases fruitful) variation in cognitive styles. In such a way, science may be presented as a thoroughly natural enterprise.

That science is understood as a natural enterprise does not imply that epistemology can be eliminated in favour of psychology, as if we could avoid discussing questions about 'how we should proceed' in forming beliefs and theories about the world, and rather restrict ourselves to the study of how humans actually proceed. We face a variety of individual cognitive styles, and in discussing epistemological issues, we assess this variety of different cognitive approaches. In doing so, and in assessing beliefs formed in different ways, we also appeal to criteria which surpass the criteria that humans are naturally inclined to use. Logical and mathematical analysis, criteria such as universality and coherence, and the variety of ways of experimenting and testing claims, for instance by 'double-blind' experiments, are important for the credibility of science, precisely because they surpass and correct the conclusions of ordinary psychological mechanisms. One might include all these elements in a psychological description of our belief-forming mechanisms, but then epistemological considerations are not so much eliminated, as incorporated in a modified psychology, which also takes into account the mechanisms by which we override ordinary psychological processes.

A philosophical view of science can be considered both as a description of and as a prescription for science. Descriptive adequacy should be tested by applying this naturalist view of science to the historical development of various scientific disciplines over long stretches of time. Not only is it worthwhile to see whether the scheme can account for actual science, past and present, but also whether it does so more adequately than other views of science, such as those proposed by Thomas Kuhn, in terms of paradigms, with a more radical emphasis on social factors, and by Imre Lakatos, in terms of research programmes, with greater emphasis on rationality. In the following I will assume that some naturalist description of science is possible, and that it has to combine social, empirical, and rational aspects. As an indication of the lines along which such a view might be developed I will adopt the understanding of science proposed by Kitcher (1993), which was briefly sketched in this section: science is understood as an interplay of various aspects (theories, techniques, questions, etc.) in a variety of interacting individual practices.

The prescriptive adequacy of such a naturalist view seems harder to defend than its descriptive adequacy. Can this view, or any other naturalist view, yield a good prescriptive model for science? If one does not take human limitations and human variety into account, the answer is 'No!' Imagine a world in which scientists could entertain at each moment an unlimited number of propositions, procedures, and goals in their individual working memories and could all carry out the same procedures equally well. In such a world, cognitive variety between individuals would be much less pronounced, much less relevant, and much less troublesome for the formation of temporary consensus. However, we are limited in our cognitive capacities. And we are social beings, who modify information when we incorporate information from others and when we offer information to others. I think that for limited social beings such as we are a naturalist view of science as a variety of individual, interacting practices, forms the basis for a fruitful attitude: respect the cognitive variety in individual practices and seek, again and again, to articulate the current range of consensus.

This attitude with respect to cognitive variety and the quest for consensus is not a rule which gives us explicit norms about questions or theories to entertain, to accept, or to reject. In lacking such discriminating norms, the proposal differs – and as a naturalist view has to differ – from attempts which seek to formulate such norms in formal or material terms, for instance in terms of greater falsifiability, or as progress in or degeneration of a research programme. On a naturalist view, the norms are themselves part of the changing variety of practices, and of the consensus practices at each moment; there are no specific criteria which could be delivered by philosophy. This does not exclude an elusive, science-defining ideal beyond the flow of practices, such as the pursuit of interesting truth (Kitcher 1993, 157–60; against Laudan 1984). Such an elusive limiting ideal fits in well with the recognition that all discriminatory judgements on the feasibility and credibility of various projects are made in relation to the current norms, which may themselves be modified in the course of further individual work and consensus-formation. Since there are no material or formal norms, there is no clear and final demarcation line between science and non-science. One cannot prevent misguided practices from being carried out, nor can one avoid the possibility that practices which later will be considered good science are currently excluded.

If science can be understood along such lines as a natural phenomenon, based on the variety of cognitive practices of individual scientists and the social interactions by which they modify the consensus about claims, questions, procedures, criteria, instruments, assessments of authority, and the like, I may have overcome one potential problem, namely an overly pretentious understanding of science, which would surpass the naturalist framework. However, I then have to face another problem: Why would such a human practice deserve preeminence over other human practices, such as astrology, sport, politics, or art? Why would science as a natural phenomenon deserve a unique place or privileged status?

A preliminary element in the defence of the importance of science should be to note the limited character of the claim. Health may be improved more by physical exercises than by exercises in physics. Emotional satisfaction may be a prime effect of music or of gastronomy, rather than of science (though it is not absent from scientific practices). Social relations require something different than knowledge, and feelings may be expressed and recognised on many occasions in non-discursive ways. Practices such as those in the arts are guided by a different goal than the sciences, and thus are governed by different notions of excellence or improvement, focusing for example on technical and evocative aspects in the performance of music. Science is not the sole practice in which we pursue some form of excellence. The claim which I seek to defend here is that science deserves preeminence as our major *cognitive* enterprise.

There are other human practices which result in cognitive claims. An astrologer, for example, might claim the ability to inform us about a person's character or about opportunities which will come up next week with respect to finances or intimate relations. The claim is that such cognitive enterprises do not deserve the same authority as the natural sciences. Such a global dismissal needs to be spelled out in more detail.

Some claims which are extraordinary and lie outside the current consensus may well deserve further scrutiny. Let me take the example of claims in parapsychology regarding telepathy across spatial or temporal distances, apparently without a mediating physical process. Such claims are at odds with the scientific consensus, but their rejection is not beyond dispute. Whether one considers exploration worthwhile will depend on one's assessment of the utility of pursuing such a project, given what others have been doing so far, what other projects one might engage in, and expectations about the feasibility and fruitfulness of such research. I personally do not consider it sufficiently promising to spend much time exploring parapsychology, since I consider the likelihood of positive results very slim and the possibilities of developing my work within the consensus view of the natural sciences more important. However, it is legitimate for some individuals to study claims about parapsychological phenomena; this is part of the cognitive variation which is encompassed in the naturalist view espoused here. In this sense the view is liberal if not to say anarchistic; there is, in principle, no external constraint on the projects to be explored.

Such a liberal attitude in no way entails that all projects deserve equal funding or equal status in curricula; many would-be scientific ideas conflict with experiences and experiments, are inconsistent or imprecise, stand in isolation from other knowledge or introduce *ad hoc* elements which seem artificial or superfluous. Some cognitive projects which aspire to be recognised as scientific fail not so much due to the beliefs they advance, but due to their lack of proper development; they do not respond adequately to new discoveries. For example, creationists advance positions which were part of the scientific consensus in geology and palaeontology some 200 years ago. Hence, one cannot say that these beliefs as such could not be part of science at some stage. However, research has moved on, and scientists have abandoned such beliefs for good reasons. Mere repetition of beliefs from the past without accommodating more recent discoveries reveals an inflexibility of mind, and hence a psychological shortcoming (e.g., Kitcher 1993, 195). Repeating previously held positions is not likely to promote epistemic goals, though it might serve non-epistemic goals, such as the well-being of certain religious groups.

There is no global criterion which delineates the proper sciences and excludes all other practices which compete for cognitive credibility, but consistency, precision, fertility, avoidance of *ad hoc*-elements, and coherence with other knowledge are among the general criteria which we use to evaluate cognitive practices. The adequacy of competing cognitive practices has to be analysed on a case by case basis, with due consideration of the modifications that ensue for other, partially unified accounts of the world. My expectation is that creation science, parapsychology, astrology, homeopathy with its extreme dilutions, and the like would all fail in comparison with mainstream science, and are not worth the effort needed to study them, but that some folk-knowledge in medicine, for instance, might be explored fruitfully, and that such an exploration might also be worthwhile.

In a piecemeal fashion we can assess claims about the relative merits of scientific and non-scientific cognitive practices. A general defence of science seems impossible, but this should not worry us too much. The same holds for some forms of scepticism, which are unanswerable, just as is a radical form of solipsism. If we abstract from everything we know about nature, including our own cognitive capacities, we may well be unable to demonstrate that certain procedures are bound to yield epistemically valuable practices. However, one can refute more specific forms of scepticism by carefully analysing the historical episodes or psychological traits appealed to. In such an analysis, scepticism is not only refuted but is also to some extent accommodated in a careful scrutiny of our currently favoured methods of individual reasoning, which might result in their modification.

The conclusion of these considerations is that science can be understood naturalistically without thereby losing its significance. We now will turn to the implications of a naturalist perspective for our views of reality and of religion. In a later section [31], I will consider limits of a science-oriented naturalism, and thereby bring to light another role for religion.

28. REALITY IN A NATURALIST PERSPECTIVE

A naturalist approach may have consequences for religion due to its *view of reality*, which may be at odds with a theological view of reality, and due to the *view of religion* that arises in its context. We will begin with the implications of a naturalist view of reality for theology.

A relatively minor issue is that any view of reality which differs from the views of reality that were prevalent when a particular religion was shaped, undermines the recognisability of the *images and metaphors* in which that religion is expressed.

With respect to the naturalist view presented here there is a further challenge to many religious images, due to its emphasis on the coherence of reality. Matter and forces are the same in outer space as on earth; organic chemistry is ordinary chemistry of a subset of all molecules, *viz.* mostly large carbon-based ones; biology does not assume a separate principle of life, humans arose in the course of a long evolutionary process, and our cognitive capacities and experiential life reside in our neurophysiological structure. Such a view of reality undermines various analogies, metaphors, and models which flesh out many Christian views of the world.[2] A duality of heaven and earth can no longer be articulated in astronomical terms, and distinctions between humans and animals, and between matter and mind have become matters of degree rather than of principle. Even the realm of personal experiences, including religious experiences and consciousness, seems to be part and parcel of nature; the distinction between personal and impersonal relations provides no basis for distinguishing supernatural and natural phenomena. This does not make such differences irrelevant or uninteresting; there is no need to belittle quantitative differences and attach significance only to qualitative ones. However, it makes such differences less adequate as metaphors or models for God's transcendence. (Metaphors for transcendence which regard the whole of natural reality are an exception, since they do not assume a dichotomy *in* the natural world; see [31].) A loss of analogies may not be too much of a problem for living religions; adherents may propose new metaphors, or continue to communicate with the help of the old ones which still function for a large part of the audience.

A naturalist view of reality obviously has implications for those theologies which understand themselves as, among other things, *explanatory* of phenomena in the world. Theologies are more than primitive or subtle attempts at explanation, but in so far as they are understood as offering explanations for natural phenomena they compete with other explanations, such as those delivered by the sciences. In this respect, a comparison is appropriate. Such a comparison does not favour a view of organisms or species as special divine creations. For example, understanding organisms as the products of design offers no account for the many less-than-optimal solutions which occur in nature, such as the Panda's thumb, which is not a true thumb but an enlarged wrist-bone, modified to strip bamboo (Gould 1980, 21–24), or the human eye, with the nerve leaving on the front side of the retina, thus saddling us with a blind

---

[2] Of the vast literature on analogies, models, and metaphors a few (Barbour 1974, Gerhart and Russell 1984, Soskice 1985) focus especially on science, religion, and their relations. In as far as the differences are relevant, I will use the term 'analogy' where words are applied to a new domain without a change of meaning or where meanings from two domains are brought into a one-to-one correspondence; I will use 'metaphor' when meanings are modified. I use the term 'model' when referring to a material or abstract partial representation or embodiment of another material or abstract system (see also [15]).

spot. 'Remnants of the past that don't make sense in present terms – the useless, the odd, the peculiar, the incongruous – are the signs of history. They supply proof that the world was not made in its present form' (Gould 1980, 28). An evolutionary approach is well suited to understand less-than-optimal solutions as the outcome of nature's tinkering, with existing mechanisms adapted to new purposes. The point is not 'that special creation is in principle *impossible*, only that it is in general unlikely, or unneeded in specific contexts' (McMullin 1993, 300; in a reflection on Plantinga's writings, see above [18]). McMullin makes it clear that scientific claims about true beliefs do not 'mean that the alternative can be logically excluded in a completely conclusive way; nothing more than overwhelming likelihood is what scientists normally intend by this sort of usage' (McMullin 1993, 306). And overwhelming likelihood they have achieved, since the evolutionary view that all forms of life on earth have a common ancestry is able to explain so many different discoveries, both in the structure of different proteins, in the fossil record, and in the study of homologies and of geographical distributions (e.g., McMullin 1993, 316ff.); special creation would leave such discoveries unexplained, although 'it would have been possible for the Creator to use similar structures' (McMullin 1993, 319). The conclusion from the success of science must be that such cognitive theological claims are unlikely.

With respect to physical processes in the non-living world, a similar argument about the likelihood of special divine activity can be made. Lightning has become dissociated from belief in the wrath of God and most believers now accept lightning rods as protective devices (Ferré 1993, 27), even though it is not logically impossible that God acts in the atmosphere so as to cause lightning to strike at one place rather than at another place.

Even when theology is not understood as explanatory to some extent, the view of reality we have may still be very relevant to theological claims, for instance about divine action, at least when such claims need certain *assumptions* about reality. The issue is not that we are comparing natural and supernatural explanations (as in the case of apparent design in organisms), but that believers propose, for instance, that there is an openness in reality which offers a possible locus for divine activity. Thus, the physical processes are not supposed to confer any likelihood on the religious belief. Rather, given the belief, the physical processes are expected to have certain characteristics which makes it possible to interpret them in a specific way.

As argued earlier [13], claims about openness in complex processes rely, in my view, in many cases on an unwarranted move from epistemological considerations to ontological ones: unpredictability does not imply indeterminacy or openness to non-natural influences, either from humans or from God. Such an influence hidden in unpredictable or unobserved but determinate processes would be at odds with the integrity of science. An exception might be processes in which there is, upon a naturalist view, a genuine element of chance. Such processes would be less problematic as a locus for divine activity within natural processes (as long as God would act so as to effect outcomes within the range of naturally possible outcomes with their frequencies). However, I do not consider this an attractive option for theology. There is no need to supplement a non-natural cause when a process is a genuine chance process; the occurrence of any of the possible outcomes may be considered explained by being one of the possible outcomes, whatever (non-zero) probability it has.[3] An appeal to chance as a locus of divine activity does not acquire likelihood as an explanation of the outcomes; it derives its credibility solely from prior beliefs about such divine activity.

Rather than focusing on a specific potential locus for divine activity, one might also consider the incompleteness of any naturalist explanation. In my view, limitations in our knowledge are not to be seized upon for religious apologetics; the absence of evidence does not count as evidence of absence. If we do not know which actual Darwinian history explains a certain feature, it does not follow that there is no actual Darwinian history. It would only be evidence of absence if we were quite sure that we had explored all the possibilities in such a way that decisive pieces of evidence could not have eluded us. Once I have turned the lights on in my room and looked around, the absence of evidence for the presence of an elephant in my room is, obviously, evidence of the absence of such a large animal. However, a similar argument about a mouse would not be valid. Similarly when we move from observations to calculations: absence of tractability does not mean that the problem

---

[3]   Salmon (1990, 62), referring to Jeffrey (1969). According to Jeffrey (1969, 106), it 'is the famous parallelism between explanation and prediction which I think breaks down for statistical explanations that impart less than practical certainty to the phenomenon explained'.

has no determinate mathematical solution, but only that this solution eludes us.

This argument, that the 'absence of evidence' should not to be confused with 'evidence of absence', may appear to be neutral with respect to religion: the naturalist could apply it to the possibility of a naturalist explanation where it has eluded us so far whereas a theist might invoke it to defend her view with the argument that the absence of evidence regarding divine intervention is not evidence of the absence of such interventions. However, this symmetry is lost once one develops examples in more detail. For instance, though looking around and not observing a mouse would not be sufficient evidence for its absence, I do have ideas about observations and tests (such as putting out cheese) which would lead to further evidence and I also have ideas about why I may have failed to observe a mouse that is present (it is small and quick); similarly, we may be unable to predict the weather two weeks in advance, but we can explain such a limitation itself quite well. We may lack evidence which informs us about the actual Darwinian history that led to contemporary hominids, but we can propose various possible Darwinian histories, develop these in detail, and check such specified possibilities against independently acquired knowledge about conditions as they obtained in the past. The challenge for a theist is to move beyond a general claim about the absence of evidence not being evidence of absence to more specific proposals about the things that might count as evidence with respect to divine intervention in natural processes or to proposals about why there cannot be any empirical evidence (see below, [31]). The overwhelming likelihood seems to be on the side of the naturalist view that natural processes are not occasionally interrupted or suspended.

The coherence of reality is not only a challenge for theology. It may well be seen as an understanding of reality which is consonant with a theistic view. Given beliefs about God's wisdom and power, one ought to expect a fundamental integrity in God's work (e.g., McMullin 1993, 323f.). Whereas individual species are not the results of distinct divine acts, the whole of natural reality may be seen in these terms. The naturalist account presented here also articulates how pervasive our limitations are. These too could be appropriated theologically as indications of the significance of our myths about our limitations, such as myths about the unavoidable (original) sin and problems of co-operation (tower of Babel), and the story of God's answer to Job.

A naturalist view portrays the richness of matter. As in the quote from Dewey at the beginning of the first chapter, mountain peaks 'are the earth in one of its manifest operations'. The propensities of matter are revealed to go way beyond such a limited result as a pile of sand, or even a mountain peak. In my view, the potentialities of matter have reached their climax so far in humans; with this climax have also come the deepest shadows so far. A naturalist view of reality does not imply that we devalue humans, but that we upgrade our view of reality. This seems to be lost sight of by opponents of a naturalist view who fear that human dignity would be lost. It is also neglected by some ardent supporters of a naturalist view, who claim that the loss of human dignity is a fact. From the availability or possibility of a naturalist explanation of humans it does not follow that humans are insignificant or equal in significance to, for instance, sponges, worms, or rocks. And whatever one's assessment of humans, the richness of matter supports, in my view, a sense of gratitude towards the reality which has given birth to us and to all these other phenomena.

29. RELIGION IN A NATURALIST PERSPECTIVE

A naturalist view of reality not only has consequences for a theological view of reality (see above), but also for the understanding of religions. Religions are phenomena within reality. Thus, they can be studied just like other human phenomena. The natural sciences in a restricted sense do not have much to contribute to the study of religions; this level of complexity and intractability requires approaches which may be less fine-grained and precise but are thereby able to take some of the richness of social interactions into account. However, even though the specific study of religions may be the business of others, such as anthropologists, sociologists and psychologists, the perspective arising out of the natural sciences offers some outlines for views of religions.

In earlier sections we have considered the implications of the neurosciences, and thus the study of those aspects of our constitution which give rise to our 'inner life', and the implications of the evolutionary understanding of humans, including their cultures and religions. Within an evolutionary perspective, one would primarily

explain the emergence of religions along lines similar to the explanations one would advance for social phenomena such as political
institutions and languages. The primary pattern of evolutionary
explanation is functional: religions arose, and therefore probably
contributed to the inclusive fitness of the individuals or communities
in which they arose, and which in turn were shaped by them. An
alternative could be that they arose as a side-effect with the emergence of some other trait. Perhaps with the rise of consciousness
questions about the origin and meaning of the world and one's
individual existence could arise, and as long as other explanations
were not available, explanations in terms of spirits and personal
powers in and beyond the world were attractive. It may have to do
with the lack of unity of consciousness (as argued by Julian Jaynes) or
as a resolution of stress when hunter-gatherers became sedentary
(Dietrich Ritschl; see [20.3]). A third possibility is that they arose as an
accidental result of some contingency in our evolutionary past.
However, this explanation of religion seems implausible given the
persistence and diversity of religions across many ecological conditions
and cultures.

As for the functional role of religion, various proposals may be
considered, such as Burhoe's view that religions made the co-
operation of larger groups of hominids, beyond close-kin, possible
[24]. Another proposal places less emphasis on the role of religion in
contributing to human co-operation, and more on its role in our
responses to intractable, apparently contingent features of our environment (e.g., Luhmann 1992, 26). Such proposals are in need of
further specification. One might test their credibility by analysing in
greater detail how religions may have arisen and may have been
sustained in the environments of various epochs, and what their
adaptive value (via culture) may have been. The functions of religions
may have changed over time as well. Here I will not defend one
particular view of the function of religions, but rather reflect on some
general implications of such naturalist views of religions as functional
cultural practices.

To say that religions are, or were, functional is not necessarily to deny
that their central terms refer to realities. However, if a religious claim
purports to be about a supernatural reality, such as one or more gods,
one might raise the question of whether the claim may be right or
wrong. For comparison I want to start with the example of observing

trees. On an evolutionary view, the adequacy of our language about trees, with notions such as bark, leaves, fire, wood, etc., is intelligible since the language has been modified in a long history of interactions of humans with trees and with each other in conversations about trees. This web of causal interactions lies behind the adequacy of our language about trees. If one came across a culture with no past experiences with trees, it would be a very surprising coincidence if they had an adequate vocabulary for trees. We refer to trees, and we seem to do so in fairly adequate ways, because our language has arisen and been tested in a world with particular ostensible trees. Now back to religions and reference. On the naturalist view there is no locus for particular divine activities in a similar ostensible way. Thus, it is extremely unlikely that our ideas about gods would conform to their reality (see above, [25]; Segal 1989, 79). Hence, an evolutionary view challenges religions not only by offering an account of their origin, but also by undermining the credibility of their references to a reality which would transcend the environments in which the religions arose.

Denying the adequacy of a transcendental reference of evolved religions need not imply that they are merely fictitious stories 'clothed with an aura of facticity', to quote again this phrase from Clifford Geertz's definition of religions [3.1]. Religions with their rituals and myths have arisen in certain environments and have been shaped by the challenges that humans, or their hominid ancestors if we dare to go back that far, faced. Elements of these myths can be seen as rooted in natural reality. Eaves (1991, 499, 501; see above [26]) gives as an example 'the experience of the "ineffable"' (since what is coded in genes, is only secondarily accessible to language and logic); he also mentions original sin and the normative contrast between nature and nature's God. With the heritage of the past and with 'the capacity to "dream", however fragmentary the dreams, and to conceive of an alternative world', we transcend the objects that are directly present to us, such as trees, but we do not transcend the natural world. In an earlier section, we also had reason to note that our sensitivity to various aspects of rituals may be deeply rooted in the structure of our brains [20.2]. Such issues can be explored further in the context of a reflection on the ontogeny of human individuals in relation to their genetic heritage and their biological and cultural environments. However, such refinements of our insights into the roles of religions in human individuals and communities would not challenge the general view of religion as presented here.

30. A RICHER NATURALISM?

In the last three sections I have presented the implications of my naturalist view for our understanding of science, reality, and religion. Now we come to consider how these explorations may be taken up in a theological perspective which not only treats religion as a phenomenon, but also as a view of, or an attitude to, reality that calls for commitment, or 'faith'. In this section we will discuss proposals which attempt to take science seriously without accepting the naturalism presented here. The authors to be considered opt for a richer view of reality, which has been called 'religious naturalism' or 'religious empiricism'. They seek to stay clear from approaches considered unattractive, such as 'reductionism', 'determinism', 'materialism', 'selectionism', and 'mechanicism', to mention just a few labels which are occasionally used pejoratively, and to find value, self-organisation, meaning, consciousness, or some other feature considered desirable, as fundamental aspects of reality.

In an earlier section [21], we referred to Thomas Nagel as someone who defends a richer view of reality when it comes to consciousness. And when John Polkinghorne (1993, 439; see [13.1]) does not so much claim room in relation to the laws of physics, but rather considers these laws downward approximations 'to a more subtle (and supple) whole', he too seems to seek a different understanding of reality in which a continuous interaction between God and particular events in the world does not disturb the coherence of processes as uncovered by the natural sciences. However, Polkinghorne retains a stronger theological dualism of God and the world than the 'religious naturalists' who will be considered here.

An advantage of a richer naturalism seems to be that its religious view of reality which emphasises notions such as meaning or value is in tune with its interpretation of reality, without appealing to any particular experiences or revelations in history (even though we may have come to this view of reality through insights and experiences in certain situations, due to certain persons). With respect to such richer forms of naturalism which seek to accommodate religion, two kinds of questions can be raised. Do they offer a plausible or at least reasonable interpretation of the sciences? And if so, do they deliver the theological fruits desired? I will focus especially on the first question, the interpretation of the sciences. With respect to the theology that arises in such a perspective, I wonder whether it is not too much a 'mystical' religiosity, accepting reality as it is, lacking opportunities to articulate a 'prophetic' sense of contrast between the way the world is and the way the world should be (see [3.3, 17.3, 26]).

Religious naturalism

> If the image of the Garden, in which humanity and nature interact with balance and mutual benefit, becomes a fundamental image of our world, it will of course be easier to see how the Machine can fit – as an inorganic simplification and servant of the organic – than it is now to understand how a Garden could come to grow in the cosmic Machine. (Ferré 1993, 95)

'Religious empiricism', sometimes called 'religious naturalism' or 'empirical theology', seeks to draw on knowledge from the natural and social sciences, including historical-critical studies of religions and their sacred texts. It assumes that 'empirical data is always relational and contextual' and 'that meaning, value, and significance are immanent, that is, within the historical, temporal flux' (Rogers 1990, 3, 5). Experience is seen as 'a rich, complex phenomenon, containing value-elements as well as sheer facts, often shading off into vague, half-lighted zones where dreaming and waking are hard to distinguish' (Ferré 1992, 223).

Among the founding philosophers one might count John Dewey, William James, and Alfred North Whitehead. Their views were propagated by many theologians teaching at the Divinity School of the University of Chicago, such as Henry Nelson Wieman, Bernard Meland, Charles Hartshorne, and Bernard Loomer (Inbody 1992; Miller 1974; Peden 1987; Rogers 1990). This (mostly American) religious naturalism has sought to relate positively to science while developing a view of reality which is adequate to all kinds of experience. Within this broader stream there are functionalists (e.g., Dewey, Wieman, and the Jewish thinker Mordechai Kaplan), who seek to understand 'God as that function or instrument in human affairs that increases human good' (Rogers 1990, 8). This is worked out in a practical and reforming spirit. Rationalists, such as Charles Hartshorne, have built superstructures of logic and metaphysics. Those of a more mystical inclination stress that life in its fullness goes beyond systematisation, remaining 'attentive to what William James has called the "More" in existence' (Rogers 1990, 13).

In a wider sense, many authors writing on science and theology, especially defenders of critical realism such as Ian Barbour and Arthur Peacocke, could be considered to be doing empirical theology, certainly when the contrast is with a theology which relies on dogma or authority. However, the 'naturalist empirical theologies' under consideration here differ from most other examples of theologies elaborated in the light of science in their tendency to deny transcendence beyond the natural; they also differ from some approaches, including mine, in their tendency to hold that the scientific view of the world itself is more spiritual, more humanistic than is often thought.

One of the labels used is 'religious empiricism'. However, this may be misleading. It is not an eliminative empiricism, *i.e.* the view that nothing exists besides sense data and what can be operationally defined on such a basis. Nor is it as agnostic as Van Fraassen's empiricism (1980, 1994). Experiences are, upon this approach, the foundation from which speculation is supposed to take off in order to develop a metaphysical view. Quite a few authors in this tradition argue for a Whiteheadian metaphysics. In searching for a metaphysical scheme they encounter the same problems as other theological and metaphysical realists who attempt to use the sciences while reaching beyond them (see chapter 3, especially [17.3]).

Religious naturalism and science

Karl E. Peters, a long-time editor of the major journal on the relationship between science and religion, *Zygon*, holds that science and empirical theology generally agree in their assumptions about the nature of reality. Both assume a naturalist world view. 'Human fulfilment and the ultimate source of fulfilment are to be found not beyond the spatial–temporal world but within it. If there are realms of being other than space-time nature and history (as in supernaturalism), they are beyond our ken and have no relevance to life today' (Peters 1992, 63). Thus, empirical theology as he sees it does without a traditional concept of transcendence. Here, we will focus on another feature of their view, namely their understanding of science and of the world.

'A second feature of the naturalist worldview, which science and empirical theology hold in common, is that reality is basically organic. By this I mean it is both relational and historical' (Peters 1992, 63). Similarly, Nancy Frankenberry claims that 'the fundamental image of nature in terms of interpenetrating fields of forces and organically integrated wholes has replaced that of self-contained, externally related bits of particles of inert matter' (Frankenberry 1992, 39). Ferré's reference, quoted above, to 'the Garden' as the fundamental image of our world, rather than 'the Machine', evokes a similar distinction between 'modern' and 'post-modern' science. Charles Birch, a geneticist, discerns 'a purpose for everything', to paraphrase the title of one of his books (Birch 1990), in a post-modern ecological world view. And the process theologian David Griffin, who takes seriously parapsychological evidence such as extrasensory perception and psychokinesis (Griffin 1989, 6), entitles a book *The Reenchantment of Science* (Griffin 1988).

The philosopher Frederick Ferré writes that one of the ideals of modern science is to explain by reduction. 'To know what a thing really is, in terms of this ideal, would be to know as much as possible about the parts that make it up' (Ferré 1993, 88). The consequences of the ideals of modern science are depressing: they leave no room for the values of spontaneity, creativity, responsibility; they leave no place for aesthetic values; and they alienate us 'from our own intuitions of meaning and our own structures of purpose' (Ferré 1993, 90). We are cut off both from nature and from the world of other people. However, ' "modern science" is of course only one of many possible approaches to the problems of "natural philosophy" ... and alternatives to it and its ideals have not been lacking' (Ferré 1993, 90). We cannot dismiss empirical testability and the power of theories formulated in mathematical concepts as mythology; we cannot go back to pre-modern forms of science. However, there are 'postmodern sciences', that 'have broken sharply with the ideals and assumptions that have been identified with modern science for long centuries' (Ferré 1993, 93). Ferré refers briefly to quantum physics, but his main example is ecology; others refer also to the work of Prigogine (see [14]). An ecologist needs analysis, but 'these analyses always become means to a wider end, the end of conceptual synthesis that preserves awareness of living systems in dynamic interaction' (Ferré 1993, 93). To understand a tree one needs to understand its cells and tissues as well as the forest of which it is a part. Ecology 'includes and transcends analysis in a holistic way that is essential to its conceptual task' (94).

To what extent has science abandoned 'the mechanistic world view', and accepted an 'organic' view of reality? I am not convinced by the analysis of science offered by Ferré and other religious naturalists.

Quantum physics excludes certain views of the universe. Perhaps the universe is not like a clockwork with springs and cogs, always in a well-defined state and, once started, for ever set on a unique course. Quantum physics, on some interpretations, introduces non-local correlations. But quantum physics does not thereby introduce into our picture of the world holism in a sense related to subjectivity or values. Something similar, it seems to me, holds for ecology. Scientists have uncovered many subtle relations between various species in a single environment. If modern science is exclusively defined in terms of analysis in terms of constituent particles, it misses such relations – and thus is *passé*. However, this is a straw man. Relations between systems and their environment, or of various systems with each other are within the domain of the natural sciences as they developed over the last few centuries; there is no need to mark such issues as signalling a shift from a world without values, subjects, and colours to an organic world. The only point is, perhaps, the place of the subject – where Thomas Nagel took exception to naturalist approaches [21].

In relation to Ferré's view of science, I consider as revealing his statement, quoted at the beginning of this section, that it is of course easier to understand how the Machine fits in the Garden than the reverse. This betrays a resistance against mainstream theories of evolution, which see more complex entities as products rather than as initial states [24]. To take another example from the development of science which is at odds with Ferré's holism: molecular processes constituting complex processes in living organisms, ranging from viruses to humans, are unveiled at an incredible rate, as testified by almost any issue of journals such as *Nature*, *Science*, and, more accessible to the general reader, *Scientific American*. This is not to deny that there are important changes in scientific analysis. For instance, one of the changes in chemistry has been the shift from analysis in terms of constituent particles to analysis in terms of three-dimensional shapes. However, analysis of amino-acids in terms of spatial structure is not less analytical and more holistic (in a sense related to values) than analysis in terms of constituent particles. And the same holds for physics formulated in terms of fields rather than in terms of particles. The transition from modern to post-modern science in the way discerned by Ferré and other religious empiricists, seems to me to underestimate the success and the potential for further development of modern science in the way it has progressed over the last few centuries, or, to express it in terms of their distinction between modern and post-modern science, to overestimate the differences and underrate the continuity between successive stages of science.

There are interesting changes in science, which have triggered various debates in the philosophy of physics and elsewhere. Ideas on space and time, substance, and determinism have acquired a new shape. However, neither these changes in science nor these philosophical discussions warrant the claim that there has been a 'reintegration of understanding with valuational intuition' (Ferré 1993, 95). Science is not modified by our 'valuational intuitions', but contemporary science seems to offer the possibility of understanding the constitutional basis and evolutionary origins of our 'valuational intuitions' [20, 24].

The order of disciplines
Can one offer an account of our world which is radically different from the way it is viewed by contemporary physics? If the focus is on current physics, the answer must be positive. Our physics is certainly not the last word. Underlying the level of particle theory there might be a quite different theory, formulated perhaps in terms of superstrings, twistors, or quantised building blocks of space-time in a, yet unknown, theory of quantum gravity. Such changes may well have consequences for our concepts of object, space, time, substance, and force, and for ideas on issues such as determinism and causality. However, such a change in physics would respect the hierarchical structuring of phenomena, and of the corresponding sciences, which is more or less the backbone of the contemporary natural sciences, from quarks to nuclei to atoms and molecules to macromolecules, and on to living organisms, followed by consciousness and culture. We might change our understanding of the foundation, ontologically speaking, but it would not affect the higher parts of the building of our knowledge. In the order of knowledge fundamental physics is not the basis for doing chemistry or biology, but

rather a kind of pinnacle, pointed but uncertain and speculative. If it were to be proved wrong, the building would not collapse, though it might need some reorganising.

A more radical alternative – and this is what religious naturalists are after – would be one which would in some way reject this overall pattern of the natural sciences, and thereby modify general expectations about the fundamental levels of reality. In discussions about the relationship between science and religion the most prominent example of such an alternative is process philosophy, which draws on the categorial scheme developed by Alfred N. Whitehead in his *Process and Reality* (1929). On this view, 'values' and 'choices' are relevant at the most fundamental level of reality. Physics is adequate for uninteresting entities, such as electrons or stones, which have a rather limited spectrum of choices. However, features of reality which show up most clearly in human relations are characteristic of the most fundamental structure of reality; the 'Garden' has priority over 'the Machine'.

The attempt to develop such an alternative view of the fundamental structure is legitimate. It would be a remarkable change in the history of ideas if such an alternative organisation of scientific knowledge would replace the consensus view, but it is not to be rejected a priori. However, there are some important constraints: such proposals will have to be able to offer alternative accounts of all well-confirmed phenomena, experiments and observations. Such accounts should be at least of a degree of detail and precision comparable to those of the currently dominant view. With respect to the proposal mentioned above, process philosophy, I am not convinced that the categorial scheme which gives a metaphysically basic role to values and choices can be developed in sufficient quantitative detail, nor do I expect it to be true or useful. I thus see no reason to abandon a materialist version of naturalism. However, naturalism cannot, and should not, categorically exclude the possibility of such a reversal of our ideas about the most fundamental structure and the relative ordering of phenomena and disciplines.

There is a dilemma for the religious naturalists. If they side with empiricism as articulated in the philosophy of science, they should abstain from erecting elaborate metaphysical schemes on the basis of our experience, or rather, they should not take any of the manifold schemes which could be constructed too seriously. If religious naturalists side with realists in philosophy of science, science enlarges our world beyond experience (McMullin 1994), but then, they will also have to accept that science forces us to a critical reconsideration of our experiences, coming up with counter-intuitive views of them; this was expressed by the embryologist Wolpert in a book entitled *The Unnatural Nature of Science* (1993). A challenge for a religious view which applies notions such as value, meaning, purpose at the most basic level may arise when science looks at the empirical material in another way than the common-sense view, and thus offers an account which respects experiences as experienced, but none the less gives an account of them which differs – by employing fewer notions related to persons, values, meaning, etc. – from the account given by the one who had the experiences.

31. A MORE TRANSCENDENT GOD?

Recent philosophers and theologians tend to think that anything that could count as *God* – as the living, loving person whom the Old and New Testaments depict as in dialogue with the creatures of history – must be in time. Their message is that the deity of the atemporalists is too remote and impersonal to be God. Yet medieval philosophers and theologians tended to think that anything that could count as *God* – as the transcendent, perfect source of all that is other than Himself – could not be in time. The medievals would say that the deity of the temporalists is too small or too creaturelike to be God. (Leftow 1991, 3)

There is one traditional way to articulate theology in a way which avoids a confrontation with the natural sciences, and that is to emphasise the uniqueness of God's mode of being and activity. This is articulated in the notion of *creatio ex nihilo*, which is not a notion that applies only to an initial creative act 'in the beginning', but which expresses that every event is created by, and wholly dependent upon God. In the course of history, this view of God has been contrasted with other views, such as that of God as a Demiurge, shaping the world from existing materials, or of God as the one who started a world left to itself thereafter – a 'deist' concept of God as a watchmaker. There is in the idea of creation a tension between total dependence upon God and the reality of creaturely – or, in the terms of this study, natural – causal processes. If the dependence of everything upon God is emphasised strongly, it may seem as if creaturely processes are not real, since God creates the world anew every instant – a view which may be called 'occasionalism'.

One resolution of this tension has been to ascribe to God a unique mode of action, by which God creates and sustains all things as their primary cause; all natural causes are real, just as are all entities and events, but they are so because they have been created by God. Such real natural causes are called 'secondary causes'. This distinction between primary and secondary causality was developed in the European Middle Ages, for instance by Thomas Aquinas, but its roots can be traced back at least to Augustine (4th/5th century). God creates everything, both past, present, and future events, and God creates them not as an amorphous bag of events but with their temporal, spatial, and causal relations, and with their creaturely freedom. The distinction between God and God's activity, on the one hand, and creatures and creaturely activity, on the other, is articulated also as a difference with respect to time: all creatures are temporal, whereas God is, upon this view, conceived as not temporal. God's eternity is not everlastingness (infinite temporal extension) but timelessness.[4]

Not all Christian thinkers accept divine timelessness. Some believe that temporality is such a fundamental feature of reality that one should not exclude even God from temporality; others hold that a genuine relation between God and God's creatures requires some temporality in God. It has also been argued that an atemporal understanding of creation conflicts with freedom, since it seems to imply that future states of affairs are already real for God.[5] The difference of opinion is not only a difference about time; it correlates with differences in the understanding of God, as was clearly expressed by Leftow in the passage quoted above.

Conceiving of divine and creaturely action in terms of primary and secondary causality results in various puzzles if not problems. A major one is that both natural and divine action are considered to be sufficient (at their own level of description). If God's creative activity is not

---

[4] Essays discussing the primary/secondary distinction can be found in books edited by Thomas (1983) and by Hebblethwaite and Henderson (1990); another introduction is an essay by R. J. Russell (1993). Historical aspects are considered by McMullin (1985a, 1988) and Burrell (1993). Among philosophical studies defending divine atemporality are a seminal essay by Stump and Kretzman (1981) and books by Leftow (1991), Helm (1988), and Braine (1988); the theologians Kaufman (1972) and Wiles (1986) lean in that direction with arguments for understanding the world as a single 'master act' of God. In discussions on science and theology, Heller and Stoeger are among those who consider such views favourably.

[5] Among thinkers defending that God is temporal, one might think of Bergson, Teilhard de Chardin, Whitehead, Pike, Lucas (1989), but also many contemporary authors writing on science and theology, such as Barbour and Polkinghorne. A few also try to have both temporality and atemporality in God, for instance in the context of a trinitarian view of God (e.g., Russell 1993a, Peters 1993).

considered sufficient, one runs the risk of conceiving of God as a demiurge who is dependent upon the co-operation of matter. However, once one allows for two different sufficient causes causing a single event, one of them seems superfluous. Thus, it is important that the kind of sufficiency and the difference between these two kinds of activity is clarified in order to avoid problems associated with 'double agency'.[6]

Accepting the whole natural world as the creation of a timeless transcendent God avoids various potential problems in the relationship between theology and the natural sciences, since it accepts the world as understood by the natural sciences as God's creation. There is no need for particular gaps within the world or for some particular form of top-down causation [13]. However, even upon such an understanding of God, theology and the natural sciences relate to each other with respect to the concept of time [31.1] and the explanation of the natural world as a whole (rather than the explanation of phenomena in the natural world). With respect to limit questions of a naturalist view of the world I will argue that science does not offer answers or evidence; this will be illustrated with a discussion on 'the anthropic principles' in cosmology [31.2]. I will conclude that a major emphasis on the transcendence of God offers a good perspective for a theological view which is consistent with science. However, it is hard to give reasons, at least in the context of a dialogue with the sciences, why one would hold such a theological position. If this is resolved through an appeal to particular events or experiences in human history, one runs into problems with respect to a naturalist understanding of human experience and history.

31.1. Divine timelessness and the temporality of the world[7]

One locus of interaction between such a conception of God and the natural sciences concerns the understanding of time. Temporal predicates are, upon the theological view considered here, applicable to creatures, but not to God. As Augustine wrote in reply to the question of what God was doing before God created the world: 'before' assumes

---

6   Other problems considered by philosophers are the relation between divine and creaturely freedom, between divine and human responsibility for evil, and the distinction between redemptive and creative actions. Burrell (1993, 111ff.) argues that resolution requires a way of conceptualising possibilities which does not conceive of many determinate possible worlds of which one is chosen.

7   The following section is adapted from Drees (1993).

that the creation took place in time, whereas time came into existence
with creation.[8] Time is, upon such a view, not a pre-existing framework, a container in which creation takes place, but rather a characteristic of creation. How does this fare in the light of contemporary
scientific knowledge?

The temporal character of our natural world has become more
manifest in the last few centuries. Whereas biological species were
considered to be fixed, we now are aware of a long history of change.
And geology and cosmology have added their discoveries to the overall
view of the natural world as a world with a history of change. But the
fact that time is characteristic of the natural world does not bear upon
the question: can we conceive of God's relation to the world in a non-
temporal way? From within the natural world, and certainly from
within the discourse of the natural sciences, it may be impossible to
answer such a question about God, but we can at least take a closer
look at the concept of time as it functions in the sciences. And, I will
argue, such a closer look reveals limitations to the universal applicability of time in the natural world in such ways that an understanding
of time as linked to the created order (rather than as a metaphysical
category applicable to everything, including God) is warranted. There
are at least three reasons for this view in relation to physics: (1) some
theories take whole histories rather than temporal processes as their
basic units of description, (2) in attempts to integrate quantum physics
and relativity theories, time is treated as an internal parameter, and
(3) in quantum cosmologies, 'time' becomes a notion of limited applicability, even within the natural world. Thus, understanding time as a
feature of reality which is not applicable to God is consonant with the
natural sciences, where time is not universally applicable either.

(1) The presence in physics of timeless descriptions, for example in
terms of trajectories in phase space or in terms of spacetimes, where the
whole is a unit including all moments, suggests that it is possible to talk
about the relation of God to this whole – and not only of the relation
between God at one moment to the universe at that moment, which
implies differentiating moments in God. Let me consider the case of
descriptions in terms of 'space-time'.

In the special theory of relativity the notion of simultaneity as having
a universal meaning with respect to a 'now' got lost. 'Past' and 'future'

---

8   *Confessiones*, Book 11, XII,14–XIV,17.

can be used as concepts relative to an observer located at some position in space-time. The problem arises when a definite article is used, speaking about 'the past' and 'the future', as if these are global concepts.[9] Thus, problems arise in theologies which insist that 'God's future' is open, or make other claims which assume the existence of a universal notion of time. As long as God lacks a specific location and state of motion, it is difficult to understand the meaning of God knowing 'the past' or influencing 'the future'.

At least three ways to get around the theological consequences of this loss of a single universal time have been proposed. One is to allow for the coexistence of more than one time in God.[10] Another, defended by Polkinghorne, is to invoke God's omnipresence. A third option is to argue that there is a physical basis for a universal time by taking into account the cosmological background radiation. I consider none of these options viable.[11] A fourth way to attempt to have a universal

---

[9] The description of the problem as one with the definite article has been taken from C. J. Isham (Isham and Polkinghorne 1993, 142).

[10] (Ward 1982, 166); analysed in Leftow (1991, 29).

[11] Some have argued that one might consider the coexistence of our time with other time series. However, if these time-series are taken to be unrelated except for their coexistence in God (see preceding note), 'multiple time sequences' are of no help with the relativity problem; they rather might refer to different universes. If one were to apply the idea of 'multiple times' to the various times arising for different observers in one space-time, these time sequences would be strongly correlated. To say that God is related to all these times would not introduce a universal notion of time which would allow for statements about God's relation to 'the future' or 'the present', but rather would be equivalent to saying that God is related – in some non-temporal way – to the whole of space-time.

Polkinghorne suggests that omnipresence provides a way out. He argues that an omnipresent God is spatially coincident with every space-time point, and thus 'has no need to use signalling to tell him what is happening and so he has instant access to every event as and when it occurs. That totality of experience is presumably the most important thing to be able to say about God's relation to world history' (Polkinghorne 1989, 82). Polkinghorne's description is ambivalent. 'When it occurs' may be read as a reference to a hidden background of universal time, making possible a reading of 'the totality of experience' as a three-dimensional present. Such a reading of Polkinghorne's solution is not in line with relativity theory, as it introduces a universal sense of now, correlated with that three-dimensional 'totality of experience'. Another, perhaps better, reading of Polkinghorne's proposal takes it that 'when it occurs' means that God has equal access to events at all space-time points – whether deemed future, past or present from any space-time point. But then God's temporality is lost; the 'totality of experience' covers four-dimensional space-time as a whole.

One might suggest that Big Bang cosmology solves some problems with respect to God's time, as there might be a way to define a global time in an expanding universe (for example, by using as the frame of reference that frame in which the background radiation is homogeneous). However, it is not clear that there is such a universal time when one moves beyond the homogeneity and isotropy of the Friedman–Robertson–Walker models. Besides, general relativity, on which the Big Bang theory is based, seems to make problems worse; there are space-times which do not allow for a definition of time that covers the whole manifold.

notion of time is to abandon relativity theory which undermines notions such as simultaneity. It might be the case that a notion of a single, flowing, universal time is possible, once general relativity as the framework for cosmology is succeeded by a quantum theory which integrates space and time as well as matter. That such a further development beyond the Big Bang theory is needed, has already been discussed [16]. Running ahead of the argument, the conclusion of the reflections on quantum cosmology will be that such a hope for a recovery of universal time will not be fulfilled. Rather, things will become worse (see below, 3).

(2) Origination of the material universe *in a fixed background spacetime* is problematic. One of the major problems is the problem of choice;[12] quantum theories which work with probabilities (e.g., per unit time) tend to introduce a plurality of origination points. This would lead to interacting 'universes', contrary to the available empirical evidence. Hence, physicists have turned to the development of theories which describe creation *of* time rather than creation *in* time. General relativity theory offers a fundamental hint in that direction. Whereas in a fixed background, time may be seen as external with respect to the system, the situation in general relativity is different. Time may be understood as an 'internal' variable. One might attempt to define time in relation to the average distance between 'test-particles' such as galaxies. Or one might use the temperature of the background radiation or features of other material phenomena. The evolution of properties of the universe in time is thus transferred to statements about the correlation between, for example, the temperature and other properties of the universe.

Thus, time in the context of relativistic space-time theories not only lacks uniqueness, but it is also a phenomenological, 'internal' construct. One might well see this as a modern-day equivalent of Augustine's view of *creatio cum tempore*, time being part of the created order. The discovery of 'internal' time, as characteristic of the theory of general relativity, has paved the way for a second discovery, the discovery of the limited applicability of the concept of time, as is typical of quantum cosmologies and quantum gravity.

(3) In traditional quantum theory, the fundamental equations describe

---

[12]   (Isham 1993). This objection to creation *in* time is not a new insight; for example, it was considered by Augustine (*Confessiones* 11, xii, 14; *De civitate Dei* xi, 6) and, centuries earlier, by an Epicurean, as told by Cicero in his *De natura deorum* i, 9, 21.

the evolution of the wave function (or state vector) in time. The properties of the system are thus described by a time dependent entity. 'Time' itself is part of the background. In some approaches to quantum gravity there might be a background structure which is sufficiently rich as to include some concept similar to classical time. However, these approaches have the same problem as indicated above for creation *in* a fixed background space-time. The main stream of research in quantum gravity and quantum cosmology has taken a different approach, drawing upon the possibility of understanding time as an 'internal' parameter.[13] The background structure is a three-dimensional space on which a wave function is defined which specifies configurations of curvature and matter. A dynamical evolution might be recovered by defining a time variable on the basis of a suitably behaving variable either out of the curvature or out of the matter fields. However, such evolutionary representations are slightly odd, compared with evolutionary equations which arise in conventional quantum theory. This deviation is an advantage in the context of the programme of quantum cosmology, the attempt to construct a genuine theory of the origination of the universe. It leads us to the idea of 'imaginary time', or, more appropriately, of the limited applicability of the concept 'time'.

In contemporary proposals for quantum cosmologies the fundamental ontology (background structure) assumes a three-dimensional manifold, rather than a four-dimensional space-time. In addition the ontology contains a collection of possible configurations of geometrical and material configurations on this manifold: superspace. 'Time' is a derivative notion, well defined only for certain subsets of, or certain paths in this superspace. 'Time' is not universally applicable for two reasons: classical space-time with the notion of time is recovered only as an approximate, fuzzy, notion, and it is only recovered for parts of reality as described by the wave function; other parts of reality do not lend themselves to an interpretation in terms of time. Hence, time is unlike traditional time at the most fundamental level of description, that of quantum gravity.

It is important to note that the relevance of these ideas cannot be restricted to considerations regarding the quantum theory of the origin of the universe. Rather, it purports to be the quantum view of the universe or, even more significantly, the quantum theory of time (and space, though in a restricted sense, since some features of space are still assumed as part of the background structure). As the quantum theory

[13] Beginning at least with B. S. DeWitt, Quantum Theory of Gravity: i, ii, *Physical Review* 160 (1967): 1113–1148 and 162 (1967): 1195–1239; see expositions by Isham (1988; 1993).

of matter or radiation is different from classical theories of matter or radiation, so is the quantum theory of space and time different from classical theories of space and time.

Since in the most fundamental theories time is a parameter which is closely tied to other physical parameters, and not applicable to all parts of natural reality, it may be in accord with fundamental science to attempt to understand God's transcendence with respect to space-time as timelessness. Natural reality is, of course, dynamic and evolving, especially when considered on an intermediate scale from a point of view within an almost Newtonian epoch. However, questions arise already when one considers larger scales, and thus has to take account of the conceptuality of general relativity. The dynamic picture may be extendable to the quantum level, the finer detail of photons and electrons. However, further down in scale, to the quantum gravity level, the conceptuality of dynamism breaks down. 'Deep down' the ontology is different. The unusual features, from the perspective of human experience, are not merely relevant to our understanding of the far past (quantum cosmology), since they have to do with quantum gravity, our speculations about the most fundamental structures of reality, space and time. And they are not just details at some irrelevant scale, because they affect, or should affect, the concepts of space and time as they are used at all levels. At the almost Newtonian level of description which is very adequate for human life on Earth, space and time may seem to be universal, infinitely extendable continua. The special theory of relativity has raised problems with respect to the uniqueness of time. General relativity also calls into question the extendability of time, as singularities may occur. And quantum gravity takes away the fundamental concept of time. The still speculative ideas at the frontier of cosmological research, and even the standard theory of space-time (general relativity), thus suggest that temporal presentations (including evolutionary ones) may be of limited validity, and not fundamental. Hence, a theological view which depicts the relation between God and the temporal, evolving world as itself a timeless relation, is consonant with contemporary cosmological insights.

31.2. Limit questions

Materialist naturalism is comprehensive: all phenomena are supposed to be part and parcel of the same reality. However, a few questions escape treatment within this framework. These are questions regarding the universe as a whole and regarding the most fundamental constituents of, or structures in reality. Earlier [2], I used an image of science adapted from Charles Misner (1977, 97): the chemist delegates a question regarding the origin of the chemical elements to an astrophysicist in the next lab, and goes on with her own work. Whereas one might be tempted to see the reductionist coherence of the sciences in terms of explanations provided by 'lower' levels, one might also view reductionism as the passing on of questions to such 'lower' levels. Questions are partially answered at each level, but new questions are generated. Some questions end on the desks of cosmologists and physicists. These scientists cannot refer them to another lab. Some of these questions are different from questions about phenomena within reality; rather, they are questions about reality. We will explore the shape of such questions, especially the question of existence ('Why is there something rather than nothing?') and of structure ('Why this structure rather than another one, or none at all?').

Why is there something rather than nothing?

In *The Blind Watchmaker* Richard Dawkins gives a lucid account of the emergence of complex organisms through a long evolutionary process. At a certain point Dawkins pauses to consider his starting-point, the molecules and atoms he assumes. Their explanation is the task of the physicists, and for that matter Dawkins refers to Peter Atkins' *The Creation* (Dawkins 1986, 15). This reference illustrates the image evoked by Misner: assumptions are passed on to the person in the next office, until they end on the desk of the physicist and the cosmologist.

For his part, Atkins takes it that elephants and humans are a product of chance given enough time and molecules. Elephants and humans are not his business; in his argument, he is concerned with the first beginnings and the basic elements. Molecules arise automatically, given atoms. Atoms arise, given the original hot mix of elementary particles. This mix of particles and radiation may have arisen by quantum fluctuations from a vacuum. And that vacuum with three spatial dimensions and one temporal one could have arisen by chance as fluctuations in a pre-geometry. There is no design or creation: the world arose by chance.

In my opinion, the appeal to quantum fluctuations does not offer a final answer. Any such scheme rests upon certain assumptions. In the case of the idea of origination by quantum fluctuations there is the assumption that some form of quantum laws hold for some form of reality, such as the 'pre-geometry' in Atkins' account. By using a language of probabilities one also assumes some measure. For instance, the probability of a certain decay is 0.5 *per day*. Even the most extreme 'nothing' of a physicist is not an absolute Nothing devoid of any properties and measures. Other proposals do not fare better. For example, Stephen Hawking's proposal for a universe without boundaries avoids questions about a beginning in time, but it does not do so without making any assumptions.[14]

A more general argument is that all scientific theories about the universe, however advanced and complete they might be, remain theories. There is no way they can ever explain why there is a reality which behaves in accordance with the theory. A mathematical theory which would explain how one could get a universe from nothing would not give a physical universe, but the idea of a physical universe. All evidence is *post factum*.[15] Reality is assumed rather than explained. This applies also to my naturalist account.

That natural reality is assumed rather than explained, is not proof for the existence of a creator. Introducing a god as an explanatory notion only shifts the locus of the question: why would such a god exist? And it is possible that the universe just happens to exist, without explanation.[16] Perhaps the craving for explanations is not appropriate here. The limit-question is there, but it does not point to a specific answer.

Why this order?

Our (observable) universe has a certain structure. It could perhaps have been different. Even if we had laws which accounted for all observations and experiments, we could still ask why these laws (or

---

[14] (Drees 1990, 72f.); Isham (1993, especially 77ff.) offers a discussion of such issues in relation to Vilenkin's proposal. The general point with respect to cosmology has been articulated by, amongst others, Heller (1987, 421) and Barrow (1988, 231).

[15] (Drees 1990, 98–101). Unless one assumes a Platonic conception of mathematics, taking it as dealing with real entities; the universe being one of those entities. But then the assumption of existence has already been made with respect to mathematical entities.

[16] Another possibility is that the explanation is not to be looked for at some deeper level, but in the requirement of self-consistency. After a story about a boy who extracts himself out of a marsh by pulling his bootstraps, this is called a bootstrap view. It is at the moment not actively pursued in physics, though it was once a serious alternative to the more common quantum field theory of the strong interactions (Gale 1974; Cushing 1985 and 1990; Balashow 1992, 366ff.). I doubt that self-consistency can ever imply existence; however, I do want to allow for the possibility that there might be only one consistent fundamental theory in physics (see the next few paragraphs in the main text).

whatever ingredients that are essential to our explanations) have been implemented in reality rather than any other laws.[17]

It might be that there are no such alternative schemes. Mathematical consistency and the finiteness (of all potential observables) have been very restrictive in particle physics (Drees 1990, 89f.). I abstain from an opinion on the claim that physics might converge on a single theory, and the subsequent claim that it might be able to show that this would be the only one possible, not only as an account of our observations and experiments but as a consistent recipe for reality. These are grand claims, but I do not see any strong objections, especially to the first part of the claim; convergence on a single theory has some credibility given the history of theories in high energy physics. However, the defence of these claims would at least assume that the laws (or symmetries, or whatever explanatory schemata involved) are to be mathematically expressible and consistent. Perhaps some other assumptions are also taken for granted; the history of science reveals our tendency to overlook the 'small print' which accompanies grand claims, small print which contains non-trivial assumptions of which people became aware only much later. The adoption of such assumptions might constitute an *a posteriori* component in the articulation of the ultimate theory. If there were to be such an ultimate theory which was not only unique a posteriori but also a priori, there would be no independent limit question about the order of the universe. Rather, the order would be given with existence (together with logical or mathematical criteria such as consistency).

Questions, not evidence: the anthropic coincidences[18]

The universe, or at least the observable universe, has characteristic features, such as its size and age, a certain average density of matter/ energy, three spatial dimensions, and certain values of fundamental

---

[17] The order of treatment, first that of existence and then that of order, is not intended to suggest that existence comes first and order is subsequently implemented. The questions of what there is and which laws apply to it are connected. For instance, whereas Newtonian mechanics allows for all imaginable angular momenta, quantum electrodynamics restricts spin to multiples of a fixed unit of angular momentum.

[18] Original articulations of the anthropic principles go back to Robert H. Dicke in 1969 and Brandon Carter in 1974; good sources are the review article (Carr and Rees 1979) and the multi-faceted Barrow and Tipler (1986). I have developed the position presented here in greater detail in Drees (1990, 78–89); the definitions follow those of Barrow and Tipler (1986, 15–22), except for the category of 'anthropic coincidences', which I introduced myself; Kirschenmann (1992) comes to a similar assessment of their limited significance, though with slightly different definitions of the terms; he has, in line with Carter (1974), the WAP referring to our location in the universe, without considering alternative universes.

constants which determine the relative strengths of the various forces. A few cosmologists and physicists have toyed with the idea that some of these features could have been different, and have calculated the consequences of such alternatives for the development of the universe. The conclusion of such thought experiments has been that most changes in such characteristic features of our universe would have led to a quite different universe, and more specifically a universe in which carbon-based forms of life, such as humans and worms, could not have developed the way they did. The universe seems remarkably fine-tuned for life. The observation that life as we know it would not have arisen if the universe had been slightly different is not itself a principle; I prefer to speak of 'anthropic coincidences' when referring to the primary conclusion of such thought experiments.

The Weak Anthropic Principle (WAP) is one of the responses to the anthropic coincidences. The Weak Anthropic Principle states that what we observe must be compatible with our existence as observers. For instance, we see a universe which has existed for billions of years, because it took billions of years to develop beings capable of determining the age of their universe. This 'principle' does not draw grand conclusions from the coincidences. Rather, it is a methodological reminder of the truism that our observations are biased in favour of situations in which we can exist. If I were to live in a train, I would always observe railroad crossings that were closed. The WAP would not explain why the crossings are closed, or why our planet has a surface temperature which permits liquid water, or why gravity is so much weaker than electromagnetic forces; it only reminds us that if the situation had been different, we would not have been able to observe it.

Some authors have combined the WAP with a belief in many actual worlds (or regions of the universe, with our observable universe being only a tiny part of the larger universe). If one assumes that all possible universes are realised somewhere somehow, then the bias expressed in the WAP explains why we happen to be where we are. Given an extremely large number of monkeys typing for an extremely long time, one might expect a flawless copy of a play of Shakespeare, as well as many more copies which are almost flawless. However, such an explanation of the origin of this work would not explain the origin of the typing monkeys (many worlds), nor the way we pick as the significant result the play (us), nor the probability of the result. All the (limited) explanatory force is carried by the assumption of many actual worlds, which is not a conclusion from the evidence, but an assumption used in addition to the evidence. There are stronger 'anthropic principles', such as the Strong Anthropic Principle (SAP), which states that the universe must have the properties which allow life (or intelligent and observing life) to develop, and the Participatory Anthropic Principle (PAP), which states that the universe exists in a definite state because it is observed by conscious beings. Thus, we would not be mere creatures, but 'central participators in the great cosmic drama' (Eccles 1979, 31). Like the assumption of plenitude (many worlds), such principles are not conclusions from the evidence, but metaphysical assumptions used in addition to it.

One more variant, in explicit opposition to the idea of many worlds, might be called the Theistic Anthropic Principle (TAP), a cosmological variant of the argument from design. As John Polkinghorne (1986, 80) wrote:

A possible explanation of equal intellectual respectability – and to my mind greater economy and elegance – would be that this one world is the way it is because it is the creation of a Creator who purposes that it should be so.

Such an apologetic argument does not work. It assumes that the anthropic coincidences are here to stay as inexplicable coincidences. However, some of them, or perhaps even all, may be explained by future scientific theories. This has happened to traditional design-arguments based on intra-cosmic adaptedness, and it has to some extent already happened to the cosmological variant with the development of inflationary scenarios in cosmology.

My conclusion, which could also be argued for by an analysis of claims about the beginning of the universe or its contingency (Drees 1990, 190ff), is that our knowledge of the universe and the limitations to our knowledge do not support metaphysical or theological claims as expressed in SAP, PAP, and TAP, or, for instance, a claim about an absolute beginning. We may develop further scientific explanatory schemes (as, I expect, will be the case for most if not all the anthropic coincidences). And, beyond each further explanation, we are left with further questions whose formulation at any moment depends on the state of science at that time.

The persistence of questions, even if one accepts a naturalist view informed by the natural sciences, may lead some to a sense of gratitude and wonder about the existence of our world. This wonder or puzzlement about the contingency of existence, and perhaps also of order and intelligibility, is something that receives an answer of some sort from faith in a transcendent God who endows the world with existence and order. However, the move is not from science to faith, as if such a God was the conclusion of an inference to the best explanation of the natural world.

31.3. No reasons for radical transcendence

So far, I have argued that a view of God which emphasises the unique, non-temporal character of God's existence and activity can be combined with a naturalist view of the natural world (see also [13.3]). However, this consistency has a price, namely in the emphasis on the otherness and uniqueness of God. It seems to leave one with empty hands when one attempts to offer grounds for adopting such a view, and the religious significance of such a view seems limited. We will briefly consider these two disadvantages.

If one defends that there is, for instance, evidence of divine design in the biological realm, or of purpose and value in natural processes [30], then the reasons for adopting a certain religious view are built in as the best explanation of certain phenomena or as an attractive reformulation of our view of reality (though a mere reformulation identifying religious and non-religious terms appears to make the religious terms superfluous). In this respect, such approaches are attractive in that they argue not merely for the possibility, but, at the same time, for the plausibility of a religious view, or at least relate it to some puzzlement in human existence. However, if – as in the non-temporalist theological view – the created world can be accepted as being self-contained in a naturalist sense – there seem to be hardly any grounds for adopting belief in anything 'more'; 'since there are no real "gaps" to fill, we may be left without an argument for God's existence of the kind that would convince a science-minded generation' (McMullin 1988, 74).

Two kinds of grounds for adopting such a position may none the less be considered. One has been referred to already: there is a puzzlement articulated in limit-questions, and especially in the question 'why is there something rather than nothing', which is to some extent answered by introducing the concept of a creator. However, a similar question with respect to the existence of that creator may be posed again, unless one argues that such a creator necessarily exists – not only necessarily given the world, but necessarily in a more radical, a priori way. This is what ontological arguments for the existence of God seek to achieve when they attempt to deduce the existence of God from the concept of God. In my view, the various variants of such an ontological argument fail to deliver existence without presupposing existence.[19] Hence, arguing for belief in an atemporal, transcendent God on the basis of limit-questions is not beyond dispute. One might as well hold, for instance, that the world just happens to exist – there may be a question, but without an answer.

Rather than turning to philosophical limit questions, one might also adopt belief in a transcendent creator on the basis of particular experiences or a particular tradition, such as the Christian one with its testimonies about God's creative activity and God's love for us, testimonies which are rooted in experiences in the history of Israel and with Jesus of Nazareth. However, such a move assumes that there is a basis in the historical realm where none was found in the physical and biological realms. This split between the domain of the natural sciences and history or anthropology neglects (or, more friendly, does not accept) the coherence within a naturalist view of reality, since it now seeks meaningful 'gaps' in the natural world, though not in the processes described by physics and biology, but in historical and psychological processes. Such an approach encounters the problems which arise when humans with their experiences and traditions are understood as part of the natural world [chapter 4].

There is one more option, and that is to abstain from giving any grounds. This way of making a virtue out of necessity seems to be the strategy of theologians who emphasise that they want to do without 'natural theology'. Coherence, or at least consistency, may be considered enough. However, this is a strategy which is at variance with ordinary scientific practice, where we not only seek to eliminate inconsistencies but also try to analyse how certain phenomena rest upon the underlying processes. For instance, evolutionary epistemology is an attempt not only to articulate an epistemology consistent with evolution, but rather to explain why (and to what extent) we can know the world by building upon our reconstruction of evolutionary processes in our past.[20]

[19] A careful defence of this conclusion, drawing on modal logic, can be found in Hubbeling (1987, 99f.).

[20] Gerhard Vollmer (1990, 6), in a foreword to a theological study of evolutionary epistemology (Lüke 1990), concludes that Lüke's theological study does not explicate why one should take a theological perspective; it is precisely on this issue of justification that he sees the most significant difference between a theological and a naturalist approach.

Even if one were to accept the mystery of existence as a ground for belief in a transcendent non-temporal God, such a philosophical concept of God is fairly empty. There is no ground to understand faith in such a God as faith in a person; nor does it inspire devotion to a way of life or a specific attitude towards the world and to other persons in the world, except perhaps for a general sense of gratitude and wonder, as mentioned above. The primary form of faith in this philosophical approach is 'belief that', namely belief in the philosophical proposition that there is a transcendent entity to which the natural world owes its existence (see [3.2] for various concepts of faith). A philosophical approach may result in a richer concept if limit questions other than that about existence are analysed and included, especially questions concerning moral and aesthetic values and the intelligibility of the universe. However, such an approach will not match the richness of patterns of worship, examples of proper ways of life, and concepts of God and God's love for humans which have arisen in religious traditions. Given such problems with an approach which focuses on the most general aspects of a naturalist view, I will in the next and final section present a view which seeks to take the particularity of religious traditions into account.

32. RELIGIONS FOR WANDERING AND WONDERING HUMANS

In the preceding section we considered a theological approach which accepts the natural world as God's creation, while qualifying God's unique mode of creative action in such a way that no problems due to a naturalist view of the natural world can ensue. A disadvantage of such an approach is that it bypasses particular religious traditions with the orientation that they may offer for religious ways of life. Earlier we considered theological views which take as primary data the richness of particular religious traditions, which were understood as evolved responses to reality [26]. A problem with these approaches is that they attempt to reach beyond an evolutionary understanding of adaptations as adaptations to local environments in order to make claims about some ultimate reality which is tolerant (Theissen), or in which 'is' and 'ought' coincide, since altruism and love express basic ontological principles (Hefner). Such claims seem to me to expect a deeper ontological foundation for tolerance or goodness in the natural world than is warranted. However, their emphasis on the value of particular religious traditions is important. Humans live in parts of the actual world, at particular times and places; their native tongue is not language, but a particular language; they are immersed in some culture. They also relate to particular religious traditions. Some people are totally immersed in a tradition; others are confronted with a variety of traditions, and seek to respond to that variety.

There are different ways of responding intellectually to the variety of religious traditions. One might attempt to find common features in underlying processes or common first principles, either through analysis of actual religions or via a more formal, for example, Kantian, approach. However, neither way of seeking common features, and thereby a basis for claims which reach beyond the particularities of traditions, seems to do sufficient justice to the variety of religions. A more promising approach is to consider religious practices in relation to their own contexts and their own history, and to see how, for instance, cosmogonic beliefs, conceptions of ethical order, and social circumstances interact (Lovin and Reynolds 1985). Such an approach in the study of religion is an obvious extension of an evolutionary approach, where organisms are also studied in relation to the environments in which these organisms function and in relation to the history of environments and organisms that resulted in the situation considered. Such a study of religions is something that surpasses the context of this book, but it forms the background of the first part of this section, where I will return to major characteristics of religious traditions, or at least characteristics which are typical of the way we mostly use the notion 'religious tradition'. Then, I will propose criteria which may be employed in selecting and modifying traditions, which are part of our heritage as wandering humans.

However, humans are not only beings enmeshed in their particular situations. They also speculate about the world beyond their local environment. In the sciences, such speculations have reached remarkable heights, resulting in the understanding of many phenomena and the discovery of new phenomena. In the speculations of science, we seem to reach beyond particularities, although the achievements of science are acquired through the study of details and not through reflections of a more general kind. In theological thinking there is a drive towards universality and abstraction which resembles the move in science from particular contexts to an understanding which covers different contexts. Wondering humans may receive answers from science, but beyond the answers arise further questions which science does not answer.

Wandering humans: a variety of particular traditions

Religious traditions are complex entities. Each one offers a particular language, with certain metaphors and concepts. When in the preface I suggested that when we stand before the divine throne on the day of judgement, God will not ask about creation 'How did I do it?', but rather 'What did you do with it?', I was using a particular religious image, embedded in a tradition. When we consider this example, we also may note another aspect of a religious tradition, namely that via its metaphors, concepts, and images it evokes a conception of moral and spiritual good life. A *way of life* may be suggested by parables, as for instance that of the Good Samaritan helping a stranger from another culture (Luke 10: 29–37), by historical narratives (such as various accounts of prophets protesting against injustice, or of Jesus forgiving those who persecuted him) and it may be articulated in commandments, such as the Ten Commandments (Deuteronomy 5: 6–21). Such a way of life need not always strengthen the conformity of the believer to the expectations of the larger community; it may also emphasise individual responsibility even where the individual goes counter to the interests of others. Such a way of life is not only a practical matter. It is oriented by an *ultimate ideal* which surpasses any actual achievable goal or situation. Thus, religious traditions include elements such as 'the Kingdom', 'Paradise', 'Heaven', 'Nirvana', immortality, emptiness, openness, perfection, or unconditional love. Such notions function as regulative ideals with which actual behaviour is contrasted in order to evaluate it.

A tradition's way of life is affirmed and strengthened by the particular *forms of worship* and devotion of that religious tradition. Worship and other forms of ritual behaviour express and nourish the individual and communal spirituality in relation to the joys, sorrows, and challenges of life, and to the conceptions and ultimate ideals of good life.

Religious traditions are not only ways of life; believers see their religious way of life as *rooted* in certain claims about historical events, ultimate destiny, or authoritative commandments. These claims are supposed to justify the way of life espoused by a tradition as corresponding to the way one should live one's life; justified because they derive from an authoritative source, because they deliver future happiness, or because they correspond to the way reality is intended to be or, deep down, really is.[21]

I assume that other languages may be equally adequate and beautiful – until I find reason to conclude otherwise – but I still have a particular native tongue, namely Dutch, which I consider very adequate and beautiful. I intend to respect other people as all being, in principle, worthy of my interest and engagement – until I find reason to think otherwise – but I am involved in more intense personal bonds with only a few friends and relatives. Similarly, I know that there is a variety of religious traditions, and I intend to grant them all initial respect. However, there is a particular tradition which I have encountered most intensely, and that is the Christian one, in a liberal Protestant form which was strongly influenced by the European Enlightenment. I have found elements of value in this tradition – in most of its parables and in some of its hymns, in a few of its representatives and in many articulations of ideals of justice nourished by it.

Just as cognitive variety is not to be dismissed in the sciences [27], so too may religious variety be acceptable, natural, and valuable in a naturalist perspective. The variety of ways of life may well be a rich resource and a colourful element in our own time. Variety is to be expected, since we deal with human experiences (of various kinds in a wide variety of contexts), and different forms of ritual behaviour and different guiding ideals of human flourishing may be entertained. However, no tradition is beyond dispute and beyond development. There is no reason to dismiss at once such complex cultural entities as religious traditions as being at odds with natural science, but neither do we have to accept our own tradition, or any other, without critical scrutiny nor as a yes-or-no package deal. Change is characteristic of our history, and there is no need to exclude religious traditions from it [chapter 2].

A particular tradition (or stage of, or element in, a tradition) may, of

---

[21] Such characteristics may also apply to 'ideologies', such as belief in a classless society (regulative ideal), in combination with indications about the proper way of life in the current stage of history (class struggle); an ideology which may be supposed to rest in, and thus derive its authority from, unavoidable historical processes; such political ideologies could be considered as religions of some sort. Rather than the question of whether the word 'religion' may be applied, the important issue is whether there are any criteria by which we can defend a preference for one view over another.

course, have to be rejected as outdated. One reason, which corresponds well with an evolutionary view, is that the actual circumstances have changed, and that therefore models of good life or forms of worship may have to change. Such is certainly the case when we consider the human condition today: we are vastly more numerous, stand in a fundamentally different relation to nature (which is threatened by us rather than that we are significantly threatened by wild animals); we are more powerful than before, and we are confronted with neighbours across the globe. In relation to such changes, traditional models and metaphors may be employed differently, or they may be understood as they always were but this may now be inappropriate to the circumstances (for example since they fuel the exploitation of natural resources).

Not only have our circumstances changed, but so have our moral and spiritual sensitivities, for example with respect to conflicts between ethnic or religious groups, slavery, or cruelty to animals. To this process of change have contributed religious traditions, changing circumstances, a wider encounter with other cultures, and philosophical insights. We evaluate traditions also by the moral and spiritual life they support. These changes have not, in most instances, much to do with science, though they reflect the general characteristic of a naturalist approach of relating the behaviour of biological organisms to the contexts in which they live.

One more reason, but not the most important one, is the cognitive credibility of a tradition. If the images which support the way of life are not recognisable, or if the claims by which the way of life is justified have become incredible (and thus do no longer justify it), then that too challenges the religious tradition, though more indirectly than challenges to the appropriateness of the circumstances of the way of life and to its moral and spiritual adequacy.

Granted that we may have to discard some traditions or may have to modify them, why would one keep alive any such tradition? The reason is, in my opinion, that they are useful and powerful. They are useful and powerful, not only for unreflective moments and persons, but also for reflective and well informed persons. No human is only a rational being who could entertain all his motives and desires consciously and intentionally; the structure of our brains is such that much goes on which is not dealt with consciously. This is the risk involved in religious forms of behaviour (since so much cannot be scrutinised consciously) and the reason for their importance: through religious metaphors and forms of behaviour we address reality especially in a way which confronts us with ideals, with what ought to be, with a vision of a better world, or with images of a paradisiacal past or an ultimate comforting presence (for similar views, see Eaves (1991), and in [26]).

At this point, authors such as Hefner and Theissen (see [26]) propose another argument: we entertain religious traditions because they are true to the way things 'really are' or to the way reality ultimately is. This seems to me to be a claim which goes – when understood in a realist way – too far beyond, if not counter to, experience. And there is also a theological reason for hesitation. If the religious ideals are claimed to correspond to the way reality really is, the crucial function of a tradition, namely in providing a guiding vision which shapes our way of life, is undermined [3.3; 17.3]. However, the identification of an ideal and ultimate reality also serves an important function. Talking about aims and values in terms of 'the way things really are' is to use a figure of speech which expresses basic trust, an appeal to a higher authority than the local environment.

Wondering humans: Limit-questions
There is another aspect of religious traditions, where we also reach beyond the local environment. Humans have, with the development of consciousness and communication, contemplated questions about the world in which they found themselves. Many of their speculative answers may have been functional; anthropologists and other scholars in comparative religious studies have found that creation myths and other cosmogonies are not merely speculative attempts at explanation, but ways of presenting and justifying moral imperatives and social structures, or in some other way are 'indications of a very general human effort to relate the changing requirements of action to a permanent and unchanging order of things' (Lovin and Reynolds 1985, 1). However, some speculations may well be useless, toy with the possibilities of thinking, or at least reach beyond what is sufficient for the circumstances of the moment. In earlier ages, answers to speculative questions may have been closely allied with the way the world was experienced, which is still to a large extent reflected in our manifest image of the world. In this manifest image, persons are the major agents from which action proceeds. Hence, it is not very amazing that animist ways of speaking about the world have become widespread; experiences with many phenomena are modelled after experiences with human agents. Sometimes, such agents are understood as residing

in the phenomena, say as spirits, and sometimes, the agent is thought of as a god who transcends the phenomena but acts through them.

Such models are still with us; animist ways of speaking about cars or computers are common, and many persons discern intentions behind bad luck such as being struck by a disease. I consider the belief in such intentions a remnant of earlier times when manifest ways of speaking were not yet corrected through the development of scientific images; such ways of speaking and thinking are interesting as phenomena but they are not credible given our knowledge of cars and cancers. However, even though earlier answers have lost their credibility and questions may have changed their appearance, humans can still be wondering persons, contemplating questions that transcend our current answers. Religious traditions offer answers to such questions, but – more importantly, in my view – they are thereby also ways of posing such questions, and thus ways of nourishing sensitivity to such questions. Earlier I quoted the physicist Misner (1977, 96) who said: 'Saying that God created the Universe does not explain either God or the Universe, but it keeps our consciousness alive to mysteries of awesome majesty that we might otherwise ignore, and that deserve our respect.' Maintaining this speculative openness is one role of limit-questions. They also may serve another role, in relation to the particular religious traditions, namely relativising them. I will come to this conclusion via a discussion of views of the relations between the two ways, the philosophical view of a radical transcendent God and the variety of particular religious traditions.

I have introduced two approaches to religion; we have considered the variety of particular traditions, each functional in its own way in certain circumstances, though none is in a position to claim to be adequate or true independent of circumstances, and we have considered religious speculations as they arise in relation to reflection on philosophical questions. How do these two approaches relate to each other?

One fairly direct claim would be that the two approaches, independently, bring us to the same conclusions. For instance, in both approaches there is a sense of mystery, of aspects of reality which cannot be fully articulated in concepts. However, the 'ineffable' in the view of Eaves reflects the fact that whatever is coded in our genes and culture is only secondarily accessible through language; this is an immanent understanding of 'mystery', whereas the openness of naturalism in its limit-questions might be linked to a mystery transcending our reality. The two may resemble each other in spirit, but they are not identical.

Another possible claim is that science offers evidence in support of a theological view. Because, as argued above, reflections on ultimate questions do not provide answers, the openness does not provide evidence in support of any particular religious point of view. Nor could the particular views of any religious tradition serve as evidence for certain answers to the limit-questions of cosmology; they do not reach that far. However, they could serve as proposals for answers to those limit-questions. Religious traditions which propose answers to limit-questions should avoid overstatement; religions should not propose answers which are at odds with what is known, nor should they wish to propose answers which upset the integrity of the world as discerned through the natural sciences. One might also opt for a more rigorous agnostic stance with respect to the limit-questions, with whatever further attitudes are deemed appropriate.

In my view, the two approaches can complement each other. I do not mean that they together result in a complete view, but I suggest that we see them as independent contributions which can be brought together in a larger world view. The openness expressed in the limit-questions may induce a sense of wonder and gratitude about the reality to which we belong. Such a cosmological approach might primarily be at home with a mystical form of religion, a sense of unity and belonging, as well as dependence upon something which surpasses our world. The functional view of religion offers some opportunities for a prophetic form of religion, with a contrast between what is the case and what is believed ought to be the case. The contrast might be seen as a consequence of our evolutionary past, which has endowed us with wisdom that is encoded in our constitution and in our culture (including religious traditions).

Not everything that is 'wisdom' of the past has the same character-istics. On an evolutionary view, the structures of our eyes and of our immune-system can be considered 'wisdom of the body' which provides some useful capacities and defences. This 'wisdom of the body' is experienced purely as a given; we could not choose to have a different eye-colour. Religious traditions are phenomena which differ from physical characteristics in that they embody an awareness of a reality which is different from the reality of our daily lives. Furthermore, this 'other reality' is experienced in such a way that it reflects upon our individual and social behaviour, for instance by promoting a quietistic acceptance or an activist rejection of social inequalities. That religions embody a sense of transcendence with respect to our situation is not a peculiar consequence of phenomena which already have the label 'religion'; rather, it is the kind of characteristic which makes us label certain phenomena religious.

Such religious wisdom is to some extent independent from the actual situation which we face. Hence, it may serve as an external reference, an apparent Archimedean position outside the actual situation, in reference to which one might judge human decisions in the actual situation. However, such 'prophetic' wisdom transcends the current situation, but is tied to an earlier one. Hence, it may not be adequate in the new situation, where consequences may be different; blind application is never justified.

Another way to articulate a prophetic element is to argue that evolution has endowed us with the capacity for imagination, for reconsidering our situation from a different perspective. This capacity has as its limit the regulative ideal of an impartial view transcending all our perspectival views. That such a point of view is inaccessible, is beneficial since it protects us from fanaticism; if one were inclined to believe that one's view could be the final one, one would not be incited to self-questioning (Sutherland 1984, 110). It is precisely in this role that the speculative approach with a radical notion of divine transcendence [31] may be of major significance in our dealings with particular traditions; this role of transcendence and the possible reasons given above for considering a tradition outdated or in need of modification relative to the given variety of particular beliefs resembles the role of the capacity for moral deliberation and for epistemologically more advanced forms of testing beliefs in reconsidering our particular psychologically constituted moral intuitions and belief-forming mechanisms [25, 27]. When considered in relation to the radical concept of divine transcendence all regulative ideals as they arise in particular religious traditions are relativised; they can never lay unrestricted claim to our allegiance.

We know, collectively, a great deal about our world. I have only given a bare outline of our knowledge, whereas its richness is in the details. Our knowledge is also limited. Certain phenomena may be intractable, even though they fit into the naturalist framework. And limit-questions regarding the whole naturalist framework can be posed, but will not be answered. The novelist John Fowles has given a positive appreciation of such limitations to our knowledge.

We are in the best possible situation because everywhere, below the surface, we do not know; we shall never know why; we shall never know tomorrow; we shall never know a god or if there is a god; we shall never even know ourselves. This mysterious wall round our world and our perception of it is not there to frustrate us but to train us back to the now, to life, to our time being. (Fowles 1980, 20)

I wonder how Fowles knows that we shall never know. He even knows *why* we do not know: to train us back to life!

'To train us back to life': the notion of such a purpose of our limitations is inadequate with respect to the evolutionary process which has saddled us with these limitations; it has simply happened that we are endowed with our capacities and our limitations. However, the emphasis on the wider context of knowledge, our lives, fits well. Our knowledge and our capacity for knowledge have arisen in the midst of life, and if we are to use them anywhere at all, it will have to be there. They allow us to wonder about that which transcends and sustains our reality, but all the time we wander in the reality in which we live, move, and have our being; to its future we contribute our lives.

References

Bibliographical resources for discussions on the relationship between science and theology are Hübner (1987), which covers the German literature on relations between science and religion for the period 1945–1987 and a substantial selection of French, Dutch, English, and American literature, (Macleod, Petersen, and Ames 1992), *Who is Who in Theology and Science*, and the quarterly *Science and Religion News* (ISSN 1048 8642).

Abraham, G. A. 1983. Misunderstanding the Merton Thesis: A boundary dispute between history and sociology. *ISIS* 74: 368–87. Extract in Cohen (1990a).

Abrecht, P. 1989. Foreword. In J. Mangum, ed., *The New Science–Faith Debate*.

Abrecht, P., ed. 1980. *Faith and Science in an Unjust World*, vol. 2: Reports and Recommendations. Geneva: World Council of Churches.

Alexander, R. D. 1979. *Darwinism and Human Affairs*. Seattle: University of Washington Press.

1987. *The Biology of Moral Systems*. New York: De Gruyter.

1993. Biological considerations in the analysis of morality. In M. H. Nitecki and D. V. Nitecki, eds., *Evolutionary Ethics*.

Allen, D. 1989. *Christian Belief in a Postmodern World: The Full Wealth of Conviction*. Louisville: Westminster/John Knox Press.

Alston, W. P. 1991. *Perceiving God: The Epistemology of Religious Experience*. Ithaca: Cornell University Press.

Altschuler, G. C. 1979. *Andrew D. White – Educator, Historian, Diplomat*. Ithaca: Cornell University Press.

Alves, R. 1980. Biblical faith and the poor of the world. In R. L. Shinn, ed., *Faith and Science in an Unjust World*, vol. 1, Plenary Presentations. Geneva: World Council of Churches.

Anderson, P. W. 1972. More is different: Broken symmetry and the nature of the hierarchical structure of science. *Science* 177 (4047, 4 August): 393–96.

Arbib, M. A., and M. B. Hesse. 1986. *The Construction of Reality*. Cambridge: Cambridge University Press.

Ashbrook, J. B. 1984. *The Human Mind and the Mind of God: Theological Promise in Brain Research*. Lanham, Md.: University Press of America.

1984a. Neurotheology: The working brain and the work of theology. *Zygon* 19: 331–50.

1988. *The Brain and Belief: Faith in the Light of Brain Research.* Bristol, Ind.: Wyndham Press.

1992. Making sense of soul and sabbat: Brain processes and the making of meaning. *Zygon* 27: 31–49.

1993. From biogenetic structuralism to mature contemplation to prophetic consciousness. *Zygon* 28: 231–50.

Ashbrook, J. B., ed. 1993. *Brain, Culture, and the Human Spirit.* Lanham: University Press of America.

Ashworth, W. B. 1986. Catholicism and early modern science. In D. C. Lindberg and R. L. Numbers, eds., *God and Nature.*

Atkins, P. W. 1981. *The Creation.* Oxford: Freeman. (Revised edition in 1992 as *Creation Revisited.*)

Bainbridge, W. S. and R. Stark. 1980. Superstitions: Old and New. *The Skeptical Inquirer* 4 (Summer): 18–31.

Balashov, Y. V. 1992. On the evolution of natural laws. *British Journal for the Philosophy of Science* 43: 343–70.

Baldini, U. and G. V. Coyne. 1984. *The Louvain Lectures (Lectiones Lovaniensis) of Bellarmine and the Autograph Copy of his 1616 Declaration to Galileo.* (Texts in the Original Latin (Italian) with English Translation, Introduction, Commentary and Notes.) Vatican City State: Vatican Observatory.

Banner, M. C. 1990. *The Justification of Science and the Rationality of Religious Belief.* Oxford: Clarendon Press.

Barbour, I. G. 1966. *Issues in Science and Religion.* Englewood Cliffs, N.J.: Prentice-Hall.

1974. *Myths, Models, and Paradigms.* New York: Harper & Row.

1988. Ways of Relating Science and Theology. In R. J. Russell, W. R. Stoeger, and G. V. Coyne, eds., *Physics, Philosophy, and Theology.*

1989. Creation and Cosmology, in T. Peters, ed., *Cosmos as Creation.*

1990. *Religion in an Age of Science.* San Francisco: Harper & Row.

Barrow, J. D. 1988. *The World Within the World.* Oxford: Clarendon Press.

1991. *Theories of Everything.* Oxford: Clarendon Press.

Barrow, J. D. and F. J. Tipler. 1986. *The Anthropic Cosmological Principle.* Oxford: Clarendon Press.

Bartholomew, D. J. 1984. *God of Chance.* London: SCM.

Bechtel, W., and A. Abrahamsen. 1991. *Connectionism and the Mind: An Introduction to Parallel Processing in Networks.* Oxford: Basil Blackwell.

Becker, J. W., and R. Vink. 1994. *Secularisatie in Nederland, 1966–1991: De Verandering van Opvattingen en Enkele Gedragingen.* Rijswijk, NL: Sociaal Cultureel Planbureau & 's-Gravenhage: VUGA.

Beer, G. de. 1964. *Charles Darwin.* Garden City, N.Y.: Doubleday.

Ben-David, J. 1985. Puritanism and modern science: A study of continuity and coherence of sociological research. In E. Cohen, M. Lissak and

U. Almagor, eds., *Comparative Social Dynamics*. Boulder, Co.: Westview Press. Extract in Cohen (1990a).

Biagioli, M. 1993. *Galileo Courtier: The Practice of Science in the Culture of Absolutism*. University of Chicago Press.

Birch, C. 1990. *A Purpose for Everything: Religion in a Postmodern World*. Mystic, CT: Twenty-third Publications.

Birch, C. and J. B. Cobb, Jr. 1981. *The Liberation of Life*. Cambridge University Press.

Blackwell, R. J. 1991. *Galileo, Bellarmine, and the Bible*. University of Notre Dame Press.

Bonner, J. T. 1980. *The Evolution of Culture in Animals*. Princeton: Princeton University Press.

Bowler, P. J. 1977. Darwinism and the argument from design: Suggestions for a reevaluation. *Journal of the History of Biology* 10 (1) (Spring): 29–43.

Boyd, R. 1983. On the current status of the issue of scientific realism. *Erkenntnis* 19: 45–90. Reprinted with shorter title in Leplin (1984) and in Boyd *et al.* (1991).

1985. Observation, explanatory power, and simplicity: Toward a non-Humean account. In P. Achinstein and O. Hannaway, eds., *Observation, Experiment, and Hypothesis in Modern Physical Science*. Cambridge, Mass.: MIT Press. Reprinted in Boyd *et al.* (1991.)

Boyd, R., P. Gasper and J. D. Trout, eds. 1991. *The Philosophy of Science*. Cambridge, Mass.: MIT Press.

Braine, D. 1988. *The Reality of Time and the Existence of God*. Oxford: Clarendon Press.

Brandmüller,W., E. J. Greipl and L. Olschki, eds. 1992. *Copernico, Galilei e la Chiesa. Fine della controversia (1820). Gli atti del Sant 'Uffizio*. Florence.

Breed, D. 1992. *Yoking Science and Religion: The Life and Thought of Ralph Wendell Burhoe*. Chicago: Zygon Books. (Essays also in *Zygon* 25 (1990): 323–51, 469–91, and 26 (1991): 149–75, 277–308, and 397–428.)

Bregman, L. 1982. *The Rediscovery of Inner Experience*. Chicago: Nelson Hall.

Brooke, J. H. 1991. *Science and Religion: Some Historical Perspectives*. Cambridge University Press.

Buckley, M. J. 1987. *At the Origins of Modern Atheism*. New Haven: Yale University Press.

1988. The Newtonian Settlement and the Origins of Atheism. In R. J. Russell, W. R. Stoeger and G. V. Coyne, eds., *Physics, Philosophy, and Theology*.

Burhoe, R. W. 1979. Religion's role in human evolution: The missing link between ape-man's selfish genes and civilized altruism. *Zygon* 14: 135–62. Reprinted in Burhoe (1981).

1981. *Towards a Scientific Theology*. Belfast: Christian Journals Ltd.

Burrell, D. B. 1993. *Freedom and Creation in Three Traditions*. University of Notre Dame Press.

Cady, L. E. 1991. Resisting the postmodern turn: Theology and contextualization. In S. G. Davaney, ed., *Theology at the End of Modernity.* Philadelphia: Trinity Press International.

Campbell, D. T. 1974. 'Downward causation' in hierarchically organised biological systems. In F. J. Ayala and T. Dobzhansky, eds., *Studies in the Philosophy of Biology: Reduction and Related Problems.* Berkeley and Los Angeles: University of California Press.

Caplan, A. L. 1978. Ethics, evolution, and the milk of human kindness. In A. L. Caplan, ed., *The Sociobiology Debate: Readings on the Ethical and Scientific Issues Concerning Sociobiology* New York: Harper & Row. Original in *Hastings Center Report* (April 1976).

Carr, B. J. and M. J. Rees. 1979. The anthropic principle and the structure of the physical world. *Nature* 278 (12 April): 605–12.

Carroll, M. P. 1983. Visions of the Virgin Mary: The effect of family structures on Marian apparitions. *Journal for the Scientific Study of Religion* 22: 205–21.

Carter, B. 1974. Large number coincidences and the anthropic principle in cosmology. In M. S. Longair, ed., *Confrontation of Cosmological Theory with Observational Data.* Dordrecht: Reidel.

Chadwick, N. K. 1942. *Poetry and Prophecy.* Cambridge University Press.

Churchland, P. 1981. Eliminative materialism and the propositional attitudes. *Journal of Philosophy* 78 (2): 67–90. Reprinted in Boyd *et al.* (1991).

Clark, J. T. 1966. Science and some other components of intellectual culture. In R. G. Colodny, ed., *Mind and Cosmos: Essays in Contemporary Science and Philosophy.* University of Pittsburgh Press. Reprinted by University Press of America, Lanham, 1983.

Clayton, P. 1989. *Explanation from Physics to Theology.* New Haven: Yale University Press.

Cohen, H. F. 1994. *The Scientific Revolution: A Historiographical Inquiry.* University of Chicago Press.

Cohen, I. B. 1990. Some documentary reflections on the dissemination and reception of the 'Merton Thesis'. In J. Clark, C. Modgil and S. Modgil, eds., *Robert K. Merton: Consensus and Controversy.* London: Falmer Press.

Cohen, I. B. (ed.) 1990a. *Puritanism and the Rise of Modern Science: The Merton Thesis.* New Brunswick: Rutgers University Press.

Collins, J. J. 1993. Historical criticism and the state of biblical theology. *The Christian Century* 110 (22) (28 July 1993): 743–47.

Copenhaver, B. P. 1990. Natural Magic, hermeticism, and occultism in early modern science. In D. C. Lindberg, and R. S. Westman, eds., *Reappraisals of the Scientific Revolution.*

Crain, S. D. 1993. *Divine Action and Indeterminism: On Models of Divine Agency that Exploit the New Physics.* Ph.D. Dissertation, Department of Theology, University of Notre Dame.

Crosland, M. P. 1975. The development of a professional career in science in France. In M. P. Crosland, ed., *The Emergence of Science in Western Europe.* London: Macmillan.

Cupitt, D. 1990. *Creation out of Nothing.* London: SCM.

288 *References*

Cushing, J. T. 1985. Is there just one possible world? Contingency vs the bootstrap. *Studies in History and Philosophy of Science* 16: 31–48.

1990. *Theory Construction and Selection in Modern Physics: The S Matrix.* Cambridge University Press.

Daecke, S. 1987. Zur angelsächsichen Literatur. In J. Hübner, ed., *Der Dialog zwischen Theologie und Naturwissenschaft.*

Danto, A. C. 1967. Naturalism. In P. Edwards, ed., *The Encyclopedia of Philosophy*, vol. 5. New York: Macmillan.

D'Aquili, E. G. 1978. The neurobiological bases of myth and concepts of deity. *Zygon* 13: 257–75.

1982. Senses of reality in science and religion: a neuroepistemological perspective. *Zygon* 17: 361–84.

1983. The myth-ritual complex: A biogenetic structural analysis. *Zygon* 18: 247–69; reprinted in Ashbrook (1993).

1987. Neuroepistemology. In M. E. Eliade, ed., *The Encyclopedia of Religion*, vol. 10. New York: Macmillan.

D'Aquili, E. G., C. D. Laughlin and J. McManus, eds. 1979. *The Spectrum of Ritual: A Biogenetic Structural Aanalysis.* New York: Columbia University Press.

D'Aquili, E. G. and A. B. Newberg. 1993. Religious and mystical states: A neurophysiological model. *Zygon* 28: 177–99.

Davies, P. (C. W.) 1983. *God and the New Physics.* London: Dent.

1992. *The Mind of God.* New York: Simon and Schuster.

1994. The mind of God. In J. Hilgevoord, ed., *Physics and Our View of the World.*

Davis, C. F. 1989. *The Evidential Force of Religious Experience.* Oxford: Clarendon Press.

Dawkins, R. 1976. *The Selfish Gene.* Oxford University Press.

1986. *The Blind Watchmaker.* London: Norton.

Dean, W. 1986. *American Religious Empiricism.* Albany: SUNY Press.

De Candolle, A. 1885. *Histoire des sciences et des savants depuis deux siècles; précédée d'autres études sur des sujets scientifiques, en particulier sur l'hérédité et la sélection dans l'espèce humaine*, 2nd. edn. Geneva: H. Georg. Reprinted by Arno Press, New York, 1981. Extract in Cohen (1990a).

Dennett, D. C. 1984. *Elbow Room: Varieties of Free Will Worth Wanting.* Cambridge, Mass.: MIT Press.

1991. *Consciousness Explained.* Boston: Little, Brown, and Company.

Desmond, A. and J. Moore. 1991. *Darwin.* London: Michael Joseph.

D'Espagnat, B. 1989. *Reality and the Physicist.* Cambridge University Press.

DeVitt, M. 1984. *Realism and Truth.* Oxford: Basil Blackwell.

Dewey, J. 1934. *Art as Experience.* London: Allen and Unwin. Reprinted as *John Dewey, The Later Works, 1925–1953, Volume 10: 1934*, J. A. Boydston, H. F. Simon. Carbondale: Southern Illinois University Press.

Dicke, R. H. 1961. Dirac's cosmology and Mach's principle. *Nature* 192: 440f.

Dieks, D. 1989. Quantum mechanics without the projection postulate and its realistic interpretation. *Foundations of Physics* 19: 1395–423.

Dillenberger, J. 1960. *Protestant Thought and Natural Science: A Historical Interpretation.* Garden City, N.Y.: Doubleday & Co. Reprinted in 1988 by University of Notre Dame Press.

Donovan, P. 1979. *Interpreting Religious Experience.* New York: Seabury.

Drake, S. 1957. *Discoveries and Opinions of Galileo.* New York: Anchor Books.

  1965. Appendix A. The Galileo-Bellarmine meeting: A historical speculation. In L. Geymonat, *Galileo Galilei.* New York: McGraw-Hill.

Draper, J. W. 1875. *History of the Conflict Between Religion and Science.* New York: D. Appleton & Co.

Drees, W. B. 1990. *Beyond the Big Bang: Quantum Cosmologies and God.* La Salle (Ill.): Open Court.

  1990a. Theologie en natuurwetenschap: onafhankelijkheid en samenhang. In H. Küng, A. van Harskamp, B. (A. W.) Musschenga and W. B. Drees, *Godsdienst op een Keerpunt.* Kampen, NL: Kok Agora.

  1991. Potential tensions between cosmology and theology. In V. Brümmer, ed., *Interpreting the Universe as Creation.* Kampen, NL: Kok Pharos.

  1991a. Quantum cosmologies and the 'beginning'. *Zygon* 26: 373–95.

  1993. A case against temporal critical realism? Consequences of quantum cosmology for theology. In R. J. Russell, N. Murphy and C. J. Isham, eds., *Quantum Cosmology and the Laws of Nature.*

  1994. Problems in debates about physics and religion. In J. Hilgevoord, ed., *Physics and Our View of the World.*

Drees, W. B. (ed.). 1992. *Theologie en natuurwetenschap: Op zoek naar een Snark?* Kampen, NL: Kok.

Durant, J. 1990. Is there a role for theology in an age of secular science? In J. Fennema and I. Paul, eds., *Science and Religion.*

Dyson, F. J. 1979. *Disturbing the Universe.* New York: Harper & Row.

Eaves, L. B. 1989. Spirit, method, and content in science and religion: The theological perspective of a geneticist. *Zygon* 24: 185–215.

  1990. Autonomy is not enough. In R. J. Russell, W. R. Stoeger and G. V. Coyne, eds., *John Paul II on Science and Religion.*

  1991. Adequacy or orthodoxy? Choosing sides at the frontier. *Zygon* 26: 495–503.

Eaves, L. B. and L. Gross. 1992. Exploring the concept of spirit as a model for the God-world relationship in an age of genetics. *Zygon* 27: 261–85.

Eccles, J. C. 1979. *The Human Mystery.* New York: Springer.

Ellis, G. F. R. 1993. The theology of the anthropic principle. In R. J. Russell, N. Murphy and C. J. Isham, eds., *Quantum Cosmology and the Laws of Nature.*

Evans, D. D. 1963. *The Logic of Self-Involvement.* London: SCM.

Evans, G. 1973. The causal theory of names. *Proceedings of the Aristotelian Society,* Supp. vol. 47: 187–208. Reprinted in A. W. Moore, ed., 1993.

Eve, R. A. and F. B. Harrold. 1991. *The Creationist Movement in Modern America.* Boston: Twayne Publishers.

Fennema, J. and I. Paul, eds. 1990. *Science and Religion: One World – Changing*

Perspectives on Reality. Dordrecht: Kluwer & Enschede: University of Twente.

Ferré, F. 1992. The Integrity of Creation. In R. C. Miller, ed., *Empirical Theology*.

1993. *Hellfire and Lightning Rods: Liberating Science, Technology, and Religion*. Maryknoll: Orbis.

Fine, A. 1984. The Natural Ontological Attitude. In J. Leplin, ed., *Scientific Realism*. Reprinted in A. Fine, *The Shaky Game*. University of Chicago Press 1986, and in Boyd *et al.* (1991).

Finocchiaro, M. A. 1980. *Galileo and the Art of Reasoning: Rhetorical Foundations of Logic and Scientific Method*. (Boston Studies in the Philosophy of Science, vol. 61.) Dordrecht: Reidel.

1986. The methodological background to Galileo's trial. In W. A. Wallace (ed.), *Reinterpreting Galileo*. (Studies in Philosophy and the History of Philosophy, vol. 15.) Washington, D.C.: Catholic University of America Press.

1986a. Toward a philosophical interpretation of the Galileo affair. *Nuncius: Annali di Storia della Scienza* 1: 189–202.

Finocchiaro, M. A., ed. 1989. *The Galileo Affair: A Documentary History*. Berkeley and Los Angeles: University of California Press.

Fleming, D. 1950. *John William Draper and the Religion of Science*. University of Pennsylvania Press.

Foster, M. B. 1934. The Christian doctrine of creation and the rise of modern science. *Mind* 43: 446–68. Reprinted in D. O'Connor and F. Oakley, eds., *Creation: The Impact of an Idea*. New York: Scribner's, 1969, and in C. A. Russell, ed., *Science and Religious Belief: A Selection of Historical Studies*. University of London Press in association with Open University Press, 1973.

1935. Christian theology and modern science (1). *Mind* 44: 439–66.

1936. Christian theology and modern science (2). *Mind* 45: 1–27.

Fowles, J. 1980. *The Aristos*. (Rev. edn.). Falmouth (Cornwall): Triad/Granada.

Frankenberry, N. 1987. *Religion and Radical Empiricism*. Albany: SUNY Press.

1992. Major themes of empirical theology. In R. C. Miller, ed., *Empirical Theology*.

Frye, R. M., ed. 1983. *Is God a Creationist?* New York: Scribner's Sons.

Funkenstein, A. 1986. *Theology and the Scientific Imagination from the Middle Ages to the Seventeenth Century*. Princeton University Press.

Gale, G. 1974. Chew's monadology. *Journal of the History of Ideas* 35: 339–48.

Geertz, C. 1973. Religion as a cultural system. In C. Geertz, *The Interpretation of Cultures*. New York: Basic Books. Originally in M. Banton, ed., *Anthropological Approaches to the Study of Religion*. London: Tavistock, 1966.

Gerhart, M. and A. Russell. 1984. *Metaphoric Process: The Creation of Scientific and Religious Understanding*. Fort Worth: Texas Christian University Press.

Gewirth, A. 1993. How ethical is evolutionary ethics? In M. H. Nitecki and D. V. Nitecki, eds., *Evolutionary Ethics*.

Giere, R. N. 1988. *Explaining Science: A Cognitive Approach.* University of Chicago Press.

Gieryn, T. F. 1988. Distancing science from religion in seventeenth-century England. *ISIS* 79: 582–93.

Gilkey, L. B. 1982. The creationist controversy: the interrelation of inquiry and belief. *Science, Technology, and Human Values* 7 (40): 67–71.

  1985. *Creationism on Trial: Evolution and God at Little Rock.* Minneapolis: Winston Press.

  1992. Foreword. In J. A. Stone, *The Minimalist Vision of Transcendence.* Albany: SUNY Press.

Gilley, S. and A. Loades. 1981. Thomas Henry Huxley: The war between science and religion. *Journal of Religion* 61: 285–308.

Gingerich, O. 1982. The Galileo Affair. *Scientific American* (August): 132–43.

  1986. Galileo's astronomy. In W. A. Wallace, ed., *Reinterpreting Galileo.* Washington D.C.: Catholic University of America Press.

Gish, D. T. 1982. It is either 'In the beginning, God ...' – or '... Hydrogen'. *Christianity Today* (Caroll Stream, Ill.) 26 (8 October): 28–33.

Glick, T. F., ed. 1974. *The Comparative Reception of Darwinism.* University of Chicago Press.

Gould, S. J. 1980. *The Panda's Thumb: More Reflections in Natural History.* New York: W. W. Norton.

Gray, A. 1880. *Natural Science and Religion.* New York: Scribner's Sons. Partially reprinted in Frye, (1983).

Griffin, D. R. 1989. *God and Religion in the Postmodern World.* Albany: SUNY Press.

Griffin, D. R., ed. 1988. *The Reenchantment of Science: Postmodern Proposals.* Albany: SUNY Press.

Gruner, R. 1975. Science, Nature, and Christianity. *Journal of Theological Studies* 26: 55–81.

Hacking, I. 1982. Experimentation and scientific realism. *Philosophical Topics* 13: 71–87. Reprinted in Leplin (1984) and in Boyd *et al.* (1991).

Hahn, R. 1975. Scientific Careers in Eighteenth-century France. In M. P. Crosland, ed., *The Emergence of Science in Western Europe.* London: Macmillan.

Hakfoort, C. 1991. The missing syntheses in the historiography of science. *History of Science* 29: 207–16.

Hall, A. R. 1963. Merton revisited, or science and society in the seventeenth century. *History of Sciene* 2: 1–16. Reprinted in C. A. Russell, ed., *Science and Religious Belief: A Selection of Recent Historical Studies.* London: University of London Press and Open University Press.

Hardy, A. 1979. *The Spiritual Nature of Man.* Oxford: Clarendon Press.

Harré, R. 1986. *Varieties of Realism.* Oxford: Basil Blackwell.

Harrison, E. 1985. *Masks of the Universe.* New York: Macmillan.

Hartshorne, C. 1967. *A Natural Theology for our Time.* La Salle: Open Court.

Hawking, S. W. 1980. *Is the End in Sight for Theoretical Physics?* Cambridge University Press.

1988. *A Brief History of Time*. Toronto: Bantam Books.

Hay, D. 1990. *Religious Experience Today*. London: Mowbray.

Hebblethwaite, B. and E. Henderson, eds. 1990. *Divine Action: Studies Inspired by the Philosophical Theology of Austin Farrer*. Edinburgh: T. & T. Clark.

Hefner, P. 1970. The relocation of the God-question. *Zygon* 5: 5–17.

    1981. Is/ought: a risky relationship between theology and science. In A. R. Peacocke, ed., *The Sciences and Theology in the Twentieth Century*. Stocksfield: Oriel Press.

    1989. The evolution of the created co-creator. In T. Peters, ed., *Cosmos as Creation*.

    1993. *The Human Factor: Evolution, Culture, and Religion*. Minneapolis: Fortress Press.

Heller, M. 1986. *The Word and the World*. Tucson: Pachart Publishing House.

    1987. Big Bang on ultimate questions. In *Origin and Early History of the Universe: Proceedings of the 26th Liège International Astrophysics Colloquium, July 1–4 1986*. Cointe-Ougree (Belgium).

    1988. Scientific rationality and Christian logos. In R. J. Russell, W. R. Stoeger and G. V. Coyne, eds., *Physics, Philosophy and Theology*.

    1990. The experience of limits: New physics and new theology. Abstract in J. Fennema and I. Paul, eds., *Science and Religion*.

    1995. In R. J. Russell, N. Murphy and A. R. Peacocke, eds., *Chaos and Complexity*. (Forthcoming.)

Helm, P. 1988. *Eternal God: A Study of God without Time*. Oxford: Clarendon Press.

Hensen, R. 1990. Noordmans: modern? In G. W. Neven, ed., *Oecumenische ontdekkingen in het werk van Noordmans*. Kampen, NL: Kok. Partially reprinted in R. Hensen, *Houtskoolschetsen: Theologische duidingen in een wankel bestaan*, ed. W. B. Drees. Utrecht, NL: De Ploeg, 1991.

Hesse, M. B. 1963. *Models and Analogies in Science*. London: Sheed and Ward.

    1967. Models and analogy in science. In P. Edwards, ed., *Encyclopedia of Philosophy*, vol. 5. New York: Macmillan.

    1981. Retrospect. In A. R. Peacocke, ed., *The Sciences and Theology in the Twentieth Century*. Stocksfield: Oriel Press.

Hick, J. 1989. *An Interpretation of Religion: Human Responses to the Transcendent*. Basingstoke: Macmillan.

Hilgevoord, J., ed. 1994. *Physics and Our View of the World*. Cambridge University Press.

Hochstaffl, J. 1976. *Negative Theologie: Ein Versuch zur Vermittlung des patristischen Begriffs*. München: Kösel Verlag.

Holmes, H. R. 1993. Thinking about religion and experiencing the brain: Eugene d'Aquili's Biogenetic Structural Theory of Absolute Unitary Being. *Zygon* 28: 201–15.

Hooykaas, R. 1956. Science and reformation. *Cahiers d'histoire mondiale / Journal of World History* 3: 109–39. Extract in Cohen (1990a).

1972. *Religion and the Rise of Modern Science.* Edinburgh: Scottish Academic Press.

Hubbeling, H. G. 1987. *Principles of the Philosophy of Religion.* Assen, NL: Van Gorcum.

Hübner, J. 1966. *Theologie und biologische Entwicklungslehre.* Munich: Beck.

1990. Science and religion coming across. In J. Fennema and I. Paul, eds., *Science and Religion.*

Hübner, J., ed. 1987. *Der Dialog zwischen Theologie und Naturwissenschaft: Ein bibliographischer Bericht.* Munich: Kaiser.

Huxley, L. 1918. *The Life and Letters of Sir Joseph Dalton Hooker.* vol. 1. New York: Appleton.

Huxley, T. H. 1893. *Evolution and Ethics.* (The Romanes Lecture, 1893). London: Macmillan. Reprinted in Huxley (1894c); in T. H. Huxley and J. Huxley, *Evolution and Ethics 1893-1943.* London: Pilot Press, 1947; in J. Paradis, G. C. Williams, *Evolution and Ethics: T. H. Huxley's 'Evolution and Ethics' With New Essays on Its Victorian and Sociobiological Context.* Princeton University Press, 1989; and in M. H. Nitecki and D. V. Nitecki, eds., *Evolutionary Ethics.*

1894. *Darwiniana.* (Collected Essays, vol.2.) New York: Appleton.

1894a. *Science and Education.* (Collected Essays, vol. 3.) New York: Appleton.

1894b. *Science and Christian Tradition.* (Collected Essays, vol. 5). New York: Appleton.

1894c. *Evolution and Ethics, and Other Essays.* (Collected Essays, vol. 9). New York: Appleton.

Inbody, T. 1992. History of empirical theology. In R. C. Miller, ed., *Empirical Theology: A Handbook.*

Irons, W. 1991. Where did morality come from? *Zygon* 26: 49-90.

Isham, C. J. 1988. Creation of the universe as a quantum process. In R. J. Russell, W. R. Stoeger and G. V. Coyne, eds., *Physics, Philosophy, and Theology.*

1991. Quantum theories of the creation of the universe. In V. Brümmer, ed., *Interpreting the Universe as Creation.* Kampen, NL: Kok Pharos.

1993. Quantum theories of the creation of the universe. In R. J. Russell, N. Murphy and C. J. Isham, eds., *Quantum Cosmology and the Laws of Nature.*

Isham, C. J. and J. C. Polkinghorne. 1993. The debate over the block universe. In R. J. Russell, N. Murphy and C. J. Isham, eds., *Quantum Cosmology and the Laws of Nature.*

Jacob, J. R. and M. C. Jacob. 1980. The Anglican Origins of Modern Science: The Metaphysical Foundations of the Whig Constitution. *ISIS* 71 (257): 251-67.

Jacqueline, B. 1987. The Church and Galileo during the Century of the Enlightenment. In P. Poupard, ed., *Galileo Galilei: Toward a Resolution of 350 Years of Debate - 1633-1983.* Pittsburgh: Duquesne Press.

Jaki, S. L. 1974. *Science and Creation: From Eternal Cycles to an Oscillating Universe.* Edinburgh: Scottish Academic Press.

James, W. 1902. *The Varieties of Religious Experience.* New York: New American Library, 1958.

Jastrow, R. 1980. *God and the Astronomers.* New York: Warner Books. (1st edn. 1978, Reader's Library).

Jaynes, J. 1976. *The Origin of Consciousness in the Breakdown of the Bicameral Mind.* Boston: Houghton Mifflin Co.

Jeffrey, R. C. 1969. Statistical explanation vs. statistical inference. In N. Rescher, ed., *Essays in Honor of Carl G. Hempel.* Dordrecht: Reidel.

Jensen, J. V. 1988. Return to the Wilberforce-Huxley Debate. *The British Journal for the History of Science* 21: 161–79.

  1991. *Thomas Henry Huxley: Communicating for Science.* Newark: University of Delaware Press and London: Associated University Presses.

John Paul II. 1979. Speech on the occasion of the centenary of Einstein's birthday, 10 November, in French. *Acta Apost. Sedis* 71: 1461–8. English translations in *Discourses of the Popes from Pius XI to John Paul II to the Pontifical Academy of Sciences 1936–1986* (Pontificiae Academiae Scientiarum Scripta Varia 66). Vatican City State: Pontificia Academia Scientiarum; and in Poupard 1987, pp. 195–200.

  1982. In H. A. Brück, G. V. Coyne and M. S. Longair, eds., *Astrophysical Cosmology.* (Pontificiae Academiae Scientiarum Scripta Varia, No. 48.) Città del Vaticano: Pontificia Academia Scientiarum. English translation in *Discourses of the Popes from Pius XI to John Paul II to the Pontifical Academy of Sciences 1936–1986* (Pontificae Academiae Scientiarum Scripta Varia 66). Vatican City State: Pontificia Academia Scientiarum.

  1988. Letter to Reverend George V. Coyne, S. J., Director of the Vatican Observatory. In R. J. Russell, W. R. Stoeger and G. V. Coyne, eds., *Physics, Philosophy, and Theology.*

  1992. Lessons of the Galileo Case. Speech to the Pontifical Academy on 31 October 1992. English translation in *Origins: CNS Documentary Service* 22 (22) (12 November): 369, 371–3.

Jones, R. F. 1936. *Ancients and Moderns.* Saint Louis: Washington University Studies.

Juengst, E. T. 1988. Response: Carving nature at its joints. *Religion and Intellectual Life* 5 (3) (Spring): 70–8.

Kaiser, C. B. 1991. *Creation and the History of Science.* (The History of Christian Theology, vol. 3.). London: Marshall Pickering and Grand Rapids: Eerdmans.

Kaufman, G. D. 1972. *God the Problem.* Cambridge, Mass.: Harvard University Press.

  1993. *In Face of Mystery: A Constructive theology.* Cambridge, Mass.: Harvard University Press.

Kelsey, D. 1985. The doctrine of creation from nothing. In E. McMullin, ed., *Evolution and Creation.* University of Notre Dame Press.

Kirschenmann, P. P. 1992. Does the Anthropic Principle live up to scientific standards? *Annals of the Japan Association for Philosophy of Science* 8: 69–96.

Kitcher, P. 1981. Explanatory unification. *Philosophy of Science* 48: 507–31; Reprinted in Boyd *et al.* (1991).

1982. *Abusing Science: The Case Against Creationism.* Cambridge, Mass.: MIT Press.

1985. *Vaulting Ambition: Sociobiology and the Quest for Human Nature.* Cambridge, Mass.: MIT Press.

1989. Explanatory unification and the causal structure of the world. In P. Kitcher and W. Salmon, eds., *Scientific Explanation.* (Minnesota Studies in the Philosophy of Science, XIII.) Minneapolis: University of Minnesota Press.

1993. *The Advancement of Science: Science without Legend, Objectivity without Illusions.* New York: Oxford University Press.

Klaaren, E. M. 1977. *Religious Origins of Modern Science: Belief in Creation in Seventeenth-Century Thought.* Grand Rapids: Eerdmans.

Kornblith, H., ed. 1994. *Naturalizing Epistemology.* (Second Edition.) Cambridge, Mass.: MIT Press.

Kripke, S. 1980. *Naming and Necessity.* Cambridge, Mass.: Harvard University Press.

Kuhn, T. 1962. *The Structure of Scientific Revolutions.* University of Chicago Press.

Küppers, B. O. 1990. On a fundamental paradigmn shift in the natural sciences. In W. Krohn *et al.*, eds., *Self-organization: Portrait of a Scientific Revolution.* Kluwer Academic Publishers.

Kylstra, F. J. and B. Klein Wassink. 1983. *Mensbeeld – godsbeeld.* Utrecht, NL: De Ploeg.

La Barre, W. 1991. *Shadow of Childhood. Neoteny and the Biology of Religion.* Norman: University of Oklahoma Press.

Lakatos, I. 1970. Falsification and the methodology of scientific research programmes. In I. Lakatos and A. Musgrave, eds., *Criticism and the Growth of Knowledge.* Cambridge University Press. Reprinted in I. Lakatos, *The Methodology of Scientific Research Programmes. Philosophical Papers, Volume I,* eds. J. Worrall and G. Currie. Cambridge University Press.

Langford, J. J. 1966. *Galileo, Science, and the Church.* Ann Arbor: University of Michigan Press. (3rd edn. 1992.)

Larson, E. J. 1989[2]. *Trial and Error: The American Controversie over Creation and Evolution.* (Updated edition; 1st. edn. 1985.) New York: Oxford University Press.

Laudan, L. 1981. A confutation of convergent realism. *Philosophy of Science* 48: 19–48. Reprinted in Leplin (1984) and in Boyd *et al.* (1991).

1982. Commentary: Science at the bar – Causes for concern. *Science, Technology, & Human Values* 7 (41): 16–19. Reprinted in M. C. La Follette, ed., *Creationism, Science, and the Law: The Arkansas Case.* (Cambridge, Mass.: MIT Press, 1983), and in Ruse, ed. (1988).

1983. The demise of the demarcation problem. In R. S. Cohen and

L. Laudan, eds., *Physics, Philosophy and Psychoanalysis*. Dordrecht: Reidel. Reprinted in Ruse, ed. (1988).

1984. *Science and Values: The Aims of Science and Their Role in Scientific Debate.* Berkeley and Los Angeles: University of California Press.

Laughlin, C. D. and E. d'Aquili, eds. 1974. *Biogenetic Structuralism.* New York: Columbia University Press.

Laughlin, C. D., J. McManus and E. d'Aquili. 1992. *Brain, Symbol, and Experience: Toward a Neuroepistemology of Human Consciousness.* New York: Columbia University Press. (Originally Boston: New Science Library, 1990.)

Leftow, B. 1991. *Time and Eternity.* Ithaca: Cornell University Press.

Leplin, J. ed. 1984. *Scientific Realism.* Berkeley and Los Angeles: University of California Press.

Levin, M. 1984. What kind of explanation is truth? In J. Leplin, ed., *Scientific Realism.*

Lindbeck, G. A. 1984. *The Nature of Doctrine: Religion and Theology in a Postliberal Age.* Philadelphia: Westminster.

Lindberg, D. C. 1990. Conceptions of the Scientific Revolution from Bacon to Butterfield: A preliminary sketch. In D. C. Lindberg and R. S. Westman, eds., *Reappraisals of the Scientific Revolution.*

1992. *The Beginnings of Western Science: The European Scientific Tradition in Philosophical, Religious, and Institutional Context, 600 B.C. to A.D. 1450.* University of Chicago Press.

Lindberg, D. C. and R. L. Numbers. 1986a. Beyond war and peace: A reappraisal of the encounter between Christianity and science. *Church History* 55: 338–54. Reprinted in *Perspectives on Science and Christian Faith* 39 (1987): 140–5.

Lindberg, D. C. and R. L. Numbers, eds. 1986. *God and Nature: Historical Essays on the Encounter between Christianity and Science.* Berkeley and Los Angeles: University of California Press.

Lindberg, D. C. and R. S. Westman, eds. 1990. *Reappraisals of the Scientific Revolution.* Cambridge University Press.

Livingstone, D. N. 1987. *Darwin's Forgotten Defenders: The Encounter between Evangelical Theology and Evolutionary Thought.* Grand Rapids: Eerdmans.

Loomer, B. 1987. The size of God. In W. Dean and L. E. Axel, eds., *The Size of God: The Theology of Bernard Loomer in Context.* Macon, Ga.: Mercer University Press.

Looren de Jong, H. 1992. *Naturalism and Psychology: A Theoretical Study.* Kampen, NL: Kok.

Lovin, R. W. and F. E. Reynolds. In the beginning. In R. W. Lovin and F. E. Reynolds, eds., *Cosmogony and Ethical Order: Studies in Comparative Ethics.* University of Chicago Press.

Lucas, J. R. 1979. Wilberforce and Huxley: a legendary encounter. *Historical Journal* 22: 313–30.

1989. *The Future: An Essay on God, Temporality and Truth.* Oxford: Basil Blackwell.

Lüke, U. 1990. *Evolutionäre Erkenntnistheorie und Theologie: Eine kritische Auseinandersetzung aus fundamentaltheologischer Perspektive.* Stuttgart: Hirzel.

Luhmann, N. 1992. *Funktion der Religion.* Frankfurt-on-Main: Suhrkamp. (Originally 1977.)

Lumsden, C. J. and E. O. Wilson. 1981. *Genes, Mind, and Culture: The Coevolutionary Process.* Cambridge, Mass.: Harvard University Press.

Mackor, A. R. 1994. The alleged autonomy of psychology and the social sciences. In D. Prawitz and D. Westerståhl, eds., *Logic and Philosophy of Science in Uppsala.* Dordrecht: Kluwer Academic Publishers.

MacLeod, R. H., R. Petersen and P. Ames 1992. *Contemporary Issues in Science and Christian Faith: An Annotated Bibliography.* Third Printing, Revised and Expanded. Ipswich (Ma.): American Scientific Affiliation.

Maffeo, S. 1991. *In the Service of Nine Popes: 100 Years of the Vatican Observatory.* Vatican City State: Vatican Observatory & Pontifical Academy of Sciences.

Mangum, J. M., ed. 1989. *The New Science–Faith Debate.* Minneapolis: Augsburg-Fortress and Geneva: World Council of Churches.

Manley, F. 1963. *John Donne: The Anniversaries.* Baltimore: Johns Hopkins Press.

Marini-Bettòlo, G. B. 1986. *Outlines of the Activity of the Pontifical Academy of Sciences 1936–1986.* (Pontificiae Academiae Scientiarum Scripta Varia 67) Città del Vaticano: Pontificia Academia Scientiarum. (Reprinted in 1987 as *The Activity of the Pontifical Academy of Sciences 1936–1986.*)

Marshall, G. 1982. *In Search of the Spirit of Capitalism: An Essay on Max Weber's Protestant Ethic Thesis.* London: Hutchinson.

Martz, L. L. 1947. *John Donne in Meditation: The Anniversaries.* London.

May, G. 1978. *Schöpfung aus dem Nichts: Die Entstehung der Lehre von der Creatio ex Nihilo.* Berlin: W. de Gruyter.

May, H., M. Striegnitz and P. Hefner, eds. 1989. *Kooperation und Wettbewerb: Zu Ethik und Biologie menschlichen Sozialverhaltens.* (Loccumer Protokolle 75/ 1988.) Rehburg-Loccum: Evangelische Akademie Loccum.

   1990. *Menschliche Natur und moralische Paradoxa aus der Sicht von Biologie, Sozialwissenschaften und Theologie.* (Loccumer Protokolle 78/1989.) Rehburg-Loccum: Evangelische Akademie Loccum.

Mayaud, P.-N. 1992. Une 'nouvelle' affaire Galilée? *Revue d'Histoire des Sciences* 45: 161–230.

McFague, S. 1982. *Metaphorical Theology.* Philadelphia: Fortress.

McIver, T. 1988. *Anti-Evolution: An Annotated Bibliography.* Jefferson, NC.: McFarland.

McMullin, E. 1967. Introduction: Galileo, man of science. In E. McMullin, ed., *Galileo, Man of Science.* New York: Basic Books.

   1981. How should cosmology relate to theology? In A. R. Peacocke, ed., *The Sciences and Theology in the Twentieth Century.* Stocksfield: Oriel Press and Notre Dame: University of Notre Dame Press.

   1984. A case for scientific realism. In J. Leplin, ed., *Scientific Realism.*

1985. Realism in theology and in science: A response to Peacocke. *Religion and Intellectual Life* 2 (4) (Summer): 39–47.

1985a. Introduction: Evolution and creation. In E. McMullin, ed., *Evolution and Creation*. University of Notre Dame Press.

1987. Explanatory success and the truth of theory. In N. Rescher, ed., *Scientific Inquiry in Philosophical Perspective*. Lanham: University Press of America.

1988. Natural science and belief in a creator: Historical notes. In R. J. Russell, W. R. Stoeger and G. V. Coyne, eds., *Physics, Philosophy, and Theology*.

1990. Conceptions of science in the Scientific Revolution. In D. C. Lindberg and R. S. Westman, eds., *Reappraisals of the Scientific Revolution*.

1991. Plantinga's defense of special creation. *Christian Scholar's Review* 21 (1): 55–79.

1992. *The Inference that Makes Science*. Milwaukee: Marquette University Press.

1993. Evolution and special creation. *Zygon* 28: 299–335.

1994. Enlarging the known world. In J. Hilgevoord, ed., *Physics and Our View of the World*.

Merton, R. K. 1936. Puritanism, Pietism, and Science. *Sociological Review* 28: 1–30.

1938. Science, technology and society in seventeenth century England. *Osiris* 4 (2): 360–632 (Bruges, Belgium: St. Catherine Press). Reprinted as a monograph, with a new preface, New York: Howard Fertig, 1970.

Midgley, M. 1985. *Evolution as a Religion: Strange Hopes and Stranger Fears*. London: Methuen.

Miller, R. C. 1974. *The American Spirit in Theology*. Philadelphia: United Church Press.

Miller, R. C., ed. 1992. *Empirical Theology: A Handbook*. Birmingham, Al.: Religious Education Press.

Millikan, R. G. 1984. *Language, Thought and Other Biological Categories*. Cambridge, Mass.: MIT Press.

1989. In defense of proper functions. *Philosophy of Science* 56: 288–302. Reprinted in Millikan (1993).

1993. *White Queen Psychology and Other Essays for Alice*. Cambridge, Mass.: MIT Press.

Misner, C. W. 1977. Cosmology and theology. In W. Yourgrau, and A. D. Breck, eds., *Cosmology, History, and Theology*. New York: Plenum Press.

Monod, J. 1971. *Chance and Necessity*. New York: Alfred Knopf.

Montagu, A., ed. 1984. *Science and Creationism*. Oxford University Press.

Montefiore, H. 1985. *The Probability of God*. London: SCM.

Moore, A. W., ed. 1993. *Meaning and Reference*. Oxford University Press.

Moore, J. R. 1979. *The Post-Darwinian Controversies: A Study of the Protestant Struggle to come to terms with Darwin in Great Britain and America, 1870–1900*. Cambridge University Press.

1985. Herbert Spencer's Henchmen: The Evolution of Protestant Liberals in Late Nineteenth Century America. In J. Durant, *Darwinism and Divinity: Essays on Evolution and Religious Belief.* Oxford: Basil Blackwell.

1989. Of love and death: Why Darwin 'gave up Christianity'. In J. R. Moore, ed., *History, Humanity and Evolution: Essays for John C. Greene.* Cambridge University Press.

Morris, D. 1967. *The Naked Ape.* London: Jonathan Cape.

Morris, H. 1984. *A History of Modern Creationism.* San Diego: Master Book Publishers.

Mortensen, V. 1987. The status of the science-religion dialogue. In S. Andersen and A. R. Peacocke, eds., *Evolution and Creation.* Aarhus: Aarhus University Press.

1988. *Teologi og naturvidenskab: Hinsides restriktion og ekspansion.* København: Munksgaard.

Munitz, M. K. 1986. *Cosmic Understanding.* Princeton University Press.

Murphy, N. 1990. *Theology in the Age of Scientific Reasoning.* Ithaca: Cornell University Press.

Nagel, T. 1986. *The View from Nowhere.* New York: Oxford University Press.

Nebelsick, H. P. 1992. *The Renaissance, the Reformation and the Rise of Science.* Edinburgh: T. & T. Clark.

Nelkin, D. 1977. *Science Textbook Controversies and the Politics of Equal Time.* Cambridge, Mass.: MIT Press. Expanded edition as *The Creation Controversy: Science or Scripture in the Schools* (New York: W. H. Norton, 1982).

Nickles, T. 1992. Good science as bad history: From order of knowing to order of being. In E. McMullin, ed., *The Social Dimensions of Science.* University of Notre Dame Press.

Nitecki, M. H. 1993. Problematic worldviews of evolutionary ethics. In M. H. Nitecki and D. V. Nitecki, eds., *Evolutionary Ethics.*

Nitecki, M. H. and D. V. Nitecki, eds. 1993. *Evolutionary Ethics.* Albany: SUNY Press.

North, J. D. 1977. Chronology and the age of the world. In W. Yourgrau and A. D. Breck, eds., *Cosmology, History, and Theology.* New York: Plenum Press.

Numbers, R. L. 1986. The creationists. In D. C. Lindberg and R. L. Numbers, eds., *God and Nature: Historical Essays on the Encounter between Christianity and Science.*

1992. *The Creationists.* New York: Alfred Knopf.

Otto, R. 1917. *Das Heilige: Über das Irrationale in der Idee des Göttlichen und sein Verhältnis zum Rationalen.* Breslau: Trewendt und Granier.

Owen, R. 1849. *On the Nature of Limbs.* London: John van Voorst.

Paley, W. 1802. *Natural Theology, or Evidences of the Existence and Attributes of the Deity Collected from the Appearances of Nature.* London.

Pannenberg, W. 1989. Theological appropriation of scientific understandings: Response to Hefner, Wicken, Eaves, and Tipler. *Zygon* 24: 255–71.

Paul, H. W. 1974. Religion and Darwinism: Varieties of Catholic reaction. In T. F. Glick, ed., *The Comparative Reception of Darwinism.*

1979. *The Edge of Contingency: French Catholic Reactions to Scientific Change from Darwin to Duhem.* Gainesville: University Presses of Florida.

Peacocke, A. R. 1979. *Creation and the World of Science.* Oxford: Clarendon Press.

1981. Introduction. In A. R. Peacocke, ed., *The Sciences and Theology in the Twentieth Century.* University of Notre Dame Press.

1984. *Intimations of Reality: Critical Realism in Science and Religion.* University of Notre Dame Press.

1985. Intimations of reality: Critical realism in science and religion. *Religion and Intellectual Life* 2 (4) (Summer): 7–26.

1986. *God and the New Biology.* London: Dent.

1993. *Theology for a Scientific Age: Being and Becoming – Natural, Divine and Human.* Enlarged Edition. London: SCM, and Minneapolis: Fortress. (First edn. Oxford: Blackwell, 1990.)

1994. The religion of a scientist – explorations into reality (*Religio philosophi naturalis*). *Zygon* 29: 639–59. In Dutch translation in W. B. Drees, ed., *Denken over God en wereld: Theologie, natuurwetenschap en filosofie in wisselwerking.* (Kampen, NL: Kok, 1994).

1995. God's interaction with the world: The implications of deterministic 'chaos' and of interconnected complexity. In R. J. Russell, N. Murphy and A. R. Peacocke, eds., *Chaos and Complexity.*

Peden, C. 1987. *The Chicago School: Voices in Liberal Religious Thought.* Bristol, IN.: Wyndham Hall Press.

Pedersen, O. 1983. Galileo and the Council of Trent. *Journal for the History of Astronomy* 14: 1–29.

1991. *Galileo and the Council of Trent.* Vatican City State: Vatican Observatory. (Revised reprint of Pedersen 1983.)

Peters, K. E. 1992. Empirical theology and science. In R. C. Miller, ed., *Empirical Theology: A Handbook.*

Peters, T. 1993. The trinity in and beyond time. In R. J. Russell, N. Murphy and C. J. Isham, eds., *Quantum Cosmology and the Laws of Nature.*

Peters, T., ed. 1989. *Cosmos as Creation: Theology and Science in Consonance.* Nashville: Abingdon Press.

Philipse, H. 1994. Churchland, Heidegger, en de kennistheoretische traditie. *Algemeen Nederlands Tijdschrift voor Wijsbegeerte* 86: 1–38.

Phillips, D. Z. 1976. *Religion without Explanation.* Oxford: Basil Blackwell.

1986. *Belief, Change and Forms of Life.* Basingstoke: Macmillan.

Pickering, A. 1984. *Constructing Quarks: A Sociological History of Particle Physics.* University of Chicago Press.

Pike, N. 1970. *God and Timelessness.* London: Routledge and Kegan Paul.

Plantinga, A. 1974. *God, Freedom and Evil.* Grand Rapids: Eerdmans.

1985. Self-Profile. In J. E. Tomberlin and P. van Inwagen, eds., *Alvin Plantinga.* Dordrecht: Reidel.

1991. When faith and reason clash: evolution and the Bible. *Christian Scholar's Review* 21 (1): 8–32.

1991a. Evolution, neutrality, and antecedent probability: a reply to Van Till and McMullin. *Christian Scholar's Review* 21 (1): 80–109.

1993. *Warrant and Proper Function*. New York: Oxford University Press.

1993a. Methodological naturalism. Paper presented at the conference 'Our Knowledge of God, Christ, and Nature', University of Notre Dame, April 1993.

Platvoet, J. G. 1993. De wraak van de 'primitieven': godsdienstgeschiedenis van Neanderthaler tot New Age. *Nederlands Theologisch Tijdschrift* 47: 227–43.

1994. Het religionisme beleden en bestreden: recente ontwikkelingen in de Angelsaksische godsdienstwetenschap. *Nederlands Theologisch Tijdschrift* 48: 22–38.

Polkinghorne, J. C. 1986. *One World: The Interaction of Science and Theology*. Princeton University Press.

1989. *Science and Providence: God's Interaction with the World*. Boston: Shambala.

1990. A revived natural theology. In J. Fennema and I. Paul, eds., *Science and Religion*.

1991. *Reason and Reality: The Relationship between Science and Theology*. Philadelphia: Trinity Press.

1993. The laws of nature and the laws of physics. In R. J. Russell, N. Murphy and C. J. Isham, eds., *Quantum Cosmology and the Laws of Nature*.

Poupard, P. 1992. Galileo: Report on Papal Commission Findings. (Presented, in French, to the pope and the Pontifical Academy of Sciences on 31 October 1992). *Origins: CNS Documentary Service* 22 (22) (12 November): 374–5.

Poupard, P., ed. 1987. *Galileo Galilei: Toward a Resolution of 350 Years of Debate – 1633–1983*. With an Epilogue by John Paul II. Pittsburgh, PA: Duquesne University Press. (Original French, 1983)

Preus, J. S. 1987. *Explaining Religion: Criticism and Theory from Bodin to Freud*. New Haven: Yale University Press.

Prigogine, I. and I. Stengers. 1984. *Order Out of Chaos*. Toronto: Bantam Books. (Originally *La Nouvelle Alliance*. Paris, 1979.)

Proudfoot, W. 1985. *Religious Experience*. Berkeley and Los Angeles: Univerity of California Press.

Psillos, S. 1994. A philosophical study of the transition from the caloric theory of heat to thermodynamics: Resisting the pessimistic meta-induction. *Studies in History and Philosophy of Science* 25: 159–90.

Quine, W. V. O. and J. S. Ullian 1978. *The Web of Belief*, 2nd edn. New York: Random House.

Quinn, P. L. 1984. The philosopher of science as an expert witness. In J. T. Cushing, C. F. Delaney, G. M. Gutting, eds., *Science and Reality*. University of Notre Dame Press.

Radder, H. 1984. *De materiële realisering van wetenschap*. Amsterdam: VU

Uitgeverij. (*The Material Realization of Science.* Assen, NL: Van Gorcum, 1988.)

1989. Rondom realisme. *Kennis en Methode* 13: 295–314.

Rawls, J. 1971. *A Theory of Justice.* Cambridge, Mass.: Harvard University Press.

1980. Kantian constructivism in moral theory. *Journal of Philosophy* 77: 515–72.

Redondi, P. 1987. *Galileo: Heretic.* Princeton University Press.

Reynolds, V. and R. E. S. Tanner. 1983. *The Biology of Religion.* London: Longman.

Ritschl, D. 1986. *The Logic of Theology.* London: SCM. (Originally *Zur Logik der Theologie.* Munich: Kaiser, 1984.)

Rogers, D. J. 1990. *The American Empirical Movement in Theology.* New York: Peter Lang.

Rolston, H. 1987. *Science and Religion: A Critical Survey.* New York: Random House.

Rouse, J. 1987. *Knowledge and Power: Toward a Political Philosophy of Science.* Ithaca: Cornell University Press.

Rudwick, M. J. 1972. *The Meaning of Fossils.* London: MacDonald.

1981. Senses of the natural world and senses of God: Another look at the historical relation of science and religion. In A. R. Peacocke, ed., *The Sciences and Theology in the Twentieth Century.* Stocksfield: Oriel Press and Notre Dame: University of Notre Dame Press.

1986. The shape and meaning of Earth history. In D. C. Lindberg and R. L. Numbers, eds., *God and Nature.*

Rupke, N. A. 1993. Richard Owen's Vertebrate Archetype. *ISIS* 84: 231–51.

Ruse, M. 1982. Creation-Science Is Not Science. *Science, Technology, & Human Values* 7 (40): 72–8. Reprinted in M. C. La Follette, ed., *Creationism, Science, and the Law: The Arkansas Case.* (Cambridge, Mass.: MIT Press, 1993).

1982a. Response to Laudan's Commentary: Pro Judice. *Science, Technology, & Human Values* 7 (41): 19–23. Reprinted in M. C. La Follette, ed., *Creationism, Science, and the Law: The Arkansas Case.* Cambridge, Mass.: MIT Press, 1983; and in Ruse, ed. (1988).

1988. *Philosophy of Biology Today.* Albany: SUNY Press.

1989. Is rape wrong on Andromeda? In M. Ruse, *The Darwinian Paradigm: Essays on its History, Philosophy, and Religious Implications.* London: Routledge. Originally in E. Regis, ed., *Extraterrestrials: Science and Alien Intelligence.* Cambridge University Press 1985.

1993. The new evolutionary ethics. In M. H. Nitecki and D. V. Nitecki, eds., *Evolutionary Ethics.*

Ruse, M., ed. 1988. *But Is It Science? The Philosophical Questions in the Creation–Evolution Controversy.* Buffalo, N.Y.: Prometheus Books.

Russell, R. J. 1985. A critical appraisal of Peacocke's thought on religion and science. *Religion and Intellectual Life* 2: 48–58.

1988. Contingency in physics and cosmology: A critique of the theology of W. Pannenberg. *Zygon* 23: 23–43.

1988a. Quantum physics in philosophical and theological perspective. In R. J. Russell, W. R. Stoeger and G. V. Coyne, eds., *Physics, Philosophy, and Theology*.

1993. Introduction. In R. J. Russell, N. Murphy and C. J. Isham, eds., *Quantum Cosmology and the Laws of Nature*.

1993a. Finite creation without a beginning: The doctrine of creation in relation to big bang and quantum cosmologies. In R. J. Russell, N. Murphy and C. J. Isham, eds., *Quantum Cosmology and the Laws of Nature*.

Russell, R. J., W. R. Stoeger and G. V. Coyne, eds. 1988. *Physics, Philosophy, and Theology: A Common Quest for Understanding*. Vatican City State: Vatican Observatory. Distributed outside Italy by University of Notre Dame Press.

1990. *John Paul II on Science and Religion: Reflections on the New View from Rome*. Vatican: Vatican Observatory. Distributed outside Italy by University of Notre Dame Press.

Russell, R. J., N. Murphy and C. J. Isham, eds. 1993. *Quantum Cosmology and the Laws of Nature: Scientific Perspectives on Divine Action*. Vatican City State: Vatican Observatory and Berkeley: Center for Theology and the Natural Sciences. Distributed outside Italy by University of Notre Dame Press.

Russell, R. J., N. Murphy and A. R. Peacocke, eds. 1995. *Chaos and Complexity: Scientific Perspectives on Divine Action*. Vatican City State: Vatican Observatory and Berkeley: Center for Theology and the Natural Sciences. Distributed outside Italy by University of Notre Dame Press. (Forthcoming.)

Sacks, O. 1990. *Awakenings*. New York: HarperCollins. (1st edn. 1973.)

Salmon, W. C. 1990. *Four Decades of Scientific Explanation*. Minneapolis: University of Minnesota Press. (Also in P. Kitcher and W. Salmon, eds., *Scientific Explanation*. Mineapolis: University of Minnesota, 1989.)

Sanders, A. F. 1988. *Michael Polanyi's Post-critical Epistemology*. Amsterdam: Rodopi.

1992. Geloof, kennis en natuurwetenschappen. In W. B. Drees, ed., *Theologie en natuurwetenschap*.

Sanders. C. and H. van Rappard. 1985. Psychology and the philosophy of science. In *Annals of Theoretical Psychology*, vol. 3, eds. K. B. Madsen and L. P. Mos. New York: Plenum Press.

Santillana, G. de. 1955. *The Crime of Galileo*. University of Chicago Press.

1965. Appendix B. Reply to Stillman Drake. In L. Geymonat, *Galileo Galilei*. New York: McGraw-Hill.

Schüssler Fiorenza, F. 1991. The crisis of hermeneutics and Christian theology. In S. G. Davaney, ed., *Theology at the End of Modernity*. Philadelphia: Trinity Press International.

Schuster, J. A. and R. R. Yeo, eds. 1986. *The Politics and Rhetorics of Scientific Method: Historical Studies*. Dordrecht: Reidel.

Schwartz, J. 1991. Reduction, elimination, and the mental. *Philosophy of Science* 58: 203–20.

Schweber, S. 1993. Physics, community, and the crisis in physical theory. *Physics Today* 46 (November): 34–40.

Searle, J. R. 1992. *The Rediscovery of the Mind*. Cambridge, Mass.: MIT Press.

Secord, J. A. 1993. Introduction. (Special issue: The Big Picture.) *British Journal for the History of Science* 26: 387–9.

Segal, R. A. 1989. *Religion and the Social Sciences: Essays on the Confrontation*. Atlanta: Scholars Press.

Sellars, W. 1963. *Science, Perception and Reality*. London: Routledge and Kegan Paul.

Sessions, W. L. 1994. *The Concept of Faith: A Philosophical Investigation*. Ithaca: Cornell University Press.

Shapere, D. 1982. The concept of observation in science and philosophy, *Philosophy of Science* 49: 485–525.

Shapiro, B. 1969. *John Wilkins 1614–1672: An Intellectual Biography*. Berkeley: University of California Press.

Singer, P. 1981. *The Expanding Circle: Ethics and Sociobiology*. Oxford: Clarendon Press.

1984. Ethics and sociobiology. *Zygon* 19: 141–58. Reprinted from *Philosophy & Public Affairs* 12 (1) (Winter 1982).

Soskice, J. M. 1985. *Metaphor and Religious Language*. Oxford: Clarendon Press.

1988. Knowledge and experience in science and religion: Can we be realists? In R. J. Russell, W. R. Stoeger and G. V. Coyne, eds., *Physics, Philosophy, and Theology*.

Sperry, R. W. 1980. Mind–brain interaction: mentalism, yes; dualism, no. *Neuroscience* 5: 195 -206.

1988. Psychology's mentalist paradigm and the religion/science tension. *American Psychologist* 43: 607–13. Reprinted in Ashbrook, ed. (1993)

1991. Search for beliefs to live by consistent with science. *Zygon* 26: 237–58.

Staal, F. 1975. *Exploring Mysticism*. Berkeley and Los Angeles: University of California Press.

Stimson, D. 1935. Puritanism and the New Philosophy in 17th Century England. *Bulletin of the Institute of the History of Medicine* 3: 321–34. Extract in Cohen (1990a).

Stoeger, W. R. 1993. Contemporary physics and the ontological status of the laws of nature. In R. J. Russell, N. Murphy and C. J. Isham, eds., *Quantum Cosmology and the Laws of Nature*.

1995. Describing God's action in the world in the light of scientific knowledge of reality. In R. J. Russell, N. Murphy and A. R. Peacocke, eds., *Chaos and Complexity*. (Forthcoming)

Stone, J. A. 1989. What religious naturalism can learn from Langdon Gilkey: Uncovering the dimension of ultimacy. In W. C. Peden and L. E. Axel, eds., *God, Values, and Empiricism*. Macon, Ga.: Mercer University Press.

1992. *The Minimalist Vision of Transcendence: A Naturalist Philosophy of Religion.* Albany: SUNY Press.

Strawson, P. F. 1985. *Skepticism and Naturalism: Some Varieties.* New York: Colombia University Press.

Stump, E. and N. Kretzmann. 1981. Eternity. *Journal of Philosophy* 78: 429–58.

Surin, K. 1986. *Theology and the Problem of Evil.* Oxford: Basil Blackwell.

Sutherland, S. R. 1984. *God, Jesus and Belief: The Legacy of Theism.* Oxford: Basil Blackwell.

Swinburne, R. 1979. *The Existence of God.* Oxford: Clarendon Press.

1981. The evidential value of religious experience. In A. R. Peacocke, ed., *The Sciences and Theology in the Twentieth Century.* Stocksfield: Oriel Press.

Terrien, S. 1978. *The Elusive Presence: Toward a New Biblical Theology.* San Francisco: Harper & Row.

Theissen, G. 1985. *Biblical Faith: An Evolutionary Approach.* Philadelphia: Fortress. (Translation of *Biblischer Glaube in evolutionärer Sicht,* Munich: Kaiser, 1984.)

1987. *The Shadow of the Galilean: The Quest of the Historical Jesus in Narrative Form.* Philadelphia: Fortress. (Translation of *Der Schatten des Galiläers. Historische Jesusforschung in erzählender Form.* Munich: Kaiser, 1986.)

Thomas, O. C., ed. 1983. *God's Activity in the World: The Contemporary Problem.* Chica, Calif.: Scholars Press.

Toulmin, S. E. 1990. *Cosmopolis: The Hidden Agenda of Modernity.* New York: Free Press.

Tracy, D. 1975. *Blessed Rage for Order: The New Pluralism in Theology.* Minneapolis: Seabury.

Trigg, R. 1993. *Rationality and Science: Can Science Explain Everything?* Oxford: Blackwell.

Turner, F. M. 1974. *Between Science and Religion: The Reactions to Scientific Naturalism in Late Victorian England.* New Haven: Yale University Press.

1978. The Victorian Conflict between Science and Religion: A Professional Dimension. *ISIS* 69: 356–76.

Updike, J. 1986. *Roger's Version.* New York: Knopf.

Van Baal, J. and W. E. A. van Beek. 1985. *Symbols for Communication: An Introduction to the Anthropological Study of Religion,* 2nd revised edn. Assen, NL: Van Gorcum.

Van den Beukel, A. 1991. *More Things in Heaven and Earth: God and the Scientists.* London: SCM. (Originally *De dingen hebben hun geheim.* Baarn, NL: Ten Have, 1990.)

Van den Brom, L. J. 1982. *God alomtegenwoordig.* Kampen, NL: Kok.

1984. God's omnipresent agency. *Religious Studies* 20: 637–55.

1993. *Divine Presence in the World: A Critical Analysis of the Notion of Divine Omnipresence.* Kampen, NL: Kok Pharos.

Van der Steen, W. J. 1993. *A Practical Philosophy for the Life Sciences.* Albany: SUNY.

Van Fraassen, B. S. 1976. To save the phenomena. *Journal of Philosophy* 73: 623–32. Reprinted in Leplin (1984) and in Boyd *et al.* (1991).

1980. *The Scientific Image.* Oxford: Clarendon Press.

1984. The problem of indistinguishable particles. In J. T. Cushing, C. F. Delaney and G. M. Gutting, eds., *Science and Reality.* University of Notre Dame Press.

1991. *Quantum Mechanics: An Empiricist View.* Oxford: Clarendon Press.

1994. The world of empiricism. In J. Hilgevoord, ed., *Physics and Our View of the World.*

Van Huyssteen, J. W. 1989. *Theology and the Justification of Faith.* Grand Rapids: Eerdmans. (Originally *Teologie as kritiese Geloofsverantwoording*, Pretoria: RGN, 1986.)

1993. Theology and science: the quest for a new apologetics. *Princeton Seminary Bulletin*, New Series, 14 (2): 113–33.

1993a. Is the postmodernist always a postfoundationalist? *Theology Today* 50: 373–86.

Van Till, H. J. 1986. *The Fourth Day: What the Bible and the Heavens are Telling Us about the Creation.* Grand Rapids: Eerdmans.

1991. When faith and reason cooperate. *Christian Scholar's Review* 21 (1): 33–45.

Vollmer, G. 1990. Geleitwort. In U. Lüke, *Evolutionäre Erkenntnistheorie und Theologie.*

Vroon, P. A. 1989. *De Tranen van de Krokodil.* Baarn, NL: Ambo.

Wainwright, W. J. 1973. Natural explanations and religious experience. *Ratio* 15: 98–101.

1981. *Mysticism.* Brighton: Harvester Press.

Ward, K. 1982. *Rational Theology and the Creativity of God.* Oxford: Blackwell.

1990. *Divine Action.* London: Collins.

Weber, M. 1930. *The Protestant Ethic and the Spirit of Capitalism.* London: Allen and Unwin.

Webster, C. 1975. *The Great Instauration: Science, Medicine and Reform 1626–1660.* London: Duckworth.

Weinberg, S. 1977. *The First Three Minutes.* New York: Basic Books.

1992. *Dreams of a Final Theory.* New York: Pantheon Books.

Westfall, R. S. 1989. *Essays on the Trial of Galileo.* Vatican City State: Vatican Observatory & Notre Dame: University of Notre Dame Press.

White, A. D. 1896. *A History of the Warfare of Science with Theology in Christendom.* (2 vols.) New York: Appleton & Co.

Whitehead, A. N. 1925. *Science and the Modern World.* New York: Macmillan.

1929. *Process and Reality.* New York: MacMillan.

Who is Who in Theology and Science: An International Biographical and Bibliographical Guide to Individuals and Organizations Interested in the Interaction of Theology and Science. Compiled and edited by the John Templeton Foundation. 1992 edition. Framingham, Mass.: Winthrop Publishing Co.

Wildiers, N. M. 1982. *The Theologian and his Universe: Theology and Cosmology from the Middle Ages to the Present*. New York: Seabury Press.

Wiles, M. 1986. *God's Action in the World*. London: SCM.

Wilkes, K. V. 1988. *Real People: Personal Identity Without Thought Experiments*. Oxford: Clarendon Press.

Williams, G. C. 1989. A sociobiological expansion of *Evolution and Ethics*. In J. Paradis and G. C. Williams, *Evolution and Ethics: T. H. Huxley's 'Evolution and Ethics' With New Essays on Its Victorian and Sociobiological Context*. Princeton University Press. (Condensed as: Huxley's evolution and ethics in sociobiological perspective, *Zygon* 23 (December 1988): 383–408.)

Williams, P. A. 1993. Can beings whose ethics evolved be ethical beings? In M. H. Nitecki and D. V. Nitecki, eds., *Evolutionary Ethics*.

Wilson, E. O. 1975. *Sociobiology: The New Synthesis*. Cambridge, Mass.: Harvard University Press.

1978. *On Human Nature*. Cambridge, Mass.: Harvard University Press.

1992. *The Diversity of Life*. New York: Norton.

Wolpert, L. 1993. *The Unnatural Nature of Science*. Cambridge, Mass.: Harvard University Press.

Yates, F. 1964. *Giordano Bruno and the Hermetic Tradition*. University of Chicago Press.

Index

308

Index